Secondary Analysis
of Sample Surveys:
Principles, Procedures,
and Potentialities

Secondary Analysis of Sample Surveys:

Principles, Procedures, and Potentialities

HERBERT H. HYMAN

Wesleyan University

JOHN WILEY & SONS, INC.

New York · London · Sydney · Toronto

Library of Congress Catalog Card Number: 72-251

ISBN 0-471-42605-9

Printed in the United States of America.

10 9 8 7 6 5 4 3 2 1

In Memory of
Sydney S. Spivack

THIRTY YEARS AGO, WHEN I BEGAN MY STUDIES IN SURVEY RESEARCH, OUR EFFORTS were focused at first on the immediate problems presented by World War II and then on the problems pressing for solution in that postwar society. It did not take long, however, to realize that those surveys yielded by-products of great potential value to social scientists. The thought of secondary analysis quickly dawned on me, and I soon began, in various ways, to promote the idea and to move toward the goal of a fuller utilization of the riches produced by survey research. I completed some secondary analyses in those early years.

While teaching at Columbia University in 1951, I offered a graduate seminar in "Methods and Applications of Secondary Analysis," in the process trying to codify the principles, procedures, and potentialities of the field and hoping that the good works that the students might produce would inspire others to follow their example. Only a few studies were published. The difficulty was not in formulating and developing the analytic procedures but in locating and obtaining the data. In those days we already had grasped the essential methodology, but the technology and organization for searching through the many completed surveys and acquiring the data were still out of our reach. Additional progress depended on the solution of these difficulties. A subsequent foundation grant to Columbia, guided by an advisory committee of which I was chairman, enabled York Lucci with Stein Rokkan and Eric Meyerhoff to conduct a major study of those critical problems. Their 1957 report and proposal for the development of the field, unfortunately, was not acted upon at the time. However, in the years since then, abundant archives have been established and the appropriate institutions have been molded. Secondary analysis now can be a viable and large-scale enterprise, but somehow progress is still impeded. Although the essential technology and organization are now available to everyone, ironically the methodology, in a codified and convenient form, still remains beyond the reach of many.

A book that would serve this need is an idea that I dreamed about many times. In my earlier book, *Survey Design and Analysis*, I examined Durkheim's classic work, *Suicide*, as "an illustration of certain methodological problems of . . . secondary analysis," but remarked that it would "not receive systematic treatment . . . in the text" because the procedures "are too diverse to be readily codified into a short statement." The long statement has been a very long time in coming to life. At last it is accomplished and, for this, I express special thanks to the National Science Foundation and, most particularly, to Charles R. Wright, former Director of the Program in Sociology and Social Psychology, whose grant permitted me to carry out the work and provided support for the essential background studies. John S. Reed helped in the conduct of those studies, especially in the survey of users of the archives, and his contributions are gratefully acknowledged. The Interuniversity Consortium for Political Research and the Roper Public Opinion Research Center allowed us to draw samples of users for the survey. Their help in this and other ways is greatly appreciated. I also express my appreciation to the many respondents who wrote such informative accounts of their experiences in secondary analysis. Eleanor Singer, Charles R. Wright, Hubert O'Gorman, and Hanan Selvin read the manuscript and their careful criticisms and good advice are acknowledged with thanks.

Herbert H. Hyman

Wesleyan University, 1971

Contents

*Secondary Analysis
of Sample Surveys:
Principles, Procedures,
and Potentialities*

Introduction

IN RECENT YEARS THE IDEA OF SECONDARY ANALYSIS OF SURVEY DATA—SIMPLY stated, the *extraction of knowledge on topics other than those which were the focus of the original surveys*—has inspired a major movement in social science.[1] Because of substantial support from public and private funds, archives of data have multiplied in number and their holdings have greatly increased. Information on many characteristics of millions of respondents from thousands of surveys, conducted in many countries and time periods, now conveniently awaits the social scientists who are thoughtful and skillful enough to grasp the opportunity. Newton, in the seventeenth century, explained his

---

[1] The *idea* of secondary analysis is not new. However, the social movement which it inspired and *concerted* activity toward the goal of full utilization of the accumulated data of past surveys are recent. This rebirth, may be dated from 1957, when a systematic report on the possibility and a proposal for funding was presented to the Ford Foundation. See York Lucci and Stein Rokkan with Eric Meyerhoff, A *Library Center of Survey Research Data* (New York: Columbia School of Library Service, June 1957, mimeo). In that same year, the Roper Public Opinion Research Center at Williamstown, Mass., the largest repository of survey data, was officially organized as a *general* archive (it had been established in 1946 to house Roper's own surveys). The movement remained in its infancy until the early sixties when funding and, correspondingly, archives and activities multiplied. To be sure, there were attempts prior to 1957 to establish an archive, to organize some bodies of survey data, cast them into serviceable forms in periodic indexes, and to promote their scientific use. An encyclopedic volume, containing the results of surveys conducted by 23 organizations in 19 countries during the period 1935-1946 was published in 1951. See H. Cantril and M. Strunk, *Public Opinion 1935-1946* (Princeton: Princeton University Press, 1951). In his preface, Cantril reminds us that "One of the reasons for establishing the Office of Public Opinion Research in 1940 was to accumulate archives of survey data for research purposes."

achievements by the remark: "If I have seen farther, it is by standing on the shoulders of giants." Now, late in the twentieth century, social scientists can also be described as standing atop a giant mountain of data, from which they might see farther back into the past, away into remoter regions of the world, and over a larger vista of problems than ever before.

Mountain climbing should have been the sport of scholars in the nineteen sixties. What in fact have been our activities in secondary analysis and our accomplishments? That our achievements have fallen short of the *prime* goal is evident to any objective observer who scans the literature.[2] Considering the vast amount of information available to illuminate many scientific problems, by now one would expect to find many more scholarly publications based on secondary analysis. However, the data seem either to have been neglected or to have produced an inadequate yield.

Obstacles and Remedies

Why has relatively little scientific wealth been extracted from the figurative mountain of gold? One major explanation is that many scholars are not skilled in the principles and procedures of secondary analysis of survey data. Lacking the skills, some cannot even start the climb. Others start but are inadequately trained for the rigors involved and never finish.[3] Some may persevere only to

---

[2] The data from past surveys must also serve as a convenient device for training students in research methods. But clearly this goal is subsidiary to that of increasing scientific knowledge and hardly requires an extensive archive. It can be accomplished with one survey that a teacher has conducted himself, and certainly with a few surveys that a teacher may obtain at small expense from the original sources. By now, even these minor labors are unnecessary, since a number of curriculum units based on past surveys are available for general use. By way of illustration, selected items from the 1952, 1956, 1960, and 1964 election surveys by the Survey Research Center have been combined into a training deck with accompanying manual which has been tested at a number of institutions. See Wm. Flanigan and D. Repass, *Manual for the Political Behavior Laboratory* (Minneapolis: Political Science Department, 1967). This was the first in a series of manuals being prepared at the University of Minnesota. A second manual provides training in the analysis of cross-national surveys and is based on Almond and Verba's comparative study of *The Civic Culture*. See Edwin Fogelman and Nancy Zingale, *Manual for the Comparative Politics Laboratory* (Minneapolis: Political Science Department, 1968).

[3] In 1963, Philip K. Hastings, the Director of the Roper Center, reported that some 2,500 scholarly inquiries had been received as of that date and presented a list of examples of completed secondary analyses based on the Center's data. At that time, about 2,800 different studies from 40 countries were on file, and 25,000 individuals received the

complete secondary analyses which do not satisfy scientific standards for publication. Worse yet, some of these may get published, thereby perpetrating *pseudo*scientific findings on innocent readers, since the errors in *other* people's surveys are no longer visible and are frequently overlooked by unsophisticated analysts. The full utilization of past survey data to increase scientific knowledge will remain an unrealized goal until these deficiencies are remedied by special methodological training. In metaphorical terms, the map showing the routes to the mountain top must be drawn in sufficient detail. Otherwise, lacking a guide, the amateur sportsman will get lost along the way. Our work is conceived as such a guidebook.

In the past, there were other major deterrents to full utilization: the heavy labors and expense involved in locating and processing data and the lack of awareness of the general opportunity. Such difficulties have declined as the

---

periodic mailings describing the materials and services available. See "The Roper Center: An International Archive of Sample Survey Data," *Public Opinion Quarterly,* **27,** 1963, pp. 590–598. The discrepancy between the extent of the materials in this one archive (now grown to over 6000 surveys comprising over 12 million respondents), or the number of inquiries received, and the number of analyses completed suggests the obstacles in the way. The Interuniversity Consortium for Political Research, established in 1962, making available another large archive of data, conducted a survey of uses that had been made of the data in the five-year period up to Fall, 1967. The list of theses and scholarly publications based on secondary analysis is impressive, as is also true of the list from the Roper Center. But in terms of *full* utilization, one may again make the judgment that the potential is far from fully realized. The report notes that many universities, "particularly those having joined the Consortium during the past one or two years, had little to report" in the way of uses. ("Inventory of Use of Consortium Data," December, 1967, mimeo.) A relevant statistic is provided by careful record keeping of the progress of requests made to the International Data Library of the University of California. In the four-year period after this archival service was established, some 400 requests were received. Of those who initially requested codebooks from particular studies in the archive, about 40% eventually went on to acquire data. Some of the attrition is due, no doubt, to the fact that the user finds after detailed inspection that the desired data are not contained within the study or to restrictions that limit the use of particular studies. But some must reflect lack of skill in knowing how to proceed with the analysis. These and other facts on patterns of use may be gleaned from a report prepared for the Council of Social Science Data Archives. See William G. Jones, *User Request Patterns at Social Science Data Archives* (Ann Arbor, Michigan: Institute for Social Research, November 1967, mimeo). For other evidence on failure in utilizing archival data and its causes, see C. G. Bell, "The Joys and Sorrows of Secondary Data Use," in R. L. Bisco, *Data Bases, Computers, and the Social Sciences* (New York: Wiley, 1970), pp. 52–60. Periodically, we shall draw upon the results of two mail surveys we ourselves conducted in 1968 of samples of clients who had recently requested data from the Roper Center or from the Inter-University Consortium at Michigan. These surveys revealed a variety of obstacles—legal, logistical, financial, technological—to secondary analysis, but also provided independent evidence of the *analytical* obstacles to effective utilization.

movement has become effective in reducing the labors and costs and has publicized the opportunity. Inventories of holdings have been printed and disseminated. To spur scholars onward, the idea of secondary analysis has been promoted by a series of conferences and publications.[4] As the movement has grown, archives of a specialized character, auxiliary to the giant general-purpose archive, have been established to serve the needs of special clientele more efficiently. The omnivorous scholar can continue to patronize the Roper Center which provides the largest and most varied menu. But the scholar who is interested in an exotic item from the developing countries, for example, may turn to the Berkeley archive; the political behaviorist to the Consortium at Michigan; the analyst of international relations to the holdings at Oak Ridge or Pittsburgh or the University of Pennsylvania; the Latin-Americanist to Berkeley or Florida; others to large European collections in Amsterdam or Cologne. In this way each may find what he is seeking with a minimum of irritation. These archives have been active in developing technologies for efficient retrieval of information relevant to a specific inquiry, and in reducing the restrictions on public use of the data.

The relationship between the user and the suppliers of data is, of course, not yet perfect. Service is sometimes slow, the price occasionally a matter for contention,[5] the quality of specific material sometimes inferior, and particular

---

[4] A privately printed brochure, *Social Science Data Archives in the United States* (Council of Social Science Data Archives, New York City, 1967) lists twenty-five archives and describes their holdings and the procedures to be followed in obtaining data. European archives have been described in such articles as Ralph L. Bisco, "Social Science Data Archives: Progress and Prospects," *Information*, **6**, 1967, pp. 39–74. For published proceedings of several conferences see: S. Rokkan, ed., *Data Archives for the Social Sciences* (Paris and the Hague: Mouton, 1966); Richard L. Merritt and Stein Rokkan, eds., *Comparing Nations, The Use of Quantitative Data in Cross-National Research* (New Haven: Yale University Press, 1966); Ralph L. Bisco, *op. cit.*; M. Dogan and S. Rokkan, eds., *Quantitative Ecological Analysis in the Social Sciences* (Cambridge: MIT Press, 1969).

[5] In our survey of users, the reaction to the charges that were applied seem unrelated to the status of the user or the magnitude of the fee. One user expresses "dismay" at the "excessive charges" of $45 for three decks of cards plus a xeroxed codebook! Another user who obtained cards from surveys in 7 countries expresses pleasure that "the cost of the materials was only $30–$40" and adds "we've stored the cards, and might use them for other analyses some day." Clearly, some users are aware of the much higher costs to produce equivalent data *de novo*, and are therefore pleased. For example, one correspondent remarks: ". . . secondary analysis has made it possible for me to explore subjects at a cost of a few hundred dollars . . . whereas collecting the data myself would have cost hundreds of thousands." Other users, by contrast, are thinking of the high cost that the archive charges for clerical labor rather than the replacement costs. As one man puts it: "the costs were probably three times what they ought to have been—using our own local rates for clerical help, card reproduction, etc., as a guideline." The complaints

delicacies still in short supply. The *response* to these present difficulties how-ever, should be temperate. To many scholars, such obstacles as persist seem small, but to a few, a small irritant still appears large. The remedy for them is a change of heart. Perhaps they can transform themselves in the image of Durkheim: His 1897 classic, *Suicide,* was a secondary analysis drawn from imperfect and inconvenient data sources, although not sample surveys. He pro-duced it by heroic labors and without the benefit of modern technology. Two tables alone required that "the records of some 26,000 suicides had to be studied to classify separately their age, sex, marital status, and the presence or absence of children. M. Mauss alone performed this heavy task."[6] Poor Mauss. If only he had been born in the IBM era, he, like other modern scholars, would have been spared that heavy manual labor. If the pun be allowed, a Mauss labored alone and produced a mountain of data. The mod-ern analyst whose labors are so eased and who is given the mountain but produces "a ridiculous mouse" should look into himself.

If he still feels put upon, he should also recall the examples of modern scholars, whose secondary analyses were accomplished before the era of the archive, although with the benefit of the IBM machine. Until mid-century, sample surveys were decentralized, often fugitive, and captured only after laborious inquires of the personnel of many agencies. The scholars of the seventies, by contrast, have comprehensive catalogues, consolidated and greatly expanded holdings, and improved technology. Brief reflection should make them sense their relative advantage and hearten them to face relatively minor practical obstacles, ever diminishing as the archives increase their effi-ciency. Many still lack the knowledge needed, together with motivation, to sustain their analyses and insure the successful completion of their studies. Where might they learn it?

There is, unfortunately, no systematic and comprehensive statement of principles and procedures of secondary analysis in the literature. Nor is there any detailed statement of the many kinds of studies to which it can be

---

of some users relate to still another set of considerations. The initial outlay to obtain raw materials from the archive is small but it may be only the beginning of a long chain of other unanticipated costs to clean the cards, to reformat the data for use in their machine room or computer center, and for tabulations.

[6] Emile Durkheim, *Suicide* (New York: Free Press, 1951), p. 39. In his preface to the English edition, the editor, George Simpson, remarks: "In the last decade of the nine-teenth century when Durkheim was conducting the investigations incorporated in this work, repositories (governmental or private) of statistical information on this, or any other subject, were either rare, skimpy, or badly put together. With characteristic energy and the aid of some of his students, especially Marcel Mauss, Durkheim realigned the available statistics so as to answer the question posed by the general problem and its internal details" (pp. 9–10).

applied.[7] In this book, we provide a comprehensive statement of the principles, procedures, and potentialities of secondary analysis. In the next section of this Chapter we shall consider how many ways we may benefit by utilizing the accumulated data of past surveys.

Benefits of Secondary Analysis

If the claims made for secondary analysis are described in an exaggerated and misleading fashion, the skeptics may be put off, the greedy may be driven to frenzied and aimless activity, and the innocent may be led into an ordeal of frustrating research. The presentation must be fair, but the genuine claims of secondary analysis should be stated, no matter how grand they may at first appear.

PRACTICAL BENEFITS

It is self-evident that solving a problem by the analysis of existing survey data, rather than by collecting data in a new survey, *economizes on money, time, and personnel*. The savings involved vary widely depending on the specifications of the original surveys and the agencies conducting the research. The length of the questionnaire and interviewing time, the number of open-ended questions and corresponding coding, the geographical location and elusiveness of the population that was within the scope of the inquiry, the design and size of the sample, the amount of pre-testing—all these and other factors enter into the calculations. However, some crude and general idea of the substantial economy can be given.

Conservatively estimated, the phases of a survey essential to producing data in a processed form ready to be analyzed consume about 40% of the total

---

[7] Several symposia extend the frontiers of the field, but leave uncultivated the large area of basic knowledge that the beginner must have. They dwell on specialized types of research designs, cross-national and contextual, by which phenomena can be examined comparatively over a wide range of societal, temporal, and ecological settings (*Comparing Nations . . .*, *op. cit.*; *Quantitative Ecological Analysis . . .*, *op. cit.*) These are fruitful but frightening designs to operate. They require great technical skill from the analyst, supersensitivity to subtle sources of error, and deep knowledge of the social environments within which the behavior is set. It would be sensible in any text to imbed them late in a graded series and to begin with simpler designs. Then the amateur would not neglect fruitful approaches which are compatible with his abilities and would only confront the most awesome designs when he is adequately prepared.

budget. The scholar who engages in his own analysis does not pay out-of-pocket for the services of high-priced analysts who consume perhaps another 50% of the budget (the remaining 5–10% going into machine work and the production of the report), so this portion of cost is the same whether he works with old or new data. And from the point of view of a sponsor or client who pays the bill, it is again a constant that he must pay to one or the other, to the primary or the secondary analyst. In 1970 in the United States, the bill for the services necessary simply to produce new data from a national sample of 1500 to 2000 cases could easily be $60,000.

To be sure, if the solution of the problem being researched requires only a few questions and measures, one can buy only a piece of a new survey, sharing the total costs with others who then amalgamate their inquiries into an omnibus survey. The amount spent is divided accordingly, and the economies netted by secondary analysis would not be so great in absolute terms. On the other hand, as will be seen later, often the secondary analyst can combine data from more than one relevant survey for the definitive study of a problem. The amount he would have to spend to produce the equivalent in several such primary surveys would be multiplied accordingly. Some of our later examples will show secondary analysts working on a problem with anywhere from 2–3 surveys up to 7–8 or more surveys. In the latter instances, the amount of money saved is truly astronomical.

Economies in time spent and personnel used are also considerable, although these also vary with the particular survey. Field work and coding alone, ignoring the time spent in planning and preparing the inquiry for the field, can easily take 3–4 months or more and can rarely be compressed into any less than 3–4 weeks in the instance of a large and elaborate survey. As we shall suggest, even a few weeks saved may sometimes provide a valuable benefit. And, of course, the time saved by not using a large staff of interviewers and coders, certainly no less than 60–70 people in a primary survey, is not to be disdained.

These economies serve not only the private interests of sponsors and researchers but also the public good. Money, competent personnel, and time are scarce resources, and if they can be allocated to new research that is essential rather than wasted to duplicate data that are already available, so much the better for everyone. There are enough unsolved problems that deserve these resources. A sponsor or researcher whose funds are meager and who knows no alternative but expensive primary research may end up doing nothing at all or doing an inadequate study, whereas he might solve his problem despite his limited means by secondary analysis. A sponsor or researcher who needs information quickly to ameliorate an urgent problem and who knows no alternative but slow primary research, may have to do without any research guidance at all or get his information too late to be applied, whereas he might shed light on his problem within time by secondary analysis.[8]

Even when one has enough time and money to undertake primary research, a prior secondary analysis may be valuable. Conducted as a preliminary, it may insure that a new inquiry is designed more effectively, suggesting to the scholar that his hypotheses are not very promising and that he should rethink his ideas, that some instruments are unlikely to be productive and others should be elaborated, that some aspects of the problem are so puzzling as to deserve special attention, that some strata in the population should be sampled more heavily and others can be undersampled. Admittedly, these benefits transcend the merely practical, and verge on the theoretical. And it is only fair to note that it is more costly to do *both* secondary and primary research than it is to do primary research alone. But certainly a practical man would quickly conclude that he gets a lot for his money. A preliminary secondary analysis may also serve to suggest to an initially skeptical sponsor that there is a topic that needs study and that survey research can contribute something of value; this may increase his readiness to support new inquiry.

SOCIAL BENEFITS

There are times and places where tensions are so high that the intrusion of a new survey may aggravate the situation, or may be used as political ammunition by those who wish to heighten a public's sense of conflict or grievance. To be sure, surveys in the past have often provided a vehicle for the expression of grievance, for catharsis, or for information which ultimately can be used beneficently to reduce the source of tension. However, the initiation of field work must be examined in its duality—as a force both to heighten and to ease tension. In recent times, this balance sometimes is tilted. The instituion of surveys has been regarded with hostility in some quarters, and even interpreted as spying and manipulation of others rather than as a neutral or humane science. The obstructions to field work have, on occasion, become so severe as to undermine any primary survey and to create an explosive issue. Under such conditions, secondary analysis may well be a boon and the optimal strategy for researchers and sponsors to follow. The information is obtained without any intrusion and exacerbation of social conflict. Of course, those who regard the accusations directed against surveys as warranted, would adjudge secondary analysis an even more insidious form of intervention.

When the atmosphere is less strained, the social benefits of secondary analysis must also be considered. The natural resource upon which *all* sur-

---

[8] On this and other benefits, see Barney G. Glazer, "Secondary Analysis: A Strategy for the Use of Knowledge from Research Elsewhere," *Soc. Probl.*, Summer, 1962, pp. 70–74.

veys depend is the willing cooperation of the population, and until now, at least in the United States, most people have been agreeable to act as respondents. Given the fund of good will toward surveys, the wearing away of this precious resource is probably a very slow process. Yet prudence would dictate that we not hasten its depletion by unwarranted intrusions on people, and not wear out our welcome any faster than necessary; ethical concerns would certainly direct us not to impose on human subjects for research purposes except when it is required.

These benefits from secondary analysis are shared by all, but there is another type of social benefit that accrues mainly to the social scientist, and that contributes to the health of the discipline and its members rather than the general welfare. To put it dramatically: secondary analysis *restrains oligarchy* in a discipline and insures that scholars of individualistic temperament are not forced to live as *organizational men*.

Whatever his ideological persuasion, a sensible sponsor or foundation official is not likely to entrust $60,000 or more to a lone scholar who has not established his credentials and his reputation in survey research. The high cost of new surveys inevitably directs the funds to the agencies and individuals of proven competence. As the money continues to flow toward these centers, "oligarchy" becomes more entrenched.

The imagery is fanciful and the analogy to political oligarchy is somewhat strained: The "oligarchs" of survey research have not inherited their power or achieved it through ruthless means. They have learned their expertness through years of work and they have earned their reputations by delivering high-quality surveys. They alone have the staffs and facilities essential to conducting new surveys. The situation does not stem from evil intent, but simply from their unique capacities to conduct effectively the large-scale data collection that is inherent in survey research.

Such oligarchs are a strange breed. They are happy to share their knowledge, to train aspiring surveyors, to provide apprenticeships and paying jobs in the enterprise, and to disclose the secrets of their trade. The young can join whenever they wish, stay as long as they want, and even live their entire scholarly lives within the corporate body using the essential resources of the agency to do their surveys. The scholars who do not find such a *permanent* existence palatable can leave the organization after a period of training, carrying their own credentials. When they need to mobilize resources to conduct a primary survey, and have the necessary funds, they can enter into a businesslike contract with one of the agencies to purchase the data which they then can analyze.

In our judgment, it is a friendly and benevolent arrangement. It is congenial to many, insures responsible management of large amounts of money, and makes new survey research possible, efficient, and effective. Nevertheless, the critical point is that it is not congenial to every type of scholar and some price is paid for the benefits. Some do not have the temperament to be organizational men even for a short time. Some do not like the entanglements in team research, or the process of entrepreneurship involved in getting large sums of money and dealing in contracts and budgets.

If *primary* surveys were the only vehicle for training individuals and for the production of knowledge, some individuals would be barred from participation or destined to an unpleasant existence. Inevitably the agencies with the facilities, along with the sponsors who provide large amounts of money to support the enterprise, maintain at least a "veto" power over the research. Secondary analysis provides an alternative avenue of training, of ascent to competence and power, and for the production of knowledge from survey data. The benefits are not merely the psychic comfort of some individuals. It may well be that men of individualistic temperament, freed from the pressures of the organizational milieu, from the grind of producing wholesale quantities of data, and from obtaining and allocating moneys can contribute fresh and different kinds of ideas. Given access to the bodies of data already available, they may enlarge the total body of knowledge in ways that would not be conceived or elaborated by men of other temperaments who work in the organizational context.

It is possible that the pure secondary analyst who has never been contaminated by any association with organized research may accomplish very little and make many mistakes. As we shall see, men who are associated with survey agencies have a built-in advantage in formulating problems for secondary analysis and in finding the appropriate data. Men who have had past experience in the actual conduct of a survey are more sensitive to the types of errors that may afflict the data they inherit. Each institutional arrangement for survey research is bound to have its special limitations as well as its advantages. But it would follow that a diversity of arrangements would be the optimal situation, and the mix of secondary and primary research comes close to the ideal.[9]

BENEFITS FOR THEORY AND SUBSTANTIVE KNOWLEDGE

Secondary analysis may seem, thus far, to appeal most to those who are driven by thoughts of personal comfort, frugality, or ideological goals. But even for those whose only thoughts are to advance knowledge—whatever the costs—it

---

[9] For a thoughtful treatment of the implications of various institutional arrangements for research, see B. G. Glazer, "Retreading Research Materials, The Use of Secondary Analysis by the Independent Researcher," *Amer. Beh. Scient.*, June, 1963, pp. 11–14.

may have great appeal. Secondary analysis benefits science in many ways, all stemming from one fundamental feature of the method. It expands the types and number of observations to cover more adequately a wider array of social conditions, measurement procedures, and variables than can usually be studied by primary surveys. Thus it produces a more comprehensive and definitive empirical study of the problems the investigator has formulated. Occasionally, new surveys are a literal impossibility or would yield no evidence at all on a problem, and secondary analysis is then truly the only avenue to understanding. Examining the wide array of materials in the course of secondary analysis also expands our intellectual horizons. We are stimulated to think about otherwise forgotten problems and also forced in the direction of higher levels of abstraction.

Understanding the Past. In an essay on "The Historian and the Pollster," written prior to 1957, Lazarsfeld remarks that "Unconsidered aspects of the past become interesting in the light of the changing present."[10] We may suddenly realize that some particular past event—a war, a law, an invention— might have provided a strategic opportunity to study some important, problematic aspects of human behavior, or might have initiated some process whose dynamics we wish to explore, or that the description of the values or climate of opinion during some previous interval might have permitted a test of such psychological forces in initiating the social changes we now experience. A contemporary crisis—a wave of intolerance or violence—may lead us to ask whether it is a new experience rooted in our present circumstances or whether it represents some continuity with the past. We would like to tie our present observations to some threads of measurement from the past, to determine if and when a pattern had formed, and how it and its determinants might have changed. Unfortunately, the time to have undertaken the surveys is also past. Remorse must have been the common affliction of survey analysts in the era before the archive. We had lost our chance, and could only feel regret or repent our mistakes. Secondary analysis restores our chances, and the archival holdings multiply them by increasing the odds that we will find at least one appropriate survey out of the thousands that were already conducted.

To be sure, the social researcher can try to construct the indicators of his desired variables from documentary records as historians have always done in an attempt to unlock the past. But these sources may be poorly suited to his purposes, especially if he is interested in the distribution of a variable throughout the general population or if his interest lies in an internal state, such as a belief or attitude or value which may be reflected only poorly in

---

[10] P. F. Lazarsfeld, "The Historian and the Pollster," in M. Komarovsky, ed., *Common Frontiers of the Social Sciences* (New York: Free Press, 1957), p. 249.

overt behavior.[11] Or he may try to reconstruct the past by retrospective questions in a current survey; but then memory errors may cause slippage between measurement and concept. It is worth stressing that, at best, such a survey design cannot carry one very far back into the past. Consider a primary analyst applying this strategy in the course of a survey conducted in the year 1967. At that point, about 40% of the American population was 21 years of age or younger; about 50% of the population was under thirty. Even if their memories were infallible, they could not report on the events of World War II or the Great Depression because they were not alive at that time. And of those who were participants in those past events, many are no longer alive to render their reports to the interviewers. For example, in 1945, at the end of World War II, more than twenty million Americans (about 15% of the population) were 55 years or older. To catch them in the net of a survey conducted in 1970, all of them would have had to live to the age of 80 and about half of them had to survive beyond the age of 90.

In this light, Lazarsfeld aptly remarks that the pollster of the past, in the capacity of "a contemporary historian, thus takes on considerable importance. What he considers worthy of a survey will, in later years, influence the range of possible historical inquiries."[12] Thus, long ago, Lazarsfeld was able to envision the potential for historical studies that lay in the secondary analysis of surveys from the past. Understandably, his worry at that time was that there might be "no data at all" on the particular problems that would emerge as subjects of future scholarly study. And that really was something to worry about before 1957. A pollster in the past might never have conducted the survey that a later secondary analyst would have desired. But even if it had been conducted, how would one come to know about it? What Lazarsfeld did not anticipate was the establishment of archives which now insure that whatever historical materials exist are known and accessible, and which reveal what an abundance and variety of data in fact exist.

---

[11] Thus Planck, who studied French value systems and tried to trace their stability over time and their distribution in the population, remarks: "The great obstacle to ascertaining the values of a period lies in the paucity of information concerning the great masses of the people as contrasted with the articulate few. What starts out as an attempt to portray the climate of opinion of an age turns out frequently to be a description of its intellectual leadership or some other limited group. It has been suggested, for example, that the characterization of the Middle Ages as predominantly spiritual in its values may have come about because the major primary sources for the period are the products of the clerical pen. . . ." Planck, therefore, turned to the secondary analysis of French surveys. R. E. Planck, "Public Opinion in France after the Liberation, 1944–1949," in Komarovsky, *op. cit.*, p. 214.

[12] Lazarsfeld, *op. cit.*, p. 250.

"Seek, and ye shall find" is truly a doctrine for the new era. To be sure, one may still confront the ultimate difficulty that no data whatsoever exist on a particular problem, but, in this respect, the secondary analyst is not completely at the mercy of the pollsters of the past, but to some degree the maker of his own fate. To some extent he makes, or more correctly, remakes, his own data. As in all secondary analysis, he must be able to see particular questions and indicators as serving diverse purposes, and endow them with new meaning and relevance for his concepts. Ingenuity and caution are required, and there is always the danger of misusing or misapplying a measure. But in the instance of historical studies, he has ample precedent and is, in no sense, engaging in radical or unusual behavior. The documents and records of the past have always been used inferentially as indicators of and keys to some hidden reality on which there are no ideal and direct measures, and inferential use of survey questions is no different in principle.

The empirical basis of our knowledge and theories thus can be broadened through secondary analysis of data from a wide variety of specific historical situations. To some, the odds in our favor may still seem pretty low, but it may be suggested that they will become progressively better. When Lazarsfeld envisioned the prospect in 1957, he realized that the acute problem might be the absence of any data at all relevant to the variables under subsequent study. He saw the solution in increasing the sensitivity of pollsters to the role they would ultimately play. Somehow they had to be made to feel the weight of the future upon them, and internalize the variety of perspectives that later secondary analysts would bring to the examination of previous surveys. To increase the sensitivity and responsiveness of pollsters, he proposed an institutional device, a "commission for the utilization of polls in the service of future historiography."

The idea had merit then and it has merit now, although to this day it has not been realized. One may suggest, however, that the establishment of archives and the promotion of secondary analysis may themselves be institutional forms which contribute to the solution of the problem. The future will inevitably weigh more heavily upon pollsters as they see their surveys being deposited in archives and held for posterity and as they observe secondary analysts actually using the surveys. Collectively, the secondary analysts will be functioning from day-to-day as a commission utilizing the data and learning of the omissions they only wish had been remedied. It is by the practice of their work that they will make their weight felt and begin to clarify dimensions along which measurements should routinely be made.

Understanding Change.   Lazarsfeld remarks at one point in his 1957 essay, "that the historian will expect that we, *today*, have initiated a series of trend studies."[13] And this suggests the way in which secondary analysis may contribute knowledge about general processes of social and psychological change. The benefit should be distinguished from the ways in which specific episodes out of the *past* can be recaptured for study by secondary analysis. Note that Lazarsfeld urged that we begin trend studies *today*, and he goes on to say that "trend data will have to be assembled over a long period of time."

His implicit hypotheses were not anchored to any particular historical event, but to events in general. His focus was the present and the distant future, as well as the past. If one is to accumulate general knowledge of the ways in which individuals and societies change over time—to build an adequate theory of the patterns individuals and groups exhibit as they age and live through chains of experiences impinging upon them in diverse sequences and at different junctures in their growth—one must be able to bring long spans of time under study.

With that extended vision in mind, Lazarsfeld urged researchers to begin such systematic empirical studies in 1957. The sooner one began, the quicker one would reach that distant goal of having studied long-term change, and by now, more than a decade would already have been brought under systematic observation. The wisdom of the strategy seems self-evident. Yet the irony is that the decade has passed us by, and we have neglected the opportunity. Indeed, a governmental commission, sensing the need and the past omission, recommended as recently as 1969 that we move *Toward a Social Report*, in the direction of developing a "comprehensive set of social indicators" which will "tell us how social conditions are changing,"[14] by trend measurements conducted on an annual basis. This was in response to a request from the President, that the Secretary of Health, Education and Welfare "search for ways to improve the nation's ability to chart its social progress," that request having been issued in 1966.

Other prestigious works of committees and foundations had previously issued the same kinds of requests for "regular trend series of social indicators," and had proclaimed the "idea of monitoring social change" in 1966, and again in 1968; one other major programmatic statement is still to be issued in 1971.[15] The argument seems unexceptionable; the hard work of thinking out the technical and conceptual problems in such research has been accomplished in good measure. However, the translation of the idea into the reality

---

[13] *Ibid.*, p. 255. (italics supplied).

[14] *Toward A Social Report*, HEW (Washington: Government Printing Office, 1969).

[15] R. A. Bauer, *Social Indicators* (Cambridge: MIT Press, 1966); E. B. Sheldon and W. E. Moore, eds., *Indicators of Social Change* (New York: Russell Sage Foundation, 1968). The forthcoming volume, under the auspices of the Russell Sage Foundation, is: A. Campbell and P. E. Converse, eds., *The Human Meaning of Social Change.*

of primary research continues to elude us. Consequently, a theory of social and psychological change suffers for lack of evidence.

What an anomalous situation! Some of the puzzle can be solved, and some of the solution, as we shall see, can be found in secondary analysis. Comprehensive measurement of changes in many respects, on a national scale and on an annual basis, is, of course, so costly an enterprise that only a government could fund it, but this can hardly account for the almost total absence of *miniature* ventures in long-term trend measurements in the decades that have passed. Certainly, funds could have been found by scholars who wished to begin the study of some particular aspect of behavior as it has changed over a long interval in some specified population in a city or region. The difficulty must be psychological, not financial.

To contemplate a study that one might begin let, us say, in 1970 and that would span a thirty-year period of social change is to embark upon a venture that would not come to fruition until the year 2000. The initial population under study would have aged, but so too would the investigator! One must have a healthy-minded attitude, and contemplate the future with great self-confidence if one is to undertake a study that is as long as the average professional lifetime of most scholars. To begin something that one may not live to see the end of requires a capacity for transcending the self and finding gratification simply in the thought that one is laying down the baselines others will exploit. Even those young enough to live to consummate their studies must be able to defer their personal gratification far into the future, if they are to find such research prospects attractive. The record suggests that there are few among us who are driven in this way to embark on a long-term primary study of trends. And even if there were more, science itself would have to wait for an indefinite period before the empirical knowledge of long-term social and psychological change had accumulated.

These apparently intractable problems can be solved by a simple turn of thought involving the idea of secondary analysis. Instead of laying down a baseline in 1970 for others to use some thirty years from now, why not reap immediate enjoyment from the baselines and trend lines that the surveyers of thirty years ago happened to lay down for us? That way the investigator and science in general can profit right now from a completed study that provides knowledge of change over as extensive an interval as would otherwise require us to wait until the year 2000. Perhaps we can only go back ten years along a particular dimension of measurement that interests us, but that is equivalent to waiting until 1980, a delay that some of us might find too long for our tastes and incompatible with our urgent needs for knowledge.

In principle, considering when sample surveys became regularly established in the United States, one can now examine about thirty-five years of social change across the nation. Every year that passes further extends the interval one might be able to span for studies of long-term change.

Admittedly, as we shall see in Chapter VI, there are serious technical difficulties in the secondary analysis of trends. Some time series do not cover the full domain of phenomena one would like to examine; some are short in duration, and others, more lengthy, show gaps and discontinuities in measurement. However, the chapter will also document a specific and elaborate study of change over a twenty-four-year period, for example; and another study for a thirty-year period.

The strategy outlined may seem to rest upon a hidden assumption: that the investigator can exchange one interval of time (for example, the thirty-year period from 1970 to 2000) for another of equal length (for example, the period 1940–1970) and that his findings would be the same. The critic might well argue that the patterns observed as people age, as societies move through time, are dependent upon the particular events they experience. Even if this were so, the strategy is not faulted. If the findings were different, this would not make the *primary* study more important for those interested in the laws of social and psychological change, although its contemporaneity might make it more relevant to practical men. The periods may be different, but neither one can be rated "better" than the other. Indeed, the study of both periods is better than the study of either one alone.

The assumption described above is really not at issue at all. And even if one were to prefer to pursue the study of long-term change in the present and on into the future, this preference is somewhat academic, since primary trend studies seem to be obstructed for the moment whereas secondary analysis is open to us all. Whether, as individuals age and as groups and whole societies experience some flux of events, there are patterns that are invariant no matter what is happening in the environment, or whether the patterns of change are themselves changeable, is really not a matter for speculation but a basic question to be studied empirically. Secondary analysis of changes over long periods in the past provides essential evidence on this basic question.[16] And such analysis should not be construed as providing only *one* unit of evidence. The past can be subdivided in many subtle ways. As we shall see in Chapter VII, a *series* of successive age cohorts, who entered into the stream of life at different historical points and who are living through some of the same events at different stages of their development, can be traced to provide a great deal of evidence on basic questions of change. Such modes of analysis are compli-

---

[16] An encyclopedic review of patterns of aging has recently been published, and it should be stressed that the findings on political, psychological, and social phenomena are based almost completely on the secondary analysis of sample surveys. See Matilda White Riley *et al., Aging and Society: An Inventory of Research Findings,* Vol. I (New York: Russell Sage, 1968).

cated and tricky, but they expand the temporal span of our observations far beyond their apparent extent. For example, when we study, through a survey conducted in 1940, individuals in their fifties, we have incorporated those who were children at the turn of the century or earlier. That distant period—the enduring influence it wrought—is in fact included somewhere in any set of trend measurements spaced between 1940 and now. When the analyst unravels the many strands contained within his aggregate data and single set of surveys, he has far more than one unit's worth of evidence.

Examining Problems Comparatively.   Secondary analysis of a series of comparable surveys from different points in time provides one of the rare avenues for the empirical description of long-term change, and for examining the way phenomena vary under the contrasted conditions operative in one society in several periods. Some phenomena or relationships between variables may endure through all the vicissitudes of time, and, indeed, such findings verge on the kind of powerful generalizations social scientists seek. Nevertheless, the surveys on which they are based suffer from a special kind of narrowness despite their broad sampling of time. They are limited to but *one* society, even if it encompasses within its wide boundaries and long history considerable variety.

The solution, obviously, is to expand the empirical base for our surveys by sampling several societies, thus providing more stringent tests of the limits of our generalizations and establishing the way phenomena vary over a much wider range of conditions than can be represented in the survey of a single society. Understandably, the desirability of comparable cross-national surveys has been stated eloquently in various writings, and the methodological problems and principles have been reviewed at length. Modern scholars hardly need to have the point belabored any longer. Yet, the irony is that the field of *primary* cross-national survey research seems to suffer from neglect, just as is the case for primary surveys of long-term change. The latter, to be sure, is almost a nonexistent species and the former is only a rare bird, there being about ten documented examples of comparable large-scale multination surveys of the general population as of 1970. Why so few? The merit of the design is indubitable. There has been ample persuasion and ample time for many researchers to act. Indeed, a reasonable judgment would be that the modern literature *about* cross-national surveys is extensive, provides detailed guidance, and has been around for a long time.[17] Severe obstructions to *primary* cross-national surveys must exist, and if this is our only strategy, the goal of a comparatively based body of knowledge will remain elusive.

---

[17] Some 1600 items are abstracted in F. Frey *et al.*, *Survey Research on Comparative Social Change: A Bibliography* (Cambridge: MIT Press, 1969). Various special numbers of

A variety of difficulties conspire against the use of this method. A cross-national survey is singular in name only. The examples in the literature involve anywhere from two to ten surveys in countries spread across several continents, and the costs are multiplied correspondingly. Since comparability is quintessential to the method, complicated administrative arrangements for conferences, communication, coordination, and decision making are usually required and tax the investigators' energies and resources. Since the countries chosen may include some where the political situation is volatile, the survey may, in fact, heighten tensions, or be construed in that way, and may be barred altogether or aborted along the way, or if forced to completion may yield poor-quality data. Since international investigators occasionally have behaved like invaders or barbarians rather than as scholars and decent guests, the hosts may make them *persona non grata*. Not only may their future surveys be bared and cooperation of indigenous scholars be withheld from them, but, tragically, the frontiers may be closed to other deserving and innocent surveyors.

If the investigators can triumph over all these practical difficulties, they still must cope with all sorts of technical problems. Words must be translated in such a way as to maintain equivalence in the instruments; concepts must be translated across cultures into their equivalents in the several societies. Otherwise the fundamental assumption of comparability on which the method rests may be jeopardized. Procedures must be adapted to the special circumstances of drawing samples, obtaining the cooperation of respondents, and eliciting the data in each country, and yet they must maintain the all-essential comparability. When the data are finally in hand, the analysts must ponder all these prior operations in evaluating the differences, and must summon up all sorts of deep knowledge of the countries in interpreting those differences that seem to be societal, rather than artifactual. No wonder there have been so few weighty cross-national surveys accomplished until now.

The moral is that we should make the most of what we have. Surveys that have been very expensive and hard to conduct and bring to succeessful completion should be exploited to the fullest by secondary analysis. Such precious resources deserve lavish attention and the highest quality of workmanship. There may be few studies, but if they are used repeatedly for diverse purposes, the data base, in effect, is multiplied. However desirable, such cross-

---

journals and a series of books are available beginning around 1953. For listings of the few major studies that have been conducted, see, for example, F. Frey, "Cross Cultural Survey Research in Political Science," in R. T. Holt and J. E. Turner, eds., *The Methodology of Comparative Research* (New York: Free Press, 1970), pp. 173–294; H. Hyman, "Strategies in Comparative Survey Research," in R. Smith, ed., *Social Science Methods* (New York: Free Press, in press).

national research is the last place for the inexperienced secondary analyst to begin his career. It may appear simple, but it is fraught with difficulties.

There is another way in which the meager data base for comparative studies can be multiplied. Surveys in different countries that were conducted initially as component parts of a comparable cross-national study are few. But a great many surveys may have been conducted as *independent* inquiries in many countries with no thought of what was going on elsewhere. And by fortunate coincidence parallel surveys with comparable data may be found. The secondary analyst must not limit himself only to studies that were arranged originally as cross-national designs. He must try to *re*arrange separate national surveys, after the fact, into a cross-national design. Since he has a great many surveys to choose from for a considerable number of countries, his chances of finding what he is after are not so poor, and he can still maintain reasonable standards as to comparability, rejecting those surveys that do not satisfy him.

The success of this strategy, of course, depends on the investigator's resourcefulness and flexibility. Some of the countries he might like to have represented in his design may lack surveys on the topic that interests him. He may have to change some of his desires, narrowing the number of countries, or substituting ones that interest him less, or modifying the original problem to suit the data. He must exercise unusual skill and good judgment in appraising comparability since it was not built into the original survey. If he is utterly mechanical and rigid in demanding complete identity or equivalence in all respects, he may find no surveys whatsoever for a series of countries that meet such a criterion of comparability and that suit his problem. The test of his skill is in checking on apparent sources of incomparability and weighing them properly, and he must be sophisticated in the way he weighs orthodox doctrines which, if applied mechanically, would hamper this strategy for secondary cross-national research. For example, primary cross-national surveys often are conducted *simultaneously* in the various countries, but careless thinking underlies the position that comparability is necessarily jeopardized if chronological time is *not* a constant. If that doctrine were applied without exception, there would be very little prospect for comparing cross-national surveys because independent surveys which might be comparable in other respects are not likely by chance to have been conducted at the very same point in all the countries. All this underscores the fact that secondary cross-national research is not for the beginner.

The use of this second strategy to enlarge comparative knowledge also protects us from reckless inferences we would be likely to make if we depended solely on *primary* research. This special benefit deserves a brief note.

Primary analysts of cross-national surveys often wish to interpret differences in their findings as reflections of enduring cultural or structural features of the respective societies. Since it is hard enough to complete *one* comparable survey in each of several countries, however desirable, it is almost inconceivable that a primary design would involve several surveys over time in all, or even any, countries. No one can really say that the national differences observed would have been the same if the surveys had been done at another time, since they may well reflect transient conditions within each society at that particular calendar point, rather than enduring features of the respective societies. To be sure, the investigator may try to pick a single time period when the gross conditions within each society are presumably "normal," but it is hard to defend such an assumption, and sometimes sudden events to which the phenomenon under study is vulnerable destroy all possibility of such an argument.

By contrast, the secondary analyst sometimes can find a series of surveys in one or more of the countries and thus determine empirically whether the pattern is stable. Indeed, we shall report one secondary analysis in which eight to eleven surveys spanning about twenty-five years were available for each of the four countries in the design. Such a case is truly a rarity in the annals of comparative secondary analysis. Another case will be cited however, in which four to eight surveys, spanning a period of about one to three years, were available for each of the three countries in the design, the descriptions thus transcending the temporary conditions at the moment that any single survey was done. Chapter VIII will review the many possibilities and procedures to be employed.

Improving General Knowledge through Replication and Enlargement. It is through the combination of surveys from different countries and time periods that secondary analysis contributes knowledge of comparative problems that otherwise would be inaccessible and permits inferences that would not be safe in the single, primary inquiry. But this is not peculiar to comparative studies. In secondary analysis, generally, the ability to enlarge and replicate the inquiry produces a survey instrument that is powerful and sensitive in illuminating a wide range of problems that would otherwise remain obscure, and gives the investigator greater protection against reckless inferences.

Consider the common experience of a primary investigator studying some phenomenon with a fancy, expensive, probability sample of the United States numbering 2000 cases. It is a powerful tool in illuminating his problem, describing and explaining it in fine detail—up to a point. But when he tries to pinpoint the phenomenon in the Negro population, he may be down to 200 cases; in the Jewish population, to 75 cases; among those with a particular constellation of characteristics—for example, young, northern Negroes—the numbers may have dwindled to as few as 25 cases. As he tries to sharpen his focus upon groups that are microscopic in size, to examine more subtle details and hypotheses, the once powerful instrument loses its power. He is either forced into reckless inferences despite the inadequate number of observations, or must admit that his survey is not sensitive enough to detect and safely measure very refined phenomena.

A solution, in principle, lies in enlarging the total sample or designing it initially so as to enlarge a particular cell at the expense of another cell of lesser interest. The first procedure may be barred to him because of costs. The latter procedure presupposes that he is driven toward only one or a few goals, and can sacrifice knowledge in some directions in order to expand it in another. Often, the analyst has many interests. He would like his instrument to serve him well in several respects, and must spread his quantum of scarce resources too thin. Worse yet, the strategy presupposes that he knows in advance exactly where he is going. Often the fruitful directions to follow are discovered only in the course of a survey, when it is too late to redesign the sampling. What is also presupposed is that the individuals who exemplify the constellation of characteristics of interest can be located in advance by some simple device and thereby easily sampled rather than screened after the fact. To the contrary: The individuals most strategic for some test may be elusive and spread thinly throughout the population rather than densely concentrated in one or a few places. There may be no sampling frame available by which to locate them in advance, and the characteristics that define some special and rare group as appropriate for study may not be observable features easily screened, but inner states and personal experiences that can be measured only by lengthy questioning in the course of a survey.

An alternative that solves many of these problems and increases the sensitivity of the research is to repeat the original inquiry a second or even a third time, thereby enlarging the total number of observations, replicating the tests, and thus safeguarding the inferences.

Replication, of course, is a classic and powerful procedure, not only making the findings less vulnerable to the errors or accidents in sampling, but also protecting them from the accidental and transient circumstances that impinged on the respondents and operated on the particular set of survey procedures. The combined findings transcend all those particularities. In a series of surveys, one may try to improve each inquiry, rather than merely replicate it, sharpening and tightening the successive phases in light of the information learned at each previous stage, but unknown at the time of the initial survey. However desirable these strategies may be, a series of surveys multiplies the cost both in money and time and may be prohibitively expensive.

With secondary analysis, the various strategies become workable. Several available and comparable surveys may be combined into one super-survey, thus enlarging the size of various cells and making the instrument sensitive enough to examine tiny groups, and complex patterns or processes.[18] Or they may be treated as replications bringing those benefits within reach.[19] Chapters IV and V will provide many instances.

When the secondary analyst enlarges the number of cases on which particular kinds of measurements have been made, or conducts an independent study of a problem in a second survey which employs the very same procedures and measurements as the first, he certainly has protected the finding from certain kinds of errors. His findings are still vulnerable, however, to whatever limitations were inherent in the particular indicator or measuring instrument that was used on *all* the cases and in *all* the replicated surveys.

Although a primary investigator cannot normally strengthen his conclusions by enlarging the number of cases or number of surveys, he is in a relatively advantaged position with respect to the number and quality of the measuring instruments he can apply. He designs items or questions that are especially appropriate to the concepts he has in mind, and he deliberately incorporates multiple indicators so as to obtain a more reliable and comprehensive measurement of each major variable. One might argue, using the term in a legitimate but special sense, that the primary analyst has replicated his tests through the use of multiple indicators, although it should be stressed that these are not truly independent tests, since they are all derived from the very same set of respondents and the very same survey. Indeed, one of the crucial difficulties in secondary analysis is that the indicators one employs may have tenuous connections to the concepts under study and may be too few in

---

[18] As we shall see in Chapter IV, some *secondary* analysts had to omit from their studies rare population groups, and this despite the fact that they were working with four or more surveys and a grand total of 12,000 or more cases. But this only makes the argument more compelling. Primary research on this scale truly is prohibitively expensive, and, by contrast, the secondary analysts could have enlarged their base by adding more surveys at little expense.

[19] How great the gain can be is described by Selvin in his treatment of Durkheim as a "secondary analyst." Selvin uses the term "replication" to include not merely the duplication of an inquiry in every respect, but also "the systematic restudy of a given relationship in different contexts." By this definition, he remarks that Durkheim's first test of an hypothesis is "followed by no less than *seventeen* replications . . . Durkheim's lavish use of replications is in sharp contrast to modern survey research, where a relationship usually appears only in a single table. One reason why Durkheim used so many replications is undoubtedly that his data came from official records; it cost him little more to study suicides in six countries than in one." Hanan Selvin, "Durkheim's Suicide: Further Thoughts on a Methodological Classic," in R. Nisbet, ed., *Emile Durkheim* (Englewood Cliffs: Prentice Hall, 1965), p. 121.

number to insure reliable and comprehensive measurement. One must take what one can find.

All this, however, is a balance sheet of the paper assets and liabilities with which primary and secondary analysts start. The way they translate their prospects is what counts. We shall report instances where secondary analysts are fortunate enough to find surveys that contain multiple indicators which do seem highly appropriate to their concepts. One can report instances of primary analysts who have predicated their conclusions upon very few indicators, perhaps even upon a single item, and where the slippage between concept and indicator was considerable. Good intentions do not necessarily make good procedures. An analyst may fail to produce an appropriate instrument, not because of lack of intent, but simply because of fallibility.

Some secondary analysts, as we shall also note, have worked with one or a few rudimentary items and only on a small sample within a single survey. And some, whether working with few or many items and few or many observations, have strained those items of all proper meaning as they stretched them to a purpose for which they never were intended. Nevertheless, general knowledge on many problems may be greatly expanded by those secondary analysts who can apply within their studies one or more of the strategies noted: the replication of tests over a series of surveys, the enlargement of samples, and the use of multiple items and operations. The possibilities and the difficulties will be reviewed in Chapters IV and V.

Elevating and Enlarging Theory.   Certainly a greatly expanded empirical base, the exploration of otherwise inaccessible phenomena, and various safeguards against unwarranted inferences all contribute to the improvement of theory, which depends, after all, upon the quality of the evidence. But there are two distinctive features built into the very activities of secondary analysis which stimulate the investigator to elevate and enlarge his theorizing.

The necessity to use indicators that happen to be available sometimes forces the investigator to measure his concepts by inappropriate means. The slippage between concept and indicator is an ever present danger in secondary analysis. The investigator is tempted under conditions of exigency to introduce serious errors. But he is also pushed in the direction of higher levels of abstraction. When an investigator focuses on a concept in designing a new inquiry, he points himself in the right direction, but his vision is narrowed. He selects the few indicators that hit the center of his target idea. The secondary analyst starts at the other end. He must examine a diverse array of concrete indicators, assorted specific manifestations of behavior or attitude, apparently tangential bits and pieces that he hopes will fit into some larger domain. He is compelled to think broadly and abstractly in order to find overarching concepts or categories within which these varied specific entities can be contained. He is likely to be more exhaustive in his definition of a concept, to think about it not only in his accustomed ways, but in all sorts of odd ways. Vicariously he is immersed in the thought processes of others, some being products of the same milieu and period, and some far removed from him in time and place. This feature of his experience takes us beyond the way in which his specific theories are elevated to higher levels of abstraction and further demonstrates that the general body of theory in any given period is enlarged by secondary analysis.

Many commentators on science tell us of the discontinuities in theory, of the fads and fashions in scientific thought and in the choice of problems. The secondary analyst may escape the narrow ways of thought in his milieu in the process of searching through archives and records. He inevitably becomes a kind of antiquarian, rumaging through all the relics from surveys of earlier periods. The scholars who conducted some of those old surveys were, of course, also afflicted by the fashions and urgent problems of their day, for there is no enterprise more afflicted by fashion than institutionalized public opinion research, geared as it has been to applied research needs and to journalism.

The point, however, is that the secondary analyst sees all at once a show of fashions from many periods, and is at least reminded of problems that are now neglected to our disadvantage.[20] He may still turn his back upon these potentially fruitful topics and return to the problems shared in the society of his fellow workers, but there is at least a chance that he may broaden his theorizing and choice of problems in light of the exotic stimulus. This may require unusual courage and character. Chapter III presents the testimony of some secondary analysts who were creative enough to profit from just such experiences.

---

[20] The periodic summaries by Hazel Erskine of poll findings in various areas document the changing interests of the agencies, and are cited in various places in our text. One such summary, concerned with research on attitudes toward freedom of speech and tolerance toward political nonconformity remarks on three periods, in totality spanning twenty years, when the issue was being studied, only to be dropped in the interim periods. "Thirty-five questions originated in the 20 peak years, as compared with only nine questions during the 15 years of comparative quiet. . . . Rarely has any research organization followed through one facet of civil liberties with a uniform question over any length of time." To be sure, this discontinuity hampers the analyst of trends and social change, but exposure to these data can serve the function of restoring interest in an important problem. See "The Polls: Freedom of Speech," *Publ. Opin. Quart.*, **34**, 1970, p. 483.

A Foundation for Realizing the Potentialities

Existing surveys can be made to yield these many benefits, but only if the researcher learns how to realize their full potentialities, how to translate the great, but vague, opportunity into the reality of successfully completed studies of specific and fruitful problems. To succeed, he surely must have knowledge of technical principles and procedures of analysis, but also he must develop familiarity with the wide range of data available, good judgment in choosing his problems, and skill in applying the technical principles to the specific data. It is not easy to provide all these elements in book form; however, all are essential to the foundation upon which the secondary analyst can build his studies. In the following sections we shall outline the contents of this book and its structure, which, although unconventional, seems to us the best form to establish that foundation.

DISTINCTIVE METHODOLOGICAL PRINCIPLES

In the following Chapters, we develop a comprehensive formulation of the *distinctive* features of secondary analysis and present them in a way which will establish a firm foundation of knowledge plus judgment and skill. Because much of routine primary analysis, notably the multivariate treatment of quantitative data, applies equally to the secondary analysis of many problems, there is no need to review such procedures here. Many students already have such background and it is adequately covered in the literature of survey research. But exactly what principles and procedures are distinctive enough to require extensive coverage?

Research Design in Secondary Analysis. Those who conduct new surveys must cope with matters of budget, time, and personnel, and with exigencies in the field. Sometimes they are severely constrained by such practical conditions, but, at least, they are free to create their total inquiry, constructing every phase of it as best they can to suit their special purpose. Understandably, the matter of research design assumes great importance for the *primary* analyst. By overall planning and intelligent allocation of his resources, leading to a specially constructed arrangement or design of all the parts of a survey, he maximizes the likelihood that the study will be brought to completion, that it will yield unambiguous findings relevant to the original problem, and that the errors that accompany all empirical research will be reduced and measurable.

The secondary analyst, by contrast, does not create anything in the sense of *physically constructing* it. All the completed pieces of the surveys are there already, predetermined for him and unchangeable. From this narrow point of view, he has nothing to design, and correspondingly, there are no principles to be promulgated. By adopting a broader point of view, we will recognize that the secondary analyst truly does create his total inquiry, though in different and subtle ways. In secondary, just as in primary analysis, the success of the inquiry is dependent on the quality of the research design employed. Its importance and its distinctiveness make it essential that research design should be a central topic in our later treatment of methodology. But since secondary analysts may not even be aware that they design their research—and indeed they do not in the conventional sense—it seems all the more important to sensitize them to this fact and to improve their knowledge and skill in this area. The many varieties of research designs, their properties, and the ways they can be created will be reviewed in later chapters, but a basic point can be made now.

The primary analyst constructs a total survey and each of its parts to suit his purposes. The secondary analyst, by exercising careful judgment, selects from the many available surveys the one or more that happen to have been constructed in ways that are most compatible with his purposes. In primary analysis, the design is achieved by the *pre*arrangement of parts of the surveys. In secondary analysis, it is achieved by *re*arrangement of a survey or the combination of several surveys rearranged as if they were components of a larger planful inquiry, and by the *elimination* of those portions of one or more of the original surveys that would frustrate or complicate the analysis.

Within the limits of his resources, the primary analyst constructs procedures that will reduce error. Again, what the secondary analyst does is select a survey with an eye to the quality and accuracy of the procedures, or he tries to attenuate error by combining surveys, or he eliminates those portions of the surveys which are most error ridden.

In primary studies, research must be designed in relation to budget. A design too large for one's resources, no matter how beautiful it may be, will never be completed. The secondary analyst lives off the financial resources of others and works only with completed studies. Even so, he faces analogous problems of scaling his design. He must also exercise restraint. Sometimes, there may be no end to the relevant surveys at his disposal, and since he may combine so many at so little cost, he may exhaust his own *intellectual* resources and be unable to complete the study. In all these ways, the secondary analyst does or should do much planning and arranging of all phases of his inquiry. In the process, he designs or creates a new totality out of the old parts. In our later chapters, we shall describe at length no less than a dozen different research designs in secondary analysis, and if one makes finer distinctions among subtypes, the designs one can employ are even more numerous.

Distinctive Problems of Error in Secondary Analysis. All survey research tries to control error, first at the point of design by the use of high-quality procedures suited to the topic, and, again, at the point of analysis, by the appraisal of the residual errors that affect the data. The secondary analyst might seem to be no worse off. In the course of analysis, he attempts to appraise the errors and, as suggested, he can even exercise control initially by proper selection, elimination, and combination of surveys and their parts. But this is an idealized, perhaps utopian, picture of his situation. Error can be a vexatious problem for him and is sufficiently distinctive that it must be given extensive treatment in our later chapters. It is the second major theme that will recur throughout the discussion of methodological principles and in the case studies presented. The general nature of the problem can be outlined here. We shall begin with the most basic difficulty.

A primary analyst may not have designed his survey well, but at least he knows what procedures he prescribed, even though he may lack complete knowledge of the exact way they operated in every place in his sample. Thus, he can make a knowledgeable appraisal of the residual errors in the data. The secondary analyst does not necessarily deal with surveys of lesser quality, more afflicted by errors. His real problem is simply that he may not know enough about the original procedures to make a sound appraisal of errors in the data.

The problem is more acute when using surveys from the distant past. When methodology was more primitive, some researchers were less meticulous in keeping records. And most were not thinking of later generations of secondary analysts reading those records. The idea had hardly dawned upon them. They knew what they were doing in their own surveys without benefit of detailed records. Once a report had been written and a reasonable interval had passed, the files could be closed and buried. Thus, whatever records once existed may have been destroyed or simply lost with the passage of time. Apart from the fallibility of memory, there may be no participants left alive to reconstruct the procedures.

Surveys from distant places in the world present similar problems. Some are from places where survey reasearch is primitive. Record keeping may be poor and in an exotic language. Transporting the records to distant archives increases the risk of loss and presents problems of expense and logistics. Communicating with the participants is difficult. A secondary analyst dealing with surveys from his own country may at least approximate an appraisal of error in light of his acquaintance with the original agency and knowledge of its general operating procedures. In employing surveys from remote countries, he may lack even such gross knowledge. Such problems obviously deter secondary analysis of discrete historical topics, trend analysis reaching far back in time, and cross-national analysis.

These deficiencies in knowledge impinge also at the point of design. Applying the criterion of quality in the selection and elimination of surveys presupposes knowledge of the procedures and assumes that the supply of surveys is lavish enough that one can be particular and that the quality of the procedures can override all other desiderata. A particular survey of dubious or unknown quality may be a rare or unique source of data on a particular substantive topic. A secondary analyst may confront all sorts of conflicts implicating the problem of error and then must exercise good judgment and special skill in design and analysis. If he feels compelled to make one or more reckless decisions at the point of design, he should try to compensate either by other protections introduced elsewhere in the design, by extra care in reviewing the residual errors, or by ingenious analytic tests of the evidence.

Even when the original surveys are explicit about their procedures and legitimate claims are made for their good quality, the proper appraisal of errors can still be difficult. Indeed, such a situation can give an uncritical analyst a false sense of security. The surveys appear to be most attractive properties to inherit and work with, and the analyst may therefore neglect to appraise how appropriate the procedures are for *his* topic. What may be harmless or a trivial source of error—perhaps even a desirable procedure— when a survey is applied to one purpose, may become a source of considerable error when that survey is converted to other purposes. Why should a primary analyst make any cautionary note about a harmless procedure or trivial detail? He may even have *praised* its utility for his purposes. Thus it is easy for the secondary analyst to discount some errors that lurk in the path of *his* conclusions.

Consider, for example, the analyst who finds some national surveys of American adults based on elegant probability samples. He takes no special note of the fact that these almost invariably are restricted to the noninstitutionalized population, excluding from their universe about 5% of adults who do not live in private dwellings. Such a practice normally could not be regarded as a source of error, but simply a minor constraint on the generalizability of the findings, the *aggregate* findings for most studies changing very little by adding into the total the small number that was missed. Indeed, it even improves the findings from some studies, for example, in voting research, since the inclusion of those in institutions would incorporate mainly individuals who for legal or other reasons are disfranchised.

The secondary analyst who recasts those surveys into a study specific to the *very old* or the *very young*, however, might find himself seriously hampered by such sample designs. Much larger and perhaps distinctive portions of these particular age groups are contained within military, collegiate, or other types of institutions, and his findings might be far from the true picture that would have been drawn if such individuals were also sampled. Admittedly, the label "in error" would not be deserved if he stayed within strict boundaries of his universe in his statements. But two of the cases reported later will show the analysts weighing, and for good cause, the probability that such fine, but restricted, samples led in obscure ways to errors in their conclusions about a particular phenomenon.

The later chapters treat many sources of error and stress the difficulties and obscurities. Even in the rare instance where the problem defied solution, the recognition of that fact by the investigator and a candid statement of his uncertainty attached to a report marks some advance in secondary analysis. Being casual and glossing over the problem in a report misleads the reader and represents worse research. The later chapters will also show ways to make careful appraisals and tests of error in the course of analysis and ways to reduce possible errors in the design stage. It is only fair, however, to note that a secondary analyst can also create by his design an *emergent* problem of error where none was present before, when the original surveys were treated as discrete and intact entities. He initiates this perverse process by the arbitrary and thoughtless way he combines fine individual surveys, eliminates portions of them, and excludes others. He has powerful tools of design at his disposal but he can handle them ineptly. However, since this error is of his own making, it is also completely within his control, and principles to insure his safe conduct will be presented.

Selection of Appropriate Indicators and Index Construction.   Another set of methodological problems is central and distinctive to secondary analysis. The choice of appropriate indicators and index construction is the third and final theme stressed throughout the later chapters.

These problems might appear to be completely covered already under our second theme. The data derived from particular questions, always being subject to response or measurement error, certainly must be inspected in that light. That indeed was implicit in our previous discussion and is fundamental to the appraisal and control of error in general. But that part of the problem, although not easily solved, is not likely to be ignored since it is a conventional issue in all survey research. There are two other facets to the problem which might be seen only dimly and therefore deserve to be highlighted by a separate designation.

A *primary* analyst must face the possibility that unreliable and biased responses cause error in the measurement of whatever variable he intended his instrument to measure. But certainly his data will have some minimal relevance to the concept under study. The instrument may reasonably be regarded as having some degree of *face* validity if the primary analyst exercised any rationality and skill at all in designing it to suit his purpose. The secondary analyst, by contrast, must search among available indicators to find the ones that fit his concepts. Earlier, we alluded to the benefits for science from being forced into this position. In the process of searching and fitting, the secondary analyst may even improve the usual measures, finding and incorporating questions that tap some important and forgotten aspect of the concept. Now we should also look at the problematic side of his situation. Within the surveys that are ideal in sampling and quality of procedures, all the questions he can find may depart to some extent from what the secondary analyst has in mind. If they surround his target concept, approaching it from various points, but none hitting it directly, then the proper diagnosis would be that he suffers from a mild condition of "slippage" that is treatable. At other times, his condition might become severe and almost uncontrollable. If the secondary analyst is narrow and rigid in his purpose, and stringent in his requirements, he may experience a real scarcity of data. Then he may stretch the available questions too far, reshaping them out of desire and desperate need to assume a meaning they cannot carry. Thus, he creates his own problem of extreme slippage between the concepts he is studying and the indicators he employs.

This end result may be described simply as an "error" in measurement, a classic example of *invalidity*. The instrument does not measure what the secondary analyst now purports it to measure. The problem could thus be treated under the omnibus heading of "error" in secondary analysis, but this would be to give it insufficient attention or to bury it. The process by which it is generated by the analyst himself is distinctive. Good judgment and restraint in selecting appropriate indicators deserves special cultivation.

The various types of slippage should be noted and strategies for reducing them should be reviewed. Obviously, one can stick rigidly to all technical requirements and original topics and concepts, and simply try to select one's indicators more carefully, sometimes accepting defeat. But it may be less obvious to some analysts that a sensible approach might be to modify some initial concepts to match the range of available indicators, to be more careful in defining the final concepts operationally, or to relax some other stringent technical requirement in order to net an appropriate question. These are strategies used by careful and productive secondary analysts.

Some forms of slippage, as we have implied, do not involve tricky switches in meaning and dangerous chains of interpretation, but are simply minor slips away from an ideal measurement to which the analysts simply should become alert. It is common, for example, that although the appropriate concept may be implicated in the question, the measurement may have been obtained for a member of the family or a time period that is not the ideal one. The amount of slippage in a given question can sometimes be checked by other questions and attenuated by combining several questions into a battery. This will suggest conventional procedures of index construction, but it is not what we intend by our reference to one other facet of the problem that will be reviewed in later chapters.

Slippage is a problem produced by a narrowness of purpose and a scarcity of appropriate indicators, common conditions in some kinds of studies. But in one class of studies, broad in purpose, the secondary analyst suffers not from a lack of indicators, but from an overabundance of them. It is absurd to suggest that when a secondary analyst escapes from a starvation diet into a situation of plenty, he is in a perilous condition. Indeed, he is very well off, but he must then cope with unusual problems of index construction, which primary analysts hardly ever face and correspondingly have little to say about.

Chapter IV will present many fruitful examples of secondary analysis in which social groups are described and compared along very broad, multi-dimensional lines by combining a great diversity of data from many surveys. Primary analysts, being able to conduct only one or a few surveys, usually have a much narrower scope and a more limited data base. The secondary analyst develops various designs for implementing such studies and for sampling surveys and items located in this multidimensional scheme. But he must also develop methods of index construction for compressing and clarifying such a volume and complexity of data and to impose order upon the final descriptions and comparisons.

THE STRUCTURE OF THE BOOK

Our systematic treatment of secondary analysis really does not begin until Chapter IV. Then it is organized in terms of major types of problems that can be studied rather than in terms of a neat statement or compact list of abstract principles and formal procedures. Chapters IV and V treat studies of a wide variety of social groups and fundamental phenomena for which past surveys provide unusually rich resources of data, and present many cases of investigators analyzing these problems. The technical principles are presented in the context of their research, shown in live action. The reader sees a procedure being used, adapted, and applied with skill and judgment.

In these chapters we have sometimes chosen one particular theme or problem and consolidated into a lengthy case study many examples of parallel secondary analyses. This device serves to suggest the plenitude of particular types of data and the special benefit from combining surveys in various ways and from continuity of inquiry. It also emphasizes how basic some technical principles and procedures are and shows the way different investigators apply them in the study of a particular problem and the solution of recurrent difficulties. But then we have also presented shorter case studies of other substantive problems, to suggest the variety of data and corresponding problems that can be studied, and again conveying how generic certain analytic principles and procedures are, no matter what specific problem is being studied. The cases cover problems germane to various disciplines—mainly psychology, political science, and sociology, but occasionally other fields. Such a selection should emphasize the breadth of secondary analysis.

In Chapters IV and V, we periodically codify the principles and procedures implicit in the cases and present them in a more abstract form. We also present brief listings of types of data that are available to increase familiarity with the resources. In connection with some problems, many investigators have seen their opportunity and grasped it. Ironically, in other areas practically no one has noticed or seized an opportunity, and only by a listing of materials that have rarely or never been studied, can we redress this neglect.

Chapters IV and V present the principles and procedures that are basic to all secondary analyses, but in the context of *relatively* simple problems. The reader enters upon his vicarious career as a secondary analyst where the life is good —where he can strike it rich and where the labors and learning are easiest. Chapters VI and VII move to more difficult problems, the study of change over time and the study of phenomena in comparative context. These, as already suggested, are very fruitful areas for secondary analysis, but demand unusually thoughtful judgment and special technical knowledge over and above the knowledge of general principles and procedures.

Studies of social groups and phenomena, when limited in time and social space, are everyday activities in *primary* analysis. The paths one must follow in solving such problems by *secondary* analysis are novel ones, but not utterly unfamiliar. Past experience as a primary analyst provides a kind of road map which will orient the mature reader as he traces the routes the secondary analysts take, and those without previous experience in primary analysis can orient themselves with the aid of the considerable literature on primary survey analysis. Thus comprehensive directions along the entire route and for every step of the way do not have to be stated in Chapters IV and V.

Studies of change and trend analysis, by contrast, have not been the common experience of primary researchers, and thus have not been codified and incorporated into books on primary survey analysis. Truly, the reader is traveling over *terra incognita*, and he needs a route that is clearly marked. Consequently, in Chapters VI and VII we have presented a more detailed statement of principles and a step-by-step sequence of procedures. The cases are then strung upon this elaborate framework.

The case studies in this book are drawn mainly from the published literature, some dating from the era before archives. The old examples remind the reader that no one is barred from secondary analysis for lack of an accessible archive. They also reveal that, although those who proceed without recourse to the archive may be taxed heavily in some ways and have less lavish re-

sources at their disposal, their difficulties of formulation and analysis, ironically, are sometimes reduced. Selecting cases from the published literature,
old or new, also permits the reader to study the original reports in entirety
and pursue points we have omitted in our treatment, especially the substance, which we have generally skipped.

The case studies based on published reports were supplemented by cases
derived from a special survey we conducted on samples of the clients of two
archives, who had requested data, whether or not they had subsequently
published. (Appendix A describes its design.) The survey broadened our
treatment of secondary analysis in several ways. Studies that promised to be
fruitful, but which had not yet reached completion and publication, could
be drawn upon for examples. The scholars who had already published, might
well have omitted from their final polished papers information about the
actual process of secondary analysis. But when cast as respondents in our
survey, they could inform us of these subtle but all-important matters. And
those scholars who had long since lost the prospect of publication because
of such intractable difficulties that they never completed their analyses were
also captured by the survey and reported their experiences. Our treatment
could at least address itself to their problems, if not solve them.

Chapters IV–VIII communicate knowledge and skill in handling the major
methodological problems distinctive to secondary analysis, and also broaden
the reader's familiarity with the range of data available and the kinds of
studies that can be accomplished.

We have not yet described the contents of Chapters II and III in the
larger structure of the book nor explained their special function in realizing
the potentialities of secondary analysis. All the devices of Chapters IV–VIII
might still be insufficient to communicate the good judgment and fine skills
that must be applied at so many stages to succeed in secondary analysis. The
discrete case studies, whether long or short, and the principles derived from
them might even have missed some subtle element that has to be blended
into the work of an analyst if he really is to have a sustained success. Therefore, Chapter III tries to discover some of that secret of success and to facilitate learning generally by a different device. We have selected a handful of
investigators, in ways to be described, whose careers in secondary analysis
have been highly productive. We have then examined the totality of their
work and supplemented this by special, personal reports. Chapter III presents
brief portraits of these analysts at work, and thus the reader begins his detailed learning with this as orientation and inspiration.

Discussions of secondary analysis tend, perhaps without intent, to make us
see the analysis of old surveys and the conduct of new surveys as two separate
worlds of activity. We then think of ourselves as having to work in one world
but not the other. The discussions may also create a kind of orthodoxy about

secondary analysis, narrowing our conception of the kinds of activities we must engage in exclusively if we are to be respected members of that world. It would be unfortunate if such views were to prevail. There is much to be gained from joining both worlds. To counteract the emphasis on previous surveys in Chapters III–VII, and the stress on a core of methodological problems and procedures distinctive to secondary analysis, Chapter II is presented as a precautionary measure. It is intended to enlarge the view of secondary analysis and show its many connections to primary research, in the hope that the reader will thereby be encouraged to make the best of both worlds.

II

Varieties of Semisecondary Analysis

MANY STUDENTS AND SCHOLARS HAVE SOME INTUITIVE IDEAS ABOUT SECONDARY analysis, but they may construe it in too narrow a way. Understandably, their conceptions tend to be shaped by the forms that secondary analysis is now taking in the era of data archives. They must broaden their conceptions so that they will not bar themselves from discoveries that could be made in the wider realm that secondary analysis can claim. We shall therefore try to provide a more informed understanding, pushing the definition of the domain perhaps to extreme limits, so that nothing potentially profitable will be neglected. As we near the boundaries of the realm, terminological arguments may start, because there are forms of research that do not fall under a simple label, which are only *semisecondary* rather than completely, secondary analyses.

Type I: Secondary Analysis by the Primary Analyst

The usual imagery of secondary analysis is of a poor scholar obtaining data from a survey that a wealthier primary analyst could afford to conduct. In the era of data banks, this is certainly the common variety of secondary analysis, the collective wealth being loaned to individuals to further knowledge. But in an earlier era, survey organizations and analysts did not destroy the data after they had served their immediate purposes. There was some primitive accumulation of wealth, even though small in magnitude, which that very same primary analyst could draw upon for his secondary analyses.

Even today, the thoughtful man should not neglect the survey data he or his organization has already saved at home and rush to get a loan from a *foreign* data bank. Apart from the small service charges, there are greater penalties he may have to pay. It is for the latter reason that we discuss an old fashioned but desirable form of semisecondary analysis. Note that it fits under the brief, introductory definition given for secondary analysis: "the extraction of knowledge on topics other than those which were the *focus* of the original surveys"—whoever the second analyst may be. Although it is not the pure, modern form, it was the classic form.

Consider an analysis reported in 1947, long before data banks were established, chosen because of our intimate knowledge of the circumstances surrounding the original surveys. Exploiting a series of six surveys conducted in December, 1945, February, April, May, June, and September, 1946 by the National Opinion Research Center, Hyman and Sheatsley, members of that organization and the primary analysts of the surveys, extracted findings from the original bodies of data on the social psychological determinants of knowledge and ignorance of public affairs.[1] The reader may feel uneasy about classifying such a case as *secondary* analysis. Understandably, he may be suspicious about the behavior of the primary analysts. He may gain some comfort by designating it only "semisecondary."

If questions appropriate to this problem were included in the original surveys, was it not done with such purposes in mind initially? Secondary analysis may seem a misnomer, masking the sins of the primary analysts who were delivering too late an installment of the original analysis they had neglected to do in the first place. Such delinquency is not unheard of in research circles. The argument seems all the more compelling when one notes that the major variables figuring in the second analysis were measured not by an incidental question or two, but by indices based on batteries of questions.

Despite the circumstantial evidence, an alternative interpretation must be considered, by which these analysts may be exonerated from crimes of bad intentions or negligence. To be sure, there was purpose behind the inclusion of such questions, but the critical point is *what* purpose? The meaning attached to the questions in the second analysis was certainly not in the focus of the original inquiries.

It is a truism that survey questions may serve *more* than one purpose; they may be treated as indicators of some complexity. As the examples

---

[1] Herbert H. Hyman and Paul B. Sheatsley, "Some Reasons Why Information Campaigns Fail," *Publ. Opin. Quart.*, **11**, 1947, pp. 412–423. The six surveys were drawn from a long string of surveys sponsored by the State Department and conducted on a monthly basis, each intended to document the response of the public to international events as they occurred and public opinion on American foreign policy.

throughout the text will demonstrate repeatedly, a new analyst by an act of *abstraction* uses questions originally employed to indicate one entity to illuminate other aspects that a former analyst did not have in mind at all. What becomes critical for the success of many secondary analyses is the validity of the relation between the old indicator and the new concept, since the second analyst has to refashion tools that were fashioned initially to serve other measurement purposes.

Indeed one may say that, up to a point, the greater the powers of abstraction, the more successful the secondary analyst. More raw materials then serve his needs. If he cannot see the original questions as serving any new purposes whatsoever, but remains firmly fixed in the ways of thought of the earlier analysts, he obviously has nothing new to study. It has all been done before. But if a second analyst is capable of following old indicators down new conceptual paths, it would seem reasonable to endow the first analyst with the same intellectual gifts.

There are other reasons for coming to the defense of analysts of such dual stature or slippery character as Hyman and Sheatsley, and for asserting that the case may at least be labeled semisecondary analysis. There is one class of questions or items incorporated in most surveys that may properly be described either as *multipurpose* indicators, or as *purposeless*. Such background or "face-sheet" items as region and size of community, sex, age, occupation, etc. clearly are descriptions of complex entities. Each is a shorthand way of referring to many aspects of the respondent's experience.

It is also correct to say that most analysts incorporate a core of such questions without the slightest conscious thought. These have long since passed into the routinized, mechanical operations of survey research because it is taken for granted that they are bound to be useful in various ways, some of which are utterly unrelated to any substantive problem. For example, the face-sheet characteristics are often used as quality controls to check on the skill with which the sampling was executed.

As we shall see later, one of the most fruitful types of secondary analyses involves the study of social groups, readily located through the classification of respondents by reference to their face-sheet characteristics. It is just because the basic face-sheet has become almost institutionalized that many different surveys can later be combined in various research designs to bring large and powerful bodies of evidence to bear on the study of the major social groupings or categories of a society.

At one point in their analysis, Hyman and Sheatsley do classify respondents by the size of their community of residence. They use this datum as an indicator of the objective availability of sources of information in the immediate environment in order to test the importance of objective versus subjective determinants of knowledge. This was certainly a use far removed from the common purposes behind the face-sheet item on residence.

Make, however, the extreme assumption that any single question serves only a unitary purpose, or is a refined indicator of only one aspect of behavior. Nevertheless, it may be related to other measures, also unitary in character, to test some hypothesis or illuminate some problem that was not on the agenda of the original analysis. It is from the *recombination* of the multiple measures in a survey that a new focus of analysis can appear.

By way of illustration, the original purposes of a study may have required the differentiated description of some phenomenon for respondents in contrasted occupations or educational categories. But by examining that same phenomenon for social groups with various *profiles* of education *and* occupation, one may transcend the original purposes and test by secondary analysis a theory of status congruence, or a theory of relative deprivation, those being in occupations below the level of their educational peers presumably feeling relatively deprived.[2] If one adds a third characteristic to the profile, such as race or region, one obtains a more refined measure of deprivation relative to peers in social or psychological proximity.

Or to take another illustration, primary analysis might have included separate breakdowns of a phenomenon for religious groups and for regions of the country. By the combination of these two face-sheet items, one could examine the influence of religious membership when, depending on the environmental context, one is placed in the position of a minority or majority in the population. Thus, by the very simple process of abstracting oneself from the earlier concrete datum, the analyst moves to the test of current theories of contextual processes, or what Katz and Eldersveld, and Tingsten before them, called "cluster effects."[3] We shall come later to the detailed discussion of secondary analytic designs for studies of social contexts, but as the example will suggest, it can all begin with the combination of simple face-sheet indicators out of which a totally new focus emerges.

To take one more illustration, each information question Hyman and Sheatsley asked might be construed as only a measure of one concrete bit of knowledge. That was the sole intended purpose the sponsor of the original surveys had in mind. But the matrix of intercorrelations then examined in

---

[2] For example, a recent secondary analysis examines a rather bizarre consequence of status incongruence, the tendency of individuals who exhibit "underrewarded" versus "overrewarded" status incongruence to see flying saucers. See Donald Warren, "Status Inconsistency Theory and Flying Saucer Sightings," *Science*, **170**, No. 3958, November 6, 1970, pp. 599–603.

[3] Herbert Tingsten, *Political Behavior: Studies in Election Statistics*, (London: King, 1937). Daniel Katz and Samuel J. Eldersveld, "The Impact of Local Party Activity upon the Electorate," *Publ. Opin. Quart.*, **25**, 1961, pp. 1–24.

the secondary analysis established whether knowledge was a generalized quality of some individuals and whether others were, as Hyman and Sheatsley put it, "chronic know-nothings." By extension, the combination of findings from their six separate surveys clarified problems that were not likely to be the focus of any single survey, and which could not have been central to the first survey in the series. The discrete reports rendered to the sponsor after each survey satisfied his immediate purposes and may be regarded as the completion of the primary analysis. As we shall see later, some of the most fruitful secondary analyses depend on combining several surveys by various designs. As a result, a problem not previously subject to analysis comes under study. Whether or not the second analyst is new on the job does not change the fact that a new focus has emerged.[4]

No doubt, some of the potentialities for secondary analysis must be in the awareness of any primary analyst. If he were sensitive, he could not help but see the manifold implications of his original inquiry. But by defining secondary analysis in terms of what is outside the focus of inquiry, even if it is in the periphery of vision, a primary analyst is encouraged toward the same goals of secondary analysis as anyone else.[5]

---

[4] Some of the earliest examples of semisecondary analysis involved the synthesis of many findings from a large number of surveys in which the investigator had participated. For example, the analysts and editors of the Gallup Poll have periodically issued volumes synthesizing the findings of a great many surveys to characterize American thought for a particular era. See, for example, John M. Fenton, *In Your Opinion* (Boston: Little, Brown, 1960) which covers the period 1945–1960. In some of these instances, the analyst supplemented surveys conducted by his own organization with surveys from other agencies. Thus, to be precise, a portion of the inquiry was semisecondary and other portions were completely secondary analysis, but the total body of data was treated in an integrated way. See, for example, Jerome S. Bruner, *Mandate From The People* (New York: Duell, Sloan, and Pearce, 1944) which marshalled data from 1937 to 1944 to characterize the American political culture of that period, and to describe the kind of post war society the American people expected and desired. A semisecondary analysis, similar in design, treated data from a large number of surveys spanning the period, 1945–1955, to characterize American thought about the United Nations and foreign relations. See William A. Scott and Stephen B. Withey, *The United States and the United Nations: The Public View, 1945–1955* (New York: Manhattan Publishing Company, 1958).

[5] One particular form of exploitation of a survey by a primary analyst cannot fall under the heading of semisecondary analysis. We have in mind the opportunity often presented to use a survey as a vehicle onto which to tie a supplemental inquiry. The analyst, so to speak, hitchhikes or takes a free ride, since the overhead costs have been covered and there remains extra space in the vehicle which would otherwise be wasted. Such an omnibus inquiry involves really two primary and independent analyses. That it is a good strategy is suggested by the institutionalization of what has come to be called "amalgam" or "caravan" surveys in which the questions of several different analysts are carried on the same larger questionnaire, each then paying only his small share of the total cost.

To convey the similarities between this first form of semisecondary analysis and the more conventional forms, we have had to examine some of the fundamental features of any secondary analysis. In one respect, however, the restudy is simplified for the original analyst, and he faces far fewer risks than a new analyst. The contrast between their respective situations may also enlarge our understanding of the general process, and suggest some of the principles and cautions to guide any secondary analyst.

It is self-evident that the searching phase of the process is much simpler for the analyst working with his own data or in the confines of his own organization. Even when a new analyst knows the very specific materials needed to treat a sharply defined problem, he still must search and hope that he will find them. Ironically, as the technology for retrieving information accelerates, the archive also grows ever larger. It must be sifted. At the end of his search, a second analyst may have a far larger data base than the analyst who uses his own agency's data,[6] but the search is bound to be more laborious and at times frustrating. The data are stored in the machine—assuming they exist—not stored in his own memory where they are immediately accessible.

But as we shall see in our discussion of styles of work, some secondary analysts start with diffuse and vague problems or ideas, their ultimate success being dependent sometimes on serendipity, or a flash of insight which leads them down a trail to a new and exciting problem and the corresponding data. The stimulant they need is not given immediately. Often it is the accidental by-product of the initial, laborious search. For semisecondary analysts of this same intellectual style, the stimulant emerges naturally in the very course of their work.

The reader can sense the paradox. How does one go searching for serendipity, for a flash of insight? Unless there is some way of improving their luck, secondary analysts of this style have to adapt to a life of chance, risking a considerable investment of effort for an uncertain return. Indeed this is their fate if their searching begins within a monstrous-size, machine-readable archive. The detailed survey findings buried within the machine cannot directly stimulate the eye or the mind. The brief general summaries of the surveys in the inventory that the prospectus of the archive or the machine

---

[6] By way of illustration, contrast the data base Hyman and Sheatsley had—six surveys—with the data base located by Schramm and his associates in 1967 for their secondary analysis of problems of public knowledge. They found 54 national surveys spanning the period from 1940 to 1967, of which 35 were subjected to more intensive treatment. Such a giant analysis would have been exceedingly difficult, perhaps impossible, to accomplish without the retrieval and processing capabilities of modern technology. See Wilbur Schramm *et al.*, *Knowledge and the Public Mind* (Stanford University, Institute for Communication Research, 1967, mimeo). A brief report of partial findings may be found in Serena Wade and Wilbur Schramm, "The Mass Media as Sources of Public Affairs, Science, and Health Knowledge," *Publ. Opin. Quart.*, **33**, 1969, pp. 197–209.

prints may be too pallid a stimulus to evoke serendipity. In the stretching out of the process, the excitement may be lost.[7]

The old-fashioned apparatus for secondary analysis perhaps is a better starting point for scholars of such intellectual style. They should browse in handbooks of marginal findings and breakdowns on various questions, in the regular journal listings of detailed findings for particular periods or topics, and in books that report detailed findings from elaborate surveys that are filed within the archives.[8] They should scan copies of the questionnaires of surveys that are filed. These are the natural forms that may stimulate flights of thought.

---

[7] In its 1968 report, the Council of Social Science Data Archives acknowledged this problem and began to innovate a solution: "Ideally, potential users should be able to interrogate a reference work at their home base. . . . At present the user must correspond with the managers of numerous archives; if his needs are unusually sophisticated, he must pay personal visits to inspect numerous codebooks." As a solution, several thousand surveys in the holdings of various archives are being described in brief, standard abstracts and will be placed on file in some machine form in many libraries and computer centers. Certainly, this will reduce the labors in searching and hopefully increase utilization. (May, 1968 Report, pp. 7–9.)

[8] For an encyclopedic listing of findings from many countries prior to 1946, see Cantril and Strunk, *op. cit.* Up to 1951, the *Public Opinion Quarterly* contained a section, "The Quarter's Polls," listing results under topical headings for questions asked in the previous three-month period. The feature was then discontinued and not revived until 1961. Since that time the *Quarterly* has published results on particular topics in a given number, rather than results on diverse topics for the narrow time period. For example, each of seven recent numbers (1967–69) has been devoted to detailed findings on aspects of Negro–white relations over the entire time span of survey research. The five volumes (1947–51) of a now defunct journal, the *International Journal of Opinion and Attitude Research*, published detailed findings for the corresponding periods under topical headings in a section called "World Opinion." A journal titled *Polls* was published in the years 1965–1968 in Amsterdam and presented detailed results by country and topical heading for the corresponding time periods, accompanied by brief, basic information on the specifications of the surveys. In the period 1943–48, the National Opinion Research Center, University of Chicago, published a semimonthly journal, *Opinion News*, containing detailed findings for the period from national surveys in various countries, plus findings from state and local polls in the United States. Each issue also contained a more analytic review of a particular topic and summarized detailed findings over a long time span from all survey organizations that had addressed research to the problem. On an irregular basis, the American Institute of Public Opinion issued a quarterly titled *World Opinion*, in the years 1945–48, which contained a summary of findings on particular topics obtained by the organizations affiliated with the Gallup Poll in many countries. The Gallup Poll has continued to publish on an irregular basis the "Gallup Political Index" containing trend data and breakdowns on selected topics from their American and foreign surveys. The Indian Institute of Public Opinion has been issuing a monthly digest of its findings since 1955. For a summary of some of its major surveys, and a review and critique of the procedures, see M. Lal Goel, *Political Participation in a Developing Nation* (New York: Asia Publishing House, in press). Merritt and Puchala

have rendered a service to the community of secondary analysts by compiling a handbook of marginal totals and trends from cross-national surveys of four Western European countries conducted by the USIA during the period 1952–63. See Richard L. Merritt and Donald J. Puchala, *Western European Perspectives on International Affairs* (Praeger, 1968). A similar, notable service was rendered by Naomichi Nakanishi and Allan B. Cole who translated and edited a three-volume compilation of marginal totals and breakdowns for questions asked in 170 Japanese surveys conducted between 1947 and 1957. A concise review and evaluation of the procedures of the various agencies helps the reader appraise the quality of the data, and the sampling specifications, mode of data collection, and other relevant features are summarized for each of the surveys. See Allan B. Cole and Naomichi Nakanishi, *Japanese Opinion Polls with Socio-Political Significance, 1947–1957*, Vol. I, Political Support and Preference; Vol. II, Political Institutions, Processes, and Legislation; Vol. III, Military Problems and Foreign Relations (Medford, Mass.: The Fletcher School of Law and Diplomacy, Tufts University and Williamstown, Mass.: The Roper Public Opinion Research Center, N. D.) A brief article lists the titles and dates of 191 surveys conducted between 1946 and 1950 in Germany under the auspices of the American Occupation and is a most convenient resource for secondary analysts interested in the problems of that period and the post-war reconstruction of a society. See Leo P. Crespi, "What Do You Think?" *Information Bulletin*, April 1950. A later index lists an additional 118 surveys, and carries the record forward to 1952. (Office of the U. S. High Commissioner for Germany, Office of Public Affairs, Reactions Analysis Staff, January, 1952 mimeo.) For abstracts of all reports of the first 72 surveys, from 1945 to 1949, under U. S. Military Government auspices plus an analytic review, see A. J. Merritt and R. L. Merritt, eds., *Public Opinion in Occupied Germany* (Urbana: University of Illinois Press, 1970). Various survey organizations have periodically published a detailed index of their cumulative findings. For example, the Institute for Demoscopy published an English edition of findings from their surveys in Germany during the period 1947–66. This edition of some 600 pages is a selection from their several handbooks in German which taken together provide a more than 1500 page comprehensive listing of marginals, breakdowns and trends from all questions asked. See *The Germans, Public Opinion Polls, 1947–1966* (Allensbach, Germany: Verlag fur Demoskopie, 1967). A similar compilation of some 1350 pages presents marginals and breakdowns from surveys conducted in Italy over a ten-year period, beginning in 1946. See Luzzatto Fegiz, *Il Volto Sconosciuto dell'Italia: Dieci Anni di Sondaggi DOXA* (Milan, Italy: Giuffre, 1956). An agency perhaps unique in the population covered was the *Purdue Opinion Panel*, founded by H. H. Remmers, which issued continuing reports of the results of surveys of national samples of American high school youth for the period from about 1940 to 1960. A series of more specialized handbooks containing individual questions and more elaborate scales have started to be issued by the Institute of Social Research, University of Michigan. The first of these on political behavior includes trends for the individual questions asked by the Survey Research Center in its election studies from 1952 to 1966. See John P. Robinson, Jerrold G. Rusk, and Kendra B. Head, *Measures of Political Attitudes* (Ann Arbor, Michigan: Institute for Social Research, 1969). Secondary analyses of a broad-ranging and synthesizing type frequently yield a comprehensive listing of findings in a given topical area. For example, the Schramm monograph (*op. cit.*) presents about thirty pages of marginal totals for questions on public knowledge. The works by Bruner, and by Scott and Withey (*op. cit.*), each contain about a forty-page appendix listing questions and marginal findings plus long-term trend data on foreign policy issues. A similar source with detailed citations of many survey questions, but perhaps uniquely valuable for those secondary analysts interested in

The searching process, however, is not completed when the appropriate *substantive* data have been located. It is axiomatic in all survey research that the conclusions have to be qualified in terms of the procedures that were employed, and errors that may obscure, distort, or even artifactually create the findings be taken into account. In this respect the semisecondary analyst again starts from a great advantage.[9]

Of course, there are some sources of error that are distinctive to secondary analysis, which emerge only as a result of the special designs that are imposed upon the original data and the need to bend old instruments to fit new purposes. From whatever data base he starts, no secondary analyst can escape from all dangers, and the distinctive error problems and solutions will be treated later. It also must be noted that one of the classic experimental solutions for the problem is especially adapted to secondary analysis. The large body of data from many different agencies permits *replication* of the original test to see whether the findings arose from peculiar circumstances or procedures. This attractive design will be treated below. It is also true that the basic documents of a survey are usually deposited in data banks, and

---

regional differences is Alfred O. Hero, Jr., *The Southerner and World Affairs* (Baton Rouge, Louisiana: Louisiana State University Press, 1965). Such materials should serve to introduce the scholar to the worlds of opportunity that become accessible, and secondary analysts of a particular intellectual style will certainly find such stimuli vivid enough to generate productive thought, and yet manageable in format and magnitude. The item index in card catalogue form which lists each and every question from all past American surveys that are held in the archive of the Roper Center is a magnificent resource. Someone searching for a particular indicator or a series of indicators that relate to some set of concepts will find it a most valuable tool for secondary analysis. But it may not stimulate serendipity, since only the questions and not the marginal findings are entered on the cards. And for those analysts whose interests are diffuse and vague, it may be too unwieldy, involving dozens of drawers and thousands of cards. The analogy might be a reader looking through the catalogue of a large library for that one book out of 50,000 volumes he knows he will want, when he sees the title. The index available to institutions which hold memberships in the Roper Center, may be found at 20 or more places, and is periodically updated to show the items that have been acquired in recent surveys. Similar indexes for British, French, Canadian, and Italian items are or will be available.

[9] Converse puts the problem in its sharpest form: ". . . once one recognizes that there are myriad sources of error beyond sampling error, this question of sufficient information becomes 'much more pressing. Indeed it is likely that the information we are presupposing typically outruns that which we possess, even when it is we ourselves who have conducted the survey study and are intimate with many of its wrinkles and frailties. Naturally, when we lack such intimacy (as is necessarily the case in wholesale use of data archives) we have no vestige of this kind of information. These are the new problems of error for the user of the archives." Philip E. Converse, "The Availability and Quality of Sample Survey Data in Archives within the United States," in Merritt and ↑Rokkan, *op. cit.*, p. 431.

constitute a readily accessible source of information on the general procedures employed and some possible sources of error. A secondary analyst of a conservative bent may even decide to narrow the field of his prospecting. He may decide to draw only upon a data bank that is like one of those old and exclusive banks that welcomed only certain depositors—the best and the richest. Pick the right data bank and get the gilt-edged survey that has already been refined so as to remove many imperfections and errors. The depositors in such a data bank have nothing to hide; they would happily demonstrate that their surveys operate by an old-fashioned gold standard, and would provide ample documentation of the procedures. Nevertheless, the semisecondary analyst still has the advantage.

Documents tell only part of the story of any survey. There are procedures critical to know before drawing a particular inference which have never been recorded and remain buried in the minds of the original analysts. Other procedures may have been recorded but remain buried in the internal files of the original agency, since they appear too trivial to place within the data bank and would only burden the storage capacities of the vault. The *semi*secondary analyst has this subtle information in mind to start with or readily at hand.[10] Admittedly, he can deceive himself and avoid the painful thought that his own data are not of such high quality as he would wish. And some subtle forms of error may escape his detection if he is not especially acute. But given the equivalent motivation and acuity, the semisecondary analyst has greater capability for the estimation of error, and the true secondary analyst must make up the handicap by vigilance and extracareful searching.

Given so many built-in advantages, one may ask why more survey researchers have not taken advantage of their opportunities for semisecondary analysis. Many speculations could be advanced, but some of the plausible explanations will underscore the general difficulties of secondary analysis.[11]

---

[10] The exceptions to this argument only emphasize the need for the analyst to be vigilant in relation to the ever present danger of error in his findings. Given the turnover in personnel, surveys from the distant past which are likely to be employed in trend designs may involve different procedures of which the current generation of analysts in the same agency are unaware. In the era before the establishment of central data banks, the difference between the secondary analyst and semisecondary analyst was not as great. The secondary analyst perforce went directly to the agency that had produced the data. Thus the internal files were close at hand, and vicariously he could learn from the staff those features of the survey relevant to the assessment of error which had never been recorded.

[11] Barriers of a structural nature might be operative. Those who are recruited into full-time survey research may perhaps be of a less theoretical turn of mind. Those on the job have less time for the abstract contemplation of their data, and, on occasion, are barred by the sponsor from using data for general publication.

Certainly some unknown portion of the research that has been done is trivial in content or sloppy in execution. The opportunities are not unlimited. To recognize the desirable prospects requires sensitivity and powers of abstraction, and to exploit those prospects requires knowledge of designs and principles of secondary analysis which have not previously been codified.

We turn to another variety of semisecondary analysis which may also enlarge our understanding.

Type II: Secondary Analysis Incorporating Primary Data

The imagery evoked by the term secondary analysis is of data already collected in a previous survey which then are used in a new analysis of a novel problem. If the data have to be specially collected that seems obviously to be a *primary* analysis. These are the usual, polar and pure types of investigation, easily identified and labeled. Confusion occurs when we find a hybrid study in which *some* old data from a previous survey plus *some* newly collected data are merged into an *integral* analysis. It is best resolved by recognizing another variety of *semi*secondary analysis.

DESIGN A: MERGING OLD AND NEW DATA INTO CONTEXTUAL DESIGNS

Consider the perplexing example of Warren Miller and his investigation of "One Party Politics and the Voter," reported in the literature in 1956.[12] As he remarks, the analysis was "based in large part on data" already collected by the Survey Research Center in its 1952 election study of a national sample of individuals, published in 1954.[13] But it also required that Miller collect, from official election records, new, aggregate data to classify the counties in which the respondents resided into those that were dominated more or less by one major party or the other. By this merger of two sets of data, old and new, individual and aggregate or collective, Miller conducted the semisecondary analysis in which he demonstrated that the political climate of the county modified the political behavior of individuals with given predispositions.

---

[12] Warren E. Miller, "One Party Politics and the Voter," *Amer. Polit. Sci. Rev.* 1956, pp. 707–725.

[13] The quotation documents that the term, "semisecondary" can be a conservative description. Obviously, such hybrids can vary in the proportions of old and new data in the mixture. The larger study is reported in Angus Campbell, Gerald Gurin, and Warren E. Miller, *The Voter Decides* (Evanston: Row, Peterson, 1954).

Again we may see a valuable opportunity for studying contextual or environmental effects on behavior by this relatively simple, yet highly imaginative, design for semisecondary analysis. It is simple since the residential location of respondents is a characteristic that is common on the face-sheet of surveys.[14] And because the respondents in most all surveys are clustered into a relatively few sample points for reasons of efficiency, collecting information on the limited number of environments does not involve heavy labors. Miller did not have to classify the 3000 counties of the United States by their political complexion; he only had to collect data for 72 counties, excluding for theoretical reasons the other 23 counties in the border and southern states from his design.[15]

---

[14] To be sure, agencies vary in the way they code residential location, some coding respondents only into broad regional and size-of-place categories; others coding the exact state, others coding still more refined units. But from the original information on the questionnaires, any size residential unit could be identified and specially coded. (Of course, the smaller the unit of description, the larger the number of units that have to be characterized and the greater the labors.) There are also puzzling theoretical questions of which environmental unit (the immediate neighborhood or the larger area) in what temporal aspect (historical or contemporary) and in what respect (political, social, demographic) is the important contextual influence. These thorny problems, however, are common to all contextual analyses, secondary or primary, although they are generally ignored. Miller's remarks and tests (see especially his p. 716) on these problems deserve careful study, and our later discussion of such designs and some of the references to be cited will provide further guidance. There is a methodological problem in such contextual analyses, also generally neglected, where the secondary analyst is at a severe disadvantage. Residential location almost invariably refers to the respondent's *current* status, and it is rare that surveys enumerate the respondent's residential *history*. Obviously, there is some crudity in most tests of contextual processes created by the fact that some respondents may have been under the influence of that environment for too short a time, and all must be influenced in some degree by the previous environments in which they lived. Also, some of the effects may be dependent on which environmental unit, in its past or present aspect, the individual takes as a reference group. The *primary* analyst who is thoughtful enough to entertain such considerations could, of course, add appropriate questions to his survey on the history of the respondent's moves and his orientations to and integration into his various environments. For a most thoughtful discussion of the kind of refinements that could be introduced see Kevin R. Cox, "Information Flow and Partisan Attitudes" in Dogan and Rokkan, *op. cit.*, pp. 157–185.

[15] Ten years later, the very same data were used by Robert Putnam for another semisecondary analysis which may be described as an *external replication* in that an independent investigator again documented the influence of the political context of the county on the voting behavior of respondents in the 1952 election. More aptly, it may be described as a *continuity* in social research in that Putnam went beyond the first study to explore the process that mediated the effects of the political environment. In regard to our earlier remarks about the conversion of indicators to new purposes, the variable of "social integration" is inferred from various indicators in the original study (e.g., home ownership and voluntary association items on the face sheet) and used along

In this particular instance, the research was also simplified because Miller had no difficulties searching for the appropriate set of survey data or appraising it. He was one of the primary analysts. Thus, the study is semisecondary in two respects and perhaps should be labeled a *demisemi*secondary analysis.[16] It provides compelling evidence on our earlier point that the most conscientious analyst may find a new focus of inquiry in his own old data. Practically nothing was left unturned by those primary analysts, as any reader of the many papers and voluminous books reporting the Michigan surveys will realize. Yet Miller remarks: the "investigation of one-party dominance was not anticipated" at the time.[17]

Those who are knowledgeable about the recent developments of data archives will realize that even such minor labors as Miller had to perform in collecting the *county* data may soon be obviated. Inspired perhaps by the very example of his study, the Inter-university Consortium for Political Research began around 1966 to collect and organize for convenient use in secondary analysis the official returns *for all counties* in the United States, for elections to various offices from 1824 up to the present period as well as voting results on public referenda and constitutional amendments. From the census, the basic characteristics of the populations of each *county* over a long historical span will also be added to the data bank. As of 1968, portions of this giant undertaking had been completed, the endless arrays of statistics checked for errors, and put into usable form.[18] Thus studies patterned *exactly* after Miller's will soon pass completely into the realm of pure secondary analysis.

---

with "primary-group relations" indicators as interpretive links in the process. See Robert D. Putnam, "Political Attitudes and the Local Community," *Amer. Polit. Sci. Rev.*, **60**, 1966, pp. 640–654.

[16] The reader should not think of the process of collecting the new data in any particular narrow way. It could involve field trips, or a supplementary survey but, in this instance, data on election results by counties could be culled from such convenient handbooks as Scammon has edited which provide the appropriate figures for all states and counties for presidential elections from 1920 onwards. See, for example, Richard M. Scammon, *America at the Polls, A Handbook of American Presidential Election Statistics, 1920– 1964* (Pittsburgh: University of Pittsburgh Press, 1965). In any case, the essential feature of this variety of semisecondary analysis is that the old survey data have to be supplemented by data collected by some special means by the analyst.

[17] Miller, *op. cit.*, p. 708 (footnote).

[18] A convenient summary of the types of aggregate data that will be available is provided in the 1968 report of the Institute of Social Research, Universtiy of Michigan. Periodic memoranda issued by the Consortium describe the progress made and the time schedule, and present for the reader some of the incredible difficulties in making such an enterprise work efficiently and accurately for secondary analysis. These provide important cautionary notes for an investigator. In noting that this work "will cost over a million

This should not be construed to mean that all *semi*secondary analyses of contextual processes have been made obsolete by the technological advance of the archives and the vast ecological resources that sooner or later will be available in proximity to the survey data. Some analysts may be concerned to locate respondents within *units smaller than counties,* regarding the more immediate environment as the potent influence on some aspects of behavior. If they wish their generalizations about such contextual processes to apply to *national samples of Americans,* they will still have to resort to *semi*secondary analysis, collecting the data by their own efforts, since the smallest units for which data are likely to be available in the Michigan archive are counties.[19]

---

dollars," Angus Campbell stresses that the archives will have to assign stringent priorities to the data bases they will be able to provide. For a critical review of some of the future difficulties see his "Some Questions about the New Jerusalem," in Bisco, *op. cit.,* pp. 42–51.

[19] It should be clear that one can combine counties into larger area units, and aggregate the county data so as to describe the character of the larger units. But one cannot *disaggregate* the county totals to describe smaller areas contained within counties. In other countries, where parallel developments of ecological data banks have occurred, the unit of description may in some instances be smaller, and/or psychologically more salient to the inhabitants. For example, in Finland the 550 communes, the smallest administrative units, are the basis for the organization of the archive, the decision being "based on the fact that communes are areas with which people identify themselves." The communes are being classified with respect to some 80 variables. Erik Allardt, "Implications of Within-Nation Variations and Regional Imbalances for Cross-National Research," in Merritt and Rokkan, *op. cit.,* p. 339. In Norway a similar ecological file using "communes" as units has been developed, this appearing to be a fairly large unit, but the smallest one for which uniform information on a range of electoral, demographic, and social variables was available. See Stein Rokkan and Henry Valen, "Archives for Statistical Studies of Within-Nation Differences," Merritt and Rokkan, pp. 411–418. In Denmark, an archive using the 1400 municipalities as the unit of description has been developed, and will provide in machine-form social, economic, and electoral data spanning the period from 1920 to 1964. See *Scandinavian Political Studies,* **1,** 1966 (New York: Columbia University Press, 1966), p. 256. A centralized resource for comparative studies of contextual effects in Central and South American countries has been established at the University of Florida as "The Latin American Data Bank." Time series of demographic, economic, and electoral data for territorial units within about ten countries are available. Since some of the basic data on file are the actual enumerations of *individuals* from the original population censuses and specialized censuses, the aggregate characteristics for very small areas can be obtained. Similarly, official electoral returns have been compiled for the smallest political subdivisions. The "Large City Data File" established by Herman Turk at the University of Southern California for a program of comparative urban studies has now "assumed a life of its own" and provides a rich resource for semisecondary and completely secondary analyses of contextual effects at this level. Measures on over 300 variables for each of the 130 American cities which had populations over 100,000 in 1960 are available describing the population, the local

The UCLA Political Behavior Archives now provide in convenient form the social characteristics of all census tracts, and the electoral patterns over time of each of the precincts in Los Angeles, as well as the results of various local surveys. Thus a secondary analyst can examine the contextual effects of various types of political atmospheres for a unit as small as the precinct and of various types of social environments for the intermediate unit, the tract. The minor labors of a *semi*secondary analysis can now be obviated at the sacrifice of generalizability beyond that one locality.[23] Certainly, some investigators will be willing to pay that price, but *semi*secondary analysis may still seem a desirable strategy to others.

There are additional reasons for regarding semisecondary analysis as the likely strategy for the study of contextual processes. In some instances data permitting an investigator to classify the particular size environmental units by the particular characteristics that suit his purposes may exist in some local archive, but the *dependent* variables of interest, particular characteristics of the respondents, may not have been measured in any of the surveys that are on file in the way that satisfies him. Thus he would be forced back to what would be still another form of *semi*secondary analysis. To collect a new body of survey data on a large sample is a more costly enterprise than to collect new information on a small number of ecological units, and is thus not as efficient a strategy, although it is an approach not to be neglected. Indeed, the growth of ecological data files in data banks may well provide a new type of sampling frame for the selection of small areal units, and the subsequent sampling and survey of individuals living in predesignated sociopolitical environments.

In other instances, the survey data as well as some data on the appropriate contextual unit may be available, but the variables by which the analyst wants to characterize the environment might not be available.[24] Again, he would

---

[23] The precinct data on political history have been aggregated so that the complex sociopolitical profile of the census tracts is available in convenient form, permitting a highly elaborate secondary analysis for this size unit. As more local archives become established and incorporate data files on small ecological units, the secondary analyst will progressively achieve more generalizable findings about social contexts. And as the primary surveys employing such a contextual design as the Katz and Eldersveld one bank their ecological information, the resources for future secondary analyses will also expand. But the rarity of such designs, and the prodigious labors of organizing such files, make this a distant prospect, and semisecondary analysis will continue to be the operative procedure in the near future.

[24] For a conceptualization of different aspects of "community contexts" and empirical evidence of their respective importance derived from secondary analyses, see Philip H. Ennis, "The Contextual Dimension in Voting," in William N. McPhee and William A.

Miller does establish that "the assumption that dominance within the *county* is a meaningful . . . locus of dominance" was warranted, but he also stresses that dominance "can be found at many different levels . . . precinct, ward, city, county, congressional district, state . . . " and that "the question of whether dominance on other levels may be more meaningful must be tested by an independent investigation."[20] That a smaller unit for contextual analysis is meaningful (though not necessarily *more* meaningful) was established for the next election, the 1956 presidential election, in a primary survey of Wayne County, Michigan by Katz and Eldersveld.[21] They stratified the congressional districts of Detroit and the precincts within them in terms of party dominance and ethnic composition and surveyed samples of respondents living in contrasted types of environments. The subtle features of this contextual analysis will not be reviewed here, but it should be noted that a county such as this one was indeed heterogeneous sociopolitically, and that the precinct context did affect political behavior. In a survey of similar design in Los Angeles County in 1965, Marvick and Bayes classified the respondents by reference to the sociopolitical characteristics of the census tracts within which they resided. The 1300 tracts (containing some 12,000 precincts) had varied character, and contextual effects at this level of analysis were demonstrated.[22]

---

polity, the economy, the health and public services, the police system and crime rates, the history of riots, and the voluntary associations and organizational texture. Plans to add information on foreign cities in a number of nations and on additional variables are under way. Under special conditions, other scholars may obtain access to these computerized files, and thus respondents could be classified in terms of the complex urban environments in which they are contained. See Herman Turk. "Comparative Urban Studies in Interorganizational Relations," *Sociol. Inquiry,* **39,** 1969, pp. 108–110; "Interorganizational Networks in Urban Society: Initial Perspectives and Comparative Research," *Amer. Sociol. Rev.,* February, 1970.

[20] *Op. cit.,* p. 708.

[21] Katz and Eldersveld, *op. cit.*

[22] Dwaine Marvick and Jane H. Bayes, "Domains and Universes: Problems in Concerted Use of Multiple Data Files for Social Science Inquiries," in Dogan and Rokkan, *op. cit.,* pp. 533–553. In both these investigations, one feature of the design should be emphasized. Given the large number of precincts or tracts within such a universe, in the first stage of the design, the investigators drew only a small sample of units, which were stratified into contrasting types, within which samples of respondents were surveyed. One other feature of the Marvick inquiry should be emphasized. Using historical data on a series of past elections, the tracts were stratified in terms of whether they exhibited a "stable" or "vacillating" pattern over time. The positive findings obtained suggest that the sheer contemporary characterization of the context omits important processes. For another demonstration that the historical characterization of the context (in this instance, the previous level of unemployment in the county) is fruitful, see A. Campbell *et al., The American Voter* (New York: Wiley, 1960), p. 383.

be forced to collect such data by some special means. Note that the characteristics on file in the Michigan archive, although not an inconsiderable number, are limited to the social composition of the population, in certain respects, and to the electoral behavior of that population. Global properties, such as institutional or organizational features of the environmental unit, may also be relevant contextual factors and the corresponding data would have to be collected.[25] Thus Katz and Eldersveld demonstrate that the activity of the precinct party leaders affects the behavior of the respondents, even when the social composition of the precincts is controlled.[26]

This is not to suggest that archival data of an aggregate type, characterizing the sociopolitical composition of the population of the areas, is of no utility. Katz and Eldersveld also found that such compositional or clustering effects were of independent significance. And one of the critical problems of all contextual analysis, secondary, semisecondary, or primary, is to avoid spurious inferences as to which of the variables characterizing the complex environment is responsible for the contextual effect. The more information

---

Glaser, *Public Opinion and Congressional Elections* (New York: Free Press, 1962), pp. 180–211.

[25] Secondary or primary analysts concerned with the *aggregate* characteristics of the population in a unit sometimes use the very same sample survey both for information on the dependent variable, the behavior of the individual under some environmental influence, and, by pooling the respondents within areas, to arrive at a sampling estimate of the composition of the population of the unit. By such a procedure, contextual analysis can be accomplished purely by the secondary analysis of a sample survey, no independent source of data being needed. Such a procedure can only be applied safely where the total survey involves a large number of individuals concentrated in each of the units. For an illustration of such a secondary analysis see David R. Segal and Marshall W. Meyer, "The Social Context of Political Partisanship," in Dogan and Rokkan, *op. cit.*

[26] Katz and Eldersveld, *op. cit.*, pp. 6–15. Here again one should note the advantages that accrue to the secondary analyst working with his own survey data. As a member of a survey organization, he can organize the special data collection on the environmental units efficiently and economically. The field staff can be co-opted to collect information on the institutional, organizational, or other global properties of the areas in the course of their regular on-going duties, by observation, or documentary research, or by interviews with elites or key informants in the areas. For an early example of the way in which the contextual characteristics of communities were obtained systematically by field workers, see Herbert Hyman, "Community Background in Public Opinion Research," *J. Abnorm. Soc. Psychol.*, **40**, 1945, pp. 411–413. Particular, hypothesized characteristics of the population central to some test of compositional effects can be enumerated by the field staff in the course of a brief census-type interview, operated jointly with some other field work activity, thereby minimizing costs, or by hitchhiking a supplementary schedule of questions onto some large-scale new survey. Thus, in order to obtain the social characteristics of their precincts, Katz and Eldersveld did a large, but brief sample survey along with the more intensive smaller survey of the political behavior.

available on the unit, the more the possibility of separating analytically the components that are confounded.[27]

It is easy to understand why, up to now, there have been few secondary analyses of contextual processes. The complete set of ingredients—particular environment units characterized in particular ways, information that readily identifies the location of respondents in a survey within those same units, and survey measures of the dependent variables of interest—have been scarce until now. But why have *semi*secondary analyses using refined contextual designs been few? Only the basic ingredients from the survey are required, and the labors of adding the one ingredient, the ecological information, are not great.

No doubt, the conceptualization of contextual processes and the corresponding design of inquiry has not been a traditional way of thought to survey researchers. But the technical problems in analyzing such multilevel data already suggested by our discussion but hardly conveyed in their full severity, have also been an obstacle. Our later discussion of such designs may heighten the saliency of such approaches, and our codification of procedures may make the design more attractive to secondary and semisecondary analysts. And as the archives become enriched by the essential ingredients, the future studies will multiply.

Semisecondary analytic designs that merge old survey data on individuals and new data on a series of environmental units can serve other purposes than the study of contextual processes. Instead of taking the attitudes and behavior of samples of individuals in particular environments as the *dependent* variables, the semisecondary analyst may use the old survey data as measures of *independent* variables to trace the subsequent effects that occur in the collectivities, e.g., the districts, as a product of the antecedent characteristics of the residents. The effects are measured by new data collection on the decisional outcomes in each of the environmental units.

In our examination of the literature and our survey of users of the archives, only a few examples of such ingenious designs for semisecondary analysis were found. The ongoing research of Pettigrew provides one example. Combining data from many surveys conducted by the Texas POLL, he characterized the

---

[27] There are, of course, valuable contextual analyses which do not try to refine the complexity of environmental factors nor to determine the particular aspect of the environment that is effective. The complex entity is taken as a configuration, and its net effects demonstrated. Speculations may be entertained as to the process, but no claim is made that the analysis provides refined evidence. These grosser types of contextual designs can be implemented by secondary analysis. For example, the polarization of classes or religious groups can be examined in small versus large towns, or sex attitudes can be examined in rural, i.e., more traditional cultures, versus urban or more modern communities. For the fruitfulness of secondary analysis using such grosser units, see Philip H. Ennis, *op. cit.*

racial attitudes of the population of county units, and related these variables to desegregation decisions, incorporating into the causal model other data on the demography of the local populations, obtained from census sources.[28]

Ongoing research by Kelley provides another illustration. Old surveys are used to compute an index of presidential popularity among the populations of congressional districts prior, but close, to the time of midterm elections. That index is used as an independent variable to account for variations in the vote for other Democratic candidates running in the districts. Other variables, such as years of incumbency of the candidates and party dominance at the local level, are obtained from independent sources and introduced into the multiple regression analysis. It should be stressed that this analysis is being conducted for all such elections from 1938 to 1942, and through 1962, since the appropriate survey data span this entire long period, and that the estimate of presidential popularity is based on *two* pre-November polls, rather than one, thereby increasing reliability.[29]

DESIGN B: MERGING OLD AND NEW DATA INTO TREND DESIGNS

That variety of semisecondary analysis in which old and new data are combined is in no way limited to contextual designs. An old survey can be supplemented by a new *survey* and the two sets of data, secondary, and primary, combined into an *integral* and powerful analysis. Much of the promise of this general form of semisecondary analysis can come about in this very way, rather than from its application to the study of contextual processes.

It is obvious that any previous survey can be taken as a point of origin for a *trend* design. A new, comparable sample of respondents from the original universe can be drawn and a new survey conducted incorporating the same indicators, thereby providing data on social and psychological changes in the specified population over time. To be sure, research involving trend designs

---

[28] Personal communication from Thomas F. Pettigrew. This is an oversimplified statement of the research, which also involves certain specialized modes for pooling data from many old surveys yet to be discussed, plus the commissioning of new surveys to measure variables in the causal model for which previous surveys provide no indicators. The example will suggest that one of the new potentialities of secondary analysis lies in its contribution to the building and testing of models of social and political processes.

[29] Personal communication from Stanley Kelley, Jr. Again we oversimplify the description of the design and the causal model, and do not go into the methodological difficulty that Kelley must cope with, that the measure for the small environmental unit, the Congressional district, has to be inferred from data on presidential popularity for *grosser* units, since the sampling is not heavy and fine enough to provide more proximate data. The problem will underscore our earlier discussion in the text of the appropriate and available units for such analysis.

may be deliberately planned from the start, and the time series may be the primary focus of a program of inquiry. Yet as weariness sets in, the time series itself or some aspect of its analysis may become neglected. Through such accidents, another investigator may inherit a valuable body of data for secondary analysis. But there are also instances where a measure had been obtained once or twice long ago with no future time perspective in sight. Its utility was seemingly realized back then and thus it was forgotten; but later events may enhance the value of reviving it and converting it to trend purposes by *semi*secondary analysis.

Enter again into the minds of Hyman and Sheatsley. In 1942, the National Opinion Research Center, of which Sheatsley was a member, conducted the field work for the Surveys Division of the Office of War Information of which Hyman was a member. Understandably, race relations became a prominent issue in connection with wartime policies, and questions on white attitudes toward segregation were asked in 1942 and again in 1944 and 1946. The immediate findings of those wartime surveys were analyzed and utilized. The purposes then having been realized, and the issue no longer being vivid, the questions fell into neglect and into the recesses of memory. After about ten years, Sheatsley and Hyman, sensitized by the 1954 Supreme Court decision and the Civil Rights movement of that period, saw the opportunity and the desirability of measuring the changes in public attitudes that had occurred during the interim by using the old baseline surveys in a semisecondary analysis. Thus began a new, long-term trend study which by now documents the social changes in these respects for a span of about twenty-five years.[30]

After 1956, the time series was the focus, and the new primary research certainly bulks much larger in the total inquiry than the data from the original base period. Nevertheless, the term semisecondary analysis seems warranted, and will sharpen awareness that old surveys can be refocused upon the problems of social change and merged with new data to create a trend design. In this particular instance, the appropriate designation would be a demisemisecondary analysis, since the original investigators conducted the

---

[30] Herbert H. Hyman and Paul B. Sheatsley, "Attitudes toward Desegregation," *Scient. Amer.*, **195**, No. 6, December 1956, pp. 35–39; "Attitudes toward Desegregation," **211**, No. 1, July, 1964, pp. 16–23; Paul B. Sheatsley, "White Attitudes toward the Negro," *Daedalus*, **95**, No. 1, Winter 1966, especially pp. 233–236. One may well ask why it took ten long years, until 1956, to realize the importance of documenting the trend. As a result, the process during the intervening years remains obscure. This neglect will underscore the fact that a long-term measurement of trends could not have been the focus of the original inquiry. It will also suggest that public opinion research has not focused on the abstract problem and systematic study of social change over long periods, but rather on the issues which are temporarily matters of public concern.

later analysis, but similar opportunity presents itself to any new investigator concerned with social change.

This form of semisecondary analysis is not the bargain that complete secondary analysis is, since the costs of collecting new survey data are considerable. However, the savings netted from the gift of the earlier data are substantial, and the design is invaluable in providing knowledge of changes from a distant past which is beyond the empirical reach of any totally new survey design. And economies can be introduced into the procedures. The sample for the new phase can be reduced in size. The new phase can be restricted to one or a few strata within the broader universe where change or stability is most likely or which are especially critical for some hypothesis, and these subsamples, if desirable, can be expanded. The instruments can be brief and perhaps piggybacked onto an ongoing inquiry where the sample satisfies the specifications, thereby saving on field costs.[31] Given the investment that is involved, the design also should be used sparingly to document changes only along significant sociopsychological dimensions that were initially measured on adequate samples by good indicators likely to retain their relevance over long periods.[32]

---

[31] This was the exact way in which Hyman and Sheatsley were able to carry out their design, the new measures for almost all the later time points being obtained by adding the basic indicator questions onto larger NORC surveys going into the field. By being connected with NORC, they had the additional advantage of access to such inquiries and there was continuity in the sampling designs employed over the long span of time.

[32] A most informative case, applying this design, is by Hodge, Siegel, and Rossi. In 1947, the National Opinion Research Center conducted a national survey of the prestige of occupations. The findings had been thoroughly analyzed and reported in much detail, and the prime purposes of the original investigators, Paul Hatt and C. C. North, and the sponsor, the President's Scientific Research Board, had been realized. Building upon this baseline, a new survey using the exact same methodology was conducted by NORC in 1963, thereby permitting the study of trends in prestige of occupations in the United States over a 15-year period. The original survey was based on a sample of about 3000 cases. The new investigators followed the strategy mentioned above by limiting the new survey to a small sample of about 650 respondents. There is irony in their remark, that the new "sample was selected according to the outmoded quota sampling methods employed in 1947," since comparability, essential to the measurement of trends, overrode the concern to obtain highly accurate estimates of national patterns in the sixties. Since the new investigators were members of NORC in 1963, although not in 1947, the inquiry is again an example of *demi*semisecondary analysis. They obviously had access to the detailed records of the original sampling design, and to qualitative data which enriched their understanding of changes in knowledge and evaluation of particular occupations. For a summary of the 1947 survey, see "Jobs and Occupations: A Popular Evaluation," in Reinhard Bendix and Seymour M. Lipset, *Class, Status, and Power* (New York: Free Press, 1953), pp. 411–426. For a detailed account, see A. J. Reiss, Jr. *et al.*, *Occupations and Social Status* (New York: Free Press, 1961). The long delay of four-

DESIGN C: MERGING OLD AND NEW DATA INTO CROSS-NATIONAL DESIGNS

Comparisons of individuals, all contained within the *same* society but contrasted in the kinds of localities within which they live, have become an important focus of current survey research. Such contextual studies can be implemented by primary analysis of specially conducted surveys, sometimes by pure secondary analysis, and, often, as outlined under Design A, through semisecondary analysis merely by collection of data on the character of the environmental units.

Cross-national studies, comparison based on huge contextual units (the national societies within which individuals live), also have become a focus of recent study.[33] They, too, can be implemented by the primary analysis of comparable national surveys especially undertaken in several societies, but apart from the practical difficulties and complexities, they are almost prohibitively expensive. Thus the idea of secondary analysis based on already available comparable surveys for several nations is very appealing, and, as noted in Chapter I, has been at the center of recent discussion. The economies are great, but, unfortunately, the number of studies available is limited. Few investigators have been rich enough to underwrite specially designed

---

teen years between the first report and complete publication was occasioned by the death of Paul Hatt, the responsibility for the monograph devolving to Reiss and his collaborators. The sad chronicle has implications for our general discussion. Hatt's manuscript was never found, and therefore it is hard to establish whether the final analysis corresponded to the original purposes of the primary investigator or was, in a sense, a secondary analysis. One other facet, not uncommon in large studies, is worth stressing. There were many parties involved in the original study and correspondingly a multiplicity of original purposes. What is *the* primary goal of a survey is inevitably clouded by such multiple auspices. For the later study, see Robert W. Hodge, Paul M. Siegel, and Peter H. Rossi, "Occupational Prestige in the United States, 1925–1963," *Amer. J. Sociol.*, **70**, 1964, pp. 286–302.

[33] One of the subtleties of contextual analysis mentioned in Ref. 14 should also be considered in cross-national research. The variable that in fact is usually treated is the *contemporary* location within a society. Those who are recent immigrants and those of foreign origins may in fact reflect the membership or reference group of a society other than the one in which they are presently located. The problem is usually ignored perhaps because it is academic for many societies where foreigners constitute a small fraction of the population. In principle, it can be controlled by purifying the samples of such individuals, although it is ironic that some cross-national surveys have neglected to incorporate such questions on the face sheet and that most inquiries which do enumerate the information neglect to report the distribution of ethnicity in their samples. In this vein, we may suggest that comparisons within a one-nation survey of respondents of different national origins may indirectly shed light on problems of comparative national studies. For some secondary analyses of ethnicity, see the studies cited in Chapter IV.

multination surveys, and therefore leave us little in the way of an inheritance. We often have to juxtapose discrete studies from different nations which happened to have some common coverage and sufficient comparability in procedures.

The possibilities can be greatly expanded, however, if we apply the general strategy of semisecondary analysis. Old surveys from one or more countries can be merged with a new survey conducted in another country, designed to be thoroughly comparable. Design B suggested that an existing baseline could be exploited for a trend study simply by designing a new, comparable survey in the *same* country. IIC in the same fashion exploits a base of comparison already existing in one country by designing a new comparable survey for *another* country.

Trend studies implicitly warn us that a phenomenon may change over time, and in semisecondary cross-national studies, *both* time and place are being varied out of necessity. But we should not be paralyzed by the thought that the differences revealed by the method might be due to temporal factors rather than national factors. The strategy should not on that account be abandoned, but simply applied more carefully and selectively. Some phenomena are not sensitive to time and clearly lend themselves to such an approach, just as they would lend themselves to *primary* cross-national surveys conducted *successively* rather than simultaneously. For other phenomena that are sensitive to situational factors and events, conducting the surveys at the same chronological point in all the countries does not equate the stimuli with the exception of one special class—world shaking events that impinge on all the countries. The successive feature of the research, whether it is built into a primary, secondary, or semisecondary design therefore rarely makes the problem any worse. It must be treated in other ways that are open to the semisecondary analysts. We shall reserve a fuller discussion of the methodological implications of timing for Chapter VIII. For now, entertain the reasonable position that simultaneous inquiry may be an illusory gain.

Given this logic, semisecondary cross-national analysis is a valid and desirable approach. Sometimes, it can even be applied to a problem for which there are a *series* of surveys available from one country which can be merged with a single new survey for another country, thus providing empirical evidence on the stability of the phenomenon. And whenever it is applied, the analyst can appraise the temporal considerations after the fact by a variety of means, just as he can and must in other types of cross-national research since he cannot accurately keep stimuli constant simply by timing.

The design is not as economical as complete secondary analysis of cross-national surveys, but it certainly is a bargain compared to doing new surveys everywhere. And further economies can be introduced. The sample in the new survey can be reduced if necessary to conform to a limited budget. The new survey can be restricted to a narrower, but strategic, stratum which can be compared with its counterpart group in the old surveys.

In the several ways described, the merger of old and new surveys can greatly enlarge the opportunities for social scientists. But semisecondary analysis is not always a boon for the beginner, and he should not leap at the opportunity to employ the design in all its forms. Studies of social contexts, especially when they involve cross-national comparisons, require great technical skill and much background knowledge of the societies, whether they are accomplished by secondary or semisecondary analysis. Chapter VIII will review the complexities.

DESIGN D: MERGING OLD AND NEW DATA INTO PANEL DESIGNS

An investigator can redefine any previous survey as the starting point not merely for a trend study but for a two-wave *panel* study of *long-term*, sociopsychological change. The very same respondents can be reinterviewed and changes at the *individual* level can thereby be documented. Primary analyses, where the panel is the focus from the very beginning, have almost without exception been limited to short-term change, because of the severe difficulties of keeping such inquires going. No one should underrate the practical and methodological problems of maintaining long-term panels.[34] However, they provide fundamental knowledge on important problems, and by using semisecondary analysis the original burdens and costs of the first wave have been borne by someone else.[35]

---

[34] But the difficulties should also not be overrated. The semisecondary design proposed is limited to a single reinterview after a long lapse of time, and thus does not present the problems of maintaining cooperation of individuals for a long series of interviews massed in a short period. And the problem of tracing the respondents may well be exaggerated. On this score, see the surprising statistics on success in tracing respondents reported by Bruce K. Eckland, "Retrieving Mobile Cases in Surveys," *Publ. Opin. Quart.*, **32**, 1968, pp. 51–64. One also is encouraged by the success of the Survey Research Center in transforming the national cross-section sample interviewed in 1956 into a long-term panel which was reinterviewed in 1958 and then again in 1960, a procedure that might well be described as a semisecondary analysis. See A. Campbell, *et al.*, *Elections and the Political Order* (New York: Wiley, 1966).

[35] Eckland reminds us that some of the difficulties in conventional panel studies stem from the investigator and his circumstances: ". . . investigators (or their agents) sometimes are too impatient to pursue a group of respondents for very long. Most of us want to produce results, and in our own lifetime. Long-range panel studies, therefore, are not very attractive. Moreover, unless "institutionalized," there usually is little guarantee at the outset that financial support will continue. . . . These conditions then seriously limit the duration of most panel studies." *Ibid.*, p. 52. It is self-evident that these obstacles are removed in panels created via semisecondary analysis.

New practical and ethical obstacles arise, however, when long-term panels are to be created for such semisecondary analyses. The potentialities inherent in most old surveys will not be realizable via the archives alone, and other attractive opportunities to use the design may have been lost forever. The basic data source of an archive is the anonymous IBM card containing only a serial number to distinguish that respondent from others. Tracing a sample of respondents would require keying that number to the prior source which actually identifies the respondents, such as the addresses on original questionnaires, or the sampling lists. These materials normally would remain in the files of the original survey organization, but with the passage of time, they are often destroyed, the IBM cards or coded information being all that is needed for most secondary analysis.[36] Where the materials are intact, and the original sample could be identified, there are ethical issues about the invasion of the privacy or anonymity of the respondent, but ethical safeguards to protect confidentiality could be devised. These obstacles would be minimal for the *demi*semisecondary analyst employing the design. The extant raw materials in his own agency are accessible to him, and he could exercise foresight about those surveys and questionnaires that are worth banking for such purposes.

The experience of Roos and Roos in applying this design to the longitudinal study of a Turkish elite is most enlightening and encouraging, although their success in that unusual context may not be directly generalizable to other settings.[37] They had access to the questionnaires from a survey

---

[36] One well-known survey agency destroys completed questionnaires from ordinary surveys one year after the primary analysis is finished, and the sampling sources after five years. However, studies which have some special utility, or those where an analyst or client expresses continuing interest, may be saved indefinitely. Another well-known organization holds the questionnaires for two years. A third agency also exercises selectivity keeping materials from surveys that promise to have lasting value. This agency, and at least one other, have expressed themselves as bound to protect confidentiality of the data and the anonymity of the respondents. Consequently, even when questionnaires are given to the original investigator or sponsor who commissioned the inquiry, the names are deleted. By the same token, the agency would be resistant to providing such names to any semisecondary analyst who might plan a panel study, although the position was taken that, if the semisecondary analyst could establish his *bona fides* and provide proper guarantees that he would safeguard confidentiality and anonymity, his request might be granted. The destruction of questionnaires is, of course, not with wanton intent, but simply because the storage space for such bulky materials becomes an acute problem and most research requirements can be met with the IBM materials. With foresight, rather than hindsight, about the design it is clear, however, many survey organizations would agree to store on a selective basis the raw data that would be especially useful for such semisecondary analysis.

[37] Leslie L. Roos, Jr. and Noralou P. Roos, "Secondary Analysis in the Developing Areas," *Publ. Opin. Quart.*, **31**, 1967, pp. 272–278. Other experiences they report are very in-

conducted in 1956 on a sample of graduates of the Ankara University Political Science Faculty, the major training institution for government adminis-
trators. Thus they were able to identify the names of some 380 respondents,
and, despite the lapse of nine years, were able to locate the current addresses
of 98% of these individuals and conduct a long-term panel study in 1965.
In Turkish society, this group is a rather small, cohesive, and visible elite,
whose location is traceable through ministerial records and other sources.
Also, it should be noted that Roos and Roos were in direct and prolonged
contact with the sponsors of the original research, a position somewhat akin
to the situation of a demisemisecondary analyst, rather than working indirectly through a large archive which banks only cards and tapes. Nevertheless the feasibility and fruitfulness of the design is demonstrated.

Given the labor and costs involved, and the practical difficulties, a wise
strategy would be to reserve the design for especially significant problems.
Since the cost of tracing a respondent is high, one might economize by rein-
terviewing only a smaller, general subsample or by restricting the panel to
selected strata in which the findings are likely to be especially informative.
A design for such semisecondary analysis that is both economical and unusually informative might be labeled *selective experimental empaneling*. The
first survey provides rich data for classifying groups of individuals multidimensionally, who exhibit *profiles* of demographic, social, psychological, political, or ecological attributes contrasted in certain respects and identical in
others; the pattern of characteristics, by definition, being *antecedent* to the
experiences intervening between the old and the new survey and the later
measures of the dependent variables.[38] By this design, the investigator at
minimum cost can identify in very precise ways samples of individuals appropriate to some experimental test who would otherwise remain buried in the
general population. If there are more cases in the experimental cells than are
needed or can be afforded, subsamples can be drawn for the new survey. If
there are too few when the cases are stratified multidimensionally, the investigator can decide to sacrifice some refinements, and consolidate some of
the cells or even to abandon his semisecondary analysis. Given the continui-

---

formative. The materials from one of the previous surveys had been destroyed. They
also describe semisecondary designs in which they used a previous survey as a basis for a
long-term trend study, and an analysis which merged contextual data with data on the
attitudes of respondents. In another design, they compared the cohort studied in the
long-term panel with another younger cohort studied for the first time in 1965. For this
semisecondary analysis, see their "Administrative Change in a Modernizing Society,"
Admin. Sci. Quart., March, 1970, pp. 69–78.

[38] The hidden hazard of regression effects from the selection of individuals with extreme
values on the dependent variable must be kept in mind.

ties that exist in survey research, and the huge archive at his disposal, he may be able to pool sufficient cases from several old surveys containing common information to implement the design.[39]

Some of the potentialities of semisecondary analyses employing such a design can be conveyed by reference to the classic study on *Communism, Conformity, and Civil Liberties* conducted by Stouffer in 1954.[40] The example should be regarded as *hypothetical* since the materials may no longer be accessible. The survey was large enough to yield substantial cells—about 5000 rank-and-file respondents, and also had the additional virtue of a supplementary sample of some 1500 community leaders. The ideological syndromes and psychological patterns that characterized the respondents at that point in their lives were measured. In effect, the leaders can also be characterized by the patterns of the mass in their communities, and the followers by the kinds of leaders in their communities. This would permit a contextual secondary analysis but it now takes on a dynamic dimension in the new design.

Note that this panel design of semisecondary analysis lends itself to the study of two rather different types of processes, the measurement of *changes* over time in dependent variables that were specifically measured in the earlier survey *or* the measurement of *new* phenomena that have developed in the interim. Both types of processes are analyzed in relation to hypothesized independent variables identified from the previous survey. Now envision some of the opportunities.

Empanelling the leaders could lead to the exploration of such questions as: Have local leaders with particular patterns of political predisposition, surrounded by communities of followers of particular predispositions, gone on to success and others, of contrasted type, to defeat, with time? Have leaders (found by Stouffer to be more tolerant than the followers) of particular types changed so as to assimilate the more intolerant position of their followers? Empanelling followers would test whether those of particular profiles have been elevated by their leaders to greater tolerance. Have those with specified ideological syndromes of the fifties flowed into particular new social movements of the sixties? By concentrating on the younger cohorts in the earlier sample, definitive evidence would be obtained on what, despite Stouffer's ingenious inferential methods, remained uncertain. Were the young of that period truly a more tolerant generation than their elders, or would they

---

[39] The variations in the time elapsed between the different earlier surveys and the subsequent survey might either be regarded as a source of difficulty to be taken into account, or as an additional advantage in tracing the unfolding of a process over time.

[40] Samuel A. Stouffer, *Communism, Conformity, and Civil Liberties* (Garden City: Doubleday, 1955).

approach the same levels of intolerance as they too experienced the trauma of more than fifteen years of aging.[41]

These few examples from the Stouffer study will suggest the many possibilities to study various types of processes unfolding or changing in relation to particular antecedent conditions by selective experimental panel designs and semisecondary analysis.

In semisecondary analyses of Type II, old and newly collected data are combined to create an *integral* study. Because of the blend produced in all the subvarieties of this type, the research cannot be described as completely a primary analysis or purely a secondary analysis of previously collected survey data. We often find in the literature another kind of study, where old survey data are used in conjunction with a primary survey to deepen our understanding of a new problem. Every good scholar, whatever his discipline and his research method, cites the previous literature and juxtaposes relevant findings from the past. So, too, the good survey researcher. Each uses the appropriate sources in the library.

It would seem that we need no special term for such forms of scholarship. Although the writing may integrate the findings of past and present surveys, the mix is separable into its component parts; some being purely secondary analysis and some being purely primary analysis, and none of it being thoroughly blended into the type of semisecondary analysis we have been discussing. Sometimes the old survey data are so scanty and their treatment so rudimentary that one might almost ignore their presence and regard the inquiry as a primary analysis. At other times, the conclusions are supported by considerable quantities of old survey data treated elaborately. In these instances, one cannot fail to take note of the contributions of secondary analysis. Between the extremes, however, there are studies which are enhanced significantly by data from previous surveys. Yet some puritanical judges would not apply the label secondary analysis.[42] By their parochial standards and

---

[41] To avoid interviewer effects resulting from their expectations, or what more recently has been called "experimenter effects," the interviewers could be kept "blind" as to the earlier characteristics of the respondents.

[42] The Stouffer Study is a case in point. By virtue of the unusually large sample, elaborate and critical analysis, and an unusual design in which the field work was split between two agencies thereby permitting an estimate of error, the survey provides impressive evidence. Nevertheless, the findings are limited to a single inquiry conducted in the summer of 1954. To strengthen the conclusions and to provide historical depth, each major analysis is buttressed by the evidence available in previous surveys. Some of the material is gleaned from publications, and all of it is presented in the form of brief summaries at the ends of the chapters. Such contributions of secondary analysis to the primary analysis should not be ignored simply because they lack the *appearance* of conventional, quantitative analysis. Stouffer, *op. cit.*

rigid criteria, the old data have not been *analyzed* at all, and they might not even take notice. Since our concern is to encourage the most effective use of the total resources of past surveys, we shall define the domain of secondary analysis in a broader way and include examples of such procedures. If they produce scientific benefits for a minimal cost and effort, they become more, not less, attractive to the secondary analyst. Our discussion will also direct attention to what are the *essential* aspects of the analysis of old surveys. Since the boundaries of the total domain cannot be drawn sharply, we shall invent another variety of *semi*secondary analysis, and avoid any accusation that an impure product has been falsely labeled as the true article, secondary analysis.

Type III: Secondary Semianalysis

Secondary analysis in the current era is dominated by the institution of the data bank, a special kind of *library* where information from previous surveys is recorded in a new format, on cards and tapes, and where the storage, searching, and retrieval of that information is accomplished through the technology of electronic computers. The analysis, in turn, can be embellished by statistical manipulation of the most elegant kind, easily added by computer routines. The investigator who enlarges his understanding of some problem by obtaining and processing previous survey data in this fashion is the very model of a modern secondary analyst. What about the investigator who uses the *conventional* library to search for information from previous surveys recorded in the traditional format—in print? He may be old fashioned and less efficient, but he is none the less a secondary analyst engaged in the same operations of searching and retrieval.[43] The words are the vocabulary of librarians.

---

[43] That there is a generation gap among secondary analysts is conveyed by these remarks in a 1967 doctoral dissertation: "Secondary analysis has long been viewed as valuable and numerous examples are found in the social science literature. . . . Such studies have conventionally been limited to only published data (which were often limited to marginal distributions). This mode of secondary analysis must be distinguished from the 'new' secondary analysis made possible by the formation of social science data archives. . . . It is important to note that by bringing together numerous data files, we have produced a new data base which will support research which any one file could not support. The researcher operating with numerous files is, of course, required to adopt a different analytic style." Douglas K. Stewart, *Support for Dissent: A Study of Trends in the United States* (Pittsburgh: University of Pittsburgh, 1967), unpublished doctoral dissertation. An early example of the accomplishments of "semianalysis" is

Secondary analysts who use old survey data in conjunction with new findings must be judged not by the mechanical routines they employ, but by whether the data are selected in arbitrary ways and then used uncritically.[44] Admittedly, the secondary analyst who searches through published surveys is subject to greater temptations to select data arbitrarily. It is laborious work, and he may very well stop his search prematurely after he finds some relevant information, and before he comes upon another body of data which might change his conclusions. Not all of the relevant surveys have been put into print. Thus there is the danger that his may be a fragmentary or *semi-analysis* of a problem and that his conclusions may be misleading. And he faces other dangers. He is like the mystery-story reader who can look at the end pages for the solution. During the very act of searching, he cannot avoid seeing the printed results attached to the relevant indicators or questions, and thus is tempted to be arbitrary in ceasing or continuing the search in relation to his preconceptions.[45]

Speier's collation of published findings from many surveys of *The American Soldier* to clarify and test the general claims of Mannheim's theory of "perspectivistic thinking." The comparisons of enlisted men and officers on a wide range of opinions are simply ordered under various conceptual headings and summarized, and are then used as empirical evidence on a classic problem in the sociology of knowledge. H. Speier, "The American Soldier and the Sociology of Military Organization," in R. K. Merton and P. F. Lazarsfeld, eds., *Studies in the Scope and Method of the American Soldier* (New York: Free Press, 1950), pp. 106–132.

[44] A most imaginative and critical use of this variety of semisecondary analysis is provided by Chamberlain and Schilling, which partakes in some degree of the integral designs that we have labeled Type II. Prior to 1953 they completed a secondary analysis of surveys in the period 1935–1950, using published findings in the *Public Opinion Quarterly* and the Cantril-Strunk volume to describe American public opinion on labor–management relations and on the use of the strike. So far it partakes of a "semianalysis." But to complement these findings, they then conducted a primary survey of a sample of knowledgeable *informants* (labor reporters, union officials, industrial relations managers, etc.), asking them to evaluate on the basis of their experience whether public opinion had influenced conduct of the parties in a strike situation. See Neil W. Chamberlain and Jane M. Schilling, *Social Responsibility and Strikes* (New York: Harpers, 1953), pp. 41–77, 113–136. In this connection one may also cite a subsequent study by Cullen, which represents a continuity in secondary analysis. From the Williamstown archive, he retrieved questions on the same issues for the later period, 1954-1965, and juxtaposed the recent findings with the analysis by Chamberlain to establish trends and stable patterns in public opinion over a thirty-year span. In the instances of most secondary analyses to be described later, the trend or replication design is accomplished by *one* investigator. Here we have a later secondary analyst building on top of the work of an earlier secondary analyst. See Donald E. Cullen, *National Emergency Strikes* (Ithaca, New York: New York State School of Industrial and Labor Relations, 1968), ILR paperback No. 7, pp. 12–23.

[45] The typology of analytic procedures, *hunting, snooping,* and *fishing* invented by Selvin

The searcher who uses the machine archive is in a safer position. Since the machine does all the hard labor and can exhaust the relevant, total universe of surveys and indicators without exhausting him, there are no brute pressures for the analyst to stop the search prematurely. The analysis is less likely to be fragmentary. And since the machine search starts only with the indicators, and the results emerge later only after tabulation, the analyst cannot do any peeking. But he is not free from all danger of arbitrariness. If the results he inspects after the initial search of 14 or 40 surveys do not please him, the machine will happily work at locating and tabulating 40 more surveys, and, if desired, still another 40.

As we shall see later, secondary analysis which involves many replications or the treatment of a diversity of findings makes heavy demands on the investigator's intellectual and technical gifts of synthesis, and requires safeguards against arbitrariness in selection. These analytical problems are central with certain designs, and become more oppressive as the potential volume of data expands. The belief that a large amount of data and many tables signify the good and complete analysis may only lead the investigator to a bigger, but poorer, analysis if he slights the problems of objective selection and careful synthesis of data. If he is not critical in examining the original data for sources of error, his is also only a semianalysis, no matter how elaborate his statistical manipulations, since he has omitted an essential procedure.

The investigator who presents limited data in simple fashion may be prejudged, from a modern perspective, to have produced a fragmentary or semianalysis. That may be true, but if his procedures have provided for objective selection of the data and critical appraisal of error, his may be the more complete secondary analysis. If he has used his limited data more thoughtfully and imaginatively, he may be the better analyst. Consider some examples where the limited treatment of old data can add a missing, but essential, feature to a new inquiry.

ADDING COMPARATIVE SURVEY NORMS TO A PRIMARY CASE STUDY

The utility of semianalysis in the solution of a persistent problem faced by primary investigators with meager resources can be documented by a series of parallel examples. In each instance, the primary investigation was confined to the case study of a restricted sample of a relatively homogeneous and presumably distinctive group. In drawing conclusions from such findings, the uncritical investigator, beguiled by the assumed deviance of his group, can

---

and Stuart needs to be supplemented by this fourth hazardous approach to secondary analysis. In tune with their phrasing we label it *peeking*.

easily indulge in "fictitious comparisons" imputing a different pattern to a comparison group he has not measured, simply on the basis of his beliefs. There appears to be no way out of the trap of what might be called the *pseudocomparative* design, unless one is rich enough to buy a true comparative design.[46] But the poor investigator can avail himself of the appropriate measures from data in previous surveys, instead of filling in the comparison cell from his imagination.

Wolfinger and his associates studied about 300 members of the radical right who participated in the "Christian Anti-Communism Crusade" in Oakland, California in 1962.[47] The questionnaire measured such features of the political profile of the group as the perception of the internal Communist threat and the threat of Russia, tolerance of Communists and other political nonconformists, sense of political efficacy, and the political and social participation and memberships of the individuals. To determine whether the findings in such respects actually distinguished the group, the investigators remark that data from Stouffer's national survey of 1954 and from the Michigan national election surveys were used as "normative data with which we compared our respondents' replies."[48] Some striking and expected differences are thus established empirically. In other respects, the comparisons disconfirm common expectations and fashionable theories notably with respect to generalized tolerance, alienation, and political efficacy. An investigator without benefit of the norms would have been free to interpret the absolute findings in terms of any fictitious comparison he could imagine, and thereby "confirm" his theories.

The empirical comparisons available from previous surveys constrain the investigator, but still leave some room for arbitrariness. Which is the appropriate comparison group for computation of the norm? In this instance, differences between the Crusaders and the *national* norms might not represent

---

[46] The investigator would be especially likely to fall into the use of such designs in studies of other societies, since it may take great resources just to work in one such place, let alone more than one. And he is inclined to regard that society as exotic or different from his own. From this point of view, cross-national *secondary* analysis is especially attractive and desirable. For a discussion of the pseudo cross-national design, see Herbert Hyman, "Research Design," in Robert E. Ward, *et al.*, *Studying Politics Abroad* (Boston: Little, Brown, 1964), p. 162 ff. The danger of a fictitious comparison can also arise in a *secondary* analysis where the investigator singles out one particular social group for special study, and assumes that it is different from other groups which he has not included in his secondary analysis.

[47] Raymond E. Wolfinger, Barbara K. Wolfinger, Kenneth Prewitt, and Sheilah Rosenhack, "America's Radical Right: Politics and Ideology," in David E. Apter, ed., *Ideology and Discontent* (New York: Free Press, 1964), pp. 262–293.

[48] *Ibid.*, p. 265.

peculiarities of the Radical Right, but simply the fact that this sample of Crusaders was mainly northern, white, college educated, and in high-status occupations. Individuals with the same demographic characteristics might differ less, or even more, from the Crusaders. By presenting *refined norms* for the corresponding strata, Wolfinger can demonstrate whether there are residual differences between the Crusaders and others which cannot be explained by reference to social characteristics. Some of these refined norms required special computations; the gross norms and other refined norms could be taken directly from the published works. Whether special tabulations and laborious computations had to be ordered is clearly not the earmark of analysis. The refined norm involves a subtle idea, equivalent to the sophisticated procedure of controlling variables and testing for spuriousness in the primary analysis of a survey.

The critical reader will realize that the magnitude of the norms reflects the particular questions that were used in the previous surveys. Obviously the critical analyst also would consider such sources of error in the comparisons and try to choose his surveys wisely, or use multiple norms based on various questions and batteries so as to attenuate the influence of question wording.[49] In this instance, Wolfinger eliminated such a source of error by adopting in his primary inquiry the very questions that Stouffer and Michigan had employed. In light of such advance planning for the coordination or integration of the old and new survey data, one might regard the total inquiry as a Type II semisecondary analysis, but it also fits under the present rubric, in using limited data from published sources with minimal statistical manipulation. Perhaps it is another example of a demisemisecondary analysis.

The same methodological difficulty confronted Grupp in his studies of political activism, based on samples of individuals taken from the membership lists of the John Birch Society and of the Americans for Democratic Action. To avoid fictitious comparison, Grupp also obtained norms from the Michigan 1964 national election study. The reader may well wonder why a semisecondary analytic design was necessary. Grupp had a comparison already built into his own primary survey, and could contrast the findings for ADA members and Birch Society members. Indeed he did make such internal comparisons, but since he was also interested in what distinguished *activists*

---

[49] The critical reader will also realize that some of the psychological measures used in the comparisons are affected by events and have shown considerable trend over time. There may be a source of error in comparing Stouffer's 1954 findings with case study data obtained in 1962. It should be noted that Wolfinger's norms come from various surveys at different time points; that some of the variables are more stable characteristics, and that such a problem could be considered in the selection of the previous surveys and in evaluating the results.

of whatever persuasion, right or left, from nonactivists, he needed the more general norms as well.[50]

In passing, it may be noted that such groups are so small within the body politic that the study could not be accomplished solely by a secondary analysis in which such individuals were screened out of a "parent survey" of the *general population*. In the Michigan national survey, there was only a handful of individuals who reported membership in any highly activist political organization.[51]

The same type of semisecondary design was employed for another study of political activists by Feigert. His primary survey was limited to a sample of officers of the New York Liberal Party questioned by mail in 1966. "To establish attitudinal and demographic deviations of . . . activists" he also used norms on characteristics obtained from the Michigan 1964 national election survey.[52] To insure that the differences did not arise from variations in ques-

---

[50] For a brief report of the comparisons of the two groups, see Fred W. Grupp, Jr., "The Magazine Reading Habits of Political Activists," *Publ. Opin. Quart.*, **33**, 1969, pp. 103–106. For the total study, see Social Correlates of Political Activists: *The John Birch Society and the ADA* (University of Pennsylvania, unpublished dissertation, 1968). See also his "Political Perspectives of Birch Society Members," in R. A. Schoenberger, ed., *The American Right Wing* (New York: Holt, Rinehart and Winston, 1969), pp. 83–118.

[51] A design to be discussed later, in which rare categories of individuals are *pooled* across several surveys to provide a large enough cell for secondary analysis, might be applied to the problem. Given the extreme rarity, many surveys would have had to incorporate the question on membership, and the combined yield might still have been infinitesimal. A secondary analysis by Lipset bears on the substantive problem. But it should be noted that he used a large sample survey of the state of California, where the Birch Society was particularly active, and examined the characteristics of those who expressed *attitudes supportive* of the Society, obviously a much larger group than enrolled members. See S. M. Lipset, "Three Decades of the Radical Right: Coughlinites, McCarthyites, and Birchers," in Daniel Bell, ed., *The Radical Right* (Garden City: Doubleday Anchor Books, 1963), pp. 421–439.

[52] For the complete study, see Frank B. Feigert, *The Hierarchical Component in a Political Organization: The New York Liberal Party* (University of Maryland, 1968) unpublished dissertation. Lest the reader think from the coincidence of topics in the three examples cited that such a design is limited to the study of a deviant or extremist group, we may cite a recent study by Wolfinger where he again employed the same design. The primary inquiry was limited to New Haven. Refined norms for the Northern United States, obtained from the Consortium, provided a base of comparison to establish that political participation was higher in the New Haven community, particularly among lower-status people. Raymond E. Wolfinger, *The Politics of Progress* (New Haven: Yale University Press) forthcoming. In one of his New Haven studies, Wolfinger wished to establish whether patterns of *ethnic* voting in that community deviated from the patterns such groups exhibited elsewhere. He thus needed very specialized comparative norms, and the procedure he employed deserves special note. Refined norms for Italians in the New

tion wording, Feigert, like Wolfinger, used the same questions as in the Michigan survey, modifying them where necessary for mail questionnaire use.[53]

In the comparative designs just described, there is another source of error which may distort the conclusions. Although his case study can explore a problem in depth, the description may be in error, because the primary investigator's limited resources may prevent him from obtaining a sample of the specialized population that is adequate in size or unbiased in character. Ironically, the primary part of the study may be more deficient in these respects than the part derived from previous surveys, which, whatever their superficiality, generally involve large and properly drawn samples and provide estimates of sampling errors. Where the primary investigator uses a mail questionnaire for reasons of economy or ease of access, the nonresponse rate may be high, and those who reply may be a biased sample. Where he conducts personal interviews, he may not have enough well-trained interviewers or funds to carry the field work far enough in time or space. Where the group is deviant in character, they may be especially resistant to participating. Thus Wolfinger reports high refusal rates from the Crusaders he approached by mail, and that his student interviewers met with many rebuffs. As he summarized it: "We were unable to use systematic sampling methods in this situation. Strictly speaking, we do not have a sample . . ."[54]

England States could be computed from the Michigan voting studies, but each such survey yielded too few cases in the cell to permit a good estimate. Consequently, he pooled three of the Michigan surveys before computing the norm. The expanded base was still only 143 cases, suggesting how much pooling may be required to obtain refined norms for groups that are rare in the general population. The pooled, refined norm based on the 1952, 1956, and 1958 elections averages out the distinctive Italian pattern in a particular election or time period, and thus is a more generalized norm. His primary data for New Haven spanned the elections from 1949 to 1962, and since he was interested in the *persistent* local pattern, the property of the pooled norm to transcend a narrow point in time was desirable. See R. E. Wolfinger, "The Development and Persistence of Ethnic Voting," *Amer. Polit. Sci. Rev.*, LIX, 1965, esp. p. 900. For other examples of the design applied to nonextremist groups, see H. M. Scoble, "Political Money: A Study of Contributors to the National Committee for an Effective Congress," *Midw. J. Polit. Sci.*, 7, 1963, pp. 229–253; W. C. Rogers, B. Stuhler, and D. Koenig, "A Comparison of Informed and General Public Opinion on U. S. Foreign Policy," *Publ. Opin. Quart.*, 31, 1967, pp. 242–252, in which the norms obtained from the continuing work of a state poll serve to compare a local elite with general population and the educated stratum in the area.

[53] The critical analyst in evaluating sources of error that obscure such comparisons would entertain not only differences in the date of inquiry and in question wording, but also in the mode of administration of the measuring instrument.

[54] Wolfinger, *op. cit.*, p. 266.

These may be intractable problems for the primary investigator, especially when he sets his sights on an elusive and unusual target group, and does not have the high-powered ammunition to penetrate that target. He can, however, be especially critical in evaluating his primary data.[55] The presence of one source of error in no way denies the value of obtaining the norms, which eliminate the risk of a fictitious comparison. He may as well solve one problem by semisecondary analysis, even if he cannot eliminate the other. Sometimes this variety of semisecondary design can also serve to reduce the risks that arise from possible deficiencies in the sampling conducted by primary investigators, although it may not be helpful for the case study of the most deviant and exceedingly rare groups in the population.

STRENGTHENING THE SAMPLE OF A PRIMARY STUDY BY DATA FROM PREVIOUS SURVEYS

In the examples just described, an otherwise empty cell in a primary study is filled by cases from previous surveys to provide a point of comparison. The cells that were included in the primary study obviously are not empty, but still may be very small in size or biased samples. Why not fill them, so to speak, from previous surveys? A most compelling example is provided in Lenski's study of the effect of religious membership and commitment on daily life.[56] In 1958, using the facility of the Detroit Area Survey, a primary survey was conducted in which a probability sample of about 700 residents of Detroit was classified along religious lines and secular patterns were measured. Despite the large and fine sampling, only 27 cases of Jews were obtained, and the number of Negro Protestants was 100, since these groups constitute small minorities in the general population. Clearly, these cells are very small to carry the full weight of any conclusions Lenski wished to draw. Further refinements of the analysis to examine the pattern among subgroups, e.g., working-class Jews, would make the situation even more precarious. Since the same universe had been sampled and surveyed beginning in 1951, and formal religion had been included in the face sheet, Lenski strengthened his samples by incorporating into his analysis cases obtained in the three previous surveys conducted in 1952, 1953, and 1957, thereby quadrupling the base for any single test, or having four independent, if small, replications to combine into

---

[55] Thus Wolfinger compares the two subsamples of Crusaders obtained by mail versus personal interviews to appraise bias, and uses other kinds of evidence to evaluate response error and sampling biases common to both procedures. Wolfinger, *op. cit.*, pp. 265–267.

[56] Gerhard Lenski, *The Religious Factor* (Garden City: Doubleday, 1961).

a stronger test.[57] These analyses are, of course, limited since only a few of the dependent variables measured in 1958 were included in the previous surveys, but nevertheless, the primary survey has been buttressed significantly.

Race and religion are frequently enumerated on the face sheets of surveys. Although Jews and Negroes are small minorities, the yield over four surveys is not negligible. The design therefore became practical, but it might be academic for the study of such a specialized and tiny group as Birch Society members. Very few surveys would have asked that question of membership, and the pool would be too small unless many, many surveys were combined.

If Lenski, despite the resources of a large probability sample and the staff of the Detroit Area Facility, faced severe limitations in his primary inquiry, how much more true this would be for a poor, primary investigator working on his own and limited to a small case study. Consider a study conducted by Abramson where he strengthened his primary inquiry by using the design. He was concerned with the political socialization of English children as it was influenced by exposure to various types of English schools. It is impressive that he was able to interview as many as 331 school children enrolled in contrasted types of English schools, i.e., public, grammar, secondary modern, and comprehensive, and to explore many of their attitudes and control such factors as class of origin. Yet as he stresses: "Since it was clear from the outset

---

[57] *Ibid.*, especially pp. 331–340. "Judgments about social relationships are far more reliable when based on the findings of two, three, four, or more independent samples than when based on any single sample of the same size and quality. . . . It is for this reason that we have so often supplemented the findings of the 1958 survey with findings from other surveys conducted by the Detroit Area Study." The case might also be described as demisemisecondary analysis, since Lenski was a member of the University of Michigan Department of Sociology, the sponsor of the Detroit Area Surveys. Thus he had foreknowledge of the surveys of previous years and easy access to the materials. As he remarks, he could plan to coordinate the 1958 primary inquiry and the earlier surveys, and he drew on data from as many as six of the other annual surveys. An anomalous fact is that one of the other surveys used was done in 1959, which *postdates* rather than predates his own work, but which was already in hand when he was analyzing his own data. This bizarre situation, however, fits perfectly well under the definition of secondary analysis. It is not as rare as one might think given the time it takes to analyze a complex inquiry (Gerhard Lenski, personal communication.) As an alternative to the illegitimate use of significance tests, Hirschi and Selvin have recently urged almost a standard use of this design. To support a hypothesis that has been demonstrated once by a particular primary survey, they urge an independent test of the finding by secondary analysis of one or more appropriate surveys that have already been filed in a data bank. They describe the institution as "a hypothesis testing service from these data libraries." For the proposal and the argument upon which it rests, that the modes by which the surveyer approaches his data invalidate the assumptions of significance tests, see Travis Hirschi and Hanan Selvin, *Delinquency Research: An Appraisal of Analytic Methods*, (New York: Free Press, 1967), pp. 216-234.

that I would be unable to obtain a random sample of English youth, it was useful to find a survey which included the type of data which I was collecting in my own study, but would also reflect the universe of English school children."[58] He therefore supplemented his intensive studies with data from a British Gallup Survey, in which a good sample of some 1800 youth had been studied, on the basis of which they could be classified by type of school and social class of origin, and some of their political attitudes analyzed.[59]

Designs for *pooling* cases or *replicating* tests that are based solely on previous surveys will be discussed again in later chapters. In the current examples, although the formal procedures are the same, they are applied to different ingredients. An elaborate primary survey or intensive case study is supplemented by previous survey data to create a stronger inquiry by secondary semianalysis.

This discussion of semisecondary analysis should have broadened our conception of the many ways in which previous surveys can be applied to new problems, and should already have conveyed some of the essential features of any pure secondary analysis. The blending of old and new data that occurs in many varieties of semisecondary analysis will also suggest, in at least some respects, that the conventional methods of analysis are common to all survey data, old or new. If what is old and new have been so submerged in the integrated body of material the investigator then examines, some basic analytic procedures must be applicable to all the data, no matter when it originated. We begin our discussion of pure secondary analysis with a more detailed treatment of styles of work and analytic procedures so that future investigators will see the many paths they can follow to arrive at new knowledge from old surveys, and the procedures they must follow along the way.

---

[58] Personal communication. A brief account is provided in Paul Abramson, "The Differential Political Socialization of English Secondary School Students," *Sociol. Edu.*, **40**, 1967, pp. 246–269. For a full report, see *Education and Political Socialization: A Study of English Secondary Education*, University of California, Berkeley, 1967, unpublished doctoral dissertation. Elder had also explored the problem by a secondary analysis of an earlier Gallup youth survey containing data on political attitudes and type of school attended, but social class of origin was not available. See Glen H. Elder, Jr., "Some Consequences of Stratified Secondary Education in Great Britain," *Sociol. Educ.*, **38**, 1965, pp. 173–202.

[59] A design employed by Kessel uses data from previous national surveys to provide *norms* for evaluating how deviant a sample is which the investigator has obtained in the course of a local, primary inquiry. Depending on the comparison, the investigator can be more precise about the generalizability of his conclusions. The norms can be obtained not only for the usual demographic characteristic, but for the dependent variables under study, by incorporating some of the very same indicators used in the previous national surveys. The design thus partakes in some degree of both the semianalytic designs mentioned. For an excellent statement of its advantages, see John H. Kessel, "Cognitive Dimensions and Political Activity," *Publ. Opin. Quart.*, **29**, 1965, esp. pp. 386–389.

III

Approaches to Secondary Analysis

IN APPROACHING A BODY OF PREVIOUSLY COLLECTED SURVEY DATA, ARE THERE some distinctive quantitative operations that the analyst must learn to employ? We have already raised this question, but a convincing answer might be provided by the following experiment. Imagine that an experimenter has collected a series of articles containing survey research findings, some based on primary analysis and some on secondary analysis. That important fact is then masked by deleting all references to the sources of the data and the dates of the inquiries. A summary of the *quantitative* analysis is then prepared for each article, to provide the raw materials for the experiment. Then, the summaries are presented in a scrambled order to a group of expert judges who are to classify them as either primary or secondary analysis.

Studies dealing with topics that are relics of the past would, of course, be omitted since they would have clues that a clever judge would detect. A judge might be nostalgic, but he would know that no recent survey would ask whether Landon or Roosevelt would be more likely to keep us out of war, or whether Willkie, Dewey, or MacArthur was the preferred candidate—topics in the surveys of yesteryear.

The result can be predicted. The judges would guess no better than chance, since quantitative procedures in both forms of analysis are the same. Both incorporate marginal distributions on single questions and distributions on indices computed from batteries of questions; breakdowns on individual items or on indices for subgroups of respondents, and cross tabulations of questions; complex elaborations of data involving three or more variables; correlations and measures of association, tests of significance, standardizations of data, and regression analyses.

All the apparatus of *quantitative* survey analysis would be likely to be found in the treatment of old or new data. And this is as it should be. The technical procedures that have been developed for the primary analysis of new surveys deal with fundamental problems that cannot be ignored just because the data are from an old survey. And even though the data are old, this does not give the analyst an excuse for a less thorough analysis. Some surveys do warrant a simpler analysis than others, but this depends on the problem, not the age of the data. The advocates of secondary analysis, after all, are asserting that some old surveys are good enough in execution and important enough in content to warrant the proper treatment of which they have previously been deprived.

This "thought experiment" has never been translated into reality, but the main conclusion seems indubitable. If one remains doubtful, empirical, if not experimental, evidence is available. The examples throughout the text will reveal the entire repertory of quantitative survey analysis, and surveys of the users of archives establish that they request all the conventional technical services such as tabulations, cross tabulations, factor analyses, correlations, construction of scales, etc.

If the stimuli for this thought experiment presented more than just the core of the quantitative analysis, it is possible, however, that the judges would perform considerably better than chance. In pure secondary analysis, the investigator generally is limited to the data that have been coded and punched. The *qualitative* analysis that normally supplements and enriches a quantitative, *primary* analysis perforce is limited since the secondary analyst does not have the original verbatim answers to open-ended questions, the comments of respondents, interviewers' reports, and similar collateral material. Stouffer's 1954 survey again provides an excellent illustration of the way in which a primary analyst can use such materials effectively. The level of public intolerance was measured by a scale, and its correlates determined by quantitative methods. However, to explore the larger atmosphere of feelings, concerns, and anxieties from which the political intolerance might have stemmed, Stouffer relied heavily on the use of verbatim materials presented in qualitative fashion.[1] In that variety of *semi*secondary analysis, where a member of the original agency conducts the restudy, he, too, has these qualitative adjuncts to analysis at his disposal—a considerable advantage. But

---

[1] Stouffer, *op. cit.*, especially Chapter III, "Is There a National Anxiety Neurosis." Stouffer also used these qualitative adjuncts as evidence about response error, an obvious problem in the climate of the fifties when individuals might fear to be candid on so controversial a question as the rights of nonconformists. See, for example, pp. 46–47.

the *pure* secondary analyst who can engage in elaborate treatment of qualitative data is rare indeed these days.[2]

If the experimental stimuli were enlarged still more, and if the selections representing secondary analysis were sampled without any restrictions, the expert judges probably would perform even better. They would be right most of the time in judging that primary investigators do not have the capacity or tenacity or longevity to carry out certain kinds of heroic research designs. Unless he were superman or superanalyst, what investigator could have planned a research program that began with a survey in 1938, was followed by five more surveys, and closed with another survey in 1962? How many investigators on their own could initiate and complete a cross-national survey covering England, Canada, Australia, and the United States? These illustrate the rare privileges conferred on ordinary men by secondary analysis. However, there are also certain penalties. The secondary analyst can be liberated from confinement in narrow space and time, but, as noted, he is constrained by the indicators that the surveys already contain. Sometimes, he may have to strain their meaning to measure variables of interest to him, and the bizarre ways in which he might use items would give additional clues to the judges.

There might be other clues presented in the experimental stimuli which the sharp judge would use to detect one of two contrasted types of secondary

---

[2] Some of our later examples will show that qualitative analysis is not merely a supplement to quantitative analysis, but that the treatment of verbatim materials may actually be *central* for the study of particular problems, notably in studies of thought processes and ideology or the organization of beliefs. One such example, discussed in Chapter V, is the analysis of levels of political conceptualization or ideology among the American people reported in the 1956 Michigan election survey which required specialized coding of verbatim answers to open-ended questions. Only the semisecondary analyst working with his own raw data or the **true secondary** analyst who works directly with the originating agency rather than the archive would be in the position to incorporate such methods. To be sure, the deficiencies of archival data in this respect can be exaggerated. With the rise of the computer and the replacement of cards by tape, primary analysts are no longer compelled to compress multiform and rich data into a small number of code categories. The archivists have been eloquent advocates for more detailed coding and less reductionism in processing qualitative materials. But the fruits of this campaign have yet to be achieved, and the coded data from many old surveys are not yet an adequate substitute for the original verbatim sources which some designs of secondary analysis require. Confusion may arise in our discussions of qualitative analysis, since the term is ambiguous and used in two different senses. Some of the later secondary analyses are qualitative in that the analyst dispenses with the numbers that are attached to the original data. In his desire to synthesize or present a complex portrait or many-sided description, he drops the language of quantity. Such a "qualitative analysis" can, of course, be based on coded data or numerical data. In its other meaning, the analysis *starts* with qualitative materials, clinical and other personal documents, and cannot proceed from data that have already lost their character by being transformed into numbers.

analysts—the casual and the compulsive. The casual analysis might be singularly devoid of treatment of errors in the data since detailed information about the original procedures is hard to obtain. The compulsive analysis, by contrast, would provide lavish details or candid admission of limitations, since the investigator would be especially concerned about errors that might lurk within the old surveys or the possibility that they are not ideally suited to his purpose. The primary analyses would probably fall between the poles.[3]

What has this "experiment in thought" suggested on the procedures that the secondary analyst must learn to employ? He must cope somehow with the obstacles normally standing in the way of adequate qualitative analysis and the treatment of error. He must be concerned about the ambiguity or invalidity of his indicators as instruments for the measurement of particular variables. If he wishes to take advantage of almost unique opportunities that previous surveys provide, then *ultimately* he must familarize himself with certain research designs, whose properties are complex and difficult to master. To be sure, he should begin his learning at a simpler level. As his skills improve, he can gradually set his aspirations toward those goals that are more distant and difficult to realize.

With respect to the core of survey analysis—the quantitative treatment of the data—there is nothing new or distinctive for the secondary analyst to learn that he does not already know from his prior experience as a primary analyst. Of course, he may begin to learn the rudiments, the fundamentals, by practicing them first on other people's surveys. That way the beginner does not jeopardize the heavy investment that goes into funding a new survey, and the task is simplified, since he does not have to master all the phases of survey research at once and is freed from the anxieties and pressures of the "real thing."[4] But then, he is learning what might be called

---

[3] There is an occasional "primary" analysis in which there is extreme attention to error. A second investigator decides to reanalyze a survey for the specific purpose of establishing that the first analysis was faulty. Clearly, one would not call such a procedure "secondary analysis" since the focus is on the original problem that the survey was intended to illuminate. For want of a better label, this rare type of activity will be called, simply, *reanalysis*. For examples, see Heinz Ansbacher, "The Problem of Interpreting Survey Data," *Publ. Opin. Quart.*, **14**, 1950, pp. 126–138; Edgar F. Borgatta and Jeanne Hulquist, "A Reanalysis of Some Data From Stouffer's Communism, Conformity and Civil Liberties," *Publ. Opin. Quart.*, **20**, 1956–57, pp. 631–650. Where a second investigator replicates a test made in one survey, by converting a *different* survey, already conducted, to his new purpose, it is clearly a secondary analysis, and many examples will be presented in the text.

[4] These are telling advantages. Nevertheless, one might question the wisdom of too heavy a reliance on such an approach to the training of survey analysts. At some point the analyst must also take on the role of study director, and learn to guide the other phases

simulated primary analysis. Since the general principles of survey analysis
have been codified and treated thoroughly in the literature, our discussion
may safely omit such matters and stress the special requirements of secondary
analysis.[5]

Although the experiment described above has suggested that there is nothing distinctive in the modes of quantitative analysis which are applied to
previous survey data, we should not jump to the conclusion that we now
know the secret of success in secondary analysis. Skill in the conventional
techniques of analysis and effectiveness in handling the special methodological challenges are certainly necessary, but not sufficient to insure accomplishment. There also appear to be some styles of thought and activity among
those investigators who profit greatly from previous surveys. We shall try to
capture some of the flavor of their work realizing that it is elusive in character
and does not follow any simple formula. Our attempt will serve to set the
later discussion of design and analysis within a larger framework.

Styles of Work Among Successful Secondary Analysts

In examining the literature, we shall find particular secondary analyses that
compel our admiration by the beauty of their design or analysis, their richness
of data and corresponding definitiveness, or the significance of the problem
they illuminate. We shall inspect such distinguished examples of succeessful
secondary analysis in later chapters. We also find particular investigators who
are persistent practitioners of secondary analysis and who succeed in making
repeated contributions to the literature. Their general productivity, if not any
single product, also compels admiration, and we shall explore some of the
secrets of their success.

For this exploration, it seems wise to omit *semi*secondary analysts of "Type
I" (see Chapter II). Their status as members of survey organizations, as
directors of many surveys, creates the special privileges described earlier. This
is not to deny personal abilities, but their advantaged situation facilitates

---

of a survey. He may never fully comprehend the contributions to error that arise in
earlier phases of the survey if he has been divorced from the actual experiences in conducting a real inquiry. And he may lack the combat training he ultimately needs to
operate the principles effectively under the pressures of reality.

[5] See for example, Morris Rosenberg, *The Logic of Survey Analysis* (New York: Basic
Books, 1968); Hirschi and Selvin, *op. cit.*; Charles Glock, ed., *Survey Research in the
Social Sciences* (New York: Russell Sage, 1967); Herbert Hyman, *Survey Design and
Analysis* (New York: Free Press, 1955).

their accomplishments. The complete secondary analyst succeeds only by his wits, and he is the pure or ideal type to examine. That he has some distinctive qualities cannot be doubted. Contrast him with the many who fail! Recall that in the survey of potential users of the Berkeley Archive, over half of the initial inquiries never reached the point of acquiring data.

Many secondary analyses thus seem to be aborted almost at the point of conception. Interruptions at later stages no doubt reflect a lack of technical skills. At the earliest, or preanalytic, stage, there might be a failure of nerve, an apprehensiveness about the analytic skill one will need and may not have, or insufficient stamina or resources to face practical obstacles. But there is also some failure in thought that stops so many secondary analysts at the point of conception, and, on the other hand, some fortunate turn of mind that ushers in success.

A lucky thought might account for the conception of one secondary analysis, but *multiple* births hardly seem attributable to chance. The fertility of some secondary analysts must depend on some special style of approach, and perhaps William James' remark about the growth of a science will provide a first clue: "At a certain stage . . . a *degree of vagueness* is what best consists with fertility." Perhaps it also holds true for productive secondary analysts.[6]

A romantic metaphor or model may clarify James' remark. An archive might be likened to an agreeable lady whose charms have been described in the most lavish terms. Many investigators, no matter what the nature of their desires, thus are encouraged to pursue her. If they are perfectionists, the slightest blemish they then observe may seem to spoil the beauty of her data and stop them from further pursuit. Among others whose desires are most particular, a few, by chance encounter, may find just the creation they are seeking, and thus fall in love with that archive at first sight. More likely they will be frustrated and turn their glances elsewhere. If they switch their affections to another archive, some will be fortunate enough to find her attractive and compatible with their desires. But if their requirements are too special, their desires too particular, they may make the full circuit of all the archives finding none that charms them. They are like suitors who travel the world, searching for so rare and ideal a creature that they can never find their heart's desire. If they really wish to find a companionable archive, they may have to scale down their demands, or pause long enough and be insightful enough to sense the hidden and manifold charms that await them, or they may have to broaden their desires.

What about those whose desires are utterly vague, completely diffuse. Perhaps they, too, profit little from each encounter with an archive. Though every prospect might please them, they cannot articulate any one desire.

---

[6] William James, *Principles of Psychology* (New York: Holt, 1890) p. 6 (italics supplied).

Their attention is focused in all directions at once and their search is unguided by any purpose. By contrast, those with only some "degree of vagueness" are more fortunate. They are purposeful in their search, but still relatively easy to please. Since their pursuit is likely to be rewarded, their affection grows. As the relationship with the archive persists, they become more familiar with her many charms and the quirks in her data, and progressively more skillful in their dealings. Each later encounter is simpler and easier. Thus a fruitful and gratifying relationship develops.

This somewhat fanciful and romantic image of the process is confirmed by the empirical data obtained from our survey of users of the archives who were asked to describe in detail their experiences. (A brief description of the survey procedures is presented in the Appendix.) Combining their own reports of the process with our inspection of the end products of their endeavors will give some evidence on that elusive problem, the secret of success in secondary analysis. The cases presented are not to imply that these particular analysts are more productive than others whom we have omitted. These are the ones who have been drawn into our sample and who have been able to articulate some of the ineffable aspects of their experience.

VARIED AND BROAD INTERESTS

Consider, for example, the work of Norval Glenn, whose association with archives resulted in no less than nine published secondary analyses in the years 1966–69. Clearly, the relationship was enduring and fruitful. With various collaborators he produced studies of differences in attitudes and behavior between Negroes and whites, between religious groups, rural and urban groups, regional groups, groups varying in education, occupation and age.[7]

---

[7] Norval Glenn and Leonard Broom, "Negro–White Differences in Reported Attitudes and Behavior," *Sociol. and Soc. Research*, **50**, 1966, pp. 187–200; Norval Glenn, "The Trend in Differences in Attitudes and Behavior by Educational Level," *Sociol. Educ.*, **39**, 1966, pp. 255–275; Norval Glenn and J. L. Simmons, "Are Regional Cultural Differences Diminishing?" *Publ. Opin. Quart.*, **31**, 1967; Leonard Broom and Norval Glenn, "Religious Differences in Reported Attitudes and Behavior," *Sociol. Anal.*, **27**, 1966, pp. 187–209; Norval Glenn and Jon P. Alston, "Rural–Urban Differences in Reported Attitudes and Behavior," *Southwest Soc. Sci. Quart.*, March 1967, pp. 381–400; Norval Glenn and Ruth Hyland, "Religious Preference and Worldly Success: Some evidence from National Surveys," *Amer. Sociol. Rev.*, **32**, 1967, pp. 73–85; Norval Glenn, "Massification vs. Differentiation: Some Trend Data from National Surveys," *Soc. Forces*, December 1967, pp. 172–180; Norval Glenn and Jon Alston, "Cultural Distances among Occupational Categories," *Amer. Sociol. Rev.*, **33**, 1968, pp. 365–382; Norval Glenn, "Aging, Voting, and Political Interest," *Amer. Sociol. Rev.*, **33**, 1968, pp. 563–575; Norval Glenn, "Aging, Disengagement, and Opinionation," *Publ. Opin. Quart.*, **33**, 1969, pp. 17–33. I omit, for purposes of this discussion, other secondary analyses by Glenn which do not deal with the study of social groups.

What a great variety of interests! To be sure, one may perceive a common theme, a unity of purpose, underlying this multiplicity of studies. Indeed there is one that can be abstracted: the study of social groups or categories within the American population. This is sufficient to give direction to the search. Yet the problem of social differentiation is so general, the theme so grand, that it can be translated into many specific investigations. If the search were frustrated in one direction, it could be pursued in another. And as we shall see in Chapter IV, an interest in this very problem is most compatible with the data of many sample surveys, since the social characteristics and group memberships of the respondent are staple items. Moreover, in the patterns to be examined among various social groups, again, Glenn is not narrow in his focus. His concern is to be comprehensive, and thus it is relevant to explore orientations toward domestic politics, foreign affairs, toward work, religion, race relations, child rearing, authoritarianism, civil liberties, and morals. Some things that one might like to know are not available, but almost nothing that is available is irrelevant. One dependent variable central to one of the studies is so general, so abstracted from concrete contents, that almost every survey question bears upon it. "Opinionation" is indexed simply by the proportion who respond to issue questions with the answer "no opinion" or its equivalent.

Contrast Glenn with another investigator whose purposes fell within the same domain but were more narrow and specific. He found "that a national sample contains too few subjects from class and ethnic groups of special interest" to him, and with respect to the patterns he wished to describe for these groups—"the nature of individual attachments to the community and to society and especially the nature of those attachments which the citizen feels impose some obligation on him"—he reports that "the questions they ask did not measure the attitudes in which I was interested."[8] Success for him required a satisfactory supply of a special combination of data which unfortunately was not available. Of course, availability implies a judgment on the part of the investigator. When is the number of cases too few, the indicator too approximate to yield exactly the variable one is seeking to measure? In the encounter with an archive, to follow our romantic metaphor, beauty also lies in the eyes of the beholder. A blemish on the data that may be only a minor imperfection to some, becomes a basic flaw to others. But this is not to suggest that productive secondary analysts must be less perceptive, or have serious defects of judgment and vision. Indeed, when we study later some of the examples produced by Glenn, we shall find that he is sensitive to the

---

[8] Nothing would be gained by reporting the names of the individuals whose purposes were frustrated and whose analyses were aborted.

deficiencies of the data, and takes account of them or compensates for them in his designs and techniques of analysis.

In the words of Broom and Hill, a secondary analyst is unlikely to continue his career for very long, unless he has brought up his "yield-frustration ratio to tolerable levels."[9] Those whose interests are broad are likely to experience not merely a tolerable, but a very high, ratio. Since the very same surveys that serve to illuminate one problem may also serve for other problems, all of which happen to interest them, their labors yield free dividends, earned without extra effort. Indeed all the studies by Glenn derive from a common pool of surveys, which he dips into again and again. The largest data base consists of about 20 surveys spanning an interval of about 20 years.[10]

Alfred Hero, Jr., has had a long and productive career in secondary analysis. He, too, has a pattern of interests in a very broad realm: American opinion on matters of foreign policy and international relations. The realm is not only broad but coincides with one of the major spheres of continuing research of most of the national public opinion and survey agencies. Understandably, the resources for productivity are great.[11]

---

[9] Leonard Broom and Richard J. Hill, "Opinion Polls and Social Rank in Australia: Method and First Findings," *Australian and New Zealand J. Sociol.*, **1**, No. 2, 1965, p. 97.

[10] Similarly, Lazerwitz, whose work will be reviewed in Chapter IV, netted some free dividends from one set of surveys, although he is properly described as a *semi*secondary analyst. As a member of the Survey Research Center of the University of Michigan, he located three of their national surveys, all of which enumerated the respondent's religious membership, observance, and other factual characteristics. Using this one data base, he produced three discrete studies, dealing respectively with the demography of religious groups, variations in church attendance and its correlates, and the changes in observance from immigrant groups to their descendants. To be sure, one may describe the work as representing a unitary study which yielded three publications. But clearly the problem and his interests were broad enough that he did not limit himself to any narrow single aspect but rather to the variety of aspects within the larger domain of religious studies. See Bernard Lazerwitz, "Some Factors Associated with Variations in Church Attendance," *Soc. Forces*, **39**, 1961, pp. 301–309. "A Comparison of Major United States Religious Groups," *J. Amer. Stat. Assoc.*, September 1961, pp. 568–579; Bernard Lazerwitz and Louis Rowitz, "The Three-Generations Hypothesis," *Amer. J. Sociol.*, LXIX, 1964, pp. 529–538.

[11] Alfred O. Hero, Jr., "Foreign Aid and the American Public," *Public Policy*, **14**, 1965, pp. 71–116; *The Southerner and World Affairs* (Baton Rouge: Louisiana State University Press, 1965); *American Religious Groups View Foreign Policy: Trends in Opinion, 1937–1969* (Durham: Duke University Press, 1971); "American Negroes and U. S. Foreign Policy: 1937–1967," *J. Con. Resol.*, **13**, 1969, pp. 220–251; "The American Public and the UN, 1954–1966," *J. Conflict Resol.*, **10**, 1966, pp. 436–475; "Liberalism—Conservatism Revisited: Foreign vs. Domestic Federal Policies, 1937–1967," *Publ. Opin. Quart.* **33**, 1969, pp. 399–408.

This is not to suggest, however, that accomplishment is easy and assured. Hero's special concerns are the trends and social changes in these phenomena over a thirty-year period, and on this problem, all sorts of vexatious difficulties might arise to plague him and errors might intrude to damage his conclusions. The "yield-frustration ratio" becomes tolerable partly because he simply has a high frustration tolerance—he withstands what others might find too intolerable—and partly because he in effect controls the errors, thus maximizing the yield of adequate data and findings. Again, a central theme in secondary analysis recurs, the attention to and treatment of error. What a catalogue of difficulties he presents:

I have made rather extensive use of the data pools of Warren Miller's Consortium as well as of the Roper Center. Until he left the Gallup Organization several years ago, Louis Vexler also ran a number of tabulations for me of A.I.P.O. polls, especially of recent ones that had not yet been deposited at Williamstown. . . . Changes in sampling and other survey technology over the years have been major stumbling blocks. For example, how can one compare opinions of the national population, or of specified demographic groups within it, over the years when sampling techniques have varied as much as, say, AIPO's? In the late thirties AIPO's samples were based on voters rather than adults generally. Southern Negroes hardly appeared in samples; Southern whites were severely underrepresented; so were lower SES and lower educational groups generally. Whereas most of the survey agencies used whites to interview Negroes fifteen and more years ago, more recently they have been more aware of distorted replies likely thereby, and hence try where feasible to use Negro interviewers. Thus comparisons of Negro opinions over time, especially in respect to issues connected with race relations, are questionable.

Changes in weighting practices likewise have made it difficult to trace trends. Thus, early AIPO surveys were not weighted to compensate for undersampling of certain demographic groups. AIPO weighting methods have changed at least twice. But one cannot weight the earlier data to make it more nearly comparable with later, since often the sampling criteria are not known.

Changes in survey questions have likewise prevented comparisons over time. . . . Even the same survey agency changes its questions to such an extent that such comparisons are often impossible.

In some cases codes have been lost. . . . In cases of some older data, it is difficult to determine how the samples were drawn or other pertinent details—virtually everybody who was around then is dead and no written record is available.[12]

---

[12] Personal communication, August 5, 1968.

The difficulties he reports may seem insuperable. Yet his completed studies will reveal that they can be surmounted, and not by repressing unpleasant matters but rather by the application of critical, although reasonable, standards of rigor. Some of Hero's findings will be reviewed in Chapter V. Chapter VI will present a working philosophy and principles for the trend analysis of imperfect data, and some case studies demonstrating the ways investigators have realized their goals of studying social change.

SERENDIPITY ALMOST LOST BUT REGAINED

Among investigators with *broad* interests, serendipity is a likely occurrence. By chance, they are likely to find some of what they are seeking, and also to discover fortuitously in the course of one search valuable bodies of data that are strategic for the study of other problems. Good fortune is likely to crown their activities if only because they are interested in many things. But *sagacity* as well as chance does contribute, as in the original fairly tale, to their happy fate. They are sensitive to the opportunities that are presented. By their skill they convert imperfect data into valuable materials. They contrast with that legendary analyst who never lost a chance of missing an opportunity.

Among other investigators with one *narrow* interest, luck alone will rarely help. Serendipity is almost surely lost unless they can do something to regain it. Sagacity, rather than chance, must be the major factor in their success. The cases to be presented will show the sensitivity with which these analysts examine the data they find, and the flexibility and insight they bring to their encounters.

The career of Glen H. Elder, Jr., captures many of the aspects of discovery and productivity in secondary analysis. As suggested, interests that are *too* diffuse and vague can be a hindrance. His experiences also show the way in which optimal breadth ultimately increases the yield, and how "free dividends" which are the accidental yield of a search can ultimately compensate for frustrations and long labors. He begins his career in the following fashion:

The diffuse approach was most descriptive of my initial relation to the longitudinal archives at the Institute of Human Development at Berkeley . . . in 1962. I had experience only with large sample, cross-sectional surveys, and did not have specific problems in mind. . . . My first step was to explore the content of the data archive and to become familiar with the studies. I soon became aware of the very real handicap of this approach, specifically the coercive influence of the available data and its scatter effect on my efforts. At that point I developed a series of projects centering on theoretical concerns . . . mainly in the area of socialization in status placement. . . . I developed a keen interest in the relation between family structure and the achievement of the young.[13]

Such an interest, although focused in character, may still be described as broad in nature and potentially a fruitful choice for secondary analysis. But then, as it became specified further, the searching process for a time was laborious and frustrating.[14]

I explored the possibility of testing the cross-national uniformity of the relationship between two aspects of the family authority structure—conjugal and parent–child relations—on educational achievement. I started my search with the hope that I could find comparable indicators of my variables in nations which offered contrasts in religious composition and in level of economic development. Descriptions of data sets at the [Berkeley] Survey Research Center were ordered by nation, and I began my review with Italy since it offered the kind of contrasts with the U.S. that I was looking for. Despite a month or more of periodic work at the data library, the results were generally discouraging (the Almond–Verba data had not been catalogued). At this point, I discussed my research objectives with the assistant director . . . and he put me on the trail of the five nation study. In contrast to my dry-run of other data on file, the discovery of relatively appropriate indicators of family relations based on fairly representative samples from five nations was most exciting. I can still recall my disbelief at the find—it seemed too good to be true.

When the problem is highly specific and requires a very special and complex combination of data, it does not inevitably come to failure, as Elder's experience conveys, but success may stem from fortuitous circumstances which occur only after prolonged labors. The critical factor that intervened to change Elder's fortunes deserves to be elevated to an explicit and general principle. He used a knowledgeable *informant* and thereby saved himself from extra labors and frustrations. Perhaps it does not require great sagacity to think of this simple procedure and some would naturally avail themselves

---

[13] Personal communication, August 22, 1969.

[14] Murray A. Strauss has suggested that comparative studies of the family and the variation in socialization as related to class and culture could be accomplished by cross-national secondary analysis, and gives as an illustration the studies by Inkeles cited by us in Chapter VIII in which data from 11 countries were available on child rearing values and occupational aspirations. Where secondary analysis will not provide adequate evidence, Strauss then urges "comparative replication," in which a previously conducted inquiry in one nation is used along with a primary inquiry undertaken in another country, classified by us as a form of semisecondary analysis. See "Society as a Variable in Comparative Study of the Family by Replication and Secondary Analysis," *J. Marriage and the Family*, **30**, 1968, pp. 565–570.

of an informant, but for those who might neglect this avenue and think only of machines as aids, it is worth stating.

The investigator, as Elder shows, must also be flexible, be willing to relax some of his most stringent initial demands:

The theoretical linkage between authority patterns in the family and achievement socialization varies according to the particular parent–child relationship—four such relationships are defined by sex of parent and child. Since the Almond–Verba data included only items measuring authority in the parent–child relationship, I had no choice but to sacrifice these important distinctions in the analysis.

But the broader sphere of interests within which the specific problem was contained meant that some free dividends were reaped from the one search:

In addition to the ASR paper, I completed two other manuscripts which examine related problems.[15]

---

[15] Glen H. Elder, Jr., "Family Structure and Educational Attainment: A Cross-National Analysis," *Amer. Sociol. Rev.*, **30**, 1965, pp. 81–96. "Democratic Parent–Youth Relations in Cross-National Perspective," *Soc. Sci. Quart.*, **49**, 1968; "Role Relations, Socio-Cultural Environments and Autocratic Family Ideology," *Sociometry*, **28**, 1965, pp. 173–196. That the very same survey can serve many and varied interests is suggested by the string of secondary analyses, albeit by other investigators, that derived from *The Civic Culture* surveys. One of these reveals an ironical fact. Elder eliminated the Negro respondents from the American sample, since they would have been an obvious and irrelevant source of variation in any comparison with the European countries. By contrast, Dwaine Marvick focused mainly on this group omitting the European countries in his study of "The Political Socialization of the American Negro," *Annals*, **361**, September, 1965, pp. 112–127. Another investigator as part of a general comparative inquiry into political culture and political socialization planned a secondary analysis restricted to respondents under age 36 in the British and Italian surveys from *The Civic Culture*. A tragicomic circumstance aborted the analysis and is perhaps worth reporting as an example of the hazards in the careers of some secondary analysts. "Before I could use the data, however, my desk was moved to a different building, and to make things easier, the movers decided that the waste-paper basket would be a handy place to put loose items—like two boxes of punch-cards. In the new building an exceptionally diligent janitor, under strict orders to empty the baskets every night, spotted the data-card boxes in the waste basket and naturally assumed they were destined for the incinerator. With great dispatch he sent them on their way." In Elder's work, the distinctive character of the universe that was sampled in Mexico, and the many operating difficulties there, introduced serious difficulties for the *comparative* analysis. Yet, these difficulties would not plague a secondary analysis that was restricted to a study of Mexican behavior, although they would require some statement of the limitations of the findings. For just such a secondary analysis, another in the string derived from *The Civic Culture*, see Wm. J. Blough, *Political Participation in Mexico: Sex Differences in Behavior and Attitudes*, University of North Carolina, Doctoral Dissertation, 1967, University Micro

In the well-stocked mind, stocked with the memories of the data from past searches which are kept alive by a diversity of interests, other secondary analyses can incubate. At the right moment, they can be brought to real life, thus producing new studies without special searching. Elder remarks:

While searching for cross-national data appropriate for my research problem on family structure and achievement, I did come across survey data which were relevant to my general interests in socialization and status placement. This exposure was most helpful later . . . when I began work on British secondary education. Items from a British Gallup Poll were used in the concluding portion of the analysis.[16]

The career of Judith Blake will provide further clues to general styles of work that lead to productivity in secondary analysis. Her interests as a demographer led her, in one phase of her work, to focus on a highly specialized area of inquiry, "family size ideals." Her search revealed that, through for-

---

Films No. 68-6718. For two additional studies, from among the many offspring produced by *The Civic Culture*, see A. W. Finifter, "Dimensions of Political Alienation," *Amer. Polit. Sci. Rev.*, **64,** 1970, pp. 389–410; E. N. Muller, "Cross-National Dimensions of Political Competence," *Amer. Polit. Sci. Rev.*, **64,** 1971, pp. 792–809. Both of these employ factor analytic methods to examine the structure of belief systems, a problem to be reviewed in Chapter V.

[16] Glen H. Elder, Jr., "Life Opportunity and Personality: Some Consequences of Stratified Secondary Education in Great Britain," *Sociol. Educ.*, **38,** Spring, 1965, pp. 173–202. Another investigator carried out similar studies partly by his own small-scale primary investigation but also by the secondary analysis of British Gallup Poll data, in this instance a four wave panel carried out over four years on a sample of 1800 British Youth. In turn, he reaped a free dividend using the data he had already employed for a study of the effects of type of secondary school to explore the effects of the intergenerational mobility of these youth on political attitudes. See Paul Abramson, "The Differential Political Socialization of English Secondary School Students," *Sociol. Educ.*, **40,** 1967, pp. 246–269; Paul Abramson and John Books, "Social Mobility and Political Attitudes: A Study of Intergenerational Mobility among Young British Men," *Compar. Politics*, **3,** 1971, pp. 402–428. The way in which Elder and other secondary analysts may reap free dividends in the course of visual searching has larger implications for the technology which the archives have recently developed to reduce the labors in retrieving specific information from a great mass of data in their files. The ideal toward which the archives have been moving and which has already been partly realized is one in which from a distance, and without benefit of direct scrutiny, the potential investigator asks for a machine search for a very specific datum or set of data. He then receives back only that information relevant to the specific inquiry. Certainly this reduces manual labor to a minimum, and is ideal for an investigator with one determinate hypothesis; but nothing else crosses his path in the process. The only free dividends he can reap are those that involve recombining those very same data. Immersion in a larger body of data and visual inspection may be more tedious but at least provides the stimulation which leads to free dividends in other realms.

tunate coincidence of interests, the major American agencies had conducted no less than 13 national surveys, spanning a thirty-year period which contained an appropriate question. From these sources she produced a series of studies.[17] But the potentialities for fruitful secondary analysis were there only because of her attitude. If she had approached these surveys with a fastidious touch, rejecting materials that had some blemish visible to her sharp eye, nothing might have been realized. As she notes in the course of her analyses: "A general question on 'ideal' family size leaves much to be desired methodologically." "There is . . . a tendency . . . for the South to be underrepresented. This bias is particularly great for the 1941, 1945, 1947, and 1952 studies." "We are unable to offer assurances concerning many refinements in the data-gathering process," etc.

In these and other ways, she shows a most acute sense of error problems. Rather than rejecting the materials, she accepts their limitations and tries in various creative ways to estimate the magnitude of the errors and their effect on her conclusions. As emphasized earlier, the proper treatment of error is essential in secondary analysis. But in her courageous style of response to the problem, Blake, like the other analysts mentioned, provides the proper example to be followed. Two new aspects of a style that leads to productivity, however, are also conveyed by her example.

---

[17] Judith Blake, "Ideal Family-Size Among White Americans: A Quarter of a Century's Evidence," *Demography*, **3**, 1966, pp. 154–173; "Reproductive Ideals and Educational Attainment Among White Americans, 1943–1960," *Popul. Stud.*, **21**, 1967, 159–174; "Income and Reproductive Motivation," *Popul. Stud.*, **21**, 1967, 185–206; "Are Babies Consumer Durables? A Critique of the Economic Theory of Reproductive Motivation," *Popul. Stud.*, **22**, 1968, pp. 5–25. "Family Size in the 1960's—A Baffling Fad?," *Eugenics Quart.*, **14**, 1967, pp. 60–74; "Population Policy for Americans: Is the Government Being Misled?," *Science*, **164**, 1969, pp. 522–529. The quotations are taken from these articles and the style of work is drawn also from a personal communication, August 20, 1968. Those secondary analysts of the seventies who become interested in problems of population control will be spared her heavy labors of searching. All the holdings in the Roper Center relevant to such problems, for the years 1938–1970, have been inventoried and cast into published form in January, 1970 with the aid of a grant from The Population Council. The questions are classified under major topics, identified by country, survey agency, date of inquiry, type and size of sample, and the face-sheet data enumerated. Such specialized bibliographies are most valuable tools in reducing labors of searching and in stimulating research. We may hope that this good example will be followed by similar publications for other important problems. See Philip K. Hastings, ed., *Population Control, A Bibliography of Survey Data: 1938–1970* (Williamstown: Roper Public Opinion Research Center, 1970). Of course, the time series continues to be enlarged and the secondary analyst of the future should not pass up measurements taken subsequent to such publications. For example, the Gallup Poll added another point to the series by repeating the question on "ideal family size" in an American survey conducted in January, 1971.

Blake's interests focused on a special, narrow area—almost a pinpointed phenomenon. As she appreciates: "I find the existence of a large number of studies extending over time and yet systematic as to the questions asked very felicitous." But if the independent variables that concerned her were as specific as the phenomenon, things might not have been so felicitous.[18] Very few of the surveys might have met a *triple* standard: a measure of the specific dependent variable of interest, a measure of a specific and elaborate combination of independent variables, and a high degree of accuracy. She, however, is interested in the broad exploration of the narrow phenomenon. The model is like a wind funnel of causality converging on a fine point, rather than like a thin tube. As she describes it: "I operate with the notion that reproduction must be viewed in the motivational context of familial and non-familial roles and status, of norms and sanctions relating to such roles and statuses, and of the socio-cultural limitation on an individual's choice of playing reproductive and non-reproductive roles." Given such a broad domain of interests, her requirements for the inclusion of other types of data are less restrictive.

As a fourth requirement, Blake might have imposed the restriction that the populations sampled in the available surveys be of some special nature, usually regarded as ideal for the study of fertility problems. What is noteworthy is not that she departed from these a priori desirable requirements simply to maximize her opportunities. By a creative turn of mind, by true sagacity, she perceived the benefits to be derived from having a universe different from that usually employed in fertility studies. By pausing long enough to consider the prospect, and by flexibility in her ways of thought, she turned an apparent deficiency into a real advantage. She sensed the hidden charms of the data:

In my opinion these data are a gold mine since they cover a period of great importance in the history of American fertility, and one during which almost no other data are available until very late in the period. Moreover, the data are for both sexes, whereas most fertility surveys (although far more detailed) related to women only. Finally, the samples do not merely comprise women

---

[18] Another respondent in our survey illustrates this point. Appleton had a highly specialized interest within the foreign policy realm, the study of opinions about Chinese representation in the United Nations. His was a case of great fortune, brought about as if by chance. He found data on this issue for the United States and for 20 other countries scattered over the time period from 1949, when the People's Republic of China was formed, up to 1960. But with respect to the independent variables which figured in his analysis of the problem his requirements were not tight. He was interested in the social characteristics of those with different positions on the issue, and in their ideological and personality characteristics. Thus he did not blight the opportunity. See Sheldon Appleton, *The Eternal Triangle? Communist China, The United States and the United Nations* (East Lansing: Michigan State University Press, 1961).

in the reproductive ages, but older respondents as well. One can thus view many, to me sociologically important facets of the total context of reproductive motivation, instead of assuming that the only important people to interview are women, aged 18–39 (the typical target of the modern fertility surveys).[19]

A large part of Richard Hamilton's work in secondary analysis has involved the study of political behavior and attitudes and their relation to class factors, and he has explored these problems on a comparative basis in France, Germany, and the United States.[20] Clearly the odds favor him. This is a very broad realm of interests, and political phenomena as well as measures of social and economic position are incorporated in many surveys. Yet, in other ways, he is severely handicapped. He wishes to go deeply into the problem, and a few staple indicators of class would hardly satisfy him:

Much of the previous work has been concerned with basic cross-tabulations of politics and major background variables . . . one more study of the relationship of class and voting . . . adds little to our knowledge. . . . We will be testing hypotheses about the "mechanisms" or "processes" which operate to bring about the original findings.[21]

Thus, his is a mixed blessing. His demands are not rigidly confined to any particular indicators which might not be available, but rudimentary information on a limited range of variables would not match the sweep of his aspirations. And there are other obstacles that stand in his way: "At many points our analysis may be considered triply hazardous: it is based on quota samples, uses indirect indicators and rests on a small number of cases."[22] What comes

---

[19] As a result, she is able to demonstrate a difference in family size ideals in older women, who might otherwise not have been studied, and thus arrive at a most interesting formulation: "We are led to ask whether such pronatalist ideals among the grandparent generation have not constituted a moral backdrop for the reproductive renaissance among the young. In the future, therefore, it may be valuable to study the familial preferences of both the older and the reproducing generation in more detail, because the former—through their moral, as well as their tangible support—may influence the reproductive performance of young people." "Ideal Family Size," *op. cit.*, p. 173.

[20] Richard F. Hamilton, *Affluence and the French Worker in the Fourth Republic* (Princeton: Princeton University Press, 1967); "Skill Level and Politics," *Publ. Opin. Quart.*, **29,** 1965, pp. 390–399; "The Marginal Middle Class: A Reconsideration," *Amer. Sociol. Review*, **31,** 1966, pp. 192–199; "The Behavior and Values of Skilled Workers," in Wm. Gomberg and A. Shostak, *Blue Collar World*, (Englewood Cliffs: Prentice-Hall, 1964), pp. 42–57; "Affluence and the Worker: The West German Case," *Amer. J. Sociol.*, **71,** 1965, pp. 144–152.

[21] Hamilton, *Affluence and the French Worker in the Fourth Republic, op. cit.*, pp. 8–9.

[22] *Ibid.*, p. 14. Just as Blake found that the apparent disadvantage of samples which did not focus exclusively on what would normally be regarded as the most relevant target

to his aid is his sharp eye for strategic and valuable data. He describes his general approach:

The first procedure is somewhat open-ended and that is simply that one comes across a deck of cards or a code book and more or less as a projective test can look through the questions and ask himself what hypothesis can I test, what theories can I illuminate making use of these materials. In order to follow through on this procedure one must have a knowledge of major theories in the field, and an ability to see that question 17 has relevance to something in Mosca, question 23 has some relevance to some question in Max Weber, and question 49 has some relevance too . . . it's this ability to project and see the possibilities and being able to put them together which makes this kind of effort a fruitful one. If one doesn't have that kind of background, one approaches this kind of open-ended procedure and comes up with nothing.[23]

Pasteur stated it well: "In the fields of observation, chance favors only the prepared mind"—but, in Hamilton's words, a mind that is not "locked within" any narrow tradition. The secondary analyst who has a rich and varied knowledge of theory can more readily perceive that an apparently trivial measure is relevant to a problem, and thus turn things to his advantage. Hamilton describes just such an episode in the course of his examination of one of the French surveys. He finds the simple question: "Do you have a garden?" and this starts a chain of associations:

In following up a discussion by Engels, the garden appeared as an important wage supplement for some workers, alleviating an otherwise seriously deprived condition. . . . Engels considered gardens to be both a direct aid to the capitalists, allowing them to cut wages accordingly, and a device promulgated by middle class reformers for diverting workers from "real solutions" to their problems.[24]

---

population resulted in serendipitous findings, so too did Hamilton. The survey of workers that he used was based on a quota sample, and about 600 of the 1600 cases were drawn from the two strata white-collar workers and foremen. This provides a point of empirical comparison and served to prevent what we have called "pseudocomparative" conclusions. In the second survey which also sampled the national population, there were only 220 workers, but again this provided points of comparison with other occupational groups, as did two other surveys of heterogeneous samples which he exploited for his monograph.

[23] Hamilton, personal communication.

[24] Hamilton, *op. cit.*, p. 14, p. 149. In a not irreverent spirit, it seems to me that whether the respondent owns a pet and the kind (canary? dog? cat? hamster?) which appears to be a frivolous feature of a style of life which the public opinion polls have periodically enumerated might well deserve a fairly deep secondary analysis. Standardizing the com-

But the mind that is well stocked with *theory* is not the only source of serendipity for secondary analysts. An alertness to *policy* implications may also turn some apparently dated and specific item into a resource for secondary analysis which produces fruitful applied research and perhaps even yields evidence of a more basic theoretical worth. Hamilton describes another fortunate moment in the course of one of his searches:

> *. . . while working on some topic (I've forgotten now what it was) I happened to be going through the 1952 Survey Research Center code book and since it was spring of 1965, the season of Viet-Nam escalation, my eye caught a question asking about a preferred policy in the Korean War, and one of the options being escalate the conflict and bomb Manchuria and China. It immediately occurred to me that this was a topic which had not only practical implications, but also which might illuminate some aspects of policy making. Particularly I was interested in the sentiments of the 38 percent of the population who favored the bombing option. I also recognized that this was of potential relevance to the working class authoritarianism hypothesis and we could test that hypothesis in a somewhat different context.[25]*

A last case study will demonstrate the way in which sensitivity to the hidden significance of apparently trivial data plus powers of abstraction and reconceptualization can improve the fortunes of a secondary analyst who was

---

parisons crudely for opportunity (within the same size urban areas and for family size and composition) might tap a latent sentiment or psychological disposition which might have considerable power in predicting the respondent's ideology.

[25] The reconstruction of the experience comes from Hamilton's personal communication. For the paper see "The Mass Support for an Air Strike: The 1952 China Case," June, 1965, mimeo. In this paper, Hamilton is tentative in his conclusions since he again found it "necessary to fall back on indirect indicators for the assumed causal variables." But he found no support for lines of theorizing that would locate endorsements of bombing among individuals who are "authoritarian," "alienated," "anomic," "inefficaceous." His evidence suggests rather that the members of the advantaged majority were more prone to support bombing partly because of a general conservative ideology and defense of national interest as well as a "latent racism which is supportive of aggressive moves against non-whites," and also because their higher education made them more accessible to media which in that period contained pro-bombing content. In their timeliness, these serendipitous findings from 1952 deserve more testing in the context of the Viet-Nam War options. Hamilton was sensitive to the problem and subsequently found an opportunity to repeat the study from a question that had been asked in 1964. It provides an example of what we shall call external replication and will be reviewed in Chapter V. Back and Gergen, the secondary analysts whose experiences will be described next, also examined questions on the endorsement of various extreme policies in the Korean War including the bombing of China, using other data from Gallup surveys conducted during the years 1950–51, as part of their special interest in the diverse effects of the aging process.

concerned with phenomena quite different in nature from those already presented. Back and his associate, Gergen, have focused on matters which certainly are most general and pervasive in human experience—conceptions of the self and the orientation toward space and time—but which would seem, in their subtle psychological quality, to defy description via the secondary analysis of surveys dealing with conventional substantive issues. Paradoxically, it has been a most productive endeavor.[26] As Back describes the process of discovery:

I started first doing secondary analysis out of interest in a somewhat vague, general problem; what do people consider to be their own essence and what changes they are willing to make. As you can see, one cannot ask direct questions on this topic, I was looking for a number of indicators which would correlate and show how a consistent stance toward the limits of the self could be established. Thus we asked the Roper Center to identify surveys which dealt with a set of topics which we thought to be related—attitudes toward bodily changes, psychotherapy, changes in oneself, adult education, dress, first impressions, etc. As you can imagine, we got a somewhat heterogeneous listing of questions. . . . At this point we asked for the surveys which had the most relevant data for the topics selected and started a regular analysis for these topics. Here an element of chance crept in: as most of the studies were commercial omnibus surveys we could profit by using some other questions which happened to be in the same studies. This gave us the means to use some ostensibly unrelated questions to establish a general attitude. . . . As the study was financed in great part by a gerontological program, we paid particular attention to changes with age. Thus we gradually concentrated on the concept of life space—i.e., the time and space which is relevant to a person; our first completed paper dealt mainly with classifications of time orientation. . . . I was interested in a basic orientation, which might express itself in many specific attitudes and opinions. However, specific components would

---

[26] Kurt W. Back and Kenneth J. Gergen, "The Self Through the Latter Span of Life," in Chad Gordon and Kenneth Gergen, eds., *The Self in Social Interaction* (New York: John Wiley, 1968), pp. 241–250; "Apocalyptic and Serial Time Orientations and the Structure of Opinions," *Publ. Opin. Quart.*, **27**, 1963, pp. 427–442; "Individual Orientations, Public Opinion and the Study of International Relations," *Soc. Problems*, **11**, 1963, pp. 77–87; Kenneth J. Gergen and Kurt W. Back, "Aging, Time Perspective and Preferred Solutions to International Conflicts," *J. Conflict Resol.*, **9**, 1965, pp. 177–186; "Communication in the Interview and the Disengaged Respondent," *Publ. Opin. Quart.*, **30**, 1966, pp. 385–398; Kurt W. Back "Aging and the Paradox of Somatic Concern," in J. McKinney and Ida Simpson, eds., *Social Aspects of Aging* (Durham, Duke University Press, 1966), pp. 306–321; Kurt W. Back and George Maddox, *Overweight* (San Francisco: Jossey-Bass, in press).

always overshadow the orientation I was looking for. . . . The variety of topics, and even the fact that some of them were quite trivial helped in investigating an orientation which was supposed to be general. We could never have justified asking all these questions in our own survey, in the hope of demonstrating the range of influence of our orientation.[27]

Back was trying to capture the individual's fundamental personal style, which ought to reveal itself expressively in responses in many content areas. Even the most trivial areas, as he stresses, should yield reflections of the self, and the wider the domain of unrelated questions over which he finds some regularity, the more compelling the evidence, because it is quintessential to the concept that the self is a pervasive integrative factor. To tap certain facets of the personality, the self-concept and the personal orientation to time and space, some questions that appear trivial or simply amusing were perceived by Back and Gergen as most appropriate. For example, questions on whether the person played the horses and poker, or participated in church raffles, or a question on whether a person believes there is no harm in drinking non-pasteurized milk, or would be willing to keep a speed-governor on his car, or exercised yesterday, or advocated the banning of boxing, or emphasized utility versus beauty in the choice of clothing. All took on serious and deep significance. A battery of questions on satisfaction with one's weight and whether one had tried to diet, repeated over five national surveys, were seen not merely as having applied research value, but as an avenue to the deeper problem of one's body and self-image, and thus led to unexpected and anomalous findings on a problem that is currently controversial, the self-regard of American Negroes and its relation to their body-image.

These case studies may guide others toward productivity in secondary analysis. This is not to suggest that all must or should take the same approach. Each must seek his fortune by his own path. But following the good examples set in certain respects can do an investigator no harm and will bring him much benefit. In their approach to error, in the way they pause and reflect—not reject—in their tolerance for frustration, in the ways they make their intellectual interests congruent with the materials available, or make seemingly inappropriate materials conform to and work in their interests—in all these respects the examples may inspire others to greater productivity. The good example cannot work magic, however. It *cannot* implant the sagacity, the keen perception, the quick and powerful mind richly endowed with knowledge—the intellectual capital by which some build their great fortune. But certainly these examples must have suggested some general

---

[27] Back, personal communication, September 10, 1968.

classes of problems which can be pursued effectively by secondary analysis, and which are far from exhausted by the work of previous investigators. In the chapters to follow, these general problems that are so well suited to secondary analysis will be presented in greater detail, and the designs and procedures to be employed will be reviewed. The many studies used as illustrations should stimulate others to their own flights of creative thought.

IV

Studies of Social Categories and Groups

LARGE-SCALE, LONG-ESTABLISHED SURVEY RESEARCH IN MANY COUNTRIES HAS produced over time a great deal of information about the major social categories or groups in various societies which are identifiable from the "face-sheet" questions, the items on the respondent's social background and personal characteristics. The face sheet and its main features have become institutionalized practice in surveys. Although inquiries may vary among agencies, whatever topics they may choose to survey, they portray routinely and with considerable uniformity the social and personal profiles of their nameless respondents. The examples in the previous chapters have already suggested some of the potentialities for secondary analysis that derive from this practice, but the lavish opportunities will now be reviewed more comprehensively. The designs by which these opportunities can be realized and the principles and procedures, as well as the difficulties, will be treated systematically.

In surveys where the universe is broad or unrestricted and the samples large and sophisticated in design, the investigator presumably obtains unbiased and adequate samples of many such groups, each one being covered over the wide range of natural conditions under which it lives.[1]

---

[1] Most surveys are restricted to the universe of noninstitutionalized adults, the definition of adult usually being an individual over the age of 21. Generalization to the *youthful* members of social groups may thus not be warranted. However, there are some surveys that incorporate individuals down to the age of 18 in their samples, and there are many specialized surveys that have focused specifically on youth and which are accessible to secondary analysts. For example, H. H. Remmers and his associates at Purdue University have conducted annual national surveys of American high school youth for a period of more than twenty years on a broad range of topics, and the potential for investigators of socialization is great. Apart from the age limits, the usual exclusion of young adults

In surveys where the face sheet is elaborate—and to some extent even where it is rudimentary—each category can be specified in terms of a set of characteristics. Thus a social grouping whose very *definition* is multidimensional, based on some special combination of features, is readily located for further study. By way of simple illustration, some indices of socioeconomic status use the joint occurrence of some level of education and some set of occupations to specify a given class.

When a group is defined by a *single* characteristics, e.g., Catholics or Jews or Protestants, men or women, the accompanying face-sheet data serve to sub-divided and refine the gross category, to match it in some respect with a comparison group, or to specify an interesting or deviant type for various purposes of study. By way of illustration, one could subdivide women into those who are housewives and those who work, Catholics into those who are poor and those who are not, or those who live in the South and those who live outside the South. The *contemporary* status set can provide the raw materials for the classification of respondents, but the *status sequence* can also be employed. Southerners who once lived in the North, the rich whose past was poor, the Catholic who became Protestant, or the Protestant who became Catholic, illustrate the more subtle classifications that can be drawn from some face sheets. In these ways, the variations in some phenomena within particular groups and between groups can be examined in relation to a complex of personal or social characteristics or a context of environmental conditions.[2]

---

who are in residential colleges or the military and of the aged who are in institutions may on occasion, if not evaluated, introduce insidious effects on the conclusions on particular problems.

[2] The reader will recognize that we are using the term social *group* in a broad and loose sense, in contrast with its narrow application to a number of individuals who *interact* with each other and where, depending on the formulation, still other criteria are met. It would be awkward to have to use throughout the chapter an omnibus phrase: groups and social categories and aggregates of social statuses. The modes of analysis being presented apply equally well to all these entities. To be sure, most face sheets emphasize social statuses, and the discussion therefore has greatest application to the study of social *categories*. But no one familiar with the many variations on the face sheet would deny the possibilities for the study of *true* groups. Union membership, service in the army, church membership, document the ways in which membership groups can be isolated for study. The *general phenomenon* of joining a group and reference group versus membership group processes can also be studied. Secondary analyses with such a focus will be treated in Chapter V, in contrast with the studies treated in this chapter which focus on *patricular* social groups and the corollary patterns. Studies which focus on *changes* over time in the behavior of a group or the changing pattern of differences between groups will be treated in Chapter VI. Studies of *age* groupings specifically will also be treated later since they implicate social change. The comparison of social groups in different national contexts will be treated in Chapter VIII.

Such breakdowns of a total sample or cross tabulations of phenomena by various social characteristics are routine in any primary analysis. In secondary analysis, they take on larger significance since the opportunities for *definitive* characterization of a group are increased. A social group that is too small in any single sample survey for the findings to have stature can be expanded by various designs which combine the data from several or many surveys. With one survey, it may not be possible to distinguish a finding that is temporary or artifactual, and therefore survey-specific, from a finding that is real and enduring, but many surveys provide the test. The secondary analyst may adopt, even flaunt, Andrew Greeley's memorable motto: "One survey does not a revolution make."[3]

With questions from many surveys, the diverse patterns of conduct, attitude, and belief of a group can be described comprehensively, whereas the description from a single survey is limited to relatively few aspects. Even when one is concerned with a particular dependent variable, it may be possible to consolidate several surveys into a more powerful body of evidence, although, as implied in the previous chapter, specialized demands for a very stringent test may be met by only a very few surveys.

The opportunities are manifold. But one important distinction must be made to prevent too generous an interpretation of the resources for secondary analysis provided by the worldwide institutionalization of the face sheet.[4] The attributes that define some groupings are so simple in nature that the *coding*

---

[3] Andrew M. Greeley, "Influence of the 'Religious Factor' on Career Plans," *Amer. J. Sociol.*, **68**, 1963, p. 671. One is reminded of Campbell's important point about "convergent validation" via the use of more than one method. The value of a correlation may be inflated by the fact that the two variables have been measured by the same method. A finding that transcends the work of a given survey organization (the particular time period, the operations in a particular survey) is protected from much of this criticism since the method components change. It may still be vulnerable, of course, to the criticism that all of the data derive from one *generic* method, the survey, rather than from two or more radically different methods. See Donald T. Campbell and Donald W. Fiske, "Convergent and Discriminant Validation by the Multitrait–Multimethod Matrix," *Psychol. Bull.*, **56**, 1959, pp. 81–105. In this light and to provide a completely balanced account of the benefits that accrue to a *semi*secondary analyst, it could be argued that however many surveys he may employ, he is confined to the data of one particular agency. A pure secondary analyst who draws upon the surveys of many different agencies does attenuate whatever errors may stem from the idiosyncratic operations of them.

[4] Information on the face-sheet practices of survey agencies in various countries in 1963 is reported in the following sources. Philip Abrams, "The Production of Survey Data in Britain,"; Marten Brouwer, "The 1963 Production of Sample Surveys in Continental Europe,"; Philip K. Hastings, "Inventory of American Production of Survey Data in 1963," in S. Rokkan, ed., *Data Archives for the Social Sciences* (Paris: Mouton, 1966).

loses none of the original information that was enumerated. Sex is an obvious example. But for some social groupings, the coded data may have lost many of the original refinements that were enumerated on the questionnaire, and the original question may itself have been rather gross in classification. An extreme example is provided by age, a continuous variable, but which may be enumerated in gross step intervals, e.g., 21–34, 35–44, etc. and which may be coded and punched into even grosser categories such as "under 45," and "over 45." A person's religious affiliation may be coded in terms of the grosser category, Protestant, or in terms of some more refined system of Protestant denominations. Depending on one's interests, the coded data may be cruder than would be ideal for one's purposes. Here again the *semi*secondary analyst has the great advantage over the client of an archive in that the original questionnaire data are more readily accessible and the original refinements of the data can, if necessary, be recaptured by recoding.[5]

The opportunities and the obstacles in the way, the designs and the procedures, will become clear as we examine some studies in detail.

Religious Groups—A Case Study in Secondary Analysis

Scholars who are interested in most fundamental social differentiations in American society—other than religious groupings—have a basic research resource at hand in the official statistics of the Census Bureau and other government agencies. By contrast, those who have a special interest in religious groups have suffered from perhaps a unique and desperate lack of data on the distribution of the population by religion and the correlates of such affiliation. Censuses of religious bodies in the United States, whatever their limitations, have not been conducted since 1936.[6] A question on religious affiliation has

---

[5] One of the accomplishments of the recent activities of the archives has been the formulation of standards for more effective coverage of social characteristics on the face sheet and to urge more refinement in the enumeration and coding of the characteristics. The capacity of modern data-processing equipment is such that there is very little need for data reduction in order to compress the original information into a form manageable by the machines, and it has therefore been urged that details not be sacrificed in future coding of such characteristics as age.

[6] For a historical review, see Benson Y. Landis, "A Guide to the Literature on Statistics of Religious Affiliation with References to Related Social Studies," *J. Amer. Stat. Assoc.*, **54**, 1959, pp. 335–357. This paper does document the plethora of studies by individuals and church groups, but their inherent limitations can also be documented. For an incisive critique of the available statistics, see N. J. Demerath, III, "Trends and Anti-Trends in Religious Change," in Eleanor B. Sheldon and Wilbert E. Moore, *Indicators of Social Change* (New York: Russell Sage, 1968), pp. 352–369.

never been included in the decennial population censuses of the past, and the 1970 census does not incorporate such a question either. In 1957, however, the Census Bureau did ask a very large national sample the question "What is your religion?" The report that followed remarked: "This is the *first* report containing nationwide statistics on religion of the population, based on data collected from individuals by the Bureau of the Census. . .". In this light, studies of religious affiliation based on the information already available from sample surveys provide a compelling proof of the unique value of secondary analysis. Bogue remarks: "Most sociologists consider religious affiliation a factor of paramount importance in explaining many aspects of human behavior. Like the factors of educational attainment, occupation, and income, it is an axis around which much of a person's life is oriented."[7] Those who share his views will certainly find secondary analysis an especially welcome tool, and all investigators can profit from the general methodological principles revealed by the studies of this one particular type of social group.

Two investigators sensed the need and the opportunity, and both of them conducted parallel secondary analyses relating to the period of the fifties.[8] The unusual agreement in the findings from these independent surveys, originally conducted by different agencies, despite the time intervals separating the surveys, is a most comforting datum. Lazerwitz combined, by means to be described below, the data from three surveys of national samples of adults conducted by the Survey Research Center in the period between Spring, 1957 and November, 1958; two contained the question "What is your religious preference?" and the other "Is your church preference Protestant, Catholic, or Jewish?" In the two earlier surveys, Protestants were asked for their denomination, and in the last survey, answer boxes were also provided for those whose religious affiliation was "other" or "none." Bogue and Feldman also combined, in ways to be described, data from nation-wide surveys of samples of about 2500 adults conducted by the National Opinion Research Center

---

[7] Donald J. Bogue, *The Population of the United States* (New York: The Free Press, 1959), p. 688.

[8] On the basis of her search, Dorothy Good reports that Roper asked a question on religious preference "at least seventeen times in the eleven-year period 1946–1956 . . . in only two cases were Protestant denominations specifically listed. During the same period . . . Gallup . . . included such a question on 77 of their surveys and . . . the Minnesota Poll asked such a question 39 times." Dorothy Good, "Questions on Religion in the United States Census," *Popul. Index*, **25**, 1959, pp. 3–16. She also reports from a local study by the Census Bureau, preceding the 1957 CPS inquiry that 95.5% of respondents "gave a codable answer immediately" to a question on religion, 1.3% gave an ambiguous answer not codable, and 3.2% refused or replied that they had no religion or known preference.

in the interval between 1953 and 1955.[9] These contained a similar question and subquestion. The estimates are presented in Table 4-1.

When one considers the sampling errors attaching to samples of such design and size, possible real changes over the time span of several years, plus other sources of error that must accompany all empirical inquiry as a result of performance in interviewing, probing, classification, and the like, the agreement represents a truly magnificent achievement. These investigators did *not* compare themselves with each other, but each compares findings from his relatively small samples with those obtained in 1957 on the one occasion when the Census Bureau asked the question of a large sample of 35,000 households. Allowing for sharp differences in the definition of the universe and the slight variation in the question employed by the Census Bureau, the agreement was very high.

But the purposes of both these secondary analyses is not simply to provide an estimate of the religious composition of the American population, but rather to examine the patterns within these groups and the differences between them. As noted in Chapter III, when one requires a particular *combination* of variables, or when one wants to examine the relationship between a face-sheet characteristic and some phenomenon or dependent variable, the number of surveys that are appropriate may dwindle. Even though the face sheet is common to many surveys, the questions relating to substantive topics change radically. In both these investigations, the corollary variables that are of prime interest, however, are also drawn from the *face sheet*, thus making it highly likely that the appropriate measures will be on every survey drawn into the analyst's pool. With this specification of his requirements easily met, he can be more selective and stringent about other technical requirements as to quality of the sample, etc. It is a strategy for secondary analysis strongly to

---

[9] Bogue and Feldman, *op. cit.*, pp. 697–709. Earlier, Lazerwitz was described as a *semi-secondary* analyst, being employed at the time by the Survey Research Center. So, too, Bogue and Feldman were semisecondary analysts both being associates of NORC. Apropos our earlier remark about the loss of valuable information by compression in coding and the advantages the semisecondary analyst may have, it is worth quoting Lazerwitz: " . . . only Protestant denominations included in this article's tables were specifically coded on the two earlier surveys. Information on additional denominations can only be obtained by an expensive recoding process" (p. 569, footnote). To be sure, it would be expensive, but more conveniently available to him than to an outsider. In passing, it should be noted that the very surveys Bogue used for the study of religious groups, NORC Surveys No. 335 and 367, were the ones employed by Wright and Hyman in their secondary analysis of "voluntary association membership," again documenting the way in which a given survey can serve multiple purposes and produce a string of secondary analyses. From this study, the combined N for the two NORC studies is 5188, although Bogue only reports the approximate size.

TABLE 4-1. *Religious Preference of American Adults as Revealed by Independent Secondary Analyses.*

	1953–1955 Bogue and Feldman	March 1957	April 1957 Lazerwitz	November 1958
Protestants	71.5	70.5	71.2	72.8
Baptists	22.0	21.1	21.8	
Methodists	17.4	16.3	17.0	
Lutherans	7.6	8.1	6.5	
Presbyterians	6.7	6.5	5.6	
Episcopalians	2.8	2.9	2.6	
Other Protestants	14.9	15.6	17.7	
Roman Catholics	21.1	22.6	22.6	21.9
Jews	3.0	3.6	2.8	3.2
Other Religions	1.4	0.9	0.9	0.7
No Religion	2.8	2.2	2.3	1.3
Religion Not Ascertained	. . .	0.2	0.2	0.1
	N = about 5000	N = 2458	N = 1919	N = 1450

be recommended, and investigators should not neglect the hidden charms in the simple facial features of any survey.

Both investigations examine the religious denominations in terms of their composition on such variables as sex, marital status, age, number of children, and the geographical location, size, and types of community in which they live, by routine and simple cross tabulations. These are very common face-sheet items on American surveys, and these analyses plus similar ones in the future could thus provide much information on the demography and ecology of religious groups. Before turning to the other characteristics examined, consider the general import of the case for some of the problems that may arise in secondary analysis and the corresponding procedures.

The entire characterization of religious denominations, some may argue, is pinned to a very narrow indicator: one question which, with minor variations, asked the person his felt affiliation or religious preference. This might hardly seem adequate to a concept so complex as religious group membership. It would seem to suggest the peculiar vulnerability of secondary analysis, the slippage between a concept and the operational measure of it that happens to be available. Is there not a gigantic difference between nominal identification and formal church membership, or participation in the life of the group and the church, or acceptance of its norms and beliefs? Certainly, the problem cannot be ignored *generally*, and secondary analysts, as earlier noted, may often have to compromise their stringent and comprehensive standards for measurement.

These particular cases, however, cannot be faulted so quickly. Recall that when the Census Bureau engaged in *primary* research on the problem and was free to fashion any indicator it chose, it asked only the one question: "What is your religion?" By this act, the census also seems to suggest that one's self-conception, one's subjective identification with the religious group, is the quintessence of the concept.[10] And a paradox is to be noted. The three surveys Lazerwitz drew upon *did* ask an additional question on "frequency of church attendance" and Bogue and Feldman had at their disposal not only

---

[10] Admittedly, there may have been exigencies governing that decision. The questions had to be hitched onto the regular Current Population Survey, and for policy reasons, the Bureau may have wished to skirt completely any investigation into formal membership in a church. In a summary of the many findings from sample surveys on religion, Erskine reports the results of a Gallup question asked in 1954: "Are you a member of a church?" Twenty-one percent said "no" which is in sharp contrast with the findings reported in our text showing that only about 3% of the nation regard themselves as having no religion. Affiliation clearly is not the same thing as membership in the minds of the people. For this and the many other findings, which incidentally show how many surveys are there to be exploited, see Hazel Gaudet Erskine, "The Polls: Church Attendance," *Publ. Opin. Quart.*, **28**, 1964, especially p. 679.

a question on frequency of attendance but also a question in which the respondent rated how important religion was to him. Lazerwitz actually presents data to show that many of those who include themselves within a religion do *not* attend a church frequently, the figure ranging from a low of 15% for Catholics to a high of 65% among Jews. From data available to Bogue and Feldman, although not in their published analysis, the same pattern is documented, plus the further fact that the proportion of each self-defined religious group who regarded religion as "very important" to them never exceeded 76%. With these data available to them as a basis for a typological classification of religious group membership or for an alternate operational definition or an index, the decision of these secondary analysts to use the one question of felt affiliation must be regarded as an advised one.[11]

The question and its specific content attempts to measure the concept they were seeking, affiliation, but does it yield good measurements? We are reminded again of the pervasive problem of error in secondary analysis. How reliable can one question so gross and vague be? Does it not probe into delicate and private matters which people will resent or be anxious about, or which they may wish to falsify? It should be stressed again that these investigators as, *semi*secondary analysts, had a built-in advantage in appraising such varied kinds of response error. They were familiar with the quality of the interviewing staffs, who had to ask the questions and probe and classify the answers, and with the past experiences of the agencies in asking this very question. Bogue and Feldman invoke their intimate knowledge and actual qualitative information in assessing the error: "These questions were answered in a straightforward and matter-of-fact way in each survey. It is the experience of NORC that such questions are among the easier items on its interviews. . . ."[12] Lazerwitz notes: ". . . that respondents very readily accepted the question pertaining to their religion."[13] They both report the same experiences as that of the Census Bureau: "only a negligible number refused to answer."[14]

---

[11] Any secondary analyst who preferred to organize his studies around American religious participation would also have no difficulty in finding voluminous data. Over a period of thirty years, the Gallup Poll has incorporated in its surveys both a question on religious affiliation and a question on church attendance in the week preceding the interview. In choosing from among alternative indicators a secondary analyst must weigh the conceptual appropriateness of a particular indicator against the errors of measurement that may accompany its use. For the time series on church attendance and a review of the errors of measurement, see Demerath, *op. cit.*, pp. 367–368.

[12] Bogue and Feldman, *op. cit.*, p. 697, footnote.

[13] Lazerwitz, *op. cit.*, p. 576.

[14] Bogue, p. 688.

Reliability of measurement (plus sampling error) can be appraised by the comparison of the results from the several surveys each investigator used. As Table 4-1 demonstrated, the instability in these measurements is negligible. All secondary analysts who use designs which combine several surveys can assess random error by such procedures.[15] And then, by averaging the results over surveys, they can produce a final estimate which is less affected by random errors. Among the three surveys that Lazerwitz analyzed, two employed exactly the same open-end question, and the third a differently worded closed question, which explicitly mentioned the three major religions, and then followed the convention that the respondent had to *volunteer* that he had "no religion" or an "other religion." Comparing the first two surveys conveys the high reliability of the very same measuring instrument, and comparison with the last survey shows that the data are not vulnerable to minor changes in question wording and field procedure. Normally, it would be unfortunate that the measuring instrument was not held constant, but this accidental experiment was exploited by Lazerwitz to his advantage.

In assessing a constant error, a *bias* in response, which might afflict all the different surveys of the different agencies, a procedure that these investigators followed can be recommended as a desirable, general practice which we shall underscore for its importance. *Report the magnitude of the groups who have to be classified into "residual" categories because of their responses or lack of responses, and include these groups in all cross tabulations.*

In all survey research, there are instances of omission of a question by some interviewers or vagueness or ambiguity in response. Some of these occurrences are distributed randomly. However, individuals who wish to conceal their true identity often take refuge in an evasive, unclassifiable answer or manifest outright refusal to reply. Thus some portion of the respondents cannot be classified into a social group. The magnitude of this residual category provides some indication of the quality of the field procedures, and if it is large produces indeterminacy in the conclusions. The question as to how the results might change if the secondary analyst had been able to classify those respondents seems imponderable.

Fortunately, in the surveys Lazerwitz used, as reported in Table 4-1, this magnitude never exceeded two-tenths of a percent, and in the surveys Bogue and Feldman used, there were no such cases. In these instances, the problem is academic. But there are other residual categories of response with which the analyst must sometimes reckon and which may on occasion create inde-

---

[15] Bogue and Feldman do not present the detailed results separately for each of their two surveys. They do report that such an analysis was made, and that the duplicate tables were compared item by item.

terminacy. Depending on the question one sometimes finds a "miscellaneous" category. To be sure, there are specific religious denominations in the United States other than Protestant, Catholic, and Jewish, but some individuals who were classified in these surveys under the rubric "other religions" might in fact belong to some small and esoteric Protestant sect and, ideally, should have been included among Protestants. What the miscellany consists of the analyst cannot specify, since all are simply treated residually in the code. Fortunately, one can establish from the tabulations that the category "other religions" is negligible in magnitude. Consider also the residual category "No religion." To be sure there are atheists and individuals who, whatever their beliefs, cannot identify with any established religious group. But there may also be individuals who may conceal their religious identity by saying they have "none." By such an answer they may feel they perpetrate less of an evasion than if they adopt within the interview the false identity of another specified religious group.[16] Again, the magnitude turns out to be negligible.

The secondary analyst who reports the magnitudes of the residual categories along with the data on the specified social groups conveys to all some sense of just how indeterminate his conclusions are. And when the magnitudes are large, the question how the characterizations of his social groups have been distorted does become ponderable, if not solved, by including the residual categories in the cross tabulations on the dependent or corollary variables. The question is how much the characterizations would change if the missing respondents were included where they belong. Having the distributions for the residual categories, one can allocate them in various ways according to any assumptions one makes about their true membership and thus simulate the "real" distributions of the social groups. Thus some plausible, if hypothetical, boundaries can be set around the obtained findings. Inspection of the distribution of characteristics in the residual categories also gives some

---

[16] This is not to deny that there may be some errors in this and other analyses of group memberships produced by the misclassification of respondents who are or who *genuinely* feel part of one group but who report themselves within the fold of another specific group. But they do not remain completely insidious sources of error to the sophisticated secondary analyst, and a good deal of subtle theorizing is required before one can adjudge all such responses as flagrant errors. The variations in their severity, nature, and the corresponding solutions as one treats different dimensions of social group membership will become clearer from the examples to be presented later. An especially informative example for the student are analyses of political groups based on questions of party affiliation or voting preference, where the residual categories may assume a considerable magnitude, depending on the time period and the country, because of fear or a doctrine that politics is a most private realm. For a brief discussion see Angus Campbell, Philip Converse, Warren Miller, and Donald Stokes, *The American Voter* (New York: John Wiley, 1960), pp. 123–125.

clue as to whether they are a mixture of types, an "undercover" group, or some genuinely distinctive type. Bogue and Feldman, as well as Lazerwitz, thus find that the smallish "no religion" group is in fact heterogeneous.

We have reserved for a dramatic climax a most interesting substantive feature of the characterization of religious groups by these investigators. It will illustrate a final problem of error and a principle for its treatment. And it leads directly into the next example in our omnibus case study of the secondary analysis of religious affiliation. The face sheets of the surveys of both agencies contained the three items: educational attainment, income, and occupation, and the analysts could therefore compare the socioeconomic achievements of the several religious groups. In order to unravel some of the complexity of these relationships, Lazerwitz combines the cells from the *two*, out of his three, surveys which asked about *denomination* to produce a larger group of Baptists numbering almost 1000 cases, thus permitting a breakdown into white and Negro subgroups. Even then, the Negro Baptists only number 226. (For the analysis of major religions, he can combine the cells from all three surveys.) Since Negroes are a relatively small population group, any *single* survey based on modestly sized samples would, as earlier noted, produce too small a cell to permit refined analysis. A subcell, Negroes who are also Baptists, would be smaller still. The strategy of pooling cases from several surveys, a design we shall observe in operation many times, provides a way of studying *rare* groups and carrying their analysis to deeper and more refined levels.

Bogue and Feldman do essentially the same type of pooling and refining operation, breaking their combined sample by color and by denomination into whites of various religions, and into Negro Baptists versus all other Negroes.[17] The two studies examine the attainment of the religious groups, but employ a different unit of analysis: Bogue and Feldman examine the attainment of the *head* of the household, and Lazerwitz examines the respondent himself. Realizing that the unit of analysis is different, that there is a time interval of several years, that the exact way the controls are applied is slightly different, and that the size of the cells on which these sample estimates are based is small, the agreement in their findings on educational achievement is dramatic. The data are presented in Table 4-2.

The ranking of the different groups in educational attainment, and the exact magnitude of their respective accomplishments, may, of course, be treated simply as descriptive data toward a comprehensive characterization.

---

[17] To be precise, Lazerwitz has some Negroes, although very few, in his other Protestant denominational groups, and has only controlled on race for his Baptists. Bogue and Feldman have controlled on race for *all* their religious and denominational groups, but have a residual group of Negro non-Baptists.

TABLE 4-2. *Educational Attainments of Religious Groups as Revealed by Independent Secondary Analyses*

	Adults with College Attainment[a] Lazerwitz, 1957		Household Heads with College Attainment[b] Bogue and Feldman, 1953-1955
	N	Percent	Percent
Episcopalians	119	53	47
Presbyterians	272	36	28
Jews	188	33	33
Methodists	730	21	21
Lutherans	328	14	16
Catholics	1270	14	16
Baptists—white	713	11	13
Baptists—Negro	226	6	4

[a] Adapted from Table 5, Bernard Lazerwitz, "A Comparison of Major United States Religious Groups," *J. Amer. Stat. Assoc.*, Sept. 1961.
[b] Adapted from Table 23-ii, Donald J. Bogue, *The Population of the United States* (New York: Free Press, 1959).

But the findings may be used toward a deeper analysis seeking to explain the relationships. To reduce errors of inference about causal factors, the analysts employed multivariate procedures and controlled factors such as race. Insofar as Lazerwitz wished to determine the educational attainment that might arise *purely* from religious affiliation, he would not want the comparisons to be confounded by the disproportionate membership of Negroes within the Baptist denomination (about one-quarter of all Baptists) and, in turn, within the grosser religious group, Protestants. By controlling on race, the inference is better protected. Without it, any finding of reduced attainment by Baptists, or by Protestants in contrast with others, might simply have reflected the handicap imposed on the Negroes among them.

The procedures are familiar to all *primary* survey researchers who engage in multivariate analyses to protect causal inferences from the danger of spuriousness. What is different is simply the pooling of cases, which if carried far enough permits more refinement and protection against the many such errors. For example, it is perfectly possible that the lesser educational attainment of Catholics back in 1954 might reflect, as Bogue and Feldman suggest, the fact that there were among them more immigrants who are correspondingly poorly educated rather than the intrinsic influence of their religion. With enough cases, the possibility could be examined.

When one moves beyond the sheer question of valid explanation to the un-raveling of the complex processes that mediate some relationship, a plenitude of cases is also necessary to separate the many possible links involved, and to avoid errors of interpretation. Thus both Lazerwitz and Bogue and Feldman document that Episcopalians, Presbyterians, and Jews are more likely to have higher incomes and higher occupations than the other religious groups. Bogue and Feldman try to explore whether this is the outcome of the greater *education* they have obtained, or because of other factors associated with religious affiliations. As they stress: "A completely valid answer . . . would require much more detailed data than are available at the present time; it would require a simultaneous cross-tabulation of religious affiliation by *single* years of schooling, by occupation (using a *fairly detailed* breakdown), by color, by sex, and by age."[18] The directive to other secondary analysts is clear and loud: More pooling!

We shall not describe the complex and most interesting way in which they attempt to examine this and other links in the process; the next case study will enlarge our understanding of the problem. But it is worth reporting their exciting conclusion:

> . . . *unique "clusters of traits" are associated with each of the various religious groups. The hypothesis that these clusters are part of a tradition or culture which is transmitted from one generation to another is plausible, and is worthy of test and study. For example, in order to explain the results of this chapter it is almost mandatory to* develop the hypothesis *that members of the Episcopal, Jewish, and Presbyterian religions place a very high value on ob-taining as much education as possible, that they strive to gain employment in the professional, managerial, or proprietary occupations, and that they at-tempt to save from current income so they can invest and increase their future income.*[19]

---

[18] Bogue and Feldman, *op. cit.*, p. 703, italics supplied.

[19] *Ibid.*, p. 708, italics supplied. This tentative conclusion is not based on uncritical thought or analysis. Apart from the various controls on spuriousness and the examination of alternative explanatory factors already mentioned, these several analysts are very careful in entertaining, and wherever possible controlling, still other error factors or variables which might account for their results. For example, they consider the paradoxical possi-bility that a relationship between social position and denomination could result from exactly the opposite causal sequence. As Lazerwitz remarks: individuals "should have advanced their social and economic lot in life and would be seeking added status through membership in the Episcopalian and Presbyterian churches" (p. 570). Bogue makes a similar point about the educational attainment of Negro non-Baptists suggest-ing that they may switch their denomination to conform to the higher status they already have achieved (p. 702). The concentration of white Baptists in the South, an economically handicapped region, is entertained as an explanation of their differential

But we must pause a little longer, before presenting the next case, to explicate an important problem and to suggest a valuable general strategy in secondary analysis. The control that Lazerwitz introduced by dividing his Baptists into white and Negro subgroups automatically served to protect his conclusions against a source of error other than spuriousness in causal analysis. Those secondary analysts who study social groups are especially concerned with drawing upon surveys that have used unbiased sampling designs and, if possible, large samples. This is what imparts definitiveness to the descriptions, and Lazerwitz and Bogue and Feldman could be very confident that sampling variance and bias could not jeopardize most of their estimates.

It is possible, however, that a sample and the subsequent survey procedures may operate very well in most areas and for most groups, but function less well in some *small, separable* portion of the inquiry. Under such conditions, a desirable general strategy that we may name and underscore is: *Localize error and contain it.* That separable portion of the data that is afflicted by error or that might be suspect should be isolated in the tabulations, leaving the remaining bulk, as it were, purified. An analyst cannot take complete comfort in the thought that a good thing is good everywhere, but he should not be too distressed if a bad thing is local in extent.

Lazerwitz follows such a procedure. He remarks on the general difficulties that the Census Bureau and other survey agencies have had in obtaining interviews with Negro males. From certain tabulations of his own data, for example by sex by race, he has some suspicion that his own final sample may have had such a bias, even though it operated admirably in so many other respects. But since about three-quarters of the Negro population are located either in the Baptist group, or are unaffiliated with the religious groups ex-

---

economic achievement. An analysis was conducted to examine the possibility that the differential economic position reflects discrimination against the group rather than some intrapsychological force. Differences in income are considered in terms of the fact that the index is total *family* income which is affected by family structure, number of secondary earners, and age of household head. And the gross conclusion about the pre-eminence of Episcopalians and Presbyterians is qualified in terms of the fact that a *residual* category "Other Protestants" may contain smaller Protestant groups, e.g., Unitarians, who would have higher attainments if they could be tabulated out. A singularly neglected source of error, the fact that the controls are crude, and that differentials cannot be examined for groups that are truly *homogeneous* and matched on another factor is considered. Only one aspect of the error problem seems to be slighted in these admirable analyses, the *response errors* accompanying questions on formal education. In the instance of these particular surveys, the bias is very small in magnitude. For 1957, in the aggregate, the Lazerwitz data overestimate adults with college attainment by less than 4%. Although various sourcs of error have been eliminated, the speculation that the religious groups transmit distinctive values and drives still has not been subject to any *direct* test. The reader will have to wait until the later episodes of our long case study.

amined (located in minor Protestant sects, other religions, etc.), the separate tabulation for Negro Baptists effectively contains most of this error, since that is the only place where it might distort the conclusions.

One should realize that the same strategy can be applied to contain a locatable source of error other than sampling. For example, if a secondary analyst knew that *white* interviewers had been assigned to Negro respondents in a given survey, possibly increasing errors in their responses, he might well decide to present that portion of his data separately.

THE PROTESTANT ETHIC—A CONTINUITY IN THE SECONDARY ANALYSIS OF RELIGIOUS GROUPS

The analyses by Lazerwitz and Bogue and Feldman are essentially broad characterizations of religious groups based on elaborate and careful exploitation of face-sheet data derived from several national surveys of probability samples. Bogue and Feldman started by drawing the socioeconomic contours of the groups, and ended with a formulation relevant to a long, lively, and important tradition in social theory on which they presented considerable evidence. As Glenn and Hyland put it: "The relationship of religion to economic and occupational success is the most viable topic of debate in the sociology of religion in the United States. The issues raised by Weber in his famous essay on the Protestant Ethic continue to evoke vociferous exchanges."[20] Understandably, other investigators have also tried by secondary analysis to present a sharper or better portrait, to clarify obscurities, or to portray the changing picture of religious groups and their achievements. Some brief case studies will enlarge the body of methodological principles appropriate to the secondary analysis of social groups.[21]

Glenn and Hyland preface their report with the cautionary remarks that "a secondary analysis of national survey data not gathered for the purpose of assessing mobility cannot provide conclusive evidence." But they continue: "However, we are convinced that the potential of such an analysis to help resolve the controversy has not been realized. All too frequently partisans in

---

[20] Glenn and Hyland. *op. cit.*, p. 73.

[21] Perhaps the earliest was reported by Hadley Cantril, "Education and Economic Composition of Religious Groups: An Analysis of Poll Data," *Amer. J. Sociol.*, **47**, 1943, pp. 574–579. Cantril may also be described as a *semi*secondary analyst. Working long before there were general archives, he drew upon two of his own surveys plus two Gallup Polls to produce pooled findings for 1939–40 based on 14,000 cases. Many years later, Irving Crespi of the Gallup Poll using pooled data from two of his surveys conducted an equivalent semisecondary analysis, thereby providing trends over a twenty-year period, making due allowance for changes in sampling design and indicators. Irving Crespi, "Occupational Status and Religion," *Amer. Sociol. Rev.*, **28**, 1963, p. 131.

the debate have judiciously selected national survey data to support preconceived conclusions."[22] In the spirit of this concern they draw upon data from as many as 18 national surveys conducted over the period 1943 to 1965, but place heaviest reliance on the four Gallup Polls conducted closest to the time of their analysis, which used national probability samples and were available from the Roper Center. Obviously, there was a wealth of data available to them, but such riches bring with them new responsibilities. An analyst must protect himself from the temptation of arbitrariness in selection of surveys. Glenn and Hyland are explicit as to their criteria, and we may elevate the procedure they employ to a general principle, which we underscore for its importance. *No Peeking!* As they put it: "In no case did we have any knowledge of the relevant frequency distributions before we selected a survey, and in no case did we exclude a survey after we examined the data."[23]

The four recent surveys were pooled, thus yielding about 6000 respondents and correspondingly substantial numbers of Protestants and Catholics, but still a rather small and shaky statistical base for describing the Jewish group. These surveys document the picture between 1963 and 1965. Juxtaposed against Bogue back in 1953–1955 they constitute not merely a replication, or attempt at deeper explanation, but also a portrayal of the enduring and changing features over the span of a decade.

In analyzing the surveys, they *first exclude* all Negro respondents. By restricting their comparisons to whites, they have controlled the variable of race just as the earlier investigators did by introducing race into every cross tabulation. We may describe this principle as: *truncating the sample.* They never had to worry again about that source of spuriousness or about possible errors in the sampling and interviewing of Negroes. Introducing a control by race into every tabulation is certainly a more tedious procedure, but it does have the virtue of yielding evidence on a particular group, about which nothing can be known if it is eliminated from all analysis. Truncating, by contrast, serves one unique function. It allows the pooling of surveys that have some element of noncomparability, which can be located and removed by the elimination of a segment of the sample. It salvages otherwise useless surveys. It may also serve to control a reckless reader who would make too much of a finding for a tiny group that was presented in the tabulations.

The analysis is confined to a comparison of the three major religious groups, the Protestants not being classified into denominations in these surveys. The analysts do, however, tabulate the characteristics of the *residual*

---

[22] Glenn and Hyland, *op. cit.*, p. 74.

[23] *Ibid.*, p. 74. There was another consideration in selecting the surveys for the analysis—their spread over time. Glenn and Hyland were concerned to examine *trends* in the position of religious groups in America.

group who report that they have "no religion" (about 2% of the total sample as in the earlier studies) and find much the same kind of heterogeneity among them as the earlier investigators reported. Interpreting this response as an indicator of *apostasy*, rather than error, these investigators provide some evidence on the effects on people of once having had a religion, but no longer having it. We will return to the important implications of this thought for the general theory and for secondary analyses of the problem. Their analysis thus cannot speak to the specific question of the economic consequences of *particular types* of Protestantism, but it does provide a most careful and refined treatment of the more general question of the effects of Protestant versus Catholic affiliation.[24] The data on Jews are also presented, but because of the small sample the analysts are conservative and treat the evidence as suggestive only.

Glenn and Hyland simply take as the indicator of the variable in the theory the respondent's reported affiliation with a major religion. But in handling the dependent variables, they have much more freedom and show the careful way in which indices can be constructed and examined, and controls introduced to avoid errors in inference and misleading conclusions. And they also pay due attention to errors arising from sampling and other procedures. Since the Catholics and Protestants are found to differ in their *current* geographical location, and the environment governs man's opportunities, they control the variables of size of community, and region, of *current* residence in comparing educational and economic attainments. One may argue that geographical mobility is itself a *voluntary* process which might be set in motion by the imperatives of one's religious values, rather than an accidental, external condition, and this is the argument of the secondary analysts in our next case. In either instance, the multivariate analysis is valuable, either to control for spuriousness or to unravel the complex causal paths that begin with religion.

Since it takes a certain amount of time to complete an education or to make one's ascent economically, and Catholics and Protestants are found to

---

[24] The limitation is not necessarily altogether bad. As earlier noted, the movement from one Protestant denomination to another *following* economic advancement makes it difficult to interpret the causal direction of analyses of status by denomination. That problem is avoided in treating all Protestants as a unitary group. And the question of which denominations should be singled out and combined to test Weber gets us into difficulties procedurally, into the murkiness of the different assertions he presents, and into the endless numbers of Protestant divisions and subdivisions in America which must be grouped. For example, the Quakers and Mennonites, on whose business acumen he remarks, are too few in any sample survey and often buried in the residual category "other Protestants."

differ in age, these investigators control age in various ways to prevent erroneous conclusions. At one point, they construct an index showing the educational attainments of only those Catholics and Protestants who are thirty or older, so as to exclude those who may still be in the process of being educated, and whose final status in that respect cannot yet be known.[25] In examining economic attainment, they control age in a more conventional way by comparing Catholics and Protestants within the same age groups. Here they show care in evaluating a source of error arising from "slippage in the units of description." What is enumerated in these surveys is the age of the *respondent* (and, of course, his religion), but the measure of economic achievement is the *family* income and the occupation of the *head* of household. Although the age of the respondents in the comparison groups may be matched, it does not follow that the age of the household heads is matched. They ponder this problem, and adjudge it to be of trivial consequence in light of various collateral findings in the surveys.[26]

---

[25] Lenski draws our attention to a most unusual aspect of this problem in the course of a secondary analysis of intergenerational mobility based on a national probability sample. This sample, like most, was restricted to the noninstitutionalized population, and therefore excluded students who were adults but who still were living in residential colleges. From any conventional point of view, one would regard it as an unbiased design for sampling the specified population, but he argues that the definition of the universe, if ignored, might well introduce errors into the conclusions about mobility. Because the offspring of the higher classes are more likely to be enrolled in colleges and thereby delayed in entering their ultimate occupations, this portion of the youngest cohort of adults would be missed since they are outside of the universe, and estimates of the mobility for different classes would be distorted. See G. E. Lenski, "Trends in Inter-Generational Occupational Mobility in the United States," *Amer. Sociol. Rev.*, **23**, 1958, pp. 514–523.

[26] The thoughtful reader may wonder if there is not some slippage between the *religion* of the respondent and that of the head of the household, whose economic attainments are being examined. The same problem arises in the two previous cases. Obviously, one could eliminate the problem by examining the occupation of the respondent, but this would exclude many family units where the respondents are housewives. From the CPS sources, however, we do know that the problem is minor, only about 5% of spouses nationally differing in current religion, and it would seem that it could not affect the comparison because of *complementarity*. All Catholic respondents with a Protestant mate are balanced by the Protestant respondents with Catholic mates. There is a kind of double entry made in both religious groups. Two other problems of measurement error are considered. A measure of economic status used mainly in the study of trends is an interviewer's rating of economic level, a common face-sheet item in surveys, designed to express the respondent's position *relative to others in his community*. Its virtue as a measure of relative deprivation may be a defect in the comparison of the absolute achievements of religious groups. Since Protestants and Catholics differ ecologically, the use of this index might have worked so that Protestants no higher in absolute terms were scored higher because of the relative nature of this scale and its anchorage to the

The categories by which educational attainment is coded in surveys frequently make a distinction between "completing" a certain level of schooling, and having had "some" schooling at that level. Glenn and Hyland, following the lead of earlier studies, use the distinction to construct an index of "educational tenacity." The proportion of those who begin college, for example, and thus have the basic resources, but who do not complete four years and drop out can be taken to express a lack of persistence. It might still depend, admittedly, on brute circumstance, but it would certainly seem to tap strength of inner motivation.[27]

This particular aspect of the Glenn and Hyland analysis deserves special review. They do find differences in economic attainment favoring the Protestants, although these seem small compared to the Bogue findings of an earlier decade, and to be declining over the twenty-year interval of their own surveys. Like Bogue, they conclude that the educational advantage demonstrated for Protestants is the main link that accounts for their economic advantage. The educational attainment, in turn, could derive from some religiously based, internalized value system, or could simply reflect the social advantages they inherited from their parents.[28] The "tenacity index," with its special sensitivity as a measure of motivation, thus assumes great importance for Glenn and Hyland. Computations for the *four* pooled surveys suggest to them that there is no greater motivation among Protestants, and thus strengthens their conclusion that the pattern of the mid-sixties simply reflects inherited advantage and the forces that advantaged parents exerted on their children. This finding seems so crucial, and is in such sharp contrast to Lenski's and Weller's findings for Detroit, that Glenn and Hyland feel the need for further confirmation. And they add to their "super survey," itself

---

community distribution. One NORC survey used mainly as a base line for studying long term trends in the achievements of the religious groups posed a problem of a large residual group which could not be classified. They were allocated on the basis of evidence available in other surveys.

[27] See Lenski, *op. cit.*, pp. 236–240. This study has an ambiguous status, in part, being a primary analysis of one specially designed survey; in part being a secondary analysis of previously available data. This index of differential drop-out from various levels of schooling was computed both on the special 1958 Detroit survey by Lenski and on a series of *previous* Detroit surveys by Weller. In the 1958 data, Lenski was able to control for the social origins of the respondents, and thus infers that the index measures motivation rather than circumstance.

[28] The differential opportunities for education in the kinds of communities in which they reside are controlled in the cross tabulations. To be sure, the advantage of the parents in turn remains to be accounted for and could be attributed to *their* Protestant ethic, but at least this would clarify the process, and distinguish between a value system inernalized in the present generation of Protestants, and one that is no longer operative but whose beneficent effects are still felt through inheritance.

based on four surveys of the mid-sixties, another seven surveys conducted in the sixties. The analyses of the *seven replications* support their first test, and thus they feel considerable confidence in attributing the educational differences to parental status. ". . . serious doubts are cast on the belief that religiously based and religiously related influences have *an important* differential effect on the worldly success of Protestants and Catholics in contemporary American society."[29]

Some uncertainty still surrounds the problem, and the Glenn and Hyland study finally comes to rest upon an inferential base. Having taken care of many possible determinants other than religious values by the introduction of controls to prevent spurious conclusions, having tapped a basic motivational aspect of the hypothesized value system by the construction of a special index on tenacity, and having defended the analysis in so many ways against the

---

[29] Glenn and Hyland, *op. cit.*, p. 84, italics supplied. One may also adduce supporting evidence from two secondary analyses by Lipset and Bendix. See S. M. Lipset and R. Bendix, *Social Mobility in Industrial Society* (Berkeley: University of California Press, 1959), pp. 48–52. However, Lenski questions these results on the ground that the failure to control for the size of community in which the individuals *were raised* handicapped the Protestants and obscured the differential achievements they would otherwise have shown. His and Weller's findings for Detroit, restricted to white males, show greater attainment for Protestants even when ethnicity and class origins are controlled (pp. 79–80). In another *semi*secondary analysis, Mayer and Sharp (a director of the Detroit Area Study) pooled six other Detroit area surveys from the years 1954 to 1959 and presented another test of the theory. The sample of 9000 cases was large enough to permit an elaborate multivariate analysis for separate Protestant denominations. With regard to our earlier remark, they grouped into a category labeled "Calvinist" the Presbyterians, Congregationalists, Evangelical and Reformed, and Dutch Reformed. It is worth noting an unusual problem in their pooled design. Income was used as an indicator of the dependent variable. Since income had risen over the six-year period and such changes might confound the comparisons and since some cells might have been disproportionately surveyed in different years, they transformed the income data first. See Albert Mayer and Harry Sharp, "Religious Preference and Worldly Success," *Amer. Sociol. Rev.*, **27**, 1962, pp. 218–227. A simpler factor may be invoked to account for some of the contradictions between studies and has to do with the crudity of measurement and the indexes constructed to represent attainment. If occupation were coded into very *broad* categories, any differentials in achievement would be obscured unless they were so gross as to cross the category boundary. For example, the category "non-manual" occupation or "some high school or better" could mask a world of differences in attainment or in social origins. What is emphasized again is the need for careful attention to measurement errors and artifacts of the procedures, and to the value of pooling surveys. Refinement of classification may produce too few cases in a cell for further analysis, and the aanlyst may therefore have to use cruder groups when the total sample is small. But if he can pool many surveys, he can then luxuriate in more refined breakdowns on independent variables.

host of errors that can invade empirical research, they reach a destination that points by successive stages of elimination to an *indirect* conclusion.

The explanation of the differences probably resides in the advantage the Protestants inherited. Alas, there is no direct measure of parental status available in their surveys. A secondary analyst is not *so* blessed by good fortune that he can receive everything he might desire in full measure to solve his problem definitively. But neither is a *primary* investigator capable of fashioning his research world to perfection. His aspiration also exceeds his resources; the complexity of some problems defies his abilities. In any case, the net difference that Glenn and Hyland find in the mid-sixties which might still be attributable to religious values is small in magnitude, setting limits on the predictive power of the theory. Secondary analysis, like primary scientific research, depends on collective and cumulative inquiry. Our next case will show that *the* missing variable can indeed be brought into the net of a secondary analyst, and that continuity in secondary analysis does produce benefits. It will also show that everything is bought at a price, and that in choosing his surveys and analytic paths a secondary analyst may have to sacrifice one desire to achieve another.

Jackson, Fox, and Crockett went back to *one* of the three national surveys that Lazerwitz had already used for his description of religious groups, and subjected it to a most intensive treatment.[30] Thus it is a slippery example to label. In one sense, it might simply be termed a "reanalysis," but it is really a brand-new secondary analysis. They tested the influence of many variables on economic attainments, measures of which were available on that survey, which Lazerwitz had omitted from his more descriptive analysis of religious groups. They chose it because of its singularity in covering the many variables required for a stringent test of the theory, especially the occupation of the *father*. It should be stressed that their evidence, however thorough, rests upon but one survey, far fewer than the other investigators had. A price was exacted by the stringent requirements.

---

[30] Elton F. Jackson, William S. Fox, and Harry J. Crockett, Jr., "Religion and Occupational Achievement," *Amer. Sociol. Rev.*, **35**, 1970, pp. 48–63. The survey drawn upon was the basis for the work of Gerald Gurin, Joseph Veroff, and Sheila Feld, *Americans View Their Mental Health* (New York: Basic Books, 1960). The same survey had been used by Jackson and Crockett for a secondary analysis of occupational mobility, since, as will become clear, it provided data on the father's occupation as well as the respondent's. See their "Occupational Mobility in the United States: A Point Estimate and Trend Comparison," *Amer. Sociol. Rev.*, **29**, 1964, pp. 5–15. It is a slippery case to label since the study directors of the original survey also conducted an analysis of The Protestant Ethic. They used an instrument so special and novel in national surveys—a pictorial or TAT test—that they may have planned initially to study the problem. See Joseph Veroff, Sheila Feld, and Gerald Gurin, "Achievement Motivation and Religious Background," *Amer. Sociol. Rev.*, **27**, 1962, pp. 205–217.

The investigators immediately *truncated* their sample, although the term hardly conveys the magnitude of an excision which eliminated more than two-thirds of the respondents. ". . . this sample was reduced to 766 white, male, U.S. born respondents, employed full-time or retired, for whom occupational information was available for themselves and their fathers, and who designated themselves as Protestants or Catholics."[31] Thus by one blow—a heavy one—they controlled any differential handicaps that might have impeded a religious group for reasons of sex, color, or immigrant status, got rid of the "slippage" problem, eliminated data which might have been of poor quality or based on a biased sample, and eliminated residual groups which were unclassifiable on the main variables. The conclusions, of course, apply to this redefined and restricted universe, and at times, refinements in analysis are hampered by the small numbers available in certain cells.

To measure differential attainment accurately, relatively fine occupational distinctions were kept. Errors in the coding of such multifarious data as occupations were carefully examined. On top of the homogeneity provided by the truncating, controls are introduced in the course of the analysis for father's occupation, age, generation in the U.S., ethnic descent, and region where *reared*. The geographical environment of their childhood was an external factor over which *they* had no control and which might have affected their prospects, in contrast with the current environment into which they might have moved in order to achieve their own goals. In these ways, the two religious groups "were equalized with respect to the starting point of the competition,"[32] and any inference that religion produces achievement was protected against spuriousness. They demonstrate differences in achievement, although generally small, favoring the Protestants: that Protestants are more likely to exhibit sharp upward mobility, and that the introduction of the controls sometimes *enhances* the religious differences, since Protestants on occasion are handicapped by their location on the starting line.

To interpret the process that underlies these obtained relationships, they then introduce into the analysis the *intervening* variable of educational attainment, still controlling for father's status, to determine whether it is via the pursuit of education that the Protestants reap their advantage. Education

---

[31] Jackson, Fox, and Crockett, Jr., *op. cit.*, p. 52.

[32] *Ibid.*, p. 51. To be precise, the controls on ethnic descent and region where reared are introduced by a further truncation. Finally, 380 cases remain for analysis. It should also be noted that the controls are introduced *jointly* and manipulated by procedures of multiple standardization and "indirect standardization," valuable but generally neglected procedures in survey research which can have much utility in the secondary analysis of social groups. For a general discussion see Morris Rosenberg, "Test Factor Standardization as a Method of Interpretation," *Social Forces*, **41**, 1962, pp. 53–61 or his more recent book, *The Logic of Survey Analysis* (New York: Basic Books, 1968).

does intervene in the process but it "is clearly not the sole channel for the effect of religion."[33] Thus the conclusion that economic success is governed in some degree by the religious values inculcated by Protestantism seems strongly supported by the combined weight of the evidence. The investigators, however, are tentative and open to alternative explanations of their findings, for good reasons which will be progressively clarified in our next case materials.

Glenn and Hyland had given us a clue to a critical problem when they treated the "no religion" group as *apostates*. These people after all may have been the products of a Catholic or Protestant upbringing, and if they could only be classified, they too should be put into the balance in weighing the merits of the theory. Another clue is afforded by the earlier discussion of the implications of having only a gross classification which lumped all Protestants together. These sharp investigators knew the interpretation of the causal sequence is complicated by the fact that some Protestants switched their denomination after their economic ascent. Since they did not know what denomination they were *prior* to their economic and educational activities, the gross classification, Protestants, eliminated the difficulty for all *interdenominational* switches. Presumably they had all started within the Protestant fold. As Jackson, Fox, and Crockett make painfully explicit, "the variable of primary theoretical interest is the religious affiliation of people *during their formative years. . . .* Since, however, a question on the religion in which the respondent was reared was not included in the interview schedule," they are commendably honest about the assumption central to the research: "it will be necessary to assume that the respondent's current religious preference reflects his religion of socialization." By using the gross classification "all Protestants" they solved a good part of the problem, but they emphasize the other necessary assumption: "Of course, the comparison of Protestants and Catholics also requires an assumption that persons have not moved between these groups *in any appreciable number*, but this assumption is much easier to swallow than the same assumption about movement among Protestant denominations."[34]

Was this entire edifice of empirical research erected on the basis of a shaky assumption, pinned to an indicator that never came close to the target

---

[33] *Ibid.*, p. 59.

[34] Jackson, Fox, and Crockett, Jr., *op. cit.*, pp. 52–53, italics supplied. In our judgment, this is not to deny completely the relevance of a religion adopted in *adult life* to the theory. Economic activity, a career, is a continuing, life-long process. The religion during childhood socialization might govern educational attainment and the beginnings of the career, but so might a conversion to another religion be regarded as *prior* to and consequential for economic activity later in life.

concept in the theory? We quickly point out that secondary analysts should not be regarded as mindless empiricists. Even when the secondary analyst thinks of a missing variable, what can he do, being at the mercy of the available data? As earlier noted, he has to relax his stringent specifications at times. But as we shall see in this instance, some scarce but golden resources might be exploited.

At least once, in 1955, perhaps more often, the Gallup Poll asked a national sample not only about their current religious affiliation, but two additional questions: "Has that always been your religious preference or affiliation?" and if no: "What was your religious preference previously?" We present in Table 4-3 the cross tabulation of the results only for *white* respondents to correspond to the population analyzed in the earlier studies.[35]

TABLE 4-3. *Changes in Religious Preference for White Adults.*

| | | | | Current Preference Changed to: | | |
Former Preference	%	N	No Change	Protestant	Catholic	Other Category
Protestant	70	948	97%		2%	Less than 1%
Catholic	25	348	92%	7%		Less than 1%
Jewish	3	37	100%			
Other Religion	2	22	95%	5%		
No Religion	1	10	80%	10%	10%	
N = 1365						

The marginal totals of the former affiliations of this white sample, or the figures on current membership which can be drawn from the table, will be seen to correspond closely to the earlier data on the religious composition of the population. It can also be seen that the assumption that switches from the religion of one's childhood are not appreciable in number is warranted. If we can rely on these figures from 1955, it would appear that the current Protestant group whose attainments are being analyzed is diluted, by perhaps 2–3%, by individuals who were not exposed to its influences in their earlier years, the Catholic group by perhaps 4–5%, by individuals who had other religious patterns in their childhood; and the movement is between the two

---

[35] It was through John S. Reed's productive searching in the course of our research that this survey was located, and I acknowledge his contribution with pleasure.

major religions essentially. Whatever minor effect this would have should be in the direction of attenuating the differences found. The same survey did ask Protestants for their current denomination and previous one, if they reported that they had changed. We do not present the data, but interdenominational shifts from the religion of childhood seem, indeed, to be much larger in magnitude—ranging from a low of about 7% to around 30%.

Given this survey, one may well ask why it has not been exploited for a secondary analysis of Weber's theory. Clearly, it adds *one* element of the complex of measures, but it lacks many of the others needed for the complete empirical study. Yet it can be exploited for a fragmentary, or what we have called a secondary *semianalysis*, which despite its simplicity serves a strategic purpose in strengthening the more elaborate analyses of other data.

Other *semi*analyses may serve also to buttress vulnerable portions of the larger structure built by the various secondary analysts. Central to the whole theory is the notion of a system of beliefs and *values* that have been inculcated into the particular religionist by his membership. Understandably, none of the studies thus far reported had any measures of such intervening variables. They drew upon the lavish resources of the *face sheet*. There might be an occasional high-quality survey on an appropriate sample which had batteries measuring the values surrounding work, worldly success, and education, but which would contain only some of the total set of measures necessary for the complete empirical analysis. Even so, a semianalysis would contribute a useful piece of information. Broom and Glenn provide an illustration. In the course of another thorough secondary analysis which is a broad-ranging characterization and comparison of Catholics and Protestants, they located a Gallup survey of a national probability sample in 1955 which asked two relevant questions: Whether the respondent enjoyed hours on the job more than hours not on the job and whether he enjoyed work so much that it was hard to put it aside.

These hardly cover the total value constellation implied by the "Protestant Ethic," and perhaps the critical dimension is not whether one likes his work, but whether he feels committed to do it well, no matter how distasteful it may be. The semianalysis is relevant nevertheless. The difference between Protestants and Catholics, without any controls introduced for other characteristics, is modest in size but significant, and in the direction of Protestants enjoying work more.

This semianalysis suggests a general way to pursue the problem. Surveys that contain more comprehensive measures of the *intervening variable*—the value system—and also satisfy other requirements can be given a thorough secondary analysis. Indeed this is exactly what Bressler and Westoff did in 1963, exploiting a survey on fertility patterns which had been conducted in 1957 on a probability sample of a highly *specialized* universe: Native-white individuals, married but once, all of whom had two children, one an infant, and who resided in the seven largest metropolitan areas of the country.[36] Correspondingly it is a young sample, the average age of the men being 28. Obviously, the generalizations apply only to this restricted universe, and not to the nation as a whole, and the interpretation hangs on the implications of these restrictions. But the advantages should not be ignored. The sample was already radically truncated, and many variables were, by definition, already controlled. (Other variables were controlled by further truncating.) The survey, for sure, had a most desirable feature. It contained a lengthy battery of thirty items measuring "a commitment to the work life . . . and a drive for success," and it also included items on educational attainment, economic attainment, and father's occupation.[37] A bargain was involved in this example: the desirable findings on values were exacted at the price of reduced generalizability.

One path to productive secondary analysis is to trace conceptually the intervening and dependent variables and thus to formulate the requirements for a complete empirical test, for a direct test of a neglected aspect of a sprawling or complex theory, or for an *indirect test of some derived implication* of the theory. This creates the framework, the mental schema, that guides a search for relevant surveys. But another way is to trace out the refinements of a *gross independent* variable. And this case provides rich illustration of just such a "search model," to use a classic term from the psychology of thought and problem solving.[38]

Within their narrowed universe, Bressler and Westoff further restricted themselves to a comparison of the values of two very small groups of Catholic

---

[36] Marvin Bressler and Charles F. Westoff, "Catholic Education, Economic Values, and Achievement," *Amer. J. Sociol.*, **69**, 1963, pp. 225–233.

[37] It may seem difficult to argue that a survey that invested in thirty questions on values and asked so many other appropriate questions did not have the problem in primary focus from the start. But it is tenable that these items were included for other purposes relating to fertility, and that the recombination of them makes it a secondary study. Certainly the universe is not the one that a primary analyst of "The Protestant Ethic" would have chosen as his target.

[38] To show how far one may take this kind of mental tracery, we pick up a lead from a paper by Benton Johnson. He argues that in the rational pursuit of their economic goals, Protestants should be more likely to endorse political parties which are favorable to business interests. Johnson also stimulates us to thought on the handling of the independent variable remarking that the "Ascetic Protestant" tradition in America has become bifurcated into more fundamentalist and more liberal denominations. We shall return to this problem when we examine secondary analyses of the political behavior of religious groups. For this formulation and a primary survey analysis of it, see Benton Johnson, "Ascetic Protestantism and Political Preference," *Publ. Opin. Quart.*, **26**, 1962, pp. 36–46.

men, those who had been educated in Catholic schools and those who had not.[39] Extending the findings beyond their concrete character, one might say that those who attended Catholic school provided a much sharper and purer test of the theory. Their parents presumably had a high commitment to their religion, and presumably they were socialized more effectively via the parochial school into the doctrines and values of Catholicism.[40]

The values of these matched groups of Catholic men, contrasted in type of schooling, are compared separately for those whose education terminated at the elementary, high school, or college level. The hypothesis that Catholic education will produce values not conducive to economic success is decisively rejected.[41]

These findings refer to a highly specialized universe, and the size of the samples in the various comparison groups is tiny almost to the vanishing point in some instances. It was presented to illustrate the conceptual processes that may underlie a secondary analysis, not to claim a definitive data yield. A brief allusion to two *semi*secondary analyses of the same basic problem by Warkov and Greeley will serve, however, to show that one can reap a mammoth yield.[42] From a 1960 survey which provided data from 50,000

---

[39] The numbers shrink rapidly from the initial sample of about a thousand. Ambiguous cases of Catholics who had a *mixed* education, partly parochial–partly secular, who comprised about one-quarter of all Catholic men, were eliminated to obtain pure types. The point is relevant to our discussion of care about crudity and error in classification.

[40] The investigators make explicit the assumptions involved—that Catholic schools indeed try and are effective in teaching a distinctive set of values. One may also raise the question of the proper interpretation of the variable. A Catholic *college* may represent the respondent's own decision and may reflect his prior motivation and values. Certainly parochial grade school reflects the parental decision, and is at a life stage prior to the formation of values and career goals. In the way the analysis was conducted however, the different causal links can be untangled.

[41] Analysis of the data on actual economic attainment—income, occupation, and intergenerational occupational mobility—also yields negative conclusions. Two methodological points should be noted. The "slippage" problem arises in a new way. The education, religion, economic data, and mobility of the husband are based on the interview with the wife, who acted as an *informant*, and the value measures come from the self-administered questionnaire to him. A methodological subtlety is that the economic scores are *relativized*, the respondent's attainments being expressed in terms of departures from the average of the total distribution. Any common bias in the direction of inflating accomplishment is thus eliminated, since absolute scores are not used. The tests might be reformulated operationally as the effect of values in producing a "competitive" advantage rather than worldly success as such.

[42] Seymour Warkov and Andrew M. Greeley, "Parochial School Origins and Educational Achievements," *Amer. Sociol. Rev.*, **31**, 1966, pp. 406–414; Andrew M. Greeley, "Influence of the 'Religious Factor' on Career Plans and Occupational Values of College Graduates," *Amer. J. Sociol.*, **68**, 1963, pp. 658–671. Both these analysts were members of NORC and were working on surveys in which they had previously been involved, although the primary purpose of the inquiries was different.

professionals, they were able to analyze the effect of early parochial education on the level of higher education achieved by this stratum of professionals, and on their occupational and income levels. From a survey of a large nation-wide sample of 1961 college graduates, numbering about 35,000, they were able to examine the influence of early parochial education on the quality of the graduate schools attended and the influence of religion of *childhood* on educational attainment, on career goals of this inchoate group, and on values relating to work.[43] Thus they gained large numbers and coverage of many of the critical variables for their secondary analyses, but all contained within a rather specialized population.

These continuities in the study of The Protestant Ethic were not presented to have it monopolize our attention but rather because they serve well to show the vicissitudes, technical problems, and prospects in the secondary analysis of social groups. They also point to a larger moral and suggest a strategy for the investigator facing a tough battle. Even a thoughtful empiricist who undertook to test the Protestant Ethic by an expensive, *primary* survey might well waste large resources in an inconclusive inquiry because he had neglected some of the many variables and subtle indicators we now know he would need. The secondary analysis becomes a kind of testing ground for the examination of the inscrutable problem. As in all theorizing, the empirical data may lead to insights one does not have initially, and at low cost, thereby improving the subsequent primary research he might undertake and protecting his investment.

We leave our discussion of the Protestant Ethic, but we shall not yet leave religious groups. A few more cases will suggest that many other problems in the sphere of religious behavior can be examined by secondary analysis, and will add to our general understanding of the way in which social groups and categories can be studied.

RELIGIOUS GROUPS IN OTHER SPHERES OF BEHAVIOR

The three surveys that Lazerwitz employed to characterize religious groups also contained, as previously noted, a question on church attendance. He did not regard religious observance as essential to the definition of affiliation, but

---

[43] In general, their findings provide only a little support for the theory in these *specialized populations and age cohorts* in the United States. Two methodological points relating to our previous discussion might be noted. With respect to the refinement of measures, they solve the "mixed" education problem by treating all those who had any exposure to Catholic education during early life as falling into the "parochial" group. In one analysis, since they had a surfeit of cases, they simply drew a 10% subsample, still leaving them with about 3000 cases, enough to introduce various demographic controls, and yet resulting in more efficient processing of the material.

he did not neglect the promise of these data for secondary analysis. This aspect of religious behavior seemed a worthy subject in its own right, and he produced two published secondary analyses from the same surveys. In the first he examines the social correlates of churchgoing by cross tabulation with all the conventional face-sheet items, and also the variations in observance among the major religious groups and Protestant denominations.[44] Because it begins with simple procedures, applied to such readily available face-sheet data, it is worth remarking that the multivariate analysis yields exciting, perhaps serendipitous findings. The Baptists are a sufficiently large group in the pooled surveys to be further subdivided by race, yielding evidence on a matter frequently raised in the literature, the question of strong religious attachment in the Negro population.[45]

Such an analysis, pinned as it is to the one question, calls for special attention to *measurement error*. There is some evidence that individuals overstate their attendance, but Lazerwitz makes the assumption that such errors are a constant over all groups, and thus do not distort the comparisons.[46] The properties of the particular question employed in such analyses also require

---

[44] Lazerwitz, "Some Factors . . . ," *op. cit.* A footnote remarking that "The opportunities for analysis of these religious data were pointed out by Dr. Angus Campbell, Director of the Survey Research Center" underscores the tactic mentioned in Chapter III. The use of a knowledgeable informant may guide a search in fruitful directions.

[45] Controlling for denomination, and comparing whites and Negroes who report a *religious affiliation*, his report documents that the Negro *religionists* are more observant. But it provides no direct data on racial differences in affiliation, since the number of Negroes and Whites who have no "affiliation," a residual group, is not reported. In passing, an interesting continuity may be noted. Among urban Christians, Lazerwitz documents that white-collar, professional, and managerial groups showed more frequent attendance than industrial workers in 1957–1958. Using a 1955 NORC survey, Hamilton independently documents the same general finding. The focus of his analysis is on the "skilled worker" category. He is concerned to see whether the patterns of behavior of this "marginal" group are closer to the middle classes or to the working classes. With respect to church attendance, they are psychologically identical to the workers. Richard Hamilton, "The Behavior and Values . . . ," *op. cit.*, p. 47. Orbach also examined differences in church attendance by the secondary analysis of a pooled sample of some 7000 cases from the Detroit Area Surveys of 1952–1957. See H. L. Orbach, "Aging and Religion," *Geriatrics*, October 1961, pp. 530–540.

[46] For evidence, see Michael Argyle, *Religious Behavior* (London: Routledge & Kegan Paul, 1958), p. 6. This monograph is based in part on the secondary analysis of survey data for both England and the United States, and provides one illustration of such cross-national designs. Apart from the treatment of measurement error, it provides evidence on the need for careful index construction, showing that some of the group and national differences reported are dependent on the cutting points used and the specific index employed in constructing measures of religious behavior. For a criticism of assumptions about the distribution of error on such a question and a most ingenious thought, see Demerath, *op. cit.*, pp. 367–368.

thought. The Michigan question, for example, asks the respondent to engage in a kind of mental arithmetic and to report the *usual* frequency of attendance over some unspecified longish interval. This procedure works to average out minor fluctuations in attendance, but may introduce memory error. By contrast, the Gallup Poll generally formulates its question in terms of attendance at church in the preceding week, which may reduce memory error, but makes any estimates based on one survey (but not if there is pooling) vulnerable to the peculiarities of the week in question, and also makes comparison between religious groups vulnerable to the phasing of their holidays and the survey dates. To control these problems, the Gallup Poll in recent years has computed annual estimates of attendance by averaging the results from surveys conducted " in 12 widely scattered weeks."

Two of the surveys contained a battery of questions on the country of birth of the respondent, of his father and his mother, and even a question on the grandparents' national origin, and provided the data for a second analysis. Lazerwitz truncated the samples, omitting Jews (because the small number prevented any further subdivision) and Negroes, thus confining his analysis to the pooled data for white, affiliated Christians.[47] These data permitted him to test the "Three-Generations Hypothesis": Immigrants in a foreign land would find essential supports in an attachment to their churches; their children—the second generation—would be weakened in their ties, but "there must result a religious revival as the third generation returned to the church to which their parents paid less attention."[48]

In order to protect against spurious conclusions—to isolate effects attributable purely to immigrant status—controls are introduced for socioeconomic status, urbanization, and sex in comparing the attendance of the several generational groups. As a result he arrives at an unanticipated *specification* of the theory. Increasing Americanization produces one pattern among Protestants, another

---

[47] In addition to the reasons advanced earlier for omitting Negroes from such comparisons, additional ones apply here. Although they themselves were asked where they were born, the subquestions on their parents' and grandparents' national origins were not asked of Negroes. The theory being tested was not couched with reference to them—the notion of their being the products of immigration in the ordinary sense of that term would seem grotesque when applied to slavery.

[48] Lazerwitz, *op. cit.*, p. 529. In the later chapter on social change we shall again turn to the concept of *generation* as it figures in secondary analysis. There the concept is applied to *age groups*, younger individuals being members of a later generation entering into a different world from that of their parents and other older individuals. Lazerwitz, however, controls chronological age in his comparisons. Thus his study focuses on the concept purified of these connections, and only tests the theory in terms of how far the individual is removed from the status of an immigrant or how close he is to being an "established" American.

pattern for Catholic men, and still a third pattern for Catholic women, and this leads Lazerwitz to propose some hypotheses which implicate the ethnicity and social origins of the various immigrant religious groups.

The unusual fact that information on the ethnicity of both the father and the mother was obtained posed a problem of classification and measurement. At first, individuals whose parents were both foreign born and those who had "mixed parentage" (one American and one foreign), were lumped in the crude category "second generation." About a third of the group were of the mixed type, and ambiguity surrounds the decision as to where to locate them on the continuum of Americanization, especially if one considers the more subtle issue of which parent was American. It is only when Lazerwitz refined the crude category, and examined those who are *pure* second-generation Americans that the patterns became clarified. What is suggested is the need for refined measurement and index construction. But we see here that previous surveys may provide the opportunities for subtle distinctions and the corresponding findings.

These several studies illustrate the ways in which the *religious* behavior of religious groups can be explored via secondary analysis, just as the studies described earlier illustrated the ways in which their *economic* behavior and attitudes can be explored. A few other cases will show that other spheres of behavior and attitudes of religious groups can also be explored by secondary analysis, and will add to our basic methodological principles.

Consider a most informative study by Wesley and Beverly Allinsmith of the voting behavior and politicoeconomic attitudes of no less than eight religious groups. Recall that all the earlier studies shed very little light on Jews, and on the smaller Protestant denominations because, despite the pooling of cases across several surveys, the size of those cells was still too small to provide dependable estimates or to allow for any breakdown of a gross category into refined subgroups. The line of strategy, however, is obvious. Pool more surveys providing that they are comparable in sample design and that each one includes the necessary measures. Unlimited growth is the principle, although one must be cautious about it, as we shall see.

The Allinsmiths pooled six surveys of the nation conducted by Gallup in 1945 and 1946, thus producing a super-survey containing almost 12,000 respondents which yields a cell of over 500 Jewish respondents, and sufficient numbers to provide a separate estimate for Congregationalists and many other small Protestant denominations.[49] All of the surveys contained a ques-

---

[49] Wesley and Beverly Allinsmith, "Religious Affiliation and Politico-Economic Attitude: A Study of Eight Major U.S. Religious Groups," *Publ. Opin. Quart.*, **12**, 1948, pp. 377–389.

tion on religious affiliation and denomination within Protestantism; plus face-sheet items on socioeconomic status, union membership, and region of residence; plus questions on vote cast in the 1944 presidential election and on domestic economic policies; plus a question on foreign policy. These formed the basis for the analysis.

Quickly, it should be stressed that these analysts faced a crisis before they could pool such large resources. The first four surveys sampled the target universe of "voters," whereas the last two sampled the universe of *adults*, irrespective of their eligibility or likelihood of voting. Southern Negroes were excluded, or underrepresented, in samples of voters, since they had a very low probability of voting in that era, whereas samples of adults or "social cross-sections" included them.[50] The Allinsmiths could have followed the strategy of "localizing and containing error" by presenting separate tabulations for Negro Baptists in the data pooled from the six surveys. The other religious groups would have been, in effect, comparable samplings over the six surveys, and the Negro cell would have been based essentially on two of the surveys. Or they could have truncated the samples of the two social cross sections, eliminating the Southern Negroes and thus making all six samples comparable before the pooling. In fact, they conducted some preliminary cross tabulations to determine whether the Negro versus white Baptists and Methodists (who also included Negroes) were markedly different on the dependent variables. The findings being negative, they treated Baptists and Methodists as unitary groups and consolidated them across all six surveys.[51]

---

[50] As late as 1948, Gallup and Roper excluded Southern Negroes from the samples they used in election predictions, thereby reducing the problem of developing screening instruments for estimating the likelihood that a respondent with a certain political preference would turn out to cast his vote. And various other biases in the sampling procedures, under sampling of given strata, served paradoxically to reduce the error in the predictions, since they also worked to eliminate individuals with a low probability of voting. But the biases which were inconsequential for those purposes might play havoc with a secondary analyst, who was unaware of these matters and who tried to use those surveys for other purposes. On the 1948 samples, see F. Mosteller, H. Hyman, P. McCarthy, E. Marks, and D. B. Truman, *The Pre-Election Polls of 1948* (New York: Social Science Research Council, 1949), Bulletin No. 60, p. 90.

[51] They also present data on Congregationalists, a group that was too small in the other studies to be presented separately. In a more detailed statistical report, data are presented for Mormons (179 cases), Christian Scientists (141 cases), and a number of other specific groups. Several residual groups are reported and cross tabulated on the dependent variables. "No religion" plus "atheist" runs 4%; "No answer" or "don't know" totals 2.6%. See "Social-Economic Status and Outlook of Religious Groups in America," Federal Council of The Churches of Christ in America: Information Service, 27, No. 20, Part 2, May 15, 1948.

The Allinsmiths find that the Congregationalists, Episcopalians, and Presbyterians are consistently the most conservative on *domestic* economic issues, by examining each of the battery of three indicators of this ideology. The test in a sense is *replicated by a series of measures* and cannot be disputed on the ground that it is an artifact of some particular measuring instrument since it is confirmed three times.[52]

The Methodists and Lutherans are found to be less conservative, and the Baptists, Catholics and Jews are found to be the least conservative groups. The Allinsmiths, like the investigators cited earlier, then ponder the problem of spurious conclusions and institute similar analytic procedures, although they adopt quite a different perspective on the problem. They hypothesize that the ideology of religious groups really derives from their socio-economic status, not their religious membership.[53] In any case, the technical operations follow the same course.

They array the eight religious groups along a dimension of socioeconomic status, again replicating the measurement by using three different indicators of the variable.[54] Among Christians, the conservative position of the denomination has an exact parallel in its social composition. But these procedures also bring to light an anomaly, a serendipitous finding. The Jews, one of the least conservative groups, rank very *high* in socioeconomic status. The Chris-

---

[52] For example, a peculiarity of one of the indicators, retrospective report of vote in a past election, which has been documented many times, is the fact that it produces more votes for the winning candidate than he actually obtained. The Allinsmiths obtain an estimate that 57% of their combined national sample voted for Roosevelt in 1944, whereas he actually obtained about 53% of the vote. Without going into the subleties of this problem, and the actual magnitude of this error considering the differences in the sample and the total electorate, etc., or the way it is distributed over the religious groups being compared, the important point is that the test is based on two other indicators which do not have the same properties or limitations.

[53] In light of our earlier discussion, one can, of course, have a more complicated causal model of the process, formulating the economic status and political ideology as variables flowing from the religious values, both being components of the larger quest for worldly success. The Allinsmiths do not raise these questions, but clearly their study can serve as a continuity in the study of The Protestant Ethic. Some might point to a problem of "slippage" in the analysis, the occupation of the *breadwinner* being used when the respondent was a housewife or student, but the measures of religion and ideology being computed on the respondent. A crudity in coding also afflicted this secondary analysis, like many others. All farmers, no matter whether they were laborers or proprietors or tenants, were coded into a common category. By eliminating farmers from the multivariate analyses involving occupation, the Allinsmiths avoided this problem of measurement error.

[54] It may be of interest to present the comparative national findings on educational attainment, one of the three indicators obtained by the Allinsmiths for their set of surveys, and by Lazerwitz for his set, keeping in mind the dozen years that intervened between

tians might be liberal because of their status; the Jews in spite of it.[55] Since the variables of status and religion are confounded in such a way as to cloud the interpretation of the findings for Christians, the Allinsmiths then follow the conventional procedure and control occupation in the religious comparison. The ideological differences are reduced markedly for Christians but Jews of high status are still much less conservative than their social counterparts among the Christian groups.[56]

These analyses thus confirm the initial hypotheses, except for the Jewish group for which they "do not appear to hold." The Allinsmiths then look a second time at these same tables in an unusual way which conveys the conclusion in a more compelling fashion and which can be of general utility in the study of social groups. Analysts, inspecting such multivariate tables, usually focus their attention on the difference *between* groups who are matched on some control variable. The Allinsmiths also focus on the differences *within* a group which has been further subdivided on a control vari-

---

the two sets and the difference in the target universe and the mode of sampling. The attribute available in both is "high school graduation or better."

	Allinsmiths	Lazerwitz
Episcopalian	65%	78%
Presbyterian	63	65
Jewish	63	66
Methodist	51	49
Catholic	43	46
Lutheran	44	43
Baptist	35	31

[55] The replicated measures of the dependent variable are especially valuable for this analysis. The 1944 vote for Roosevelt could have been a most peculiar, and ambiguous, measure of domestic liberalism for Jews. In contrast with earlier eras and other groups, Jews voted overwhelmingly for him in that election, presumably because of the special circumstances of World War II and his leadership in the fight against the Nazis. The other indicators of domestic ideology, however, did not implicate this particular attitude. For a discussion which draws incidentally on the Allinsmith findings as well as on another unpublished secondary analysis which pooled *nine* surveys from 1940 to 1944 to produce a large enough Jewish cell, see Lawrence H. Fuchs, *The Political Behavior of American Jews* (New York: Free Press, 1956), pp. 74–79.

[56] These comparisons, of course, still leave uncontrolled other social characteristics, e.g., region and urban location, which might account for the differences. However, it would be a hasty judgment to suggest that the Allinsmiths have drawn a spurious conclusion. Their hypothesis is quite specific claiming to test only whether religious differences in ideology can be explained by status. Insofar as they persist, they nowhere make the firm inference that doctrinal factors are the explanation. What in the cluster of membership characteristics accounts for the outcome is left moot, although they do speculate as to the nature of Jewish group membership.

able. They remark: "It is not a case of all Episcopalians thinking one way." However, Jews are then seen to behave uniformly despite the *internal* differentiations in status. There is in their words a "group coherence." To use an old-fashioned term, the membership characteristic "Jewish" is *"prepotent,"*—it overrides class membership. As a mode for studying the strength of group identification, or for drawing inferences as to which of the individual's multiple group memberships functions as his reference group, it is a promising, but neglected, procedure easily applied to many secondary analyses.

A last finding from this secondary analysis of 1948 gives support to a conceptual distinction which appeared in the scholarly literature of that early period, and which has continued to be influential up to the present. George Horsley Smith had reasoned back then that there were *two* kinds of liberalism, one relating to domestic economic matters, which the low-status groups would support, and the other including international matters and noneconomic issues which the high-status groups would endorse.[57] At least two of the six surveys contained one indicator of this second realm, and Smith joined with the Allinsmiths in its analysis partly to strengthen the empirical evidence available from his own studies, and partly to determine how the religious groups would array themselves along this dimension. The Protestant denominations that had been the most conservative Christian groups on domestic economic issues were most liberal on the internationalism question used as the indicator, and the Jewish group was most liberal of all, thus bolstering the theory and enriching the description of religious groups.[58]

---

[57] G. H. Smith, "The Relation of 'Enlightenment' to Liberal-Conservative Opinions," *J. Soc. Psychol.*, **28**, 1948, pp. 3–17. This was itself a secondary analysis of Gallup Polls from 1942 to 1946. The distinction is central to S. M. Lipset's well-known paper, "Working-Class Authoritarianism" in *Political Man* (Garden City: Doubleday, 1960), pp. 97–130. This latter study is based also on secondary analysis of survey data from many countries.

[58] Other comparisons of the voting behavior of Protestants and Catholics, controlling occupation, are provided by Lipset's secondary analysis of surveys conducted during each presidential election from 1936 to 1960, and during the Congressional elections of 1954 and 1958. He remarks, "most of the available surveys do not contain detailed denominational information for Protestants, or if they do, the size of the sample interviewed is too small . . . " and controls cannot be introduced. Jews are so few in number in each survey that no analysis is reported. By truncating the sample and eliminating Southerners and Negroes, Lipset controlled these variables from the start, but, of course, the sample sizes are further reduced, ranging from about 550 to 1400 cases. Thus only a crude control for occupation can be introduced by dividing the remaining sample into manual, nonmanual, and farmers, but the possible errors arising from such crudity in measurement are carefully considered by Lipset and empirically checked with the data of one 1964 survey of some 10,000 cases, permitting finer breakdowns. Since the surveys deal with different specific dependent variables and since Lipset is also concerned with

A final case study by Broom and Glenn further enlarges our knowledge of religious groups, and is the first illustration of a different design for secondary analysis, one of a class that may be described as *Synthesizing* designs. They draw upon data from seven surveys of national samples conducted between 1953 and 1961, all of which contained a face-sheet item by which respondents could be classified as Protestant, Catholic, or Jewish. The surveys, however, dealt with different topics, and taken as a whole contained 40 questions covering 10 topics such as religious beliefs and behavior, domestic political issues, international relations, attitudes toward work, discipline of children, race relations, and authoritarianism.[59] Obviously, the coverage is wide and spaced out in time, and the analysis moves toward the goal of comprehensive description of the variegated patterns of American religious groups.

Seven is, indeed, a lucky number among gamblers, but for secondary analysts it is no insurance of good fortune. Eleven surveys containing more than 40 questions and ranging over more than 10 topics and 8 years would have been better yet. As the empirical base grows bigger, the proof gets better and the description more definitive. The synthesizer, the pooler, and the replicater all face the same question as the gambler. When should they stop? Is there one correct point at which to end the combining of surveys? The problem was academic formerly, when there were few surveys to be found, but it is real at present, and it is bound to become more acute in the future as the data banks become richer and richer. In truth there appears to be no end, and the conclusions of such secondary analyses—like primary research—are always open to revision in the light of new empirical evidence. But there is at least one principle to guide us. Rich secondary analysts face essentially a moral dilemma. They must be *fair* in the way they initially select and then add or eliminate surveys for such designs. They should choose their surveys

---

trends, they are not pooled, but they may be regarded as a series of nine replications of the general problem. Thus the disadvantage of small numbers and grossness of categories is offset by the time span and many tests which reproduce the Allinsmith basic finding. See S. M. Lipset, "Religion and Politics in the American Past and Present," in Robert Lee and Martin Marty, eds., *Religion and Social Conflict* (New York: Oxford University Press, 1964), especially pp. 91–105.

[59] Broom and Glenn, "Religious Differences in. . . .", *op. cit.* One of the surveys was a 1953 NORC survey employing a quota sampling design and is drawn on essentially because it contained a five-item scale on authoritarianism. The other six were Gallup Surveys, all of which were based on probability samples. Given the phasing of the surveys, the measurements on the different topics refer to different time periods in the eight-year interval, and some topics are covered more comprehensively and more reliably than others. Obviously if the data had been pooled into some kind of unitary analysis, differences arising from content of the variable, time, universe, and mode of sampling would have all become mixed and obscurity would surround the meaning of the findings.

blindly—not peeking at the results before they make their decisions—and only by criteria of relevance and quality of information.[60]

Before turning to the distinctive features of the design and analysis, it should be noted that the comparisons on three questions on domestic economic issues, and on three questions on foreign policy, asked some ten to fifteen years later than the Allinsmith surveys, confirm the earlier findings, and also strengthen those conclusions against spuriousness. Results on these indicators are presented for Protestants and Catholics residing in non-Southern metropolitan areas, and since Jews are concentrated in these same areas, this effectively controls the comparisons. The fact that Jews show more of both kinds of liberalism cannot be explained in terms of ecological factors.

Broom and Glenn follow a familiar course in the early stages of their design and analysis. "Most nonwhites in the United States are Protestant, and therefore they are excluded from our analysis so that differences associated with race will not obscure interreligious comparisons.[61] Following truncation, the religious groups are compared on each of the 40 questions or indicators of the different variables, first without any additional controls, and then by the introduction of region and size of residence separately, and finally jointly.[62] They thus end up with a set of 40 comparisons of three religious groups, at each level of refinement introduced into the classification of the groups. If they could pool all the data, things would be simplified, but they are not dealing with the same indicator or same variable from survey to survey or within a survey. By the same token they cannot conceive of these 40 items or the ten subsets of items as replicating one another. Indeed the prime

---

[60] Broom and Glenn remark that the surveys had already been chosen for the independent purpose of a secondary analysis of another topic, and as noted earlier in our text "no peeking" was their general practice. Apart from the profit in using the same raw materials for more than one product, clearly there was no arbitrariness or bias in the selection of surveys so as to predetermine the findings on religious differences. They realize the open-ended character of the findings with their comment, "We have hardly tapped the available data, and we hope that others will follow our lead" (p. 188). A secondary analysis involving a cross-national design, to be discussed later, provides a good illustration of the open-ended character of the replicated design when the data base is large. Alford based the American part of his secondary analysis of class voting on *five* surveys between 1952 and 1962. In a subsequent article, he further replicated the study using *three* more surveys conducted between 1962 and 1964. He handled the design in a fastidious way, using all the relevant surveys that had since become available, not eliminating any on arbitrary grounds. See Robert R. Alford, "Class Voting in the Anglo-American Political Systems," in S. M. Lipset and S. Rokkan, eds., *Party Systems and Voter Alignments* (New York: The Free Press, 1967), pp. 81–89.

[61] *Ibid.*, p. 188.

[62] The controls are only introduced for Christians, since the small number of Jews—about 60 per survey—prevents any further subdivision of the group.

purpose is comprehensive description of the patterns or difference, and thus each comparison plus the gamut is presented for inspection.

Now some work of synthesis has to be accomplished. The broader the domain and the more multiform the description, the more unwieldy the findings become and the more difficult they are to capture and convey. The abilities of a primary analyst at synthesis are rarely taxed in the same degree. A survey's primary focus is one phenomenon, or one hypothesis, even if it is examined by multiple indicators and even when it is complex in structure. It has a built-in principle of order and unity. For the secondary analyst, the synthesis must be accomplished by some special work, some device.

Broom and Glenn impose some order without losing the details of the description by a classification and presentation of the 40 tests under ten topical headings and a discussion of each. But they do not stop there. Their method for summarizing large amounts of diverse data involves the construction of a *formal or abstract index* which can be applied to each of the 40 tabulations no matter what its content. Clearly the process of abstraction has to go very far. The final index is formal—it is stripped of concrete content. Like a standard deviation which simply describes the uniformity of something or anything that has been measured over a group, or a correlation, they compute an *index of the dissimilarity* between two religious groups on each item.

The dissimilarity of Protestants and Catholics, or Protestants and Jews, or Catholics and Jews, averaged over items within a sphere or over 40 items; or the *relative* dissimilarity of Christians as compared to the dissimilarity of Christian and Jew; or the *relative* dissimilarity of two groups on matters such as drinking versus child rearing; or the *relative* dissimilarity of grossly defined groups versus groups matched on a control variable—all these things can be compactly presented by the computation and manipulation of such an index. Such average indices or ratios of indices do not describe the specific contents contained within the summary measure, nor the sign or direction of the difference. The index synthesizes and allows orderly, multiple comparisons. Whatever its limitations, it is appropriate to the overarching hypothesis in the entire program of studies. Do religious groups (and other social groups) show distinctive patterns over many spheres, or has that been lost in the process of "massification" of American society?[63]

---

[63] Their index of dissimilarity is part of a larger tradition out of which developed various summary statistics for measuring the distance or difference or similarity between the profiles or patterns of scores of contrasted individuals or groups or concepts. For examples, see R. B. Cattell, "rp and Other Coefficients of Pattern Similarity," *Psychometrika*, **14**, 1949, pp. 279–298; Charles E. Osgood and George J. Suci, "A Measure of Relation Determined by Both Mean Difference and Profile Information," *Psychol. Bull.* **49**, 1952, pp. 251–262. From another tradition of research, inquiry into the residential

The major types of designs for secondary analysis thus far revealed by our case study of religious groups may now be listed in convenient form. They apply to the study of other social groups as well as to the study of a wide variety of problems. And we shall add other designs to our list as we go along.

Designs for the Study of Social Groups

Design 1: Secondary Analysis of the Single Survey.   A test of a hypothesis involving social groups that demands a most unusual combination of data sometimes can only or best be met by the analysis of a single survey. In that case, generality and extensiveness of data may have to be sacrificed in order to achieve the stringent requirements of any test at all.

Design 2: Pooling of Multiple Surveys.   Several surveys, all of which contain identical or equivalent indicators, are consolidated into one unitary survey, and subjected to a unitary analysis. A convention followed by most analysts who pool their data is worth noting. In trying to give a precise, simple statement of their findings, they generally locate them temporally at a point midway among the several surveys. Thus Lazerwitz informs the reader that his is a description of religious groups in America as of December, 1957, although the surveys were conducted in the spring of 1957 and the fall of 1958.

Design 3: Internal Replication with Multiple Surveys.   A primary or a secondary analysis of a *single* survey may itself be a replication of a previous study, and that previous study might itself have been either a primary or a secondary analysis. The investigators might be the same or different over the several studies. Cumulatively over a span of time, a chain of replications is built, and the separate studies become linked. These we shall call *external replications*. Other examples of that design will be presented in Chapters V and VI. We shall incorporate, however, an entry in our list and designate it as Design 4: *External Replication by the Secondary Analysis of a Single Survey.* By contrast, when several previous surveys, all containing identical or equivalent indicators are incorporated within a single design—contained as

---

distribution and segregation of class or racial groups, we also find demographers developing indices of dissimilarity to summarize the evidence on the residential patterns of contrasted groups. See for example Karl Taeuber and Alma Taeuber, *Negroes in Cities: Residential Segregation and Neighborhood Change* (New York: Atheneum, 1969).

internal parts of a common secondary analysis—we shall distinguish this as
internal replication. Originally, the surveys themselves were *independent* of
each other, and this desirable feature should not be overlooked. All that is
implied by the term internal is that the chain of proof is forged all at once,
the secondary analyst having the links from the several independent surveys
conveniently available. The reader will realize that an external replication of
a previous study may contain within itself an internal replication if it includes
more than one survey.

In contrast to pooling, each survey is treated separately, but all represent
parallel analyses of the same problem.

It is almost inconceivable that *primary* research would employ an internally
replicated design. One large-scale survey is expensive, two or more become
prohibitive in cost. On occasion, however, a primary survey may be *split in
half*, and an element of internal replication designed into it, although on a
reduced scale. Classic but rare examples are provided by the Stouffer study
of *Communism, Conformity, and Civil Liberties*, in which a sample of about
5000 cases was divided into two half-samples, each interviewed by a different
survey agency using the same instrument, or the Lazarsfeld and Thielens
study of *The Academic Mind* in which about 2500 respondents were divided
into two half-samples, each surveyed by a different agency. At modest cost,
the routine use of parallel questionnaire forms on equivalent subsamples,
each about 1500 cases, by the Gallup Poll constitutes an example, and provides an almost unique resource for the secondary analysis of particular
problems which we will discuss later.[64] But these are rare primary designs
and hardly on the scale of the internal replications of secondary analysis.
Three, six, seven, nine, even eleven surveys are easily within reach, as earlier
documented. The cases swell to much larger numbers, and transient circum-

---

[64] Stouffer, *op. cit.*; Paul F. Lazarsfeld and Wagner Thielens, Jr., *The Academic Mind*
(New York: The Free Press, 1958). An earlier example is provided by a 1946 study in
which the Gallup Poll conducted the larger part, sampling about 3000 respondents, and
the Survey Research Center the smaller part, sampling about 600 respondents. For a
summary see, L. S. Cottrell and S. Eberhart, *American Opinion on World Affairs*
(Princeton: Princeton University Press, 1948). The term *internal replication* has been
used by Hirschi and Selvin to apply to a procedure introduced during the *analysis* of a
single survey, in which it is divided into parts or subsurveys each of which is analyzed
separately and the consistency of the findings determined. The results for the subsurveys do constitute replicated tests based on the internal parts of a larger entity. Such
a subdivision of a single survey can be prearranged from the start by design, or introduced after the fact. In either case it is to be contrasted with the practice we describe
where the parts are *whole* surveys and the totality is a set of parallel surveys. Unfortunately, some confusion is inevitable since the label "internal replication" may be
appropriate to all three practices. See Hirschi and Selvin, *op. cit.*, p. 99.

stances and situations are transcended in the time span brought under study, whereas the split-half designs of primary research are invariably anchored to a narrow point in time.[65]

Secondary analysts often mix pooling and replication in one study. Thus Glenn and Hyland pooled four surveys and treated seven others as replications.[66] Bogue and Feldman, and Lazerwitz, first treated their several surveys as replications, and only pooled them after inspecting the separate findings. Such a two-stage, mixed design combines the virtues of both procedures. Any trend in the aggregate data, any differential trends in subgroups, and the stability or unreliability of the findings are revealed to the analyst before they are obscured in the merger of the data from several surveys. A rare and tiny social group in the single survey, however, does not lend itself to both designs, since the cases are too few to permit any analysis or any confident interpretation of the discrete findings, and pooling has to be applied right from the start. Where the questions, the indicators used to measure the particular variables, change across surveys, replication is an essential procedure. Before one can regard them as *interchangeable* indicators of the same variable and employable for pooling the data, one needs some empirical support for that assumption and the replication provides the answer.

Design 5: Intrasurvey Replication—Multiple Indicators. One survey may contain several different indicators of the same variable, and the separate and parallel analyses of each might be described as intrasurvey replication to distinguish it from the replication provided by the separate analysis of the same indicator on several surveys. (Of course, the indicators may be combined into a scale or index, a kind of "microscopic pooling" of measurements rather than cases or surveys, and one analysis conducted on the basis of the more reliable measurement.)[67] Where each of several surveys includes the same array of multiple indicators, one gains double and lavish benefits. The Allinsmiths gained the reliability of three indicators of ideology *plus* the stability

---

[65] The internal replication, in its formal or mechanical features, is identical to the design used in the secondary analysis of trends, although the comparable surveys used in the study of change are generally spaced out over a much longer time span. The analyst, however, starts from different perspectives, in the one instance looking for systematic changes over the time series whereas in the other instance he is looking for the stable features in the data and regards the fluctuations over time as indicative of unreliability or temporary instability.

[66] A trend design was brought into the mix also. An outlying survey, some 20 years earlier, is compared with the pooled and replicated data from the multiple surveys of the later period.

[67] One should not underrate this design nor jump to the conclusion that a composite index is the best procedure. See R. F. Curtis and E. F. Jackson, "Multiple Indicators in Survey Research," *Amer. J. Sociol.*, **68**, 1962, pp. 195–204.

from the larger numbers of cases and the severally staged surveys which they pooled. Intrasurvey replication can thus be combined with the pooling of surveys or the replication of surveys if the resources are lavish enough.

Design 6: Truncating the Sample. This is an auxiliary design which, as the examples suggest, can be coupled with any of the other designs for the study of social groups. Excluding the respondents in some specified category simplifies and sharpens the analysis, reduces various forms of error, and increases the stock of surveys the analyst can draw upon for pooling or replication.

Design 7: Synthesis of Multiple Surveys for Broad Characterization of Groups. In the one example of this design, the diverse data were synthesized by a *formal index* which condensed and simplified the many comparisons of religious groups. Since synthesis can be accomplished in various ways, we shall label this first variety, 7a. Our next case study will show some of the other ways of operating this design.

There is one other aspect implicit in the previous cases worth special emphasis. *Multiple uses of the singe survey* might even be designated as a general strategy for secondary analyses. Many of the designs presented are ways the secondary analyst can use multiple surveys to improve the study of a *single problem.* But we did observe a common practice on the part of investigators to exploit a particular single survey to study more than one problem. The general advantage of multiple surveys, whatever way they are arranged in a design, is that they transcend the limitations of the single survey. If the conclusions on one problem are weakened by the use of only a single survey, so too might the conclusions on many problems be weakened. Reckless application of the strategy might even produce a large edifice of social science erected on the narrow foundation of a single survey. Such excesses are certainly not to be recommended, but optimal use of the strategy has many advantages.

Clearly the investigator is blessed who can profit in many ways from one survey. How efficient and economical and what a large return he reaps from the labors of one search. But there is more to be said for the strategy! Some surveys are gilt-edged—they truly enrich the deposits in the data bank. Their procedures insure measurements of high quality; the samples well designed and large in size; the coverage of variables wide. Secondary analyses that stem from a single survey of such quality may even be better than those that stem from poorer data drawn from several surveys. Each subsequent secondary analysis can build upon the knowledge from the previous ones, as to the errors that were unearthed and appraised, and as to the intricate structure of attitude and behavior within which the new phenomenon may be contained. The benefits from multiple uses of the right, single survey cannot be ignored.

Of course, the conclusions still rest upon a single survey with its inherent limitations. But if an investigator were to base his multiple studies upon a single *set of surveys*, judiciously chosen, that limitation would be lessened, and the benefits of multiple use would continue to accrue. Intensive cultivation of the single survey or set of surveys combined with the extensive use of many surveys would appear to be an ideal long-term strategy.

Social Classes—Other Case Studies in the Secondary Analysis of Social Groups

The following briefer case studies will exemplify the principles already presented, suggest their wider applicability, reveal new designs for the study of social groups, and expand our awareness of the many substantive problems that can be illuminated by secondary analysis.

In 1947, Genevieve Knupfer painted a vivid "Portrait of the Underdog" in American society by drawing upon the published results of surveys of that time.[68] By its very title one senses a new variety of synthesizing design for the study of a social group, which we shall add to our list and label 7b: *Synthesis by Qualitative Characterology*.

Knupfer sought to describe in a broad and fundamental way a particular social type, the low-status person. There was already in that era a large amount of survey data to be synthesized. Now, some twenty-five years later, the volume of data would make almost insuperable demands on the synthesist. Knupfer had to bring some order to the data. Her image of the type guided and helped her, and almost dictated the mode of synthesis she employed. She had a prevision of the motif, the thread of unity that runs through the diverse data. There is presumably a *character structure*. Its central feature in her view is a kind of constricted quality, a withdrawal from participation and involvement, a narrowing of horizons—almost of the total life space. She thus highlighted in her picture this pervasive feature, and tried

---

[68] Genevieve Knupfer, "Portrait of the Underdog," *Publ. Opin. Quart.*, **11**, 1947, pp. 103–114. This in fact is a *semi*secondary analysis in more ways than one. By her association with the Bureau of Applied Social Research, she was able to draw upon unpublished results of surveys with which she had been involved. Since the research was conducted long before the era of archives, her work also frequently involved "semianalysis," drawing upon marginal tabulations, and commonly reported breakdowns by socioeconomic groups, which were presented in periodic summaries in the *Public Opinion Quarterly*.

to convey the structure, the way "different aspects . . . cluster together." She painted her "picture" in words, not in numbers or tables or discrete findings or abstract indices, in order to show the wholeness, the figure of the man.

She was freed from the burdens of unraveling causes by her very formulation of the problem: "The constant interaction of the different factors involved makes it difficult to distinguish between cause and effect . . . all these factors continually influence one another so that we cannot attempt to show where one begins and the other ends."[69] But her burden was to show somehow the structure of things, and the central quality that really pervades many realms of life. She had to present many facets of the person and incorporate diverse data. Otherwise she would hardly convince the viewer that the quality is all-encompassing. Our name for the design is intended to suggest that the mode of treating the data is not quantitative, and that the synthesis relies on a theory of personality or character structure.[70]

Such qualitative approaches are not easy to codify. No detailed sequence of procedures can be spelled out. The end product can be inspected to see if the picture is vivid and the structure clear. There are, in addition, a few general principles that may be recommended. The canvas of data must be big if one is to claim that the portrait is comprehensive and reveals some pervasive quality. Also, one would like some assurance that the data were not an arbitrary selection that distorted the portrait. Knupfer's footnote is comforting: "Since this paper was written a large number of new data pertaining to listening and reading habits has appeared. They all corroborate the general trends reported here."[71]

One cannot demand much more in the way of specificity about the items to be included in the portrait, but in another respect a principle of specificity could be stressed. Knupfer's portrait is big and vivid, but one wishes he knew *who* was sitting for the painter. She names him the "underdog," the low-status person, but as she tells us: "there may be manual workers, farmers, and

---

[69] *Ibid.*, pp. 103–104.

[70] Her portrait is a *collective* one, based on combining data on low-status groups from different surveys. The features therefore come from different individuals, although all of them are exemplars of the same social type of person. It is somewhat like the quaint and intriguing experiments of Francis Galton in "composite photography," in which different photos were superimposed on one another to make a composite or simulated person, and the "blended result," as he remarked, "is sure to be artistic in expression." In contrast to this approach, there are occasional secondary analyses which are inspired by personality theory but which are *clinical* studies of the whole, *real* person based on the examination of all of his answers to an elaborate and varied set of questions. See, for example, Babette Samelson Whipple, "Mrs. Jones' Ethnic Attitudes," *J. Abnorm. Soc. Psychol.*, **40**, 1945, pp. 205–214.

[71] Knupfer, *op. cit.*, p. 109 footnote.

small business men in the lower group. . . . 'Low' is used in a *purely relative* sense. The definition varies: sometimes it may be the lower half, sometimes the lower tenth of the population . . ."[72]

The portrait has no firm anchorage in social space, and its value, the price tag one would put upon it, is correspondingly reduced. If one would like to paint the "Portrait of the Underdog of the Seventies" or "The Top Dog," and to hang them all side-by-side, creating a picture gallery for the viewing and comparison of social groups, it is hard to know whom to paint to match or pair against Knupfer's indefinite subject. Orderly comparisons of social groups require designs that are more systematic and quantitative than qualitative characterology, since one would want comparable coverage of the main features in the profile of each group, and would want to represent them using some comparable scale. For these reasons, the design may serve best for the synthesis of data on a single social group. Certainly, in the rare instances when it has been used, the analyst has focused on one group, perhaps suggesting also that the work involved may be too heavy and the data too unwieldy for double syntheses.[73]

The sharper definition of a stratum or class group prior to the rendering of its portrait is shown in a secondary analysis of 21 Australian surveys from the years 1951 to 1961 by Broom and Hill. The fact that the final synthesis is quantitative may be separated from the operations for the definition of the groups. Their ultimate portrait could have been qualitative in form, even though the prior definition of the group was by precise, quantitative means. By an intercorrelational analysis of such items as occupation, interviewer's rating of standard of living, subjective class identification, and education, they arrived at a composite index of social rank which they regarded as relatively valid, refined, and having discriminative power. It should be noted that they *truncated* their samples initially, eliminating respondents in farm and mining areas because of their ambiguous social position and the crudity of the categories, and that, following the methodological analysis, respondents with inconsistent ranks on the various indicators were eliminated and the most heterogeneous stratum further refined by excluding additional cases.

---

[72] *Ibid.*, p. 104, italics supplied. The problem of the crudity of measurement hinders the synthesist here just as it does other kinds of secondary analysts, if the face sheets are inconsistent or gross in the indicators and codes for social stratification. The problem of sampling also enters, the designs of that era possibly being biased in leaving out the lowest of the underdogs who are difficult, in any case, to locate and obtain for interviews.

[73] Knupfer did contrast her underdog with the "over dog" or higher-status group periodically, but it is interesting to note that almost invariably such comparisons were on *specific* variables and presented in the language of *quantity*, in percentages in the text, rather than in words.

Over half the respondents were finally eliminated, and therefore the analysts stress that they "prefer not to generalize about the attitudinal correlates of social strata . . . in Australia."[74]

The three strata finally defined precisely by these procedures were examined on 40 items taken from 16 of the surveys. In contrast with the qualitative synthesizing approach of Knupfer, Broom and Hill's approach is quantitative, reporting a coefficient of association between each item and social rank, organizing the results under major themes to give coherence and order. They compressed, by this series of statistics or indices in convenient summary form, a great mass of data and tables.

Thus they accomplished their work of synthesis. Although it does not reach the ultimate in unity and compression, two points must be stressed. In listing *every one* of the 40 coefficients, they remark: "There is no reason why items showing small associations should be ignored. It is as important to the advancement of sociological understanding to show that phenomena are unrelated as to show that they are closely related."[75] The coefficients are computed twice, once over all the strata, and secondly, for the polar extremes in rank, omitting the large middle stratum. The latter coefficients are considerably higher in magnitude. The moral is clear. Qualitative characterologists in their drive toward synthesis may sometimes produce sharper portraits by the extremeness of the group they select, without adequate specification of that fact, and by the inadvertent omission of incongruent details. Broom and Hill's design may not produce as clear a synthesis, but one has confidence in the conclusion that there are "consistent patterns in which social rank is associated with life style and awareness of current issues and events, called 'strata correlates,' and with a commitment to private enterprise and laisser-faire, called 'class interest' themes."[76]

We may contrast the difficulties of synthesis of 40 indicators over 16 surveys for three groups that Broom and Hill faced and their solution, with the situation Hamilton faced in his secondary analyses of American class differences. In one study, he drew upon one SRC survey, truncated it, and compared only two groups: white-collar workers or "the lower middle class," with skilled industrial workers, to test whether working-class values or middle-class values and reference groups would be adopted by the white-collar workers who have been hypothesized in the past to be on the margin of the middle class. In a related study, he drew upon two NORC surveys, truncated them, and compared three occupational categories: At one pole were white-collar

---

[74] Broom and Hill, *op. cit.*
[75] *Ibid.*, p. 101.
[76] *Ibid.*, p. 106.

workers; at the other pole were semiskilled industrial workers; in the middle was a marginal group, skilled craftsmen and foremen who were examined to see whether they would be closer in their profile to the "lower middle class" or to the industrial worker. In the first study, only a few indicators are employed and there is no work of synthesis necessary. In the second, about 28 discrete indicators are examined. Nevertheless, these readily are classified into five areas, and the class profiles on these five features are not too unwieldy to be presented. Thus Hamilton can present clear portraits and test his theory without carrying the work of synthesis beyond the point of a profile.[77] Broom and Hill have to compress their more diverse and voluminous data by using a formal index. Hamilton's mode of operation, *synthesis by the device of a profile,* for purposes of notation will be listed as design 7c.

A continuity in secondary analysis is provided by Glenn and Alston who follow Hamilton's example but are concerned, not just with two or three groups, but with "an almost comprehensive classification" of occupational groups. They present characterizations of eight groups drawing upon 113 different questions from 23 different American national surveys conducted between 1953 and 1965. Their goal is to examine the similarities and differences in the patterns, but the profile is so multifaceted, comprising 17 features, that some summary index is needed to synthesize the data.

In brief, they score the frequency with which any occupational group gives a "high status" response to each item, average these scores for each of the 17 features, and finally compute one grand average for all features combined. In this fashion, they compress a multitude of information, can describe the homogeneity of any group, the "cultural distance" between groups, and the general uniformity or diversity of scores over the whole occupational structure. They confirm Hamilton's finding. The index for skilled workers shows them closer to other manual workers and more distant from white-collar workers. But by virtue of the much wider sampling of variables, seventeen features of the profile versus five, they can document some departures from the general pattern. "Only on three topics, then, do skilled workers appear to be unambiguously 'middle-class.' "[78] We shall skip other interesting and more involved findings. One last issue, however, might be raised.

---

[77] Hamilton, "The Marginal Middle Class . . . "; "The Behavior and Values of Skilled Workers," *op. cit.* One of the NORC surveys employed was the same one that Bogue and Feldman used, that Hausknecht used, and that Wright and Hyman used—again showing how a string of analyses may come from a single survey.

[78] Glenn and Alston, *op. cit.,* p. 373. The three were: reading and exposure to media, attitudes on child rearing, and "political values." Obviously, if the analysis had employed only a few very broad and gross occupational groups, instead of the eight, the index score for any group would have shown more internal heterogeneity, and the cultural

All of the surveys drawn upon were national in scope, and most were based on area probability sampling designs. Thus the findings have considerable generality, both in terms of the sampling of a considerable time span, and also in terms of the wide geographical environment within which the occupational groups are sampled. What we have distilled in effect are the patterns that transcend time and locality, making them more truly "cultural." Some of the internal heterogeneity of an occupational group may, however, represent other powerful sources of cultural differences. Some of the skilled workers may be Southern, some Northern, for example. The occupational comparisons, if one wished, could easily be made within subcultural areas rather than for the nation at large, by recourse to other face-sheet items. A neglected item available on many surveys is the type of *industry* within which the worker is located, and insofar as work-life is more precisely defined both by the occupational role and by the nature of the work itself, a secondary analysis could be based on a dual measure.

The case study of social classes has added to our previous list of designs for the secondary analysis of social groups. Three modes for combining diverse data from multiple surveys into a broad characterization were labelled synthesis by *qualitative characterology*, by *profiles* and by *formal or abstract indices*. These three approaches do the work of bringing order or unity out of multiplicity, and of compressing the data available on the different features of the group, but they do not solve a critical problem. Another approach is needed which, unfortunately, none of our characterologists can yet provide. We shall label it 7d: *Synthesis based on taxonomic principles.* We can suggest the critical need, and what that design of the future will be, even if we and they cannot yet realize it.

The characterologists have given us several effective ways for synthesizing the data they have already selected. They have also specified principles for

---

distance between groups would have been less. This analysis again reveals certain general procedures: The reliability of the score in each area is protected by the multiple indicators. The surveys were chosen "blindly," so as to provide a fair test. Some might feel there is a problem of slippage in that female respondents were included and the occupational classification is based on the head of the household. Or one might operationally redefine the analysis as a test of the extended cultural influences on family members stemming from the occupation of the head. An imponderable problem in this and most such secondary analyses, because of the rarity of the appropriate face-sheet data is the *duration of experience* within the occupation. Presumably the patterning is produced by prolonged exposure, but all that is known is the *current* occupation of the household head. The concept of culture also implies a *persistent* pattern, but the use of multiple surveys over a span of a dozen years insures that the findings cannot be regarded as mere transient phenomena, although exactly how long a pattern must persist for it to be "cultural" remains arguable.

selecting data and surveys from the larger body of material that is available and relevant to the variables or concepts under study. But they do not tell us how to select the *concepts* themselves that must enter into a comprehensive characterization of a social group. What features must be included if the portrait is to be complete? Ten or seventeen features of a profile obviously make a more rounded figure, a more complete gestalt, than five, and the cases already presented clearly establish that the omission or addition of a feature can change the conclusions. How many features are essential remains an unanswered question. The use of 40 or 113 *indicators* only speaks to the question of reliability of measurement. It begs the question of the number of features or concepts which are then to be measured in a reliable fashion. In their searching, the characterologists no doubt proceed rationally, with some sense of the relative importance of given variables, and with aspirations toward the comprehensive. They can then order or classify the finds from their searching under headings or features, and whatever disputations might occur can be resolved by rearranging the items and the headings.[79] When all this is done, they still lack a model of the complete man to guide their search. This is what we emphasize by the idea of a scientific classification or taxonomy of social psychological features.[80] Primary research might well be needed to describe a feature within the taxonomy for which no survey data are available, but this would at least signal a deficiency in the secondary analysis and spur investigators to remedy it.

The acute need and the groping toward a solution are conveyed in the work of John S. Reed who cooperated in our endeavors by keeping a diary during the course of his secondary analysis. His was a broad characterization of the culture of the South. Some of his diary entries follow:

After a trip to the Roper Center in late April, two things were very clear to me: . . . The need for a taxonomic scheme is overwhelming. There are hundreds of items which strike me as "interesting" but I have absolutely no basis for selecting from them. . . . I have been reading the "national character" literature. . . . Everyone laments the absence of a non-arbitrary check list of attributes to examine.

---

[79] For empirical tests of the effect on the conclusions of the number and types of headings under which questions are classified and of the possible overweighting of the general conclusions by disproportionate numbers of questions from given features, see Glenn and Simmons, *op. cit.*

[80] These thoughts have been stimulated by a paper by Daniel Katz on the ways in which primary survey research could enrich scientific psychology. He urges "a social psychological taxonomy of human behavior," a "definition of relevant variables and parameters," and then the use of surveys for the "gathering of descriptive data about the people of a society on a systematic basis." See Daniel Katz, "The Practice and Potential of Survey Methods in Psychological Research," in Glock, *op. cit.*, especially pp. 149–173.

Later a new entry:

Returning to the taxonomic problem, I may have found a solution which will let me duck it. It's basically an editorial idea . . . a series of essentially discrete chapters, each one a discussion of one particular aspect of the "mind of the South" . . . Thus: (1) The Agrarian South (2) The Parochial South (self-conscious?) (3) The Puritan South (religious?) (4) The Repressive South (the closed society?) (5) The Militant South (belligerent?) (6) The Nostalgic South (pessimistic, defeated?) (7) The Ordered South (hierarchical?) (8) The Kinfolk South (familistic?) (9) The Chivalrous South (manners? sex roles?) (10) The American South (patriotic?) Perhaps more.

The chapters listed certainly implicate many important institutional sectors and psychological phenomena, but later entries show that closure had not yet been achieved. There was no taxonomic principle to assure him that he had come to the end of his search.

While at the Roper Center in July, I was reading through its folders and came across a request for data on regional loyalty or regional identification . . . I may get these studies—either for the introduction, the "contented" chapter, or the "parochial" chapter.

In September he writes:

I suggested yesterday that my organizing principle for my manifold dependent variables be in terms of institutions . . . economic life, politics, family, education, religion. . . .

But, periodically, he contemplates a radically different principle of classification, one that implicates more *social-psychological* variables and *formal*, or content-free features. The entry, "The Homogeneous South" is made and formulated in terms of the greater uniformity in attitudes and behavior, or "the lack of cross-stratum variability." Later his thinking reverts to this same kind of principle with the entry: "Another formal variable—ideologization: the notion being that Southerners are supposed to be less coherent ideologically. . . . Hero suggests operationalizing this as the inter-correlation of policy items."

Reed's diary presents the dilemma of the secondary analyst who labors toward synthesis, toward comprehensive characterizations of social groups, without the aid of some commonly accepted taxonomy of characteristics.[81]

---

[81] The diary presents a great deal of other information on logistical and data-processing problems, on modes of multivariate analysis, especially multiple test-factor standardization to determine how much of the regional difference is "cultural" or residual, after structural factors are controlled by standardizing the distributions, and on the oscilla-

Despite his labors, he could not resolve the riddle of a comprehensive scheme. The final study necessarily dealt with a limited number of variables selected by reference to a series of methodological and theoretical criteria. We have little to suggest at present in the way of principles other than to urge the analyst to be broad and systematic in whatever is his formulation.

Additional Designs Revealed in Studies of Other Social Groups

There is no need for thorough treatment of other social groups. The detailed case studies of religion and class fortunately provide illustrations of most of the designs, the principles and procedures, and the difficulties involved in such secondary analysis. The examples we shall present now are not intended to cover the total range of possibilities for enlarging our substantive knowledge, but mainly to remedy omissions of a methodological nature in the previous presentation. To be sure, there has been a strange neglect of the opportunities, considering the rich data available to characterize other groups that figure prominently in discussions of social structure. Very brief review of a few references will remind secondary analysts of the potentialities.

NEGLECTED OPPORTUNITIES

Howard Beers noted, almost twenty years ago, that there already existed *published* compendia of results from over 300 polls tabulated by some criterion of *rurality*. Although no archive yet existed, and his suspicions were well founded for that era "that the representation of farmers in national polls may not be adequate at all strata of rural society," he conducted critically a secondary *semi*analysis characterizing the rural-farm group in many respects and comparing their profile with that of urban occupational groups.[82] Not

---

tions back and forth from searching and inspection of data to conceptualization and problem formulation. Unfortunately, only the portions most relevant to the discussion of synthesizing designs can be presented here. The fruitfulness of such diaries for the codification of the many complexities of secondary analyses seems documented in compelling fashion by Reed's labors on behalf of the research, and others ought to follow his good example. See John S. Reed, Unpublished Diary, 1968–69. The secondary analysis to which it corresponds is: "The Enduring South (Lexington, Mass.: D. C. Heath, forthcoming 1972).

[82] Howard W. Beers, "Rural-Urban Differences: Some Evidence from Public Opinion Polls," *Rural Sociol.*, **18**, 1953, pp. 1–11. Quota sampling designs were the common

until years later, do we come upon another secondary analysis which constitutes an external replication of Beer's study, a continuity in research, and an updating of the evidence.

Glenn and Alston drew upon 92 questions from 20 surveys for the period 1953–1965 to characterize farmers and compare them with other nonrural occupational groups.[83] Since they could work with archival materials in the new era, they conducted multivariate analysis and controlled various characteristics which were confounded with farm status in Beer's analysis, and thus drew more confident conclusions. Their surveys from the later period also are less vulnerable to criticism since they are based on probability sampling designs. It is comforting that the conclusions of the later study confirm the earlier picture of some residual and persistent difference in rural society and culture.

Rural and urban dwellers are only two polar types of groups that can be located by the common face-sheet item on place of residence. Suburbia seems to be the new way of life for many Americans, whose responses to that existence could be documented by the secondary analysis of many surveys. Again there appears to be a strange neglect, and one finds only occasional analyses in the literature.

There are technical difficulties arising from crudities in sampling suburbia and in coding of the community of residence.[84] The face sheet often does not include information on length of current residence and previous place of residence, so we may not know whether the suburbanite has been exposed long enough to register the effects of his social environment. There are, however, enough surveys from which to choose one or more with the appropriate refinements. For example, in one of the rare secondary analyses, Greenstein and Wolfinger examined the claims and explored the dynamics of a theory of "suburban Republicanism," that movement to the suburbs is accompanied by a shift toward political conservatism.[85]

---

practice, and there were many reasons for viewing the sampling of rural population with special suspicion. Even in the modern era of probability sampling designs, when clustering is an essential economy, conservative analysts wonder about the errors in the sampling of remote and thinly populated rural areas and geographical regions. For a cautionary treatment, see Philip Converse in Merritt and Rokkan, *op. cit.*

[83] Norval Glenn and Jon Alston, "Rural-Urban Differences . . . " *op. cit.*

[84] In some of the Gallup surveys, suburban residents were simply coded in terms of the size of the central city of which the suburb was a satellite, and no separation can be made between the central city and suburban respondents in that category. In other Gallup surveys the coding indicated both the size of the actual community and the fact, when applicable, that it was a satellite of a large city.

[85] Fred Greenstein and Raymond Wolfinger, "The Suburbs and Shifting Party Loyalties," *Publ. Opin. Quart.*, **22**, 1958, pp. 473–482.

The Michigan Survey of the 1952 election that they selected permitted a multivariate analysis in which groups were successively matched in education, occupation, income, race, religious affiliation, and union membership, but contrasted in suburban or metropolitan residence, and then compared on politics. By truncation, a gross control on region was also introduced, and the influence of ethnicity was also examined. These analyses strengthened the claims of the theory, but, as the authors carefully note, other more subtle forms of selective migration still vie with environmental conversion as the explanatory factor. The survey, also, contained information on length of residence (although not on community of origin), and it was found that Republicanism was more characteristic of those who had been exposed to the suburban milieu for longer periods, and could *not* be explained by the fact that the earlier waves of migrants were recruited from higher classes. The theory of conversion is thus strengthened considerably. The study illustrates how far one can go toward deep exploration of a problem by judicious selection of a survey with subtle face-sheet data, and suggests that a single survey may be recast in the form of a *"quasipanel"* design.[86]

One other secondary analysis of suburbanites illustrates a new design, and we shall therefore review it later in somewhat greater detail. But first, we shall list a few other social groupings which lend themselves to study. The literature reveals very few secondary analyses which are characterologies of the *Negro* population or comparisons between Negro and white groups. Here again there appears to be a strange neglect, as one considers the prominence of problems of race relations especially in recent writings, and the importance of the issues for social policy. To be sure, the current concern has inspired large-scale primary surveys in the recent period, but if one wishes to have historical baselines by which to assess change or the persistence of social-psychological features of the groups, secondary analysis seems a valuable avenue. Perhaps again the understandable concerns about the methods employed to sample the Negro population in earlier surveys, or the difficulties in executing the samples effectively, or the concern about the response errors that might have arisen from the frequent assignment of white interviewers to Negro re-

---

[86] A replicated design using surveys from several different historical periods would strengthen the evidence and illuminate one commonly neglected problem in theorizing about suburbia. The model that migrants into suburbia are converted by the sociopolitical milieu of their hosts must also take into account the fact that the migrants depending on their numbers and successive waves also become a substantial part of the milieu which affects the next group of migrants. Obviously the balance of forces in the suburb shifts with time, depending on the numbers and the speed of the rate of conversion. By replication, one obtains a more generalizable picture of the effects of the dynamic process. The passage of some ten years has multiplied the resources for such analyses.

spondents have deterred investigators.[87] Caution must be exercised to avoid error, but certainly this does not preclude analyses based on judicious selection of high-quality surveys and careful treatment of data.

Hyman and Reed examined an assertion that had been given wide currency: that there is a "Black Matriarchy." Although there is a great deal of statistical evidence from census sources on the *objective* datum—father-absent families, and their distribution in the population—only the most meager evidence is available on a more *psychological* aspect of the concept, whether wife or husband, father or mother, has the more dominant role within the intact Negro family. They sought to shed light on that problem by a replicated design, drawing on three surveys which taken together span a considerable time period. The critical fact was that they did not limit themselves to the Negro sample, but compared the Negro and white groups. The findings of considerable maternal dominance within the Negro family might have led to an unwarranted and "pseudocomparative" conclusion. But in the perspective of the findings on white families, they can draw the truly comparative conclusion that there is "little evidence for any social-psychological pattern of matriarchy peculiarly characteristic of the Negro family."[88]

Broom and Glenn, by contrast, synthesize a broad-ranging characterization of Negro and white groups on the basis of ten national surveys conducted during the years 1950–1961 which contained 32 questions which were classified under 8 main features.[89] Another secondary analysis comparing Negro and white groups illustrates a new design and will be summarized shortly.

---

[87] For evidence on the racial composition of interviewing staffs in the early era, see Mosteller, *et al.*, pp. 134–135. For evidence on the effect of assignment of white interviewers to Negro respondents in that era, see Hyman, *et al.*, *Interviewing in Social Research* (Chicago: University Press, 1954), pp. 159–162, where it is established that in matters unrelated to race, the effects may be small or negligible, although they are substantial on issues involving such relations. For a report on the interviewing problems in the more recent era, see Morris Axelrod, Donald R. Matthews, and James W. Prothro, "Recruitment for Survey Research on Race Problems in the South," *Publ. Opin. Quart.*, **26**, 1962, pp. 254–262. This report reflects the experience in a 1961 survey of a sample of about 600 Negro adults in the South. Parallel surveys were made of a sample of about 300 Negro college students, and of a sample of about 700 white Southerners. By virtue of the size of samples, the care in the field procedures, and the comparative design, the study presents an obvious target of opportunity for secondary analysts, and is accessible through the archives. But there are also other studies which have much potential in their size and quality of data and accessibility through the archives. For example, the Michigan 1964 election study incorporated a supplementary sample of Negroes producing a combined total of over 400 Negro respondents for analysis and comparison with the white national sample.

[88] Hyman and Reed, *op. cit.*, p. 352.

[89] Broom and Glenn, *op. cit.*

There are other types of social groups and categories which deserve more ambitious study: *regional* or *ethnic* groups, groups of persons differing in the amount and kind of formal *education* they have had, for example.[90] Still other groups locatable by the face sheet have been almost totally neglected— for example, *veterans*, those who have experienced membership in the military services. The *widowed* could be located from the face-sheet item on marital status, specified by age and sex, and characterized in many ways by the use of pooling and one of the synthesizing designs. The reader can explore such possibilities for himself, and can bring most of such analyses to successful completion if he thoughtfully applies what has already been presented.

Additional examples and details would certainly reveal some new particularities of the principles already presented. Although we have stressed the general need for vigilance with respect to error, and the difficulties of unearthing obscurities in the procedures of long-past surveys which, if left unnoticed, may distort the conclusions, we have not illustrated every insidious instance of the problem. It might, for example, serve some secondary analyst well if we have reviewed the fact that the sampling designs of some of the Gallup surveys, and of other agencies, employ weights to correct for biases, these weights introduced by the duplication of cards. This procedure increases the accuracy of the conclusions a primary analyst obtains, and serves the secondary analyst in the same way, to protect his results from sampling biases. But in one respect, he may be worse off. His confidence may be unduly inflated by the apparent size of the cells he examines. He may not know that many members of his social groups may simply be cardboard cases rather than real ones.

---

[90] For studies of regional groups, see, for example, Glenn and Simmons, *op. cit.*; Reed, *op. cit.*; George Robert Boynton, "Southern Conservatism, Constituency Opinion and Congressional Voting," *Publ. Opin. Quart.*, **29**, 1965, pp. 259–269; S. C. Patterson, "The Political Cultures of the American States," in N. Luttbeg, ed., *Public Opinion and Public Policy: Models of Political Linkage* (Homewood, Illinois: Dorsey Press, 1968), pp. 275–292. For an analysis of errors that might have been peculiar to Southern samples and their responses in the 1964 elections surveys, see W. D. Burnham, "American Voting Behavior and the 1964 Election," *Midwest J. Polit. Sci.*, **12**, 1968, pp. 33–36. For a most elaborate study of educational groups, see Charles Herbert Stember, *Education and Attitude Change* (New York: Institute of Human Relations Press, 1961). For an elaborate characterology of Americans as a group, and of many social subgroupings within the nation, see G. Almond, *The American People and Foreign Policy* (New York: Harcourt Brace, 1950), especially Chapters IV–VI. For a similar elaborate characterology of Canadians as a group, and comparisons of many subgroups, see Mildred A. Schwartz, *Public Opinion and Canadian Identity* (Berkeley: University of California Press, 1967). For an example of a study of a particular ethnic group, see Bruce M. Russett, "Demography, Salience, and Isolationist Behavior," *Publ. Opin. Quart.*, **24**, 1960, pp. 658–664.

Although we have presented many examples of the different types of designs, not every ingenious way of translating these designs into reality has been described. An analyst, for example, may imagine that he can only pool surveys that sampled the same geographical universe, even though he is aware of the possibilities of truncating one of the surveys before throwing it into the pool. It might have helped to note an instance where ingenious investigators have pooled a regional survey with a national survey to build up one cell when the samples of that stratum were compatible.[91]

Not every particular can be described. By his flexibility and sensitivity, the reader can modify and apply effectively what has already been reviewed. And the later chapters will present other applications of the general principles and add to our assortment of designs. We have, however, one new design and one radical variation on the pooling design to present before we move to the next chapter.

Design 8: The Exact Counterpart Design—Comparison of Social Groups Precision Matched on a Combination of Characteristics. A study by Tomeh of suburbanites will illustrate this new design.[92] She started by pooling data from the Detroit Area surveys. The universe here includes the metropolitan area, and therefore provided, especially when many samples were pooled, more than adequate numbers of contrasted individuals in three categories: the central city, an "outer ring" of the city, and the suburbs. The restricted universe, in contrast with a national survey, introduces by definition some element of homogeneity among all the respondents. All are in the ambience of one place, the Detroit metropolis. From the published account it is not clear whether residence had already been coded according to the refined scheme, or whether special recoding was required. Even so, it is obvious that the clerical labors would be simplified if one only had to classify addresses and communities within one area rather than the addresses of a sample scattered all over the country.

There are very few, if any, continuing survey operations which confine themselves to sampling a particular metropolitan area, but there are many long-established surveys of *states*, such as the California, Minnesota, Texas, and Iowa Polls. This type might well be an optimal choice for the secondary analyst of suburbia. Some desirable homogeneity has been introduced; some generality is retained. The surburban stratum relating to major city centers

---

[91] Boynton, *op. cit.*

[92] Aida K. Tomeh, "Informal Group Participation and Residential Patterns," *Amer. J. Sociol.*, **70**, 1964, pp. 28–35. To some extent this may be described as a *semi*secondary analysis, since Tomeh was a doctoral candidate at the University of Michigan and was in proximity to the Detroit surveys and the directors of the operations.

would be large, and whatever labors of recoding residence were called for would be simplified.

Tomeh's findings relate only to Detroit, but since her pooled data span the period 1951–1959, her generalizations are not narrowly confined in time. She tested whether suburbanites differed in their informal social relations by examining the frequency of *specific* types of interaction, and in the level of general social participation as measured by a composite index. Since she wished to determine whether the pattern derived from "the very nature of their location," from the suburb's "greater potential for enhancing informal interaction among the residents," she wanted to control the individual characteristics of the respective populations, and this led to her distinctive design.

Tomeh had a large pool of almost 2500 respondents. Thus each suburbanite could be precision matched with an individual urbanite who was an exact counterpart on *seven* face-sheet characteristics which might determine social participation: on age, sex, marital status, race, education, religious affiliation, and whether migrant or native to Detroit. As a result, the three final comparison groups each contain 267 respondents.[93] It is worth stressing that pooling is used in this design not to build up the statistical base for comparison, but to provide sufficient bodies or cases for the very demanding procedure of screening and matching of groups. Cases are thrown away, not added.

In contrast with the introduction of multiple controls by cross tabulation, and by a long series of partial contingency tables, which is unwieldy and cannot be compressed into summary form, this procedure leads to but *one* table or comparison, in which all of the seven test variables other than residence have been controlled. The power of compression is very great, but certainly it has other virtues as well. Like the classical experimentalist who equates his subjects, the controls are many and joint in character and thus imposed in a powerful way. But what is finally lost by the procedure, whether it be the classical experimental design or this quasi-experimental version, are the *specifications* that the conventional survey analysis presents. The effects on the phenomenon of an independent or experimental variable, such as residence, in *interaction with a specific level* of another variable, such as race or sex,

---

[93] In the instance of the variable, education, the match was in terms of an interval rather than the exact magnitude of schooling completed. Since this indicator served to measure socioeconomic status, occupation and income were not incorporated into the matching procedure. The loss of cases stems partly from the fact that individuals for whom exact counterparts did not exist in the other two environments had to be dropped. Tomeh does report, however, that she did have some duplicate matches, which she eliminated at random, since she wished to have the "experimental" groups identical in the distribution of characteristics.

have been lost to sight in the final summary table. And we cannot weigh the mian effect of a variable like sex or race versus the effect of residence since all the particularities have been submerged in the table.

The design achieves its gains at a price.[94] However, one can, as Tomeh did, employ both designs in tandem or in a series—presenting conventional tables specifying particular relationships of variables and the differential effects— and also presenting the summary table based on the overall precision-matched groups. By these two modes of analysis, Tomeh establishes that suburbanites are more likely to have frequent social relations with friends and neighbors, and thus to show higher levels of general participation on the overall index. The differences cannot be attributed to the seven personal characteristics, but she also documents—by the conventional analysis—that the effects of subur- bia are small compared to the independent contribution that personal charac- teristics make, and that suburban effects are differential in magnitude for particular kinds of individuals.

The same design was applied by Marvick to explore whether Negroes are socialized into politics in such a fashion that they exhibit very distinctive views of the political order and their role in it. The comparative study of *The Civic Culture* by Almond and Verba fortunately contained a great many indicators of such beliefs in national samples of five countries, and Marvick, by a secondary analysis limited to the American sample, conducted a study of "The Political Socialization of the American Negro." Apart from the intrinsic interest of the findings, the distinctive way in which he operated the design in tandem with another procedure deepens our understanding of its implications.

Only 100 Negroes had been interviewed, and given the tiny size of the group, none of these was expendable. But there were ample numbers of whites to permit precision matchings on five variables: region, size of com- munity, age, family income, and sex. This yielded a final group of 100 whites, each of whom was an exact counterpart of one of the 100 Negro respondents in all five respects.[95]

---

[94] The counterpart design has many parallels to a design employing multiple standardiza- tion. Both achieve compression or summarization; both lose the identity of the sub- groups. In the former instance the groups are equated by selection and matching of cases; in the latter instance by the introduction of mathematical weights during the analysis. Thus, the latter procedure throws away no cases. Truncating as a design also has obvious parallels to precision matching.

[95] Dwaine Marvick, *op. cit.* All five variables were dichotomized, yielding 32 profiles of individuals who had various combinations of *high* and *low* scores. The matching was done in terms of these intervals. It is important to note Marvick's remark on the "im- possibility—using the kinds of matching procedures noted—of securing a good match between Negroes and their counterparts on either occupational or educational counts;

Comparisons between these counterpart samples on the multiple indicators available reveals "those aspects of Negro political socialization that seem distinctive for the ethnic group. . . ." Some may feel such a design pushes the logic of controls and the concept of spuriousness to such an extreme that it distorts social reality. A configuration of handicaps are part of the distinctive social plight of American Negroes, and to compare them with that unusual group of whites who are characterized by the same handicaps hardly presents a realistic comparison of Negroes and whites. Marvick, however, plays the analysis *two* ways. In some instances the findings from the comparisons of the counterpart groups make his conclusions even more compelling. And in every table, Marvick also presents the findings for the "national white cross-section" thus permitting an analyst to draw conclusions about the distinctive pattern when the handicap is obliterated, and when the handicap is allowed to operate. He also presents the Negro–white comparisons separately for Southern and Northern strata, thus specifying the relationships by region rather than submerging them in the summary comparison of the national counterpart groups.

We turn to one final design for the study of social groups. It is a variation on the conventional pooling design so radical and controversial in approach as to be distinguished and reviewed in some detail.

Design 9: Characterization of Multi-Dimensional Social Groupings—Pool's Principle for Pooling.   In the course of work on the 1960 presidential election, Ithiel Pool and his associates developed an unusual approach to the broad characterization of social groups. They were concerned with immediate applications to the understanding and operation of election campaigns and

there were simply not enough whites in menial job categories or with limited educational backgrounds, once age, sex, region, income, and residence area dimensions were stipulated" (p. 117). And this despite the fact that there were 870 bodies to choose from. Obviously if such individuals could have been found in America, they would have been bizarre representatives of the white population and the social realities of the nation in 1960. One specific direction in which the counterpart design might be extended fruitfully would be to obtatin the matches between individuals contrasted in some respect from among those living in the very same areal sampling segments. These "ecological counterparts" would provide controls not only on residential context and status characteristics, but also on the kind of local stimulation that might occur in a political campaign, and thus would permit rigorous tests of the influence of some independent variable on behavior. Such a design is feasible given the facts of cluster sampling and the modern practice of coding and punching an identification number for the sampling unit. The thought is suggested by the pioneering studies by Wayne Dennis in which he used street directories to draw control groups from the immediate neighbors of some experimental group that was under study. See, for example, his "Registration and Voting in a Patriotic Organization," *J. Soc. Psychol.*, **1**, 1930, pp. 317–318.

the prediction of elections, and with more basic contributions to Political Sociology and the simulation of social processes. We shall ignore these matters and present only their general approach to secondary analysis.[96] In brief, they wished to characterize a large number of social groups, defined on the basis of the face-sheet data, in terms of the *combination of seven social factors*, each measured at several levels: region, socioeconomic status, size of community of residence, sex, religion, race, and political affiliation. Thus, for example, a particular category might be the "upper status-urban-Eastern-Protestant-white-male-Democrat."

The complete factorial arrangement—all the possible combinations produced by the seven factors each measured at several levels—would have produced 3600 distinctive social groups. Apart from the fact that some groups would probably have been infinitesimal in size (for example, upper-class, Southern-Negro-Republicans or Jewish-Negroes) or perhaps nonexistent, and that the analysis might have become utterly unmanageable and beyond all comprehension, certain combinations were not of interest. The final analysis proceeded on the basis of 480 multidimensional groupings, although at times further consolidation was desirable and only 15 grosser groupings or, in their words, "macrotypes" were used.

Whatever phenomena or features might have been examined to characterize these groups, it is self-evident that *one* survey would yield too few cases to permit any reliable description. The ordinary national sample broken down into almost five-hundred subdivisions would yield on the average 3–4 respondents to represent a social group. If the fifteen macrogroups were employed, a social group on the average might contain 100 respondents, but one defined by an unusual and rare combinations of factors would practically vanish. Obviously, the solution is to pool a large number of surveys. In fact, they pooled 65 surveys spanning the period 1952–1960, producing a super-survey of about 130,000 respondents, thus yielding 480 groupings which averaged about 200 cases in each cell. Another secondary analyst interested in multidimensional groups, whether he used more or less factors and levels, would confront similar difficulties and have to employ the same kind of super-pooling design.[97]

---

[96] Ithiel deSola Pool, Robert P. Abelson, and Samuel L. Popkin, *Candidates, Issues and Strategies: A Computer Simulation of the 1960 and 1964 Presidential Elections* (Cambridge: MIT Press, 1964). A briefer treatment is presented in Pool, "Use of Available Sample Surveys in Comparative Research," *Information*, **2**, 1963, pp. 16–35.

[97] They pondered for example the need to introduce an eighth factor, age, but if this had been introduced at three age levels, the number of subgroups of the samples would have jumped to 1440 cells. This and other variables which might have entered into the definition of groups were tabulated as if they were "dependent variables" or features of the

There was, however, another reason for drawing so many surveys into the design. Their aim was to provide the broadest possible characterization or profile of features of each social group. This led to the identification of 50 features or what they called "issue clusters," varying from such general concepts as "civil rights," "neo-fascism," and "New-deal philosophy," to such specifics as "attitude toward Israel" or "attitude toward Truman." In part, the 50 issues are an ad hoc collection of variables which were thought to bear a relation to their problem of understanding the 1960 election, rather than a comprehensive classification of features based on taxonomic principles. But in its attempt to present a multiform characterization based on 50 features, and in the solution employed, it provides a new model and design for the secondary analyst engaged in grand synthesis.

A given survey might have contained measures of 4 or 5 features, but to cover all 50 features, they needed to combine the information from a great many surveys. Moreover, each single survey, no matter how comprehensively it might have covered many features, would have been too flimsy in terms of the sizes of the 480 social groups. The need to combine surveys, and by *pooling* no less, was forced upon them from both directions—to enlarge both the characterization and the size of the groups who were characterized. If the findings from different single surveys had been presented as replications, each social group would have been so small that the evidence would have been too weak and variations in results impossible to interpret. They had to pool from the start.

But how many surveys could be pooled, if they had imposed the requirement that the *indicator* of a feature, the question employed to measure the issue cluster, had to be *identical* over all surveys. Certainly all 65 surveys did not cover every one of the 50 features. Even if they had been lucky enough to find 10 surveys that had exact replicated indicators of a given feature, this would, by pooling, still only yield on the average about 40 cases to represent a social group, a fragile statistical base for reliable description. The presentation of a profile of features, some based on a pool of several surveys, others based on a pool of some subset of other surveys from the total set of 65, would thus still be shaky evidence. Pooling across many surveys was the only solution. But it was obstructed, unless one were to give up the demand for identical indicators and make the assumption that different questions were *equivalent* indicators of a more abstract concept or "issue cluster."

Forced to pool on the basis of this assumption, they predicated it not merely on the inspection of the conceptual similarities of questions, but also

---

groups, thus yielding evidence on the degree to which a factor might have been a correlate of the differences found in the comparison of groups.

on empirical evidence as to the commonality of the items. And here one encounters the controversial and radical aspect of the design. In the normal instance, the empirical evidence of the equivalence of questions is established by having *pairs* of measures on the same set of *individuals,* and computing some measure of correlation, or association, or covariance. The measures are correlatable because each pair is obtained from one person. Pool did this where a given survey contained several indicators measuring a sample of the same individuals, but it could not carry him very far toward establishing the equivalence of many indicators from different surveys of samples of different individuals. There appears to be no continuity of units (certainly not the same individual units) to link the measures into correlatable pairs. However, by regarding the sub*groups* as units, there was a continuity across different surveys, and Pool had a basis for pairing the measures and establishing their equivalence. In effect, the correlations are computed for a set of groups (the 15 macrogroups), rather than a set of individuals.

Pool remarks, "survey researchers are apt to find this innovation disturbing," but certainly we are all familiar with instances where the unit of correlation is not an individual. For example, in ecological correlations the units are a set of areas, each comprising many individuals. The implication of this cross-survey approach to equivalence, the exact meaning of the correlations obtained for groups, is a subtle matter which must be handled cautiously, but it opens up new possibilities for the secondary analysis of refined multidimensional groupings and for comprehensive characterization based on many surveys. The methodological problems remain to be explored and examined in detail. It should not be rejected because of its unfamiliarity, but neither should it be accepted uncritically. Within our survey of users of the archives, one analyst's experience in applying the procedure was unsatisfactory, but another investigator, with work still in progress, so far finds the method satisfactory.[98]

One brute fact will surely operate to reduce the enthusiasm of many secondary analysts for the design, even though it becomes well grounded methodologically. Although the unit cost of obtaining a single survey is low, and an infinitesimal fraction of the cost of conducting a new survey, the total

---

[98] John B. Williamson, personal communication; Thomas Pettigrew, personal communication. In work growing out of Don Campbell's paper on the multitrait, multimethod matrix, Rees and Paisley, pursuing the implications, argue in favor of just such correlations of independent data sets. The continuity of unit for the pairing of observations is provided whenever two populations can be "profiled" or divided into equivalent groups on the basis of demographic attributes. Matilda B. Rees and William J. Paisley, "The Convergent-Discriminant Matrix: Multitrait-Multimethod Logic Extended to Other Research Directions," July, 1968, Stanford University, mimeo.

costs of obtaining the data from as many as 50 surveys would run into several thousands of dollars. And the computational procedures are elaborate enough to add another substantial cost. This is not a design for the poor secondary analyst.[99] He still has at his disposal eight other designs for the study of social groups, many of them most economical in operation. And he can study many problems other than social groups and their characteristics. We turn to some of these new realms of exploration.

---

[99] Pool is not explicit about the details by which the matrix of data, in this instance 480 cells by 52 issue clusters, is manipulated and the findings synthesized, but clearly very elaborate computer processing is required.

V

Studies of
Fundamental
Phenomena

SURVEYS HAVE ENUMERATED STATUS CHARACTERISTICS OF THE RESPONDENTS routinely and thereby provided a basis for comprehensive study of social categories and groups. So, too, surveys routinely have provided information on social, psychological, economic, and political patterns of thought and behavior. Some of these items of information also have become institutionalized parts of the face sheet; others are staple questions asked periodically in the body of the questionnaires of many agencies because of continuing or recurrent interest in a particular topic. Sometimes an underlying phenomenon must be abstracted from and traced by a series of questions on varied topics, each of which is the transient expression of the more fundamental variable. From these several sources, the prevalence and stability of fundamental phenomena can be established definitively because the many surveys in which they are contained are based on satisfactory samples of the nation and span long time periods. The variations in the phenomena can be traced back to their social determinants for sure, because of the luxuriant face sheet. But so, too, the consequences and interplay with other processes can often be traced because of the collateral information contained within the body of the survey.

This in no way should suggest that the secondary analyst should allow his attention to be monopolized by those face-sheet items and other questions which appear with monotonous regularity. As suggested in Chapter III, the sensitive investigator will see that an apparently trivial and exotic question which was asked only rarely may provide a strategic opportunity for study. Certainly, it is all the better if relevant surveys and questions are plentiful, but the unique opportunity should not be neglected. Consider these tasty tidbits that have appeared in a few rare surveys: a question on one's "first name"; a question on whether people can be trusted; questions on who Karl

Marx was, asked in England, Germany, and the U.S.; a question on whether man is descended from a monkey; a question as to whether the person feels that life is meaningless; a question on the nature of happiness; a question on whether there will always be poverty asked in the thirties and again in the sixties in the U.S.; the question "if you could be born again, would you rather be a man or a woman?"; a question on whether the person engages in hunting; a question on whether catastrophes are God's will; a question on whether men or women are more easily led astray.[1] Most of our illustrations will be of fundamental social patterns and processes that have been measured in many surveys, but these odd examples may alert investigators to the wider possibilities.

The designs and the technical problems and corresponding principles, understandably, are parallel to those already reviewed. The characterization of social groups implicates their attitudes and behavior. The study of attitudes and behavior, in turn, carries one back to their social location. There is thus an element of arbitrariness in whether a particular study belongs in our previous or our present discussion. Often, it belongs in both places, although the approach of the analyst tilts the problem one way or the other. An analyst may have a focus on a particular social group, and be quite loose and broad in the elements he brings into his characterization. Another analyst may focus on a specific social phenomenon and be loose and broad in tracing its social location. A third analyst may have a highly specific hypothesis which implicates one particular phenomenon and one particular social category, and indeed his study consists equally of both approaches. Thus it will not be necessary to present the full details of many studies, since, often, we will be on familiar methodological ground. We shall try to emphasize the new, but inevitably, given the overlap and intertwining of subject matter, there may be some repetition of the previous chapter, and even some overlap with future chapters.

We shall use some broad and simple headings to bring some order to the discussion of a vast array of phenomena. Some of the illustrative studies do not fall readily into one particular category, because of their complexity, and the classification itself is not intended as refined or definitive, but only as a convenient framework for the discussion.

We begin with a realm that provides a bridge between the topics of the last chapter and the phenomena to be treated in this chapter.

---

[1] Those who ask what's in a name are referred to Alice S. Rossi, "Naming Children in Middle Class Families," *Amer. Sociol. Rev.*, **30**, 1965, pp. 499–513. For a summary of periodic questions in the realm of moral conduct and belief which seem to have been generally neglected by secondary analysts, see Hazel G. Erskine, "The Polls: Morality" *Publ. Opin. Quart.*, **30**, 1966, pp. 669–680.

Affiliation and Identification with Groups

The preceding chapter focused on social categories—groupings in which membership or nonmembership is determined simply by the presence or absence of a particular status, whether racial, regional, rural-urban or socioeconomic. But, as noted earlier, a social group can be defined in a more stringent way, for example, to refer to a number of individuals who interact with each other rather than to a sheer statistical aggregate of people of a common status, or to individuals who identify themselves as members of a group rather than merely those who have been classified within a social category on some external basis. Earlier, we stressed that membership groups and reference groups in the strict sense could also be studied by secondary analysis. We turn now to some illustrative studies. These will underscore the fact that social groups, in the multitudinous senses of the term, are a major focus for secondary analysis.

VOLUNTARY ASSOCIATION MEMBERSHIP

Social scientists have long been interested in the phenomenon of individuals joining together in voluntary association for the collective pursuit of some goal or interest. There are other kinds of groups, but surely this is one important type. Many assertions about the phenomenon—its frequency in different societies, its social correlates, and its functions or consequences—can be found in the literature stretching far back in time to such classic writers as Tocqueville or Dicey and on up into the present. Despite this old and enduring concern, the only empirical evidence on the magnitude and distribution of association membership in the American population up until the mid-fifties was based on studies of specific local communities or areas, often inadequately sampled. Considering the interest in the phenomenon, it is paradoxical that no one had made it the primary focus of a special, national survey. And considering the hypothesized diverse effects of membership, it is also surprising that a measure of the variable had not been obtained frequently or routinely for the purposes of analyzing many surveys on a variety of topics. Fortunately, it had not been completely ignored and that was sufficient to begin to remedy the deficiency. By a secondary analysis of two NORC surveys conducted in the fifties on national probability samples, Wright and Hyman presented estimates of the prevalence of voluntary association membership in the adult American population and its social correlates and functions.[2]

---

[2] Wright and Hyman, *op. cit.* Arnold Rose by a secondary analysis of a French national survey for 1951 provided similar information for that country. See his *Theory and*

The study combined several designs. At its heart was design 3, *Internal replication*, achieved by the parallel analyses of a national survey from 1953 of some 2800 adults and another national survey from 1955 of some 2400 adults, supplemented by three NORC surveys of large probability samples of the adult populations of three communities of different sizes and geographical locations. All of these surveys had asked one or two questions on voluntary association membership. In testing the relationship between socioeconomic status and membership, perhaps the most central proposition in the literature on the phenomenon, they employed design 5: *intrasurvey replication* via multiple indicators. Since the face sheets of surveys routinely include many such measures, the tests were replicated using some five different indicators of status, such as income, occupation, and education. Finally, in appraising the error in tests of other correlates of membership, the size of the *residual categories* of persons whose status was indeterminate was presented in accordance with the specific principle and procedure previously emphasized. For example, persons whose race or religion had not been ascertained were examined and their numbers reported. The error factor surrounding such findings could thus be evaluated as negligible.

Various kinds of errors that might affect the measurement of the *correlates* of membership were therefore appraised. The sampling errors and other sources of unreliability that might affect the measurement of membership were taken into account both by the design of the samples and the replication of the tests over the two national surveys. But certainly the validity of the findings or possible biases in the estimates of membership must be appraised in terms of the specific questions used to measure voluntary association membership. In this connection it should be stressed that the two na-

---

Method in the Social Sciences (Minneapolis: University of Minnesota Press, 1954), p. 74. Findings on the prevalence and social distribution of voluntary association membership, and also on its functions, implicitly serve an important methodological purpose. In such notable studies as *The Authoritarian Personality* and the early Kinsey reports, the samples of individuals were drawn through the vehicle of organizations which provided convenient clusters of respondents of various characteristics who were among their members. The bias in using such sources as sampling frames for inquiry can be inferred from the evidence on how rare such membership is and how peculiar is its social distribution, and also from evidence on the functions of such associations in producing individuals who differ in knowledge, activism, opinionation, and ideology. In order to evaluate the probable bias in the sampling employed in *The Authoritarian Personality*, Hyman and Sheatsley had actually reported a brief semisecondary analysis of the phenomenon of voluntary association membership based on a 1947 NORC survey, but had not labelled it explicitly as such a study. See Herbert H. Hyman and Paul B. Sheatsley, "The Authoritarian Personality—A Methodological Critique," in Richard Christie and Marie Jahoda, eds., *Studies in the Scope and Method of "The Authoritarian Personality,"* (New York: Free Press, 1954), p. 62.

tional surveys were replicas of each other in sample design, in the survey agency involved, and correspondingly in the modes of interviewing and the composition of field staff and its allocation to particular classes of respondents, in the location of the question on membership in the sequence of questioning and in a surrounding context of topics unrelated to the phenomenon, and in the way the face-sheet measures of social correlates were enumerated and coded. The two surveys, however, did *not* replicate the *question* itself, but varied it. Through accident, a kind of multiple operationism characterized the range of measurement instruments in the two surveys and the supplementary local surveys. And this was a stroke of good fortune, since one could establish how much the aggregate and subgroup findings depended on the type of questions used—open-ended versus a card question suggesting various types of associations, a question which enumerated the memberships of the family unit versus the memberships of the respondent himself.

These variations in instrumentation become all the more important as one realizes the ambiguity surrounding the very concept of a "voluntary association." In the one national survey, the question was so structured as to include union membership; in the other survey, union membership was excluded. It is a moot point whether unions should be classified as *voluntary* associations. Whatever the proper verdict may be, the analysts could fit data appropriate to each concept posited, on the basis of the several surveys available.

The uncertainty that might surround any one set of empirical results on a fundamental, but somewhat ambiguous, phenomenon was thus given boundaries by the replicative features built internally into the design—by the several surveys and, within them, by the multiple indicators, and by the multiple operational approach to the definition and measurement of the dependent variable. The uncertainty became even more precisely bounded by subsequent *external* replications. Hausknecht drew upon a Gallup survey conducted in 1954 on a national sample. His secondary analysis of the data, yielded by a third and somewhat different measurement procedure, could be compared with the 1953 and 1955 NORC findings.[3] Two other secondary analyses subsequently appeared and provided evidence from surveys in the years 1952 and 1957, thus serving to reduce the uncertainty in the findings still further.[4]

---

[3] Murray Hausknecht, *The Joiners* (New York: Bedminster Press, 1962).

[4] Robert Lane, *Political Life* (New York: Free Press, 1959), p. 78. These data, which reveal a much higher estimate of membership than either the NORC or Gallup findings, are sometimes cited to suggest the capriciousness of the estimates and their susceptibility to measurement error. It should be noted that the survey employed involved a small subsample of 585 respondents interviewed as part of an immediate post-election survey in November, 1952. In addition, the instrument was a card question which listed a

The findings, by virtue of their generality and rarity and the high interest in the phenomenon, have continued to be cited by many scholars over the years. With the passage of time, however, those who had to rely on the old evidence were forced to make a giant leap inferentially from the data of the early fifties to the facts about America as it approached and entered the seventies. There might be good grounds for speculating that the phenomenon's prevalence and its social patterning, have remained stable, and one might also invoke the empirical evidence of the several surveys analyzed. But those several surveys, although spaced in time, all date back to what is a narrow and perhaps a bygone period, and the hypothesis that the phenomenon has changed is also plausible. We shall not spin out speculation about social change here, since that is the subject of Chapter VI. We aim only to show the way in which a chain of external replications can be forged by *successive secondary* analyses, and to describe the principles and procedures that are critical.[5]

In 1969, Wright and Hyman began a search for appropriate national surveys which, by secondary analysis, could serve to update the 1953–1955 findings. Thus the inferential leap that scholars would have to take for their current assertions would be shortened; and, depending on what stability the replications revealed, confidence in drawing conclusions would be bolstered or qualified. The more recent the surveys, the shorter the leap, of course. But other desiderata also guided the search. Whereas variation in the procedures or instruments employed over a series of *closely spaced* surveys generally yields clear evidence on reliability of measurement and error, such variation in surveys widely spaced in time creates obscurity. The real change in the phenomenon and its patterning which results from the long passage of time, is confounded with the changes produced by the different procedures. Contemporaneity might have to be sacrificed for comparability between the old

---

whole series of types of associations and examples thereby aiding recall. Reference should also be made to the fact that labor unions are counted, in contrast with the 1955 NORC survey. If the results were rescored to eliminate those whose membership is exclusively in a union, the prevalence of membership would drop by a considerable amount. From one of the same surveys he had already employed for his other secondary analyses, Lazerwitz reported estimates of voluntary association membership for a national sample in 1957, and the relationship to religion and residential location. See Bernard Lazerwitz, "National Data on Participation Rates Among Residential Belts in the United States," *Amer. Sociol. Rev.,* **27**, 1962, pp. 691–696.

[5] For an excellent treatment of the methodological issues in such widely spaced replications and the fruitfulness of the approach, see O. D. Duncan, *Toward Social Reporting: Next Steps* (New York: Russell Sage Foundation, 1969). Duncan urges that *primary* surveys be undertaken which replicate old and available baselines, a strategy that we have alluded to in our discussion of semisecondary analysis, but the technical issues are the same.

and the new surveys and the clarity of conclusion that would follow. If one could also find *several recent, closely spaced* surveys to serve as internal replications to test unreliability and measurement errors, that would be ideal.

The search yielded only six national surveys, conducted in the years from 1958 to 1967, that seemed appropriate. Two of these fortunately were ideal and carried the main weight of the analysis. Two others, which were less appropriate for the design that took shape could provide supplementary evidence to piece out the trend and the analysis of social correlates.[6]

A NORC survey conducted in 1962 provided unambiguous evidence on stability or change in the seven-year period from 1955, since it replicated that earlier inquiry in sample design, general field procedures, question wording, context within the larger questionnaire, and the enumeration and coding of the correlative social characteristics. Another NORC survey conducted in 1958 was different in approach from the 1962 survey and, of course, was four years away in time from 1962. But fortunately it provided unambiguous evidence on the changes in the five-year period from 1953, since it replicated that earlier inquiry in all essential respects.[7] Wright and Hyman had luckily drawn a nice hand from all the decks, having *two pairs* of surveys, thus "internally" replicating within the recent study the test of long-term change. Two other NORC national surveys conducted in 1960 and 1967 added other links to the chain, but provided only approximate evidence difficult to appraise because of elements of incomparability.[8] Perhaps the best way to describe this nest of designs is as two external replications at once, and thus also an internal replication.

---

[6] H. Hyman and C. R. Wright, "Trends in Voluntary Association Memberships of American Adults: Replication Based on Secondary Analysis of National Sample Surveys," *Amer. Sociol. Rev.,* **71,** April, 1970, pp. 191–206.

[7] To insure comparability, the recent surveys had to be truncated since the universe included individuals 18–21 who had to be eliminated from the estimates. These individuals had not been coded separately, but the existence and accessibility of the original questionnaires meant they could be sorted out manually and their corresponding cards removed from the deck before tabulation. A number of other ambiguities arose from the coding of the recent surveys, but since the original questionnaires were available, they could also be checked and resolved. One element of comparability deserves special note. Given the special interest in Negro–white differentials in membership, and changes in this respect over time, it was important that comparability in the assignment of Negro interviewers to respondents be maintained, and fortunately the NORC practice in this respect was long established and stable over the span of time. The tests that were made appeared to indicate there were no obvious biases in the sampling of the Negro stratum and that the estimates of change were based on comparable groups.

[8] The 1960 data came from the American survey which had been conducted as part of the five-country cross-national inquiry by Almond and Verba on *The Civic Culture.* As previously noted, this simply adds to the multiple births it already produced and shows the

SUBJECTIVE CLASS IDENTIFICATION

Our first example dealt with social groups in the sense of the individual's actual *membership* and showed how such a phenomenon could be studied by various secondary analytic designs. Ignoring the issue of errors of report and measurement, the phenomenon under study was objective in nature and referred to the voluntary interaction of individuals in a wide variety of organizations.[9] The example to be presented now deals by contrast with normative *reference* groups. An individual may define himself as part of a group or category, whether or not he is in fact a member, and thereby cast himself under the spell of its norms and remove himself psychologically from another sphere of group influence. Although the phenomenon under study is different in substance, we shall see that the same kinds of designs and principles of secondary analysis are applicable.

Eulau availed himself of the presidential election survey that had been conducted by the Survey Research Center in 1952 to examine the influence of class position as measured both by objective criteria and subjective identification.[10] The combined influence of a membership group and a reference group could be explored since such face-sheet items as occupation, income, and education had been enumerated and the respondents had also been asked whether they felt they belonged in the "middle class, lower class, working class or upper class." The effects of the reference group, when it coincided with or departed from the objective class position was explored for some seven different dependent variables in the domain of political behavior, since the original inquiry, naturally, was exceedingly rich in its coverage of that domain.

---

amazing fertility of some surveys for secondary analysis. The 1967 survey had been conducted as part of a new inquiry by Sidney Verba extending their previous work in comparative political behavior. At the beginning of 1970, these data, unlike the earlier Civic Culture materials, had not yet become available in the archives since they were still in primary analysis. Such a time lag is not uncommon and can be critical for secondary analysts of social change, especially when relevant surveys are so few as in this instance. Verba's courtesy in making the materials available to us in advance of publication is gratefully acknowledged.

[9] Membership, of course, may imply only a minimal level of interaction with others in the organization. However, the surveys which have incorporated a measure of voluntary association membership have generally added subquestions on the specific type of association, on holding office within the association, on attendance at its meetings, etc.

[10] Heinz Eulau, "Identification With Class and Political Role Behavior," *Publ. Opin. Quart.*, **20**, 1956, pp. 515–529. The study may be somewhat closer to a *semi*secondary rather than a pure secondary analysis. Eulau conducted the research during a period of residence at the Survey Research Center, and thus had close proximity to the original materials and was in propinquity with the original analysts, the obvious benefits of a semisecondary analyst accruing to him as a result.

At this stage of his studies, Eulau basically employed Design I, the analysis of a *single* survey, but because of the rich resources it contained, design 5, the use of multiple indicators within that survey to replicate the tests and explore certain particularly interesting facets of his theory, was also employed. It should be noted that the sample was radically truncated. Eulau eliminated almost a third of the respondents whose objective class position was ambiguous, e.g., farmers and housewives, or whose subjective class identification was other than "middle" or "working" class. Then, on the basis of the subjective class and an index combining the several socioeconomic indicators, the remaining respondents were classified into four groups, those whose membership and reference group was consistently working class or middle class and those who had affiliated themselves with these respective classes even though their objective position did not entitle them to such membership.

Eulau might have regarded all seven dependent variables as replicated tests of the same basic hypothesis, but instead he introduced a sharp distinction between *behavioral* and *attitudinal* variables, arguing that the taking on of a *non*membership reference group might be sufficient for adopting and exhibiting the *normative attitudinal* pattern of the group, but that interaction and experience within the group was essential to build up the capacity to *perform* in accordance with its norms. To be sure, in each of the subdomains, the tests were replicated over a series of specific indicators, some of which were based on single questions and others measured by indexes which had pooled information from several questions, for example, the well-known Michigan scales of "citizen duty" and "political efficacy."

The results of the secondary analysis were consonant with his theory, but there was one inherent limitation. All the findings referred to 1952, and might well be bound to that narrow point in time. Considerable evidence now exists that the polarization of classes in America has varied over the very time interval, 1944–1956, within which this 1952 survey was contained.[11] Objective class interests might be more or less implicated by the economic circumstances at the time-point of the study, and class identification or actual mem-

---

[11] Philip E. Converse, "The Shifting Role of Class in Political Attitudes and Behavior," in Eleanor E. Maccoby, Theodore M. Newcomb, and Eugene L. Hartley, eds., *Readings in Social Psychology* (New York: Holt, 1958), pp. 388–399. To be sure, some of the dependent variables were based on questions which had a broader temporal reference, or no apparent time reference at all and were thus somewhat less time bound. For example one behavioral index asked about regularity of voting in all the elections since the respondent had reached his majority. Items in the scales were couched in terms of the long-term sense of efficacy and duty. But nevertheless, these may well have some connection to current experience, and other items clearly referred to the specific context of 1952.

bership might well become more or less salient depending on the blandness of the particular political campaign and the candidates involved.

Eulau was sensitive to these problems and was able to test the stability of his findings by a subsequent *external* replication which became possible when the Michigan Survey in the 1956 election became available to him.[12] The sample design, the general field procedures, and the survey organization were comparable over the two surveys and in these respects the replication is exact. Again, as in the previous instance, by radical truncation, over one-quarter of the cases were eliminated because of ambiguity as to their class position, but the residual samples employed in the two surveys may be regarded as comparable. There were some minor changes in the questions and the corresponding indices used to measure objective position and subjective class, which Eulau describes and discounts, but the measures of the dependent variables were comparable. The 1956 replication confirmed the earlier findings and thus strengthens the generality of the conclusions. To be sure, one may still regard these two elections as having something in common, and the title Eulau chooses for his work does caution us that he deals with the "Eisenhower Years." He himself only forged two links in the chain of external replications, but there is no reason why other links could not be added by external replications based on surveys in the years since Eisenhower.

Some Brief Examples of Other Patterns and Processes Studied by Secondary Analysis

We cannot possibly treat in detail all the phenomena that have been studied by secondary analysis, and it would be retracing already familiar ground with respect to designs and principles for analysis. The case studies just presented served to illustrate *external* replication, a most valuable design that might otherwise be slighted. At this point we shall list briefly some of the varied phenomena that have been studied, simply to expand and sharpen the awareness of the reader. We shall then select a few for more detailed review, either to illustrate new designs and principles or procedures, or because they appear fundamental in nature and especially fruitful areas for secondary analysis.

Social Mobility. Our case study of "The Protestant Ethic" makes it clear that data on intergenerational mobility are available in sufficient amount in

---

[12] Heinz Eulau, *Class and Party in the Eisenhower Years* (New York: Free Press, 1962).

past surveys to warrant secondary analysis. A variety of investigators have exploited such materials, not only to study differences between religious groups, but also to estimate the general magnitude of the phenomenon in particular societies, trends over time, and various social determinants of the phenomenon, and to test hypothesized attitudinal and behavioral consequences that may follow upon mobility. By way of illustration, two secondary analysts have studied the effects of mobility on voluntary association membership, using sample surveys of particular American communities. A secondary analysis of a local survey examined the effects of mobility on various dimensions of prejudice, introducing into the relationship the additional specifying variable, the reference group or subjective class of the mobile person. Many determinants and consequences of mobility have been explored by Lipset and Bendix, using surveys from a range of industrial countries.[13]

Religious Behavior. In our discussion of studies of religious affiliation, we noted that investigators generally used the face-sheet question on religious preference or identification as the operational definition of the concept, even though additional questions on church *attendance* were generally also available. Such information, as we noted in Chapter IV, has not been neglected and has been used for a number of secondary analyses of religious behavior. Over many years, questions on religious beliefs have been asked in surveys in the United States and elsewhere, and these also have been exploited for occasional secondary analyses.[14] Such studies and the technical problems of error were reviewed earlier.

---

[13] Richard F. Curtis, "Occupational Mobility and Membership in Formal Voluntary Associations: A Note on Research," *Amer. Sociol. Rev.*, **24**, 1959, pp. 846–848; D. J. Vorwaller, "Consequences of Social Mobility: An Analysis of the Additive Effects of Social Class Statuses of Origin and Destination," unpublished Ph.D. dissertation, University of Michigan, 1967. For a briefer account see D. J. Vorwaller, "Social Mobility and Membership in Voluntary Associations," *Amer. J. Sociol.*, **75**, 1970, pp. 481–495. Seymour Martin Lipset and Reinhard Bendix, *Social Mobility in Industrial Society* (Berkeley: University of California Press, 1959); Joseph Greenblum and Leonard I. Pearlin, "Vertical Mobility and Prejudice: A Socio-Psychological Analysis," in Reinhard Bendix and Seymour Martin Lipset, eds., *Class, Status, and Power* (New York: Free Press, 1953), pp. 480–491. See also Abramson and Books, *op. cit.*

[14] See Lazerwitz, *op. cit.*, for data on America: Hamilton, *op. cit.*, for French data; Argyle, *op. cit.*, for English and American data; for another analysis of French data on religious behavior and belief and comparisons with other countries, see Russell E. Planck, "Public Opinion in France After the Liberation, 1944–1949," in Mirra Komarovsky, ed., *Common Frontiers of the Social Sciences* (New York: Free Press, 1957), pp. 217–226; Erskine, *op. cit.*, for a convenient summary of aggregate and subgroup estimates over time for America. See Demerath, *op. cit.*, and our Chapter IV, on the error problems. Questions on knowledge of various facts about Christianity have also been asked occasionally but seem to have been neglected by secondary analysts.

Voting Behavior.   In light of the history of survey research in the United States and elsewhere, it is evident that voting behavior has been a major focus of inquiry, and correspondingly, the secondary analyst has fallen heir to a great deal of data on this fundamental phenomenon from many different elections and countries. Some of our case studies have already demonstrated the products. There is an obvious paradox. Why would there be any need for *secondary* analysis? The potentialities of the data should have been realized already by the primary analysts. In fact, the nature of the enterprise has been such that the goals of the primary investigators have often been realized once they presented their predictions of the outcome of the particular election and some basic brief descriptive findings and breakdowns by social categories. The richness of the materials rarely has been exhausted by the problems that were the focus of the primary analysts.

To be sure, in the more scholarly sector within the total enterprise, the goals of the primary analysts have been the thorough and comprehensive treatment of voting behavior and related political phenomena, leaving less in the way of free dividends for secondary analysts. But even their findings can be enlarged upon by secondary analysts who can conduct replications for other times and places. And these inquiries are so rich that they admit of new and neglected focii. Sometimes an untouched problem can be formulated and studied by the simple rearrangement and combination of variables. By way of illustration, it is hard to think of a more elaborate analysis than that conducted under the program of electoral research of the Survey Research Center. Early in the course of that program, a scale of "citizen duty" and another of "political efficacy" were developed to tap two major dimensions of political roles, and these figured strongly in the analysis of the 1952 study. Eulau and Schneider simply combined the information from the two scales into a more comprehensive superscale of "political involvement," which classified *individuals jointly* in terms of whether they had internalized the role of the dutiful citizen and also evaluated that role as efficacious. This procedure was then applied to a truncated sample from the 1952 inquiry. Their secondary analysis of the double-faceted role, its social determinants and effects, may be regarded as different from the primary, but discrete, analyses of each of the original scales.[15]

---

[15] Heinz Eulau and Peter Schneider, "Dimensions of Political Involvement," *Publ. Opin. Quart.*, **20**, 1956, pp. 128–142. It should be noted that the procedure they followed was to pool the information so as to produce a *scale score* which located the individual on the new dimension, and that they ignored the particular typology or pattern that yielded the new score. For example, an individual with a high sense of efficacy and a low sense of duty seems to be a very different moral type from an individual with a low sense of efficacy who is nevertheless impelled by a high sense of duty. Yet these typological dif-

A secondary analysis of the Michigan surveys by Segal illustrates another avenue to a new product. He pooled their election surveys over the years 1952 to 1964, thereby transcending the particularities of specific elections and accumulating enough cases (over 5500) to examine by a multivariate computer program the social-structural bases of party support. Thus he was able to allocate that support among various multidimensional social groups, classified in terms of the combinations of some six conventional social characteristics. From the multidimensional treatment and the multiple surveys employed, he produced something not contained within the analysis of the discrete social characteristic and discrete surveys.[16]

That untapped information within the single political survey or emergent product from multiplying or combining several such surveys can lead to new secondary analysis is illustrated by Bonham's study of *The Middle Class Vote* in England. By pooling the four surveys the British Gallup Poll had conducted during the 1950 election, and then building a separate pool from the four surveys conducted during the 1951 election, Bonham captured enough cases to refine the gross category, middle class, into nine occupational groups each of which was represented by a substantial number of cases, and to examine their party preferences and voting behavior in a series of elections. It should be stressed that the design involved not only pooling, but also internal *replication*, since the analysis is conducted separately for each election. Since the samples in the 1950 and 1951 surveys were asked retrospectively about previous voting, the replication, in a sense, is extended to cover a third election, that of 1945, and the analysis of the 1950 election is itself duplicated by comparing the contemporary report from the 1950 sample with the retrospective report about 1950 obtained from the 1951 sample.[17]

---

ferences are submerged in the analysis, and both are given the same scale score on "relatedness." Still another secondary analysis could be spawned by this more typological mode of approach.

[16] David R. Segal, "Social Structural Bases of Political Partisanship in West Germany and the United States," in Wm. J. Crotty, ed., *Public Opinion and Politics* (New York: Holt, 1970), pp. 216–235. I omit from the present discussion the parallel cross-national analysis based on a pooled sample of almost ten thousand German cases. There is, of course, a subtle question raised by this case which will present itself more and more in the era of computer programs of multivariate analysis. Obviously, any investigator can feed the same survey that was previously treated by primary analysts into his computer, and study the very same problem previously studied, only applying a more elegant or sophisticated mode of statistical manipulation of the data. We shall classify such studies as simply "reanalyses." In the instance of the Segal study, however, it appears to be secondary analysis by virtue of the pooling of surveys from several periods and several countries.

[17] John Bonham, *The Middle Class Vote* (London: Faber and Faber, 1954). The monograph illustrates a number of the basic problems and procedures of secondary analysis.

Game Playing and Gambling Behavior. From three different American surveys prior to 1948, a team of investigators replicated a secondary analysis of the social correlates of participation in games of chance, strategy, or skill. This, by inference, gave support to various hypotheses about the socialization processes that lead to such behaviors. By contrast, Tec focused her entire secondary analysis on gambling behavior—participation in (whatever the bettors may think) purely a game of chance, drawing upon 1954 national survey data from Sweden on Betting Pools.[18] Extensions of these lines of secondary analysis to more recent data and to surveys from other societies, for example, England and Italy, are feasible. As a source of evidence on matters of social policy and legislation and on social-psychological theories about the determinants and functions of such behavior, survey materials appear to have been generally neglected.

Communication Behavior. The size of the audience for various classes of media—newspapers, radio, television, etc.—and for specific media within these classes, and the social composition of these audiences have, understandably, been major concerns of commercial survey research for many years. These data rarely find their way into scholarly analyses, although Knupfer drew some of the features of the "Portrait of the Underdog" from such

---

The sample was truncated to omit respondents whose occupations clearly were not within the middle classes. But there were acute problems of classifying such ambiguous individuals as the retired, the unemployed, housewives, and those in certain marginal occupations. These were not eliminated but allocated on the basis of various assumptions. The reliability of the findings was further checked by comparing the four surveys in the given year, before pooling them. Corrections for errors in reporting voting preference were introduced also, the magnitude being inferred from comparisons with the voting returns. Without stretching the concept too much, one may describe one of the early publications of the Michigan studies as a "semisecondary" analysis. The analysis of the group differences in voting behavior in the 1954 Congressional elections were replicated by going back to the 1948 and 1952 election surveys they had previously conducted, thereby observing whether the differences were enduring or varied with transient factors. See Angus Campbell and Homer C. Cooper, *Group Differences in Attitudes and Votes* (Ann Arbor: Survey Research Center, 1956).

[18] Brian Sutton-Smith, John M. Roberts, and Robert M. Kozelka, "Game Involvement in Adults," *J. Soc. Psychol.*, **60**, 1963, pp. 15–30; Nechama Tec, *Gambling in Sweden* (Totowa, N.J.: Bedminster Press, 1964). Skimming a few of the general sources in the literature will reveal how little evidence has been systematized on the participants in such behaviors and how much psychoanalytic, psychological, anthropological, economic, and other forms of theorizing has been indulged in. See for example the article on "Gambling" in the *International Encyclopedia of the Social Sciences*, or a special number of the *Annals* (May, 1950), or Eric Larabee and Rolf Meyersohn, *Mass Leisure* (Free Press, 1958), or the chapter by Philip Ennis "Leisure" in Sheldon and Moore's *Indicators of Social Change* (Russell Sage, 1968).

sources. Questions on the sheer *exposure* to different classes of media have also been incorporated into many noncommercial surveys for general analytic purposes; occasionally questions are included on the *uses* individuals make of the media to obtain specific types of information—local, national, political, scientific, medical, etc.; and occasionally entire surveys have focused on the problem of public knowledge and its varied sources including the media and other forms of communication. This broad range of materials has been exploited, but only rarely, by secondary analysts. Such studies, of course, are analyses of the problem of *knowledge or ignorance,* its functions, and its patterning among social groups, as much as they are analyses of communication behavior. Since the questions have also been repeated over time, the secondary analyses sometimes focus on trends in such behavior and they belong equally well in our next chapter on secondary analysis of social change.

The primary analyses of the original studies often have been thorough. Nevertheless, there is room for secondary analysis. From the combination of surveys, each of which mapped only one smaller region of communication behavior, the larger domain can be mapped by the secondary analyst and the specificity or generality of behavior can be established. From the examination of surveys over time, the persistence or change in communication behavior can be established by secondary analysis. For example, Wade and Schramm replicated their analyses of the uses of different media for political information by various social groups, drawing upon the four national studies the Survey Research Center had conducted in the presidential elections of 1952 to 1964. Drawing upon two other national surveys, they also examined the media as sources of public knowledge of health and science information.[19] These analyses demonstrate how much error can occur if one does not interpret a question or indicator precisely. The findings on a particular medium vary with the type of information the public is seeking and have changed over time, and they also depend on the exact metric of the question, whether the person is asked about use per se, frequency of use, trust in the source, etc.

---

[19] Serena Wade and Wilbur Schramm, "The Mass Media as Sources of Public Affairs, Science, and Health Knowledge," *Publ. Opin. Quart.,* **33,** 1969, pp. 197–209. For a more detailed account see the monograph, Wilbur Schramm, *et al., Knowledge and the Public Mind* (Stanford: Institute for Communication Research, 1967). Such studies are, of course, not limited to the United States or to the more developed countries. If anything, secondary analyses of surveys of communication behavior in transitional societies may be especially critical and establish a different internal patterning of the domain and a greater potency of media exposure in producing changes in value systems. For such a secondary analysis of a Costa Rican survey, see F. B. Waisanen and J. T. Durlak, "Mass Media Use, Information Source Evaluation, and Perceptions of Self and Nation," *Publ. Opin. Quart.,* **31,** 1967, pp. 399–406.

McCombs and Wilcox, by an independent secondary analysis of some of the very same surveys, plus some additional surveys, document the same dangers of error in overgeneralizing the meaning of a specific indicator, and also reveal another type of error that might be perpetrated by the thoughtless analyst of *changes* in communication behavior.[20] In the years under study, television was born and has since grown to saturate American households, whereas the supply of other media has been stable. In interpreting the changes in the use of media, the authors suggest that the relative reliance on TV versus other media must be expressed not in absolute terms, but in ratio to its availability to the population. In order to avoid erroneous conclusions, the rate of use must be refined or standardized in terms of opportunity.

Occasional panel studies spaced before and after the occurrence of particular events such as political or information campaigns may sometimes approximate in design a true field experiment which could provide a test of the effect of a stream of communication on a large group or sample of individuals. To be sure, the design of proof is a very elusive problem, and there are all sorts of difficulties in controlling or estimating extraneous variables, such as the influence of repeated testing, sensitization from the pre-test, stimuli which have intruded other than the one isolated for study, and—depending on the interval—maturation or natural processes of growth and change. The secondary analyst might well be cautious and conceive of these panel surveys as *quasi*-experimental designs, but he should not ignore the opportunities.

These brief examples will suggest some of the many possibilities for secondary analyses. We turn now to the detailed review of one important, broad class of phenomena which will also illustrate several new designs.

Fundamental Dispositions—Beliefs, Attitudes, Cognitions, Language, Thought, and Knowledge

It has been the very nature of the enterprise that public opinion polling has focused on the topical issue, the current event, the reaction of the moment. Over the years, myriad responses of the public to every imaginable occurrence—imminent event, impending policy, immediate situation, or notable

---

[20] Maxwell McCombs and Walter Wilcox, "Media Use in Presidential Election Campaigns," *News Research Bulletin*, American Newspaper Publishers Association, No. 14, June 21, 1967.

personage—have been collected. Literally a mountain of data on man's dispositions toward the flux of life, and on his quotidian thoughts and feelings, await the secondary analyst. Yet who but the surveyor who collected the information would bother himself to remember some of the findings in their narrow, specific, and concrete form? Who but the most omnivorous historian would care about the exact responses to some particular issues that are now long gone and thus seem to be the trivia of the past.

Alas, who cares any longer about the awareness and feelings the public exhibited in 1946 about Henry Wallace's criticism at that point of American foreign policy toward Russia? Who cares now how many individuals then approved our sending arms to Argentina in 1946? Who cares now how many people believed back then that the Greek government of 1947 was in danger of being overthrown by Communists? Or how many in 1957 knew who Nehru was? Who cares, for that matter, how many Americans went to church on a certain Sunday in 1939? Or what proportion of American adults in 1954 knew who ruled Jerusalem in the time of Jesus? These concrete data fade into insignificance with the passage of time, and there are thousands more such bits of information stored in the memory of the machine. To be sure, there are periodic questions that are pointed toward matters of specificity and yet of great importance—questions about war or peace, poverty, crime, child rearing, etc. These shining examples should not be forgotten, but thousands of other questions seem only to clutter our minds. Nevertheless, the secondary analyst may and should revive them in human memory if he can somehow elevate the concrete data to greater significance. By an act of abstraction or conceptualization and some corresponding designs and empirical procedures, he can sometimes use such items effectively as indicators of more general and enduring psychological dispositions toward classes of objects, toward persistent features of experience, toward social or political institutions; as expressive of fundamental phenomena of a cognitive or intellective nature; or as indicative of more fundamental psychological traits or even of larger constellations and the structure of personality. Our omnibus heading is intended to cover secondary analyses of this very broad and promising sphere of inquiry into a range of basic inner states and processes that underlie and regulate behavior.

Such analyses perhaps come too easily to some. Analysts are always conceptualizing or abstracting. Some are virtuosos in performing tricks of drawing the general out of the specific, capturing the latent meaning underneath the manifest, translating the concrete into the abstract. Some constraints must be applied to such an analyst to prevent arbitrariness and to give him the warrant to ignore the transient situational determinants of the response or the specific referent in the question or the conditions of measurement that affect the reliability and meaning of the datum. As suggested in the examples of communication behavior, overgeneralizing the meaning of a specific indicator or question on the use of a mass medium results in error. As one can imagine, the number of people who went to church on a particular sunny day in June, 1939, might reflect the weather as well as their religious values. Perhaps also their desire to appear in the ranks of the pious might affect the truthfulness of their reports.

To be sure, a particular question may have no temporal or concrete reference contained within the wording of it, and thus pertain to a more general state of the individual, but, even so, it may be afflicted by errors of measurement and reflect in part the temporary feelings of the individual. It is also true that an occasional analyst may extract findings of scientific worth from a question treated only in its concrete implications. By way of example, one scholar in our survey of users of archives was doing a secondary analysis of a time series of questions on overweight and dieting to study its significance for problems of nutrition and health.[21] But more often than not, the scientific worth lies in the abstract implications, and Back and his associates employed these very same questions in an attempt to penetrate the mysteries of

---

[21] Johanna Dwyer, personal communication. The face sheet often contains a *single* question which has been found over the years to provide a reliable enough measure of a given, fundamental phenomenon. Secondary analyses of such a simple datum can provide valuable information. But these instances are not exceptions to the argument in the text, since they do not relate to *dispositional* concepts but to phenomena that are in the nature of discrete experiences that have been hypothesized as powerful determinants of attitude and behavior. By way of illustration, the phenomenon or variable of the stage of the life cycle the person has reached, or his exposure to an incomplete family milieu, can be measured by one or a few simple face-sheet items. Depending on the analyst's concerns, such cases can be pooled across surveys or a replication or synthesizing design can be employed to trace the concomitants of the experience. But even in such instances, the inference can be treacherous, and there are multiple aspects implicated in the phenomenon itself. An illustration is provided by a secondary analysis by Scheuch of German surveys conducted during the years 1953–1956. It was an easy matter to classify mothers who had no husbands within the household and to introduce the control of income level, and then to contrast them with mothers in intact families. Many consequences were traced by synthesizing the data over many surveys. Yet, as he stresses, the incomplete families under study mainly represented, because of the era, father absence as a consequence of World War II casualties. And he hypothesizes that the meaning of such "socially acceptable" father absence might be very different from voluntary defections and breakdowns of the family, leading to correspondingly different consequences. He notes further that such broken families may be able to lean on the organized supports provided for war widows. Certainly, there is an obvious follow-up study in another era which would serve to tighten up the conclusions, but this secondary analysis vividly shows how much complexity may be masked by an apparently unambiguous measure of a phenomenon. See H. Treinen and E. Scheuch, "Deprived Families," in *Low Income Groups and Methods of Dealing with Their Problems* (Paris: OECD, 1965), pp. 191–249.

the concept of the "body-image" and beyond that the "self-regarding sentiment." The protection of such inferences inheres in the lavish supply of questions and measures available, and the designs and procedures that can thus be applied to obtain evidence at a high level of generality.[22]

Sometimes a *single* survey contains a battery of questions related to some domain. Then by procedures of scale or index construction, sometimes already accomplished by the primary analysts, the secondary analyst has in hand a proven measure of a disposition that has revealed itself in the pattern of answers of the respondents.[23] Then the simplest of our designs, 1: *the quantitative analysis of the single survey*, suffices to describe the broader phenomenon and trace its correlates and consequences. By way of illustration, the study by Eulau exploited two batteries of 4 items, each of which produced a Gutmann scale, all contained within a single survey, and thereby gave confidence that he was measuring the *system* of beliefs about the act of voting and about other political institutions of representation, rather than a specific discrete cognition.

---

[22] A secondary analysis of attitudes toward national security makes this point, and provides a cautionary note. Bobrow stresses the need to "reduce the 'buzz and confusion' of responses to numerous specific questions to a limited number of hypothetical dispositions . . . we look for dispositions which apply beyond the scope of particular survey items. . . . The answers to specific survey questions are thus primarily useful as *indicators* of these hypothetical dispositions. The fact that we need such structural knowledge, whether we call it a pattern or a hypothetical disposition or a factor . . . is indicated by the way all of us keep making implicit assumptions about underlying structure . . . . Much of the 'bird talk' now in vogue ('hawk,' 'dove') assumes such a pattern." By factor analyses of two surveys, each of which contained a very large battery of questions in the spheres of defense policies and international conflicts, he found a much less simple and somewhat different structure than would be expected. Davis B. Bobrow, "Organization of American National Security Opinions," *Publ. Opin. Quart.*, **33**, 1969, pp. 223–226.

[23] John P. Robinson and his associates at the Survey Research Center have compiled from the literature of academic studies and large-scale surveys three handbooks of scales and indices, each based on a series of questions of presumably homogeneous content, and then summarized the properties of the instrument and the evidence on its quality. The utility of this work, of course, goes far beyond secondary analysis, and provides the investigator who is beginning a primary survey with an array of instruments to choose from, whose utility has been established and for which some comparative norms are available. But the secondary analyst in search of a survey which contained measures of some fundamental disposition is blessed by such a gift. And careful study of these handbooks will comfort those who are worried about the quality of short batteries in survey research. The evidence on the regularity with which these instruments function, the obtained correlations and findings, all give confidence. See John P. Robinson *et al.*, *Measures of Political Attitudes; Measures of Occupational Attitudes and Occupational Characteristics; Measures of Social Psychological Attitudes* (Ann Arbor: Institute of Social Research, 1968–1969).

Sometimes the single survey yields too thin a supply of questions to measure a general disposition, but by combining surveys that are replicative or by some form of synthesizing related data across surveys, the analyst can establish regularities at the aggregate or subgroup level which transcend the specific moment, which are less vulnerable to criticisms of unreliability, and which reflect broad dispositions. Thus Greyser and Bauer remark that there are many commercial surveys which document reactions to specific advertisements, but they wanted to tap a more general disposition toward the institution of advertising, and most commercial surveys were not commensurate with this concept. A search of the Roper archives netted some nine relevant surveys extending from 1938 to 1964. By synthesizing the strands of data, they could draw conclusions about the stability of American attitudes toward the institution of advertising, and document a general acceptance and approval of the institution.[24]

Sometimes, the analyst is so fortunate as to have lavish resources of a series of questions with common content both within a single survey and across several surveys. Then it seems eminently reasonable to infer from the regularities observed that some fundamental dispositions are operative, since the only commonality is the thematic thread that runs throughout the diversity of measuring procedures, transient circumstances, and specific referents of the questions. To be sure, what remains obscure is the recognition of the *theme* itself, the nature of the latent disposition. Articulating or identifying the elusive entity that is the psychic cement for all the diverse bits and pieces can be a highly speculative venture, unless the analyst has some special kind of design to help him along. Some examples will suggest the opportunities, the difficulties, and some new designs.

IDEOLOGICAL PATTERNS OF ATTITUDE AND THOUGHT

Literally hundreds of questions have been asked of national samples over the years that may be regarded as specific instances of a liberal or conservative attitude on some particular political or economic issue.[25] With such resources,

---

[24] S. A. Greyser and R. A. Bauer, "Americans and Advertising: Thirty Years of Public Opinion," *Publ. Opin. Quart.*, **30**, 1966, pp. 69–78.

[25] Erskine's convenient 1964 summary indicated that almost 400 questions had been asked in the years 1935–1963. Apart from the handy reference tool she provides—the listing of each question by date and survey agency, the aggregate findings, some breakdowns and trends—her summaries of the rise and fall of interest in particular domains of inquiry, of which this is only one example, provide most interesting evidence on the discontinuities in research and may be regarded as contributions to the sociology of knowledge. In this instance, it is clear from her summary that the survey organizations showed a marked decline in interest in this ideological area after 1956. See Hazel G. Erskine, "The Polls: Some Gauges of Conservatism," *Publ. Opin. Quart.*, **28**, 1964, pp. 154–168.

analysts have examined the patterning of answers to a series of questions asked of individual respondents in a given survey, the patterning for subgroups over many surveys, and the stability or change in these patterns over time. Thus they have been able to draw inferences about fundamental ideologies, *systems of thought, belief, and attitude* that set broad directions for the individual's political behavior.

The early secondary analyses of G. H. Smith and the Allinsmiths, already reviewed in our discussion of religious groups in Chapter IV, had established that the total domain of politicoeconomic attitudes was not organized in terms of one master principle, one ideological system disposing toward liberalism or conservatism of every kind, but rather that there were at least *two* kinds of liberalism: one relating to the region of domestic *economic* attitudes, and the other to international attitudes and other *non*economic domestic issues such as civil liberties and tolerance. Individuals and social groups who were liberal on one of these dimensions were usually conservative or illiberal on the other dimension. Clearly, one could still argue for generalized dispositions in the politicoeconomic sphere, if not for any single all-encompassing disposition.

In a subsequent secondary analysis, Smith pooled two other large surveys from 1947, thereby netting some 6000 respondents for an *external replication* of his previous study. Each respondent was scored by appropriate questions on both internationalism and on domestic economic liberalism, and the earlier basic findings were confirmed, although some new and unexpected findings also emerged.[26]

Smith had employed rather simple quantitative techniques of analysis. By inspecting the way in which discrete attitudes occurred jointly or intercorrelated within individuals and subgroups, he inferred the organization of attitude. Using data from that same historical period, Williams and Wright

---

[26] Smith had reasoned that the generalized economic liberalism of the poor reflected their class interest and that their generalized illiberalism in other spheres simply reflected their lack of education and enlightenment, the normal accompaniment of their poor life chances. By contrast, the economic conservatism of the higher-status groups reflected their class interest, and their liberalism in the other sphere reflected their greater education and enlightenment. In his second analysis, he was able to put the theory to a direct test, since the surveys contained a battery of information questions by which he could score knowledge or enlightenment. As expected, enlightenment correlated with noneconomic liberalism within all classes. But in *all* classes, the more enlightened individuals were more conservative economically. His interpretation was that informed individuals of that era—even the poor—were more likely to believe that their class interests were best served by the status quo. In part this was functional, since Smith argued that poor, but knowledgeable, individuals were likely to be mobile and become successful. But he argued it also reflected the extra schooling they had received and the traditional values they had internalized in the process. G. H. Smith, "Liberalism and Level of Information," *J. Educ. Psychol.* **39**, 1948, 65–81.

applied more precise quantitative techniques of factor analysis to determine the structure or organization of attitudes. Their secondary analysis was based on the panel study that had been conducted during the 1948 election on a sample of about a thousand respondents in Elmira.[27] Factor analysis was applied to the matrix of intercorrelations from some 25 questions covering a wide range of attitudes toward domestic and foreign issues. Obviously, the end product is dependent on the contents of the items that enter into the analysis, but it is interesting to note that the findings give general confirmation to the conclusions that Smith had arrived at by less exact means.

Two major factors again emerged as the organizing principles for this realm. Factor I named "Threat Orientation," referred essentially to a pattern of liberalism and tolerance or illiberalism and intolerance toward minorities and deviants within the society, toward other nations and foreigners, and an optimistic and trusting view about the intentions of others and the threat of war. Factor II named "Group Identification," referred essentially to identification with a particular social class and political party and the corollary support of the kinds of domestic economic policies that would go with upper-class-Republican allegiances or the opposite allegiances. In their study, these two ideological dispositions were found to be *independent* of each other. Liberalism really was two dimensional.

This early secondary analysis of the substantive and theoretical problem of the nature of American ideology also had a *methodological* goal. At that time, most factor analyses of mental or attitudinal organization had been based on homogeneous groups of subjects, generally volunteers who were highly educated college students, tested under rather artificial conditions. The authors were concerned to see whether the structure of opinions derived from more natural measurements on samples of the heterogeneous adult population would be different, and whether this structure would vary with level of education, thereby permitting an evaluation of the generalizability of earlier factor-analytic studies. Therefore, the factor analyses were repeated separately for the three educational strata in the sample. The same structure was extracted in each instance, suggesting that the basic pattern of ideological organization into two clusters is invariant, although the authors do note that there seems to be more integration of discrete attitudes, a tighter organization, among the educated.[28] This most interesting finding, suggestive of the determinants of mental organization, of the incorporation of ideas into a sys-

---

[27] Robert J. Williams and Charles R. Wright, "Opinion Organization in a Heterogeneous Adult Population," *J. Abnorm. and Soc. Psychol.*, **51**, 1955, pp. 559–564.

[28] Carlyle Dewey has been engaged in a secondary analysis of developmental processes as these affect the level of attitudinal organization. Using the Purdue Polls of national samples of high school students, he has compared the internal consistency of attitudes among tenth graders and twelfth graders, replicating the inquiry from two different sur-

tem of thought or ideology, foreshadows the findings of subsequent studies to be presented below.

Findings on the structure of politicoeconomic attitudes, on the number and nature of the fundamental dispositions that organize a large domain, their internal relations and their contents, certainly seemed substantial. They had been replicated by independent secondary analyses, by simple and by elegant statistical manipulations. Yet, they referred to a specific era—pre 1948. Just as discrete attitudes may change over time and under the impact of experience, so too, one may at least speculate, the organization of attitudes might itself change over time. This interesting problem also lends itself to secondary analysis.

The hundreds of questions asked over the span 1937–1967 in this domain gave Alfred Hero, Jr., the opportunity to conduct a series of replicative or trend studies and to examine whether or not the patterns of organization persisted.[29] In general, he confirms the fact that there have been only "feeble correlations" between attitudes on domestic politicoeconomic issues and foreign policy attitudes over these many years, although these linkages have varied in magnitude (presumably from a zero association to a modest association) in different periods. He does note, however, that there are three aspects of domestic attitudes that have "constituted limited exceptions to this paucity of stable statistical linkages with foreign affairs."

Americans who favor cuts in federal expenditures on domestic welfare programs have shown a corresponding negative attitude on foreign policies that involve expenditures. More specifically those who have favored expanded programs of federal aid to education have been "consistently more liberal in their international thinking." One might label this disposition, which seems to tie the two separate spheres of liberalism together, a "*fiscal* liberalism," or, depending on one's point of view, the "spendthrift" disposition, and the congruence of foreign and domestic attitudes that implicate spending money is perhaps a new, and understandable, principle of organization.

Previous investigators of attitude organization had observed that tolerant or liberal attitudes toward minorities within the society, although part of the domestic sphere, accompanied liberal attitudes in the foreign policy sphere. Hero reports confirmation of this pattern of organization, although he suggests that the "linkages of racial and international liberalism-conservatism have been . . . a relatively recent phenomenon, especially outside the South."

---

veys. Long ago some studies of the increased congruence of attitudes with age were conducted on small and unrepresentative samples, but such a secondary analysis serves to test the problem on much more adequate samples. (Personal communication.)

[29] Alfred O. Hero, Jr., "Liberalism-Conservatism Revisited: Foreign vs. Domestic Federal Policies, 1937–1967," *Publ. Opin. Quart.*, **33**, 1969, pp. 399–408.

These secondary analyses, by virtue of the extensive data and coverage of time, give impressive evidence that politicoeconomic attitudes are organized ideologically, in the sense that the individual's discrete attitudes cluster or hang together in more general patterns or systems of some apparent consistent political tone. However, the inferred psychological dispositions have changed in their content and structure over time, and no single disposition was found to be the all-pervasive determinant of the totality of politicoeconomic attitudes. Without denying the evidence, some would not regard it as indicative of an *ideology*, since their definition of such entities is more restrictive, and all would recognize that the nature of the larger entities which give internal coherence to the attitudes remains elusive, and has simply been posited without any direct report from individuals as to the way they think.[30]

The attitudes they exhibit suggest to the observer that they are, in Campbell and Converse's apt phrase, "propelled by ideological concerns," but we do not actually know what frames of reference they themselves use for organizing their beliefs and opinions. On this problem, we must turn to a new design which can indeed contribute essential evidence, and which has even wider utility.

DESIGN 10: CLINICAL STUDY OF A SERIES OF VERBATIM ANSWERS OF THE RESPONDENT TO REVEAL PATTERNS OF ATTITUDES, THOUGHT, AND LANGUAGE

In an attempt to study the organization of political attitudes, the "connectedness" of the ideas of the respondent, and the kinds of concepts or ab-

---

[30] In this connection, Hero and other secondary analysts have drawn upon a question which has been asked many times over the years. Respondents are asked to identify themselves as "liberals" or "conservatives," and sometimes other categories have been provided as well. The results deserve thorough secondary analysis for many problems. For example, one may conceive of the subjective identification involved as an avenue to the study of the "self-concept" or for the study of reference group processes. Some have used the fact that a considerable proportion of the sample will not classify themselves—ranging from about 6% to 36% depending on when and how the question was put—as evidence against the existence of *ideological* organization of attitudes, since the argument goes that they will not accept those particular ideological labels. By cross tabulation of the subjective identification against specific attitudes, one can document that self-styled ideologues of either persuasion often hold, as a group, varied attitudes, changing with time, and that some of the attitudes seem incongruent with the label the person has assumed. Yet Hero finds considerable differences in the profiles of the two self-designated groups, in the direction expected, and a cautious reading of the material would convince some that the terms have considerable meaning to the bulk of Americans and are used by them in rough but accurate ways. For some of the data, see Erskine's convenient summary, *op. cit.* and Hero, *op. cit.*

stractions, if any, that pervaded his thinking, Campbell, Converse, *et al.*, in their primary analysis of their 1956 national election survey, examined the answers to a series of open-ended questions on politics and assigned each respondent an overall rating or code to designate the degree to which he organized his ideas in terms of the kinds of abstract concepts that they designated as "ideological."[31] Such a clinical procedure applied to a lengthy protocol obviously provides direct evidence on the clarity and style of thought and language, and on the explicit connections between attitudes.

There is no need here to argue the fine points of the definition of a term like "ideology," or the criteria employed to designate a particular level or type of ideology. One can operate this design according to one's own standards. For those who seek an approach that goes beyond statistical, quantitative, inferential methods to identify belief systems or general dispositions, this clinical design provides direct penetration of the respondent's psyche. It should be stressed that for Campbell *et al.* such a coding scheme was "sufficiently clear to insure satisfactorily high inter-rater reliability" and that their fruitful analysis was based on a relatively short sequence of eight questions.

The design may at first be confused in the reader's mind with the design we earlier labeled "Synthesis by Qualitative Characterology" (design 7b) which was exemplified in Knupfer's work. However, a sharp distinction in the approach and procedures should be made. In design 7b, the analyst does not work in clinical fashion with the protocol from *individual* respondents. Frequently, he starts with quantitative and group data, but the end product is a synthesis expressed in qualitative form. Here, by contrast, he starts with qualitative data on the individual, but the end product is a quantitative statement or count of the number of individuals who fall into some specified diagnostic category, and this quantitative datum may, in turn, be related by quantitative methods to other characteristics.

The particular model of the design that we presented was developed in the course of a survey by the primary analysts to suit their special problem, but there is no inherent limitation on its application to a wide range of problems by secondary analysts, although there are practical obstacles. Long ago Samelson applied such a clinical procedure, calling it the "ballot method" to a secondary analysis of ethnic attitudes. Her remarks in her treatment of the respondent, "Mrs. Jones," are worth quoting:

When a ballot has 'meat on its bones,' the student of public opinion will find that, at its best, results obtained by the ballot method approximate those

---

[31] A. Campbell *et al.*, *The American Voter* (New York: Wiley, 1960), pp. 188–265. By more conventional intercorrelational analysis, they also found no relation between the domestic and foreign spheres in 1956 (p. 197).

yielded by a brief case history . . . by inferring from the way in which the first few questions were answered the existence of a fundamental frame of reference in terms of which Mrs. Jones answers . . . and by inferring the existence of certain fundamental character traits . . . it is possible to obtain a feeling of congruence, to sense a stable attitudinal structure. . . . Is it dogmatic to say that it is only through a study of configurations, either of a single respondent's ballot or of those of many interviewees, that we can hope to extract the full value from public opinion questionnaires.[32]

Ringer and Sills adapted this design to a *semi*secondary analysis of the social and psychological sources of political extremism, based on a survey the Bureau of Applied Social Research had conducted in Iran. "Inasmuch as these interviews, which took from two to three hours to complete, were much richer and more extensive than most survey interviews, they were subjected to case history analysis."[33] The answers to four open-ended questions revealed the ideology, the "perspectives" in their word, and a coding system was developed to classify individuals into those who were extremists either of the "revolutionary left" or "nationalistic right." The rest of the political spectrum was divided in terms of other types, including a category of individuals who were nonideological or members of the "apolitical center." From this base, the analysts were able to analyze certain variables that distinguished extremists of either type, and other variables that distinguished one kind of extremist from the other. It is notable that high education characterized the Iranian ideologues. The Michigan investigators and Williams and Wright also had found that education was a correlate of more highly structured systems of attitude.

One last example of this design will reveal the practical obstacles to its use, the way they were circumvented, and the way in which this design can be combined with other designs. The Michigan findings had been based on the examination of political attitudes expressed during the course of the 1956

---

[32] Babette Samelson, "Mrs. Jones' Ethnic Attitudes: A Ballot Analysis," *J. Abnorm. and Soc. Psychol.* **40**, 1945, pp. 205, 214. Riesman and Glazer have also recommended this approach and suggest a general schema for analyzing what they call the "residues" of surveys, those disregarded "things gotten in the very process of acquiring manifest opinions." From clinical examination of respondents' completed questionnaires they classify such residues into three categories: those that are clues to his class, to his style of response, and to his underlying character structure. See David Riesman and N. Glazer, "Social Structure, Character Structure, and Opinion," *Internat. J. Opin. Attit. Res.*, **2**, 1948, pp. 512–527.

[33] Benjamin B. Ringer and David L. Sills, "Political Extremists in Iran: A Secondary Analysis of Communications Data," *Publ. Opin. Quart.*, **16**, 1952, pp. 689–701. These investigators were members of the Bureau, had participated in the primary analysis, and, most important, had direct and immediate access to the original interviews.

election. On the basis of their clinical readings of the protocols, Campbell, Converse and their associates had concluded that only a small minority of Americans—perhaps no more than a tenth of the population—exhibited an ideology in their sense of a pattern of attitudes systematized and bound together by some modestly abstract set of ideas. Field and Anderson reasoned that the Michigan findings might well reflect the blandness and nonideo-logical character of that particular presidential contest, and therefore sought to conduct an *external replication* by the secondary analysis of an appropriate survey conducted in an era when ideological matters might be more salient to the population.[34] The Michigan findings that the few ideologues in the population were mainly people of education, and their related theorizing that the organization of opinions around abstract ideas was a function of basic cognitive capacities and long-established training, would suggest that transient stimulation from the environment makes little difference, but an empirical test is critical. Anderson and Field pinned their analysis to the Michigan survey in the 1964 election, when Goldwater's candidacy (in contrast with Eisenhower's) provided as compelling an ideological stimulus as one might need for the test. For other reasons which will become clear, they supplemented their findings by analyzing the 1960 and 1956 election survey interviews, thus incorporating an *internal* replication as well. Their substantive findings, therefore, relate to larger questions of social change. The case could thus be reviewed in our next chapter, but it is perhaps the best illustration of the clinical design, as modified under the conditions of exigency that may be present in *pure* secondary analysis.

A primary or *semi*secondary analyst has *immediate, direct access* to the original interviews, which seems to be the essential requirement for the application of the method. As pure secondary analysts Anderson and Field were not in the same fortunate position. Whether they could have ultimately gained possession of the original interviews, in this particular instance, is not clear. Certainly in many other instances, a secondary analysts would be barred by circumstance from applying the design in its normal fashion, and Anderson and Field did not, in fact, work with the original protocols. They sur-

---

[34] John O. Field and R. E. Anderson, "Ideology in the Public's Conceptualization of the 1964 Election," *Publ. Opin. Quart.*, **33**, 1969, pp. 308–398. Converse, in a subsequent paper, presented further evidence on behalf of the earlier conclusion based on data from the Michigan study of the 1960 election. A variety of measures of the existence of ideology, other than the articulate statement of abstract political ideas, were employed. This paper also provides most interesting evidence of the "two kinds of liberalism" pattern and of the "spend-thrift" disposition previously described. See P. E. Converse, "The Nature of Belief Systems in Mass Publics," in D. E. Apter, ed., *Ideology and Discontent* (New York: Free Press, 1964), pp. 206–261, especially pp. 222 and 229.

mounted the practical obstacle in a way which suggests a valuable strategy and may insure the utility of the design for future secondary analysts.

The original coding system that had been applied to each of the eight questions employed in the three election studies fortunately had been exceedingly detailed. Field and Anderson read each respondent's protocol *at second hand,* identifying and classifying his level and type of ideological thinking on the basis of the themes the original coders had noted and categorized. By their system of scoring what we might describe as "derived protocols," and using the most lenient cutting point, about one-third of the national sample in 1964 might be regarded as exhibiting an "ideology," a much higher proportion than the one-tenth the Survey Research Center had identified in the 1956 sample. Thus it would seem that ideological thought is not only a function of basic, enduring dispositions, but of political stimulation and events. The analysts showed admirable care before jumping to such a conclusion.

In any replication intended to evaluate social changes in a phenomenon, either the procedures should be constant or any variations in them should be evaluated as possible artifactual causes of the change. The sample design, the instruments or questions involved, their context within the interview before or after ideology has been artificially enhanced by the line of previous questioning, all seem to have been constant over the inquiries from 1956 to 1964. In the instance of a variable measured by richness of word and thought, whether or not style of interviewing and amount of probing were constant would also be critical. Here again one might regard this as likely by virtue of the constancy of the agency involved and the corresponding stability in composition and training of its field staff. What is still critical is the very *scoring* of ideology, derived in one instance from the coded data and in the other from the original protocol. The conventions in scoring or rating the respondents have obviously changed and might account for the apparent change in the phenomenon. Therefore, Field and Anderson reanalyzed the 1956 data applying their own procedures to those respondents and threw in for good measure a secondary analysis of the 1960 Kennedy election. It is only after this essential procedure that they concluded that ideology is in part a function of the level of stimulation. The number of "ideologues" their scoring identified was 21% in 1956 (in contrast with the earlier estimate of 11%), 28% in 1960, and 35% in 1964.

The "true" magnitude of the phenomenon is, of course, still open to arguments of definition, depending on just how much systematization and depth and style of thought are equivalent to *ideological* thought. Even when such matters can be diagnosed from coded sequences of data, one should realize that the coding systems of some agencies are too rudimentary to lend themselves to such modes of analysis. The applicability of the method, at best, is limited to a small number of surveys, until agencies increase the sensitivity of their codes and apply less reductionism in coding the variety of answers. But the modified design does have some applicability. In the interest of more definitive study of this fundamental phenomenon, one might therefore urge an equivalent study from political surveys conducted between elections. After all, the most bland campaign is still a time of intense stimulation, and one might speculate that very few Americans are disposed to think ideologically during more quiet and uneventful periods in our history. As Field and Anderson remark, "despite the unusual ideological cleavage of the 1964 contest, a lenient technique for locating Ideologues comes up with only a third of the national sample."

SPECIALIZED SYSTEMS OF BELIEF AND ATTITUDE

These last studies bring us quite directly to our next subtopic, studies of *knowledge, language, and thought*, since ideology was treated not merely in terms of the direction and organization of attitudes, but also in terms of cognition and thought processes as revealed through the style of language. But we pause a bit longer on studies of attitudes. Our discussion thus far has focused on systems of belief and attitude that are of very *broad* range or scope. Each of the two kinds of liberalism encompasses a huge region of dispositions on many issues. Also, our discussion has centered mainly on *formal* matters of the level and extent of mental organization, and has been rather devoid of content. We should certainly not neglect the opportunities for the secondary analysis of selected, smaller belief systems and organizations of attitude that are not so narrow as to be trivial and which exert some directive influence on problems of importance. Some examples of such "middle range" systems will suggest the opportunities.

Beliefs and attitudes about war may well be incorporated into some larger ideology, but to blunt our understanding of the disposition toward this particular institution by losing it in a larger thicket of attitudes would seem a scientific sin. Erskine's convenient summary of such questions reveals that this has been a continuing area of inquiry for many years, and consequently regularities and differences in attitudes toward the four most recent wars in which America participated lend themselves to study.[35]

---

[35] Hazel G. Erskine, "The Polls: Is War a Mistake," *Publ. Opin. Quart.*, **34**, 1970, pp. 134–150. This particular summary, like some of her others, goes far beyond a mere listing and may well be described as a secondary analysis. An unexpected finding, for example, is that younger adults, although some may be more vociferous, have been *less* opposed to the Viet Nam war as a population group than older people. John Mueller has conducted a comparative secondary analysis of these data for the Korean and Viet Nam wars, but since the major findings relate to trends in attitude, they will be reviewed in Chapter VI.

The reader will recall from Chapter III that Hamilton, in the course of searching for data on an unrelated problem, had stumbled upon a 1952 question on American support for a widening of the Korean war and a "tough" policy of initiating bombing of Manchuria and China. He subsequently came across a very similar question, asked again by the same agency, the Survey Research Center, in their 1964 national survey in which the tough policy issue of "invading North Vietnam" was posed. His secondary analysis of these data—admittedly based on a single question but nevertheless replicated in two surveys—reveals a striking consistency in the social groups who endorse "tough initiatives" in both situations, suggesting that there is a more generalized, bellicose disposition and that it has some of its roots in particular social settings.[36] Education did not seem to diminish the tendency, and youth, surprisingly, seemed to increase it.

Support for *civil liberties* for all or intolerance toward political nonconformity and the respective attitudes toward personages and groups identified with such policies may be treated as part of the larger package of liberal–conservative attitudes, but the discrete belief systems involved certainly seem deserving of special secondary analysis. And the data are voluminous. Polsby, by a secondary analysis of such questions gleaned from various surveys, was able to shed considerable empirical light on the nature of the phenomenon and to cast into doubt some plausible, but faulty, explanations of McCarthyism which had been erected without benefit of evidence. His evidence suggests also that the attitudes were not tightly organized into a unified system, but rather multidimensional in structure.

S. M. Lipset, by parallel analyses of questions that had been asked about Father Coughlin, McCarthy, and the John Birch Society over a span of three decades, was able to analyze the social sources of these political movements, and thus established that there was considerable variation in the groups and dispositions that these apparently similar extremist political movements drew upon. Lewis Lipsitz analyzed three surveys conducted between 1952 and 1954, each of which contained a lengthy battery of questions on authoritarianism plus some more directly political questions including attitudes

---

[36] Richard F. Hamilton, "A Research Note on the Mass Support for 'Tough' Military Initiatives," *Amer. Sociol. Rev.*, **33**, 1968, pp. 439–445. The use of the very same question in the Michigan election study of 1968 presented an unusual opportunity to conduct still another replication and to examine aggregate and subgroup trends in relation to the events of the several periods and wars and to link the observed changes to the changing position of the mass media. Spurred by this opportunity and by the crisis in Cambodia in spring, 1970, a student of Hamilton recently conducted a secondary analysis. See James D. Wright, "Support for Escalation in Viet Nam, 1964–1968: A Trend Study." Unpublished master's thesis, University of Wisconsin, 1970.

toward McCarthy. By the internal replication of tests within each survey and between surveys, he provides a great deal of evidence. He finds also that the domain is not totally organized in a unitary or consistent way, and shows least structure among the lower classes. Correspondingly, he notes that the location of authoritarianism in the lower or higher classes depends very much on which dimension is being examined, and that whatever "working-class authoritarianism" is demonstrated is mainly a function of educational disadvantage. These few secondary analyses suggest how much can be accomplished.[37] One can only regret that more analysts have not been attracted to the problem, and that the survey agencies, as Erskine's summaries show, seem almost to have abandoned their interest in the domain despite their lavish study of it in the fifties.

The preferences or aversions for exemplars of particular political ideologies have been used as indicators of dispositions toward extremism. The Gallup Poll has also asked national samples annually to report the man (sometimes woman also) they most admire.[38] By 1970, there were already twenty-two

---

[37] Nelson W. Polsby, "Toward an Explanation of McCarthyism," *Political Studies*, October, 1960, pp. 250–271; S. M. Lipset, "Three Decades of the Radical Right: Coughlinites, McCarthyites, and Birchers," in Daniel Bell, ed., *The Radical Right* (Garden City: Anchor Books, 1964), pp. 373–446; When the emergence of George Wallace as a presidential candidate in 1968 presented the opportunity for an external replication, Lipset and Raab conducted a secondary analysis of his supporters. S. M. Lipset and E. Raab, *The Politics of Unreason* (New York: Harper and Row, 1970). Lewis Lipsitz, "Working-Class Authoritarianism: A Re-evaluation," *Amer. Sociol. Rev.*, **30**, 1965, pp. 103–109. The findings by Lipsitz seem compatible with Hamilton's finding that "authoritarianism" in dealing with peoples one is at war with may well be a distinctive dimension that does not behave in the same way as the more conventional scale. See, also, Herbert H. Hyman and Paul B. Sheatsley, "Trends in Public Opinion on Civil Liberties," *J. Soc. Issues*, **9**, No. 3, 1953, pp. 6–16. One might note in this connection that there have been occasional questions asked over the years on attitudes toward the Ku Klux Klan which seem to have been neglected by secondary analysts studying the problem of extremism. In this context, a brief secondary analysis by Diggins suggests how much can be done even with a few brief questions handled with a sensitive eye to limitations of the data and the historical context of interpretation. He unearthed a question in which Americans in 1937 and again in 1939 were forced to choose between Fascism and Communism, and another question which forced them to state which dictator they liked best—Mussolini, Stalin, or Hitler. By cross tabulation with the face-sheet items, he was able to "shed some light on the social and religious prisms through which Americans viewed Fascism and Communism in the late thirties." See John P. Diggins, "American Opinion on European Dictatorships, 1937–1939: A Statistical Note," mimeo, n.d.

[38] The Gallup Poll has occasionally run such a popularity contest in cross-national surveys, sometimes forcing, for the decade that has passed, a choice of "outstanding personality of the sixties (or fifties)." Under such conditions the question may well be an indicator of parochialism or "ethnocentrism" in its classic sense. President Kennedy won the con-

such surveys available. The question is very similar to one that has been used for more than half a century in scholarly studies to tap the "ego-ideal." Presumably the characteristics in the most admired personage have been internalized within the self as values and ideals which guide the individual's conduct and strivings. The very lengthy time series might yield, by secondary analysis, considerable evidence on political attitudes and also on problems of personality and the self-concept.

Beliefs and attitudes toward *racial and ethnic groups* may also be regarded as a separate belief system or set of dispositions important enough for special secondary analysis, and the opportunities are indeed profuse. The data were so voluminous that Erskine's convenient summary had to appear in eight installments in the *Public Opinion Quarterly* in 1968 and 1969, at which point she still remarked that the surveys "have by no means been exhausted." Pettigrew reports that he has built up a specialized data bank from racial questions that had been asked, and that the deposits as of 1968 included "approximately 200 surveys."[39] These are now beginning to be thoroughly analyzed by a variety of designs, including design 9, *Multidimensional Pooling*.

Many of the questions asked in this area prior to 1959 have been treated by Stember, and the results of his secondary analyses are reported in two monographs, which will be reviewed in Chapter VI.[40] Stember, after inspection of the many questions, decided that they arrayed themselves along no less than *six* dimensions of prejudice, and he remarks: "inconclusiveness in existing research may, in part, be the result of treating prejudice against a given minority as a unitary variable. The usual assumption has been that it is possible to isolate an abstraction called 'prejudice' without distinguishing among its actual components. But may this be assumed?"[41] Since he is skeptical of the assumption, he examines his major problem, the relation of formal education to prejudice, separately for three of the major components, and also scrutinizes whether the relationship is modified by the atmosphere and context of the times.

An unusual procedure in handling the variable, formal education, should be noted. Stember treats education essentially as a quantitative variable, as

---

test as the most outstanding personality of the sixties in nine countries. Only in Spain did he lose—taking second place to General Franco. See their news release, January 15, 1970. In 1969 in America, Evangelist Billy Graham and Vice-President Spiro Agnew took second and third place in the annual contest, being surpassed in the admiration of Americans only by President Nixon. (Gallup Poll Release, January 4, 1970.)

[39] Thomas Pettigrew, Personal communication.

[40] Charles Herbert Stember, *Education and Attitude Change*, New York: Institute of Human Relations Press, 1961: *Jews in the Mind of America* (New York: Basic Books, 1966).

[41] Stember, *Education . . .* , *op. cit.*, p. 2.

most analysts do. All face sheets make distinctions between amounts of schooling, although the categories vary in the degree of refinement with which increments in years of schooling are coded. But Stember also speculates that *type*, rather than amount of education, may be an important aspect of the variable. Two different colleges, for example, may provide very different kinds of education. He finds only one survey containing measures of prejudice which lends itself to such an analysis prior to 1959, the period of his research. What should be stressed, however, is that this insight could well be followed now by other secondary analysts. In the decade since then, fortuitously, other surveys have provided such distinctions in their code categories. For sure, many surveys (for example, those of NORC) have enumerated the actual name of the respondent's school or college, although the information has generally not been coded. By recoding the original interviews, the problem could indeed be studied.

STUDIES OF LANGUAGE

Converse, and Field and Anderson by proxy, had examined the lengthy verbal reports of respondents, analyzing their linguistic behavior for such signs of ideology as the use of particular verbal symbols and a coherent pattern of abstractly stated political thought. In a phrase that is very apropos of our new topic, the Michigan investigators remark that ideology is a "medium of political *translation*."[42] Simply put, it is a language. But in these works, the study of a particular language is a vehicle to carry us toward the study of attitude and belief systems. It is obvious, however, that along the way we have arrived at findings that could be valuable in their own right and that relate to a topic long regarded as fundamental, a topic that lately has created fashionable fields for scholarly inquiry, sociolinguistics, and psycholinguistics. Indeed, what could be more true and obvious but that many surveys yield large samples of the spoken languages of very large and representative samples of individuals. Of course, much of the spoken word has been lost in the processing of data or ignored by the analysts, in contrast with the rich recordings of speech by linguistic scientists. But consider the paltry samples linguists of the past have used—three informants for one city, five or twenty-five for another. What the surveys have lacked in coverage of the word, they may have counterbalanced in the sampling of the speakers.

Crude critics from outside the survey profession have recognized this state of affairs. They often say we analyze words, not deeds. But the insiders seem not to have realized the *benefits* that could derive from such a formulation of

---

[42] *The American Voter, op. cit.*, p. 202 (italics supplied).

the enterprise. Indeed, the secondary analysis by Schatzman and Strauss that proceeds from such a formulation exists in almost splendid isolation.[43] Perhaps only Whitehead can explain our neglect of the opportunity when he tells us: "It requires a very unusual mind to undertake the analysis of the obvious."

There are, however, practical obstacles to secondary analysis of language, and a review of the one example will set the problem in sharper perspective. Schatzman and Strauss employed design 10, the clinical study of the verbatim answers of the respondent, in *strict* form, to determine class differences in communication and linguistic behavior. They sought lengthy and accurate data on speech, and the survey they fortunately located was highly appropriate for this purpose. A random sample of about 300 individuals in the population of several local communities in Arkansas who had experienced a natural disaster had been interviewed by NORC to study their reactions, and their answers were recorded on tape and then transcribed. The protocols averaged twenty-nine pages in length.

Schatzman and Strauss obtained direct access to these transcripts. It is self-evident that a pure secondary analyst of linguistic behavior would have to work directly with the original protocols, rather than apply the design by proxy, since conventional codes classify the content of what is said and usually ignore the exact language in which it is put. Certainly such problems of access create practical obstacles to the utilization of the design.

Given the demanding task of analyzing these lengthy documents, Schatzman and Strauss truncated the sample, stratified the remaining cases, and then drew matched subsamples of ten "upper" and ten "lower" class individuals, restricting their analysis to these two small groups.[44] Where there is a wealth of cases, subsampling is obviously an efficient wrinkle to introduce into the design, although one may not wish to carry it to such extremes. But the reader may worry about the reverse problem. How many surveys can be found which provide *any* lengthy interviews which have been tape recorded and transcribed? Obviously they are rare, but the survey they chose was certainly not unique. Similar disaster studies had been conducted in other regions of the country, and Schatzman and Strauss were able to replicate their analysis subsequently on subsamples from other areas and to confirm the fact that their findings were not peculiar to Arkansas.

---

[43] Leonard Schatzman and Anselm Strauss, "Social Class and Modes of Communication," *Amer. J. Sociol.*, **60**, 1955, pp. 329–338.

[44] One especially relevant restriction was applied. Cases where there were more than seven probes per page were eliminated "to avoid a rigid question–answer style with consequent structuring of interview by the interviewer's questions."

The two analysts worked *independently*, preparing a profile of the linguistic behavior and the revealed patterns of thought and interpersonal communication of each respondent. "Agreement upon coding scores was virtually perfect," and they report practically no overlap in patterns of lower and upper class behavior. It is not clear whether each rater worked "blindly" not knowing the class of the respondent whose behavior he was judging, but such a procedure can easily be incorporated into such designs of the future.

The utility of the design and the prospects that await other analysts can only be conveyed by detailed reading of the article. The partial summary of the class patterns suggest the many findings. "The difference is not simply the failure or success—of lower and upper groups, respectively—in communicating clearly and in sufficient detail for the interviewer's purposes. Nor does the difference merely involve correctness or elaborateness of grammar or use of a more precise or colorful vocabulary. The difference is a considerable disparity in (a) the number and kinds of perspectives utilized in communication; (b) the ability to take the listener's role; (c) the handling of classifications; and (d) the frameworks and stylistic devices which order and implement the communication."[45] It should be added that they conclude that the variations in speech and in the communication behavior within the interview reflect the way these respective classes normally perceive and think about the world and relate to others.

The nature of the sampling of individuals, the replication in other communities, and the procedures employed in the analysis contribute to valid and generalizable findings from this secondary analysis. But this was the language and thought produced by the stimulus, "Tell me your story of the tornado," the opening question in the interview. One may speculate that the phenomena are specific to this kind of experience, that this was implicitly a test of mental and linguistic performance in relation to the specific task that was set and the events that were brought to mind. What aspects of language and thought would be revealed when individuals talk about other kinds of experiences in response to other verbal stimuli? Such speculations should not be construed as criticisms, but simply as reminders that such secondary analytic designs should be applied to other surveys which set very different tasks, and that the present findings could be supplemented and broadened.

Admittedly, there are very few large-scale surveys which employ narrative questionnaires and tape-recordings of entire interviews. But there is no reason

---

[45] *Ibid.*, p. 330. Riesman and Glazer had also argued from the inspection of survey data and from interviews with professional interviewers and survey researchers treated as informants that there were characteristic styles of communication between respondents of particular classes talking to middle class interviewers. See *"The Meaning of Opinion," op. cit.*

to think that the design is limited to that rare kind of survey. It could be applied profitably, as Converse showed, to a shorter sequence of open-ended questions, and the surveys could be chosen by the secondary analyst from the work of agencies where the interviewers are well trained to record *manually* the answers in verbatim form. It is certainly worth trying.

Studies of language and thought initiated by the stimuli in an interview need not be limited, however, to the answers to open-ended questions. Survey researchers may have neglected the linguistic phenomena implicit in the responses, but they have been unusually sensitive about the verbal *stimuli* they themselves present to the respondents. They generally agonize over the exact syntax and wording of their questions before arriving at a final formulation. Sometimes they are so agonized by their dilemma that the final survey incorporates a special procedure which potentially provides a new class of designs suited to the secondary analysis of language and thought. It is almost like the "imbedded design" used in children's pictorial puzzles and in experiments on perception. It is not noticed until brought to attention but then it is obvious to sight. As has been found in such experiments, the mere act of labeling will help future secondary analysts to see the subtle entity in a clear light, and we shall therefore give it a number and name.

DESIGN 11: ALTERNATE FORMS OF THE QUESTIONNAIRE TREATED AS AN EXPERIMENTAL DESIGN FOR THE STUDY OF LANGUAGE

Sometimes researchers have systematically varied the questionnaire used in a survey so as to observe the effect on responses of manipulating the verbal stimuli. Rather than resolving their dilemma by choosing one form of an instrument, they have used a "split-ballot" allocating two or more different forms of the instrument to random subsamples of respondents. The Gallup Poll used such a procedure routinely over many years, the notation K or T indicating the fact. NORC has employed it whenever there was special interest in testing the effect of some context of issues or information presented earlier in the questionnaire on the response to a later question, or in testing the effect of the syntactical forms in which a question might be cast. It has also been employed to test the effect on attitude of identifying a particular policy position with a prestigious public figure, and in this instance there is an exact parallel to classic experiments on prestige suggestion. Sometimes the introduction of an emotional word or symbol, rather than a person, has been examined in this way and again the parallel to experiments in the modification of attitude is clear.

Whenever the researchers have applied such designs, they have used the results either to describe the range of error attached to the estimate of some phenomenon, to increase the accuracy of an estimate by averaging the results from different ballots, or to improve the methodology of future inquiry. The great bulk of such findings, however, remain unanalyzed and have not been abstracted or codified for their bearing upon the phenomena of language and thought. Such procedures clearly are rather elegant field experiments on very large numbers of experimental subjects in which the manipulations are ways of testing the meaning of language to the listener and its effects on his thinking and attitude, just as the earlier design is a way of testing his active use of language. Thus designs 9 and 10 are obviously corollary.

The occasional results that have already been reported in the literature could be reexamined for the light they shed on language processes, and the endless experiments that have been conducted as part of normal routine operations, but never reported, could be exploited by secondary analysts.[46] Even when the experiments have been reported, it is notable that the results have been analyzed in only gross ways for the experimental subsamples. The differential effects on the educated stratum or other social groupings subjected to the several experimental treatments have remained buried in the aggregate data.

This experimental design, although not previously exploited for the secondary analysis of language, has been used in the secondary analysis of problems of knowledge, and we shall return to it shortly. Some of the more conventional designs have been used in studies of *thought* processes, however, and are relevant to our immediate discussion, since it is very difficult to

---

[46] Early works on public opinion and survey research dwelled on problems of question wording and reported some of the results of such experiments, but the problem seems to have dropped from sight in recent writings, perhaps because of the emphasis on the use of batteries of questions rather than on the vain attempt to find a single, magic, perfect question which would serve as a measuring instrument. In this proper change of emphasis, the value of experiments on question wording for the study of language need not be lost. For early writings, see, for example, Hadley Cantril, *Gauging Public Opinion* (Princeton: Princeton University Press, 1944), Chapter II; Stanley Payne, *The Art of Asking Questions* (Princeton: Princeton University Press, 1951). Skimming these pages will show, for example, that the opposite of "allow" in the public mind is not "forbid"; that the phrase "or not" is not equivalent to the explicit alternative to a statement; that words designating various equivalent magnitudes or gradations or probabilities are often not interpreted in that way. Long-experienced survey researchers have a great deal of implicit knowledge of these and other linguistic phenomena, and might well be exploited as informants in a special survey designed to explore there experience systematically. A recent paper documents that the Institute for Demoscopy in Germany has made extensive use of split-ballot designs in a program of experimentation on measurement techniques, and their accumulated studies provide additional materials for the secondary analyst. See E. Noelle-Neumann, "Wanted: Rules for Wording Structured Questionnaires," *Publ. Opin. Quart.*, **34,** 1970, pp. 191–201.

separate studies of language and thought. Language is often regarded as the reflection and expression of thought, as in some of the examples already reviewed, but one of the reasons for the interest in language is that thought is often regarded as governed by, and therefore a reflection of, language. In the major example we shall review, thought also becomes inseparably tied to attitudes and behavior, as was the case in Converse's work on ideology. After all, the dispositions and actions we adopt, however much they may be governed by such factors as motives, needs, and group influences, are also in some degree clarified by the aid of language and reflection.

V. O. KEY'S WORK: A CASE STUDY OF THOUGHT PROCESSES

Our example comes from the work of V. O. Key, the distinguished political scientist. Is it not encouraging for us that he turned, toward the end of his life, to secondary analysis of surveys for evidence and answers to complex, theoretical problems? He had never been identified with primary survey research. He had run the gamut of many other empirical methods, ecological studies of voting records, historical and institutional studies of politics, for example, and they had rendered him notable service. Yet, when he raised in his final work "the perverse and unorthodox argument . . . that voters are not fools," he sought evidence to support the argument from the secondary analysis of sample surveys.[47] As the subtitle of this work will emphasize, *Rationality in Presidential Voting, 1936–1960*, he was concerned with a matter that has always been central to the study of thought processes: he sought to trace the persistent force of *reason* upon American political behavior through the synthesis of data from many surveys spanning a long time period.

Although the monograph has a specific focus on thought processes as they govern voting behavior, it also provides many illustrations of the three major features of any secondary analysis: the construction of appropriate indices of new concepts from the available data, the evaluation and if possible control of error in the data, and the arrangement of one or more surveys into a design that will provide the most unambiguous and powerful evidence on the problem. On all these matters, Key's work is an elaborate and exciting study, and no doubt would have been even more thorough if his untimely death had

---

[47] V. O. Key, Jr., *The Responsible Electorate* (Cambridge: Harvard University Press, 1966). The previous work, *Public Opinion and American Democracy* (New York: Knopf, 1961), was an attempt at a definitive characterization of the American public's views, their sources, and their linkages to government, on the basis of secondary analysis of a great volume of data from many different surveys. Although it will not be reviewed here, it provides many examples appropriate to the discussions in this and our previous chapter.

not interrupted the work in progress, which then had to be completed by Milton Cummings from rough notes. Thus it deserves detailed review.

In constructing his indices, Key starts from the implicit assumption that even individuals endowed with rationality can perpetrate folly in deciding upon some future, novel course of action such as a vote in a given election. What would be truly irrational would be for them not to learn the errors of their ways, for them not to profit from past experience. He describes the electorate as "an appraiser of *past* events, *past* performance, and *past* action. It judges retrospectively, it commands prospectively only insofar as it expresses approval or disapproval of that which has happened before. Voters may reject what they have known; or they may approve what they have known."[48] This longer-range process has to be brought under study.

Therefore, panel studies limited to the vicissitudes of thought and attitude during a particular political campaign do not provide appropriate data for an index of political rationality. Similarly, aggregate voting records cannot reveal the patterns of *individual* behavior from one election to another. In the period under study, there were no panel studies that traced the behavior of voters over two elections, but there were a great many surveys beginning in 1936 which asked samples how they were planning to vote or had voted in a given election, and also a retrospective question on how they had voted four years before in the previous presidential election. From these voluminous materials, Key builds the core of his index. He isolates for a string of seven pairs of elections, beginning with 1932 and 1936, and ending with 1956 and 1960, groups of "standpatters" whose choices or voting remains consistent over the pair, and a group of "shifters."[49] A standpatter may, of course, persist in his behavior out of an emotional and unthinking loyalty, and a shifter may simply be a volatile and capricious person. Alternatively, both of them may be thoughtful individuals. The problem for Key is to add into his core index some additional data which will demonstrate the grounds of rationality for the particular behavior. And the polemic part of his argument is that other analysts have prejudged the meaning of these behaviors. In a way, he

---

[48] Key, Jr., *The Responsible Electorate*, p. 61 (italics supplied).

[49] Not until the late fifties do we find a long-term panel study in the United States, permitting us to trace change or stability over several elections. See Converse, "Belief Systems," *op. cit.* The reader will realize that at each election there is a group of "new voters" who cannot be employed in the computation of the particular index. They are employed by Key in other ways for his analyses, which we will not review. Key and others might also argue that *long-term* trends in the approval of a president's actions during his four years in office (in contrast with the ebb and flow of feelings about an unknown candidate during a campaign) is appropriate material for constructing an index of rationality. A trend study based on such information will be reviewed in Chapter VI.

suggests that the voters are damned if they do shift, and damned if they don't. For the standpatters, "editorial writers and other journeymen political philosophers reserve their most severe scorn. It may be quite as sensible, though, to remain steadfast in one's party loyalty as to move across party lines. In any event a certain caution is prudent if one is tempted to look with scorn on so many people."[50] In a similar vein, he takes up battle against the image of the shifter as an uninterested, uninformed, nonideological person who therefore is subject to whatever tides are flowing. And his weapons in this two-front war must naturally be empirical in nature.

In brief, by examining the profile of social characteristics and attitudes of each group, he documents that among shifters the directions in which they switch are congruent with their policy preferences and their group, i.e., class, ethnic, or religious, interests, whereas "on issue after issue those with views consistent with the outlook of their party stood pat. . . . The standpatters do not have to behave as mugwumps to keep their consciences clear; they are already where they ought to be in the light of their policy attitudes."[51] In addition, shifters generally show no lesser degree of education, nor are they recruited disproportionately from among those who report little interest in politics, or those who express no opinions on various issues. In effect, the indices of rationality underlying stability or change in voting are predicated on various accompanying social and psychological characteristics whose meanings seem clearly compatible with the exercise of reason, knowledge, and self-interest, applied correctively in the light of past experience.

The tests of rationality, based on such indices of the profiles of various groups of voters, are replicated from the surveys conducted in seven different election years. Within each of these intervals, several surveys are either examined as replications or are pooled to build up the size of the cells. These surveys are drawn from the work of different agencies. Within each survey, there are multiple tests based on the various individual questions or face-sheet characteristics that are indicators of rationality. There are three levels at which the evidence is progressively strengthened by the combination of data: by multiple indicators within a survey, by multiple surveys pooled or compared, and by comparison of batches of tests and surveys from different elections. The power of the findings is thus greatly enhanced. They cannot be undermined as narrowly limited by the quality of work of a given agency, or the particularity of some single measure or time period, or the accident of some one small sample. The compounding of evidence over time also has other benefits. Key's string of surveys is coextensive with the growth of mod-

---

[50] Key, Jr., *op. cit.*, p. 18.
[51] *Ibid.*, pp. 52–53.

ern survey research. Whatever constant errors or biases in sampling and measurement afflicted all the surveys of 1936 have certainly been reduced as the agencies became more sophisticated and skilled in the practices of their research. And by cautious comparisons of the trends over time, Key can also observe whether rationality has been rising or waning, or is harder or easier to exercise under given conditions, although he must watch for artifacts that obscure the changing and differential phenomena.

The conclusions can still be attacked by arguing about the logical nature of the indices and their compatibility with the concept of "rationality," or by questioning whether the magnitude of the scores are commensurate with Key's judgment that the electorate is rational. How many must manifest rationality; how many may deviate without impairing the diagnosis? And one can still raise the problem of errors in the measurement of the component items that have entered into Key's indices and appraisal. On the larger question of the definition of concepts and the construction and evaluation of indices appropriate to the study of "rationality," we shall say no more, since these are subtle philosophical and psychological issues that go far beyond any discussion of secondary analysis.[52]

On the problem of error, one is compelled by admiration to make some additional comments on Key's sensitive and comprehensive treatment of the quality of data, since this is so critical to the success of any secondary analysis. Beyond the control on error which Key builds into his own work by pooling and internal replication of measures and surveys, he adds in whatever evidence the literature from *primary* survey research provides. However, he also examines most carefully the bias that may strike at the very heart of his index, the classification of types of voters, since the recall of a vote in a previous election and the statement of a vote in a post-election survey are risky measurements. He appraises very carefully the meaning of other items that he employs, such as a question on voting intentions rather than votes cast, and an interviewer's rating of class. He examines the quality of the surveys from the primitive beginnings of such research upon which he must draw.[53] In these and other ways, his treatment of error provides an example to be followed by other secondary analysts.

---

[52] In this connection, however, Key entertains a procedure developed in primary research, "deviant case analysis." A cell or group that deviates from his hypothesis, that seems to exhibit irrationality, e.g., unskilled workers who voted for the Democrats in 1936 and who switched to the Republicans in 1940, is examined in a more intensive way to resolve the paradox.

[53] Apropos of a theme we have stressed, it is interesting that he only can find one Gallup Survey for 1936 with a recall question on the 1932 vote. Documentary evidence about the nature of this prehistoric survey is nonexistent. Perforce he uses it to extend the time series, but with as much caution as he can marshall.

Key's work does not exhaust the literature of thought processes, although it is a field which secondary analysts enter only rarely. For example, studies by Back and Gergen, described in Chapter III, deal in many ways with such fundamentals of thought as the orientation toward time, the scope of the ideas that individuals entertain, their impulsiveness in leaping to conclusions, their provisional handling of problems or searches for "final" solutions. To be sure these ways of thought are in turn seen as rooted in some personal style, and thus their studies, as noted, move us to even broader and deeper personality predispositions. Their studies, like Key's, also show how imaginative the analyst must be to abstract from existing questions indices of elusive, psychological functions, and how the evidence must be compounded from may questions and surveys.[54] Some suggestion of their approach was already presented, and we must now turn to a new realm of phenomena for secondary analysis, which like thought, attitude, and language can be a fundamental guide for the individual.

STUDIES OF KNOWLEDGE

The number of surveys that include batteries of questions measuring level of knowledge or ignorance about foreign countries, events, public figures, and domestic politics; about geography, history, words and other kinds of "schoolbook" information; is endless. William James and, later, Robert E. Park distinguished two kinds of knowledge, and the surveys implicitly make such a distinction. Not only do they obtain "knowledge about," but they often measure "acquaintance with" aspects of the environment. Where have people traveled, whom have they met—such questions document knowledge of a sort acquired by personal and first-hand acquaintance, and still other questions tap *vicarious* acquaintance, knowledge obtained at second hand, through hearsay, diffusion, etc. The opportunities for studies are manifold, and the phenomenon is obviously of fundamental importance for theory as well as practice.[55]

---

[54] It should be stressed that the principle: "No peeking" advanced in our discussion of the study of social groups has equal applicability to studies of phenomena. As Back notes, some surveys which contained relevant data on aspects of the self and on psychological functions were not used, but he stresses that his selection of surveys was made without any knowledge of the results therein contained. Personal communication.

[55] That it is relevant to social reformers, educators, and politicians is self-evident. For a review of its importance in social theory, see, for example, Louis Schneider, "The Role of the Category of Ignorance in Sociological Theory: An Exploratory Statement," *Amer. Sociol. Rev.*, **27**, 1962, pp. 492–508.

In 1947, Hyman and Sheatsley, by semisecondary analysis of only a small string of six NORC surveys, were able to explore on a national scale some patterns of public knowledge and the psychological barriers to public enlightenment. How much greater the data base would be now, twenty-five years later.[56] Schramm and his associates found no less than 54 national sample surveys in the period 1940 to 1967 that appeared useful for examining the public's knowledge; 35 of these promising enough that they were subjected to secondary analysis, and three so rich in data that they were given special intensive treatment.[57]

In our introductory discussion of the study of fundamental dispositions, we suggested that the findings from a single question about some item of opinion or knowledge are not of much use to the scholar concerned with the regularities of such phenomena, since the meaning of the results may be specific to the content or the measurement procedure rather than indicating anything of a general nature. As Schramm remarks, such results "contribute to news rather than to science." They may help the man of practical affairs, but it is hard to elevate a concrete finding from a single question on, for example, knowledge of the difference between a vitamin and a calorie, or a question on the chemical component of an atom bomb, or a question on knowledge of the meaning of the abbreviation F.B.I., or even a question on the knowledge of who the incumbent vice-president is, to any abstract significance.

If batteries of such questions are asked within the *same* survey, one can then examine the more generalized patterns of knowledge that an *individual* exhibits, score the depth or breadth of his knowledge more reliably, and relate his general cognitive equipment to his other characteristics as measured on the face sheet or elsewhere in the questionnaire. If many surveys contain questions of knowledge, even when there is only one or a few items per survey, by juxtaposition or combination, it is possible to examine more generalized patterns for the *aggregate* public or *sub*groups, and relate these patterns to features of the changing environment and other social factors. One can also piece together from the different surveys a string of analytic findings at the

---

[56] Hyman and Sheatsley, *op. cit.* In the period from 1947 to 1962, Erskine finds that some 110 questions were asked, but notes that interest in this area of inquiry has declined markedly in recent years. See, for example, Hazel G. Erskine, "The Polls: Textbook Knowledge," *Publ. Opin. Quart.,* **27,** 1963, pp. 133–141. On acquaintanceship, see her summaries, "Exposure to International Information," *Publ. Opin. Quart.,* **27,** 1963, pp. 656–662; "Exposure to Domestic Information," *Publ. Opin. Quart.,* **27,** 1963, pp. 491–500.

[57] In contrast with Erskine's count (for a shorter time period) of some 110 questions, Schramm later found about 300 questions important enough to be reexamined. Some of the difference in the estimate arises because the same question repeated in different years may variously be counted as one or several entries.

individual level, thus strengthening the evidence on the determinants. The rich source materials make all these modes of analysis a realistic possibility, and can be exemplified in the two studies mentioned.

One of the surveys that Hyman and Sheatsley used contained a battery of five questions testing knowledge in the sphere of foreign affairs on matters that had been raised to international prominence at that time, 1946. The criterion of knowledge was simply reported awareness or acquaintance with the facts. About a third of the public scored low or zero on this *simple* test, and another third scored relatively high. There appeared to be a generalized disposition toward ignorance or knowledge in many individuals. The inter-correlations (as well as the scores) showed that persons who were uninformed on one item tended to be uninformed on the other items, and led the analysts to label them, as noted in Chapter II, "chronic know-nothings." They spec-ulated that there is "something about the uninformed which makes them harder to reach, no matter what the level or nature of the information." To be sure, this was pushing the evidence hard, since all five items were in the one sphere of *foreign* affairs. It is possible that the phenomenon would not extend to all domains of knowledge but, unfortunately, that survey did not include batteries of information questions in other areas.

The survey did permit them, however, to test and circumscribe the location of the source of the ignorance. It could stem from an environment that was *generally* impoverished in the supply of all kinds of information, the source then being outside of the individual rather than within the self. As an index of the quality of the contemporary environment and the accessibility to in-formation that it provided, Hyman and Sheatsley used the face-sheet item on size of community, and found that this had only a modest influence on the respondent's knowledge, thus strengthening the inference that the major explanation lay *within* the individual.

These were people who remained "know-nothings" despite their advantaged environment and their current opportunities to learn. As one pondered this over the years, a companion secondary analysis seemed in order, and it is strange that it has not been accomplished. One could easily identify the man who is a "know-it-all" despite his life within a *dis*advantaged environment, and then seek to determine what inner forces impel him to overcome the ob-jective handicaps to knowledge. Perhaps a pure secondary analysis could not push deep enough toward the explanation, but then there would always be the possibility of a *semi*secondary analysis (Type II, design C—see Chapter II) using the design of Selective Experimental Empaneling to explore the inner depths of this admirable type of "know-it-all."

The same survey which permitted the identification of the "know-nothing" and of those with higher levels of information contained a battery of eight items on the level of *interest* in recent, prominent international events and continuing issues of foreign relations. Some of the items dealt with matters of overpowering importance in 1946 (and even today) such as our relations with Russia, the atom bomb, the United Nations—then a newly born light and hope in the world. Intercorrelations of these items, and an index based on all eight, again revealed wide individual differences and a generalized disposition on the part of a smallish group to be highly interested in a great many such matters, and a contrasted group who were apathetic and whose interests could hardly be engaged by even such powerful stimuli. Classifying respondents in terms of this disposition showed that it went far to explain their level of knowledge, the uninterested reporting much less awareness of specific events incorporated in the test battery, and scoring much lower on the general knowledge index.

We shall return shortly to the way in which the five other surveys in their string were exploited by Hyman and Sheatsley to enlarge understanding of the factors affecting public enlightenment. But it may be suggested that the most simple design, conventional quantitative analysis of the single survey, when it is fairly comprehensive in scope, may carry one fairly far on the phenomenon of knowledge. The descriptive findings had provided *conservative* measures of generalized ignorance and apathy toward information, since the scoring conventions had been so lenient,[58] and the combination of indirect and direct tests had pointed strongly to the source of the difficulty being the inner man. But, of course, the findings from a single survey in 1946 suffer from an inherent limitation. The domain within which ignorance and apathy had been traced was special, even though it was the broad region of foreign affairs, and the inner man had only been partially dissected. We turn to the work of Schramm and his associates whose lavish data base enlarged and extended the analysis of the problem.

Their thirty-five national surveys, spread over a span of more than twenty-five years, *taken together* measured public knowledge over a very wide domain. Each survey, with minor exceptions, however, contained very few questions. So the generality of the individual's knowledge could rarely be determined by any direct modes of analysis such as intercorrelations or scores on an index of knowledge. Yet their findings are relevant to that problem.

It is only fair to state first that they established some considerable source of *specificity* in knowledge, since the proportion who had no knowledge about

---

[58] The errors in sampling and measurement also worked, in this instance, to make the descriptive findings compelling. As the analysts remark, the size of the group of "know-nothings" is probably underrepresented because the "claim to awareness was accepted at face value, without any check on his actual knowledge" and polls in 1946 certainly and perhaps even now "consistently tend to over-sample the more literate, higher socioeconomic groups in the population." Hyman and Sheatsley, *op. cit.*, p. 414 (footnote).

or acquaintance with different items varied widely, suggesting either that this is a function of the difficulty of learning, the amount of stimulation and specific information to which individuals are exposed, or that some things are just more relevant and interesting to some people than other things.[59] Even a person disposed toward ignorance might occasionally become excited about something. It is hard to account for the vagaries of knowledge in the multitudinous data without postulating such specificities: In 1945–1946, 21% of the nation had some correct knowledge of the Bill of Rights, and 35% could name both their Senators. In 1948, 61% had heard something of the Taft–Hartley Act, and in 1952 the figure was 72%, but only 27% had heard of Truman's four-point program in 1950. In 1964, less than one person in five knew what Senator Goldwater's religion or President Johnson's religion was, but 80% knew where Goldwater came from, and, given the fame of Texas, 94% knew where Johnson came from. It is ironical that 79% had heard of the John Birch Society, but only 42% of Americans for Democratic Action. Such variations and specificities in the cognitive maps of Americans are documented again and again in the array of data presented.

Schramm and his associates demonstrate, however, that no matter what the question "there is almost certain to be a sizeable number of persons unable to answer." The speculative model one might advance is that of a hard core of "know-nothings" contained within these fluctuating masses, surrounded by additional numbers whose ignorance is a sometime thing dependent on the specificities noted above. And there is an important finding at the level of description of the group that strengthens the argument. "The proportions of know-nothings on given questions are likely to be much greater among certain segments of the population than among others."[60] Even though the very same *individuals* are not asked the many questions scattered over the surveys, the analysts are able to trace a continuity, a generalized ignorance for a particular *type* of individual or group of persons who are sampled throughout the many surveys. There must be something about the enduring characteristics of the group, metaphorically speaking, embodied in its inner nature,

---

[59] Schramm and his associates make admirable use of the occasional questions that have been repeated sometimes as often as five or six times over a single decade. On items of a historical or basic nature, unlikely to be temporarily elevated to attention by media, there is an incredible stability to the estimates of the extent of public knowledge. What is suggested, over and above the demonstration of the reliability of such simple measurements, is that such kinds of knowledge are likely to be very stable, established components of the cognitive structures. By contrast the time series on other questions, "radioactive fallout," the nature of polio, etc. show dramatic rises in public knowledge, presumably reflecting the influence of events and the supply of information in the environment. Schramm *et al., op. cit.,* pp. 21–26.

[60] *Ibid.,* p. 16.

that disposes such people toward ignorance, just as there was something in the inner nature of the concrete individuals whom Hyman and Sheatsley identified. Formal education, as expected, is what differentiated the type, but the potency of its effects is perhaps unexpected. "So powerful is education as an indicator of public knowledge that from it alone one can predict as much as from all the other demographic characteristics." When Schramm and his associates inspected some 80 different questions of knowledge asked of national samples, they found that "the proportion of people in the lowest educational group with no knowledge of those items was perhaps five and one half times the proportion in the highest educational group."[61] In terms of the formulations of Chapter IV, Schramm establishes by replication and synthesis that one of the features characterizing the uneducated as a group is a persistent and wide-ranging pattern of ignorance. The ignorance is not confined to textbook knowledge, so it is more than just a matter of what facts were learned in school and remembered. What is suggested is that the better educated have learned the skills and interests which dispose them to absorb the information later presented in their adult environments. And the uneducated have not had the earlier opportunity to learn the skills and interests which they will need later if they are to incorporate the information that becomes available to them.[62]

A good deal of the difficulty thus seems to lie in the dispositions created by the past histories of the individuals, and therefore is not remedied by simple manipulations of the contemporary environments. Hyman and Sheatsley, by semisecondary analysis of other surveys in their string, actually tested some of the barriers and vehicles to public enlightenment. They were able to graft design 11 onto several of the surveys treating the variations that had

---

[61] *Ibid.*, pp. 36, 39.

[62] It is worth recalling that one of the features Knupfer described in her "Portrait of the Underdog" was a much lesser "participation in thought life," the lower-status person using print media much less, and less inclined to expose himself to serious content in the media. In her identification of the group of underdogs, as earlier noted, there is no sharp system of criteria, and the group obviously includes those who have various combinations of low education and low economic level. However, Schramm and his associates by multivariate analysis demonstrate that the well-educated person remains knowledgeable whatever his occupation and income, although among the uneducated, occupation and income do make a difference presumably creating new opportunities and incentives to obtain information. The findings seem to transcend national boundaries. In his secondary analysis of French data, Hamilton also found that the unskilled workers were less likely to expose themselves to serious news in the print media. Parallel to Schramm's findings, when the comparisons are controlled by education, among the better educated the occupational differences disappear, but interest in certain kinds of political information persists among some occupational groups who have had *little* education. *Affluence and French Worker, op. cit.*, pp. 94–96, and p. 113.

been introduced into the questionnaire as *experimental designs* to test the effect of disseminating information. Examples of this rare design are few and thus worth brief review.

In two of these surveys, a battery of questions followed the sequence of first asking individuals if they were aware of a certain item of information. Then the gist of the information was communicated by the interviewers to *all* respondents, embarrassment being avoided by some such phrase as "well, you remember." Then the sample was asked some relevant attitude question which presumably was dependent on the knowledge of the facts. One realizes that this pattern of questioning implicitly was an experimental test of the effect of communication on attitude, and the conditions governing the absorption of information.

If the sheer cognitive content to which an individual is exposed is enough to change him, then the individuals who previously had been ignorant, but who were subsequently enlightened experimentally, should exhibit the same attitudes as those who had already informed themselves through natural means. But in the two surveys reported, and in others alluded to which followed the same paradigm, the evidence from these experiments on several thousand respondents was that the attitudes differed between the two groups, both now equally enlightened but distinguished by their previous level of knowledge. Attitudes cannot be changed so easily by such manipulations, and the inference is drawn that those who had previously absorbed the information naturally were those who found it congenial to their already existing attitudes.[63]

Another one of their surveys, involving a split ballot, implicitly contained a more rigorous experimental design to test the effect of disseminating information. In the course of other survey research, it had been documented that individuals who saw American self-interest as being benefited by our foreign-aid programs were more likely to hold favorable attitudes toward those programs. Consequently, in a later survey the national sample was split into two equivalent halves, each containing about 600 respondents. The "experimental" half was informed in the course of the questioning of the benefits that would follow from a loan to England, the prestigious supporters of it, and the guarantees against risk of loss of the money. The "control" half was told nothing, and both groups were then asked their attitudes.

There was a definite effect in that approval was 14% higher in the group that had been enlightened experimentally than in the equivalent control group. But more refined analysis revealed that the potency of the communication was dependent on the prior disposition of the individual. The experi-

---

[63] Hyman and Sheatsley, *op. cit.*, pp. 417–418.

mental *and* control groups were further subdivided on the basis of another measure in terms of their hostility to England. For those who had a *friendly* attitude, approval of the loan was 25% higher among those who had been enlightened than among individuals within the control group with the same attitudes. But among those with hostility, the experimental and control groups differed by only 1%, suggesting that such communication did not override the barriers to attitude change.[64] Split ballots and other relatively common variations introduced into the questionnaires of ordinary surveys can be recast into such experimental tests.

In the course of reviewing studies of fundamental phenomena, two new designs have been added to our list, and the value of designs involving replications has been reemphasized. That leads us quite naturally to the topics of our next chapter, since the major avenue to the study of social change is via replication. Admittedly, we could linger almost indefinitely over the topic of fundamental dispositions. We have slighted those occasional secondary analysts who have tried to explore even deeper and broader dispositions, orientations toward such central aspects of human experience as time and space and the self, and to study the way these are part of the organization of personality.

We have slighted those who have examined other psychological systems such as values or such blends of ideology and personality as authoritarianism; and those who have examined orientations toward such basic institutions and roles within them, such as work and child rearing; and those who have studied such diffuse states of affect as happiness or optimism or such unpleasant states as sadness and pain; and still others who have tried to describe the fundamental cognitive and perceptual structures by which men confer order and meaning on their experiences, such as their imagery of the world and of human nature; and those who have tried to examine intellective processes, modes of thought, and problem solving, from such common everyday lines of survey questioning as demand the entertaining of assumptions, the conjuring with hypothetical situations—the "iffy" questions—and which then press the respondent to reason on the basis of that prescription,[65] or from

---

[64] *Ibid.*, p. 419–421.

[65] A dramatic example is provided by two questions asked of a national sample of adults in Denmark in 1963 which reads in English: "*If you disregard* your own political party membership and *if you disregard* your own other sympathies, *then* what party do you think has shown the best results since the last election and which in your opinion has shown the worst results?" *Polls,* **1,** 1965, No. 1, p. 16 (italics supplied). Over 50% of the sample answered "don't know" to each question. This incredibly high magnitude does not seem on the surface related to the difficulty of the discrimination involved, but rather to the complex "if–then" construction which requires the respondent to sus-

sequences of questions which juxtapose ideas that bear a certain logical relationship and whose observed association then measures what might be called popular "psycho-logic."[66]

Unfortunately, it is the rare secondary analyst who has tried to study such subtle psychological phenomena. The examples are too few and this chapter already too long. A secondary analyst can realize these opportunities with the methodological principles already at his disposal, and the works of such men as Back and Gergen, Elder, and Inkeles mentioned in earlier chapters provide examples. We shall return to some of these possibilities in later chapters which show secondary analysts studying the way such phenomena vary in different times and places.

---

pend his feelings and make what in the purest sense is an *objective* judgment. More evidence on the nature of the difficulty comes from a cross tabulation by the respondent's own party affiliation. The judgments are in fact highly correlated with his membership, although the question instructed him to disregard such factors. It seems that ordinary individuals cannot think in such fashion. The same kind of finding can be documented in American surveys for questions which instruct respondents to make a given assumption before expressing an attitude. Whether certain types of individuals are more able to suspend subjective considerations and follow logical sets of instructions could be explored by more refined secondary analysis of such materials.

[66] For a serendipitous finding in this sphere, showing the way in which logically contradictory expectations may be commingled, and an early instance of a brief semisecondary analysis, see Paul B. Sheatsley, "Expectations of War and Depression," *Publ. Opin. Quart.*, **13**, 1949, pp. 685–686.

VI

Studies of Change

THE CENTRAL THEME OF THIS CHAPTER HAS ALREADY BEEN SOUNDED MANY TIMES in this book. Chapter I introduced the idea that the surveys accumulated over the thirty-five-year history of the research enterprise could reopen a door to the study of the past which otherwise would be closed to later generations of analysts. But it also sounded a note of caution. Knowledge of the procedures used might be matters of unrecorded history and progressively fade from human memory with time, thereby confounding the later analyst's attempts at proper interpretation of his findings. Errors might become buried, forgotten, or repressed. Conscientious analysts who would enter such lost worlds would have to abandon *some* hope and prepare themselves, if not for hell, for a severe ordeal.

Chapter II sounded a new and hopeful note, suggesting that old baselines could be combined with new primary surveys into *semi*secondary analyses of trends and social change. In Chapter III, several of the exemplars of the successful secondary analyst further restored our hopes by providing models of the investigator of social change who is neither paralyzed by the difficulties nor negligent in his handling of them.

The case studies of Chapter V went further. They demonstrated that a series of surveys arranged in replicative designs could serve in the study of social change, and presented some of the detailed procedures and problems of such secondary analysis.

Chapter IV, however, extolled the virtues of combining surveys by pooling, and its message may cause the analyst to neglect change, unless countered now. The persuasive argument was advanced that the pooled results attenuate the random errors of different surveys and transcend the vicissitudes of the situation within which a given survey was conducted. However, they also transcend the temporal setting of that moment. Pooling fits the style of the *generalizer*. Carried to its extreme, to the pooling into a super-survey of many surveys spread widely over time, it is ideally suited to the grand generalizer who seeks a finding that remains invulnerable to all the minor fluctuations of measurement and time, and who regards the variation as error or irritant rather than evidence. There is also room for the *particularizer*, who prefers a design that will reveal the process of change rather than obscure it.

Consider the case of one analyst whose style, to be sure, is not one extreme or the other, and who is certainly sensitive to the merits of alternative designs. He was fortunate enough to be able to draw upon a rich French data bank containing the results of about 100 surveys conducted over a decade, all containing a question on satisfaction with De Gaulle's performance of his office. Contemplating this wealth, his *prime* response was: "What is perhaps one of the most promising research strategies involves building large cumulative samples from a single question or a set of related questions for which the pollsters have created a 'time series'."[1] And so he builds a super-survey containing 17,245 interviews by pooling ten surveys, thereby insuring big enough cells that he can examine the enduring regional variations in support of De Gaulle. The first reaction of another analyst might have been to seize upon the "time series," to examine *temporal* rather than regional variation, and to stress replication rather than pooling. Of course, neither strategy precludes the other, and an analyst can incorporate both into a total endeavor with the balance tilted as he will.[2]

This chapter is intended to add some additional balance to the strategies that might be followed, and to present essential details for those who will focus on change. New cases involving replication have been chosen so as to emphasize the use of the design in the specific study of change.

Secondary analysts of change have profited from the common practice of survey organizations to repeat particular questions or similar indicators of certain variables on different surveys. The practice, however, shows great variation and the time series fall into a number of different classes.

---

[1] H. Rosenthal, "The Popularity of Charles De Gaulle: Findings from Archive-based Research, *Publ. Opin. Quart.*, **31**, 1967, p. 381.

[2] Rosenthal in fact does combine both approaches. And he follows the strategy mentioned in Chapter IV, of treating the surveys as replications first to check the stability of the findings before pooling them into "a large sample where time . . . effects are ignored." One of the most attractive features of the analysis is a subsequent comparison of regions *over time* to see whether a process of polarization or convergence is occurring. But it does seem fair to suggest that the balance of interest is more in the direction of pooling than in studying change.

Some analysts have had the good fortune to inherit data on the very phenomena that interest them, derived from a great *many* replications, the time *intervals* between surveys being *short* and the *total duration* of time spanned being *long*. Rosenthal's one-hundred French surveys measuring the ebb and flow of De Gaulle's popularity from month to month and over a decade provides one such illustration. The same kind of time series is available for the equivalent American variable, satisfaction with the President's performance of his office. The question has been asked some 300 times over the last twenty-five years and the four corresponding presidencies. Various investigators exploited this bonanza, and Mueller's secondary analysis will be described later.[3] The time series on this variable is perhaps the single, most lavish one available, but it is not a unique instance.

Several indicators of attitude toward American involvement in the Korean and Vietnam Wars, taken together, have been asked perhaps fifty times of national samples by several different survey organizations. The series spans a twenty-year interval and two different wars, although there is an obvious discontinuity, the measures falling into the two clumps of time of the respective wars. Whenever an issue has been regarded as topical or newsworthy, and also of continuing or recurrent importance, and the corresponding attitudes and beliefs as changeable and responsive to events, the agencies have generated time series that are long, and contain many and frequent points of measurement. Expectation of war asked during times of peace, basic tendency toward isolationism or internationalism, attitude toward the United Nations, the saliency of foreign versus domestic problems, attitudes toward the Soviet Union during the cold-war period of the forties and fifties, are examples of this first and most lavish type of time series. Occasionally, secondary analysts have taken advantage of these data for their studies.

But attitudes and beliefs are not the only entities within this category. What is obvious, but often unnoticed, is that the *face-sheet* characteristics—religious preference, church attendance, size of household, number of children, union membership, voting behavior, party preference, etc.—have been measured for years and years, many times and frequently, not because they are topical or conceived as labile phenomena. Indeed, the imagery is that they are unchangeable or relatively rigid. The time series flows simply out of routinized, institutionalized practice, because these characteristics may figure analytically in the breakdown and treatment of data. A thoughtful secondary

---

[3] John E. Mueller, "Presidential Popularity from Truman to Johnson," *Amer. Polit. Sci. Rev.*, **64**, 1970, pp. 18–34. A similar question on approval of Adenauer's general policies during his office was asked about 100 times over about a fifteen year interval and asked about another thirty times during Erhard's chancellorship. See, *The Germans: Public Opinion Polls, 1947–1966* (Allensbach: Verlag für Demoskopie, 1967), pp. 256–264.

analyst may, however, make them the central object of study and examine empirically the *changes* in such behavior and patterns of social structure.

A second type of time series has been generated by the survey agencies for other variables which are regarded as of continuing interest, but not conceived to be subject to short-run influences. The series may be long with many points, but the measurements are *infrequent*. For example, on an annual basis for many years the Gallup Poll has asked American national samples whether they are abstainers or drink alcoholic beverages, thus generating a time series over twenty years long, with many points, but one whose slow periodicity or infrequency of measurement does not yield direct empirical evidence on short-run fluctuations in the estimates and/or unreliability of measurement. Similarly, the Michigan Surveys of Consumer Finances, conducted for a period of more than a dozen years provide many such time series relating to consumption patterns, economic behavior, and attitudes. Other examples of this class of data are questions asked in Germany once or twice a year on whether the respondent is interested in politics and discusses politics, generating a time series of some ten points over a dozen years. Another question posed in West Germany, always in December, asks the respondent whether he anticipates the year ahead with hope or apprehension. It is almost a pure example of this type of time series—twenty points spaced carefully over twenty years.[4] The American time series on "ideal family size" provides another example—at least thirteen measurements over a twenty-five year period. Blake's analysis of these data will be reviewed shortly.

Several other patterns of repeated inquiry by the survey agencies may be presented together, since the time series, however they may vary, are more rudimentary, and all hamper the secondary analyst to some degree. Occasionally, one finds a time series of *long* duration, but with relatively *few* points of measurement, and marked *discontinuities* in study. There may be wide empty spaces in it, and a thin scatter of points. Occasionally, the series may be enriched by some clusters of points when, for a short time, interest was high and there were frequently spaced measurements, but only temporarily. Such irregularities of various sorts reflect the natural style of the agen-

---

[4] The reader will realize that some of these phenomena may be subject to seasonal variation or have some calendric character. Sometimes the agency has standardized the point of measurement, thereby insuring constancy in the measurement of trend or change, but perhaps running the danger of an unfortunate choice of an unrepresentative period of measurement. At other times the agencies have experimented with the phasing of the inquiry, permitting some estimate of this factor. Sometimes annual trends are confounded with seasonal variables, but the actual problem may be less worrisome than one might think. For example, the Gallup national trends on drinking seem affected very little by whether one is talking about drinking in June or November.

cies, whose interests and activities are governed more by the topical than by systematic prolonged attention to a problem. And some of the time series might even have died completely if not for an occasional semisecondary analyst within the agency who saw the benefits from reviving an item out of the dim or forgotten past.

The civil rights and race-relations area provides many examples. A battery of questions on support for racial integration in various spheres had been asked by NORC of national samples in 1942, and a few of these questions had been repeated during the war years, but the time series was then interrupted and not revived until 1956, after which point occasional measurements and clumps of points using the same instruments cover the period up to about 1965. The decade between 1946 and 1956, as well as the Dark Ages before 1942, will always remain *terra incognita* to the secondary analyst, but nevertheless the data allow him to describe a trend over a long time span and estimate the short-run fluctuations.[5] This would hardly be described as bad fortune, although compared to the analyst of presidential popularity an investigator may suffer from *relative* deprivation.

The time series on other aspects of this belief system present the same mixed fortune to the secondary analyst, although they have a different character. The measurements may be many and frequent, but the duration of the series is shorter. For example, a question on the respondent's belief in the inevitability of integration begins in 1956 and about half a dozen measurements describe the trend over the subsequent years, but the long early period remains a blank, and the most recent years may well be seeing a cessation of interest in the use of the question. A question on the perception of the speed with which integration has been proceeding—too fast or too slow—was asked

---

[5] Sheatsley remarks that "during the seven years from 1935 to 1942, only four questions bearing even indirectly on the subject seem to have been asked by the national public opinion polls of that time." P. B. Sheatsley, "White Attitudes toward the Negro," *Daedalus*, Winter, 1966, p. 217. As noted in Chapter II, the revival of the time series beginning in 1956 is best described as a semisecondary analysis, the later measures being obtained deliberately to tie into the already available baseline. Attitude toward various forms of social insurance provides another example of this last type of time series. Schiltz found no less than 39 surveys of American samples spanning the thirty-year period, 1935–1965, but all sorts of technical difficulties plague the analysis of the trends and the interpretation of specific findings, including such a fundamental problem as lack of information on the exact dates of the surveys, the size of samples, and the exact question wording in the very early surveys. How much can be accomplished, nevertheless, by meticulous handling and thoughtful judgment applied to such bodies of data is conveyed by the monograph, especially the technical appendix. See M. E. Schiltz, *Public Attitudes Toward Social Security, 1935–1965* (Washington, Government Printing Office, 1970), Social Security Administration, Research Report No. 33.

by Gallup at least eighteen times between 1962 and 1968, and is illustrative of the shorter, but lavish, time series on racial questions in recent years reflecting the current importance of these problems.

Attitudes toward civil liberties and tolerance or intolerance for political nonconformity provide another example of a domain in which the time series have been shaped irregularly by oscillating interest and neglect of the agencies. Questions tapping this domain were scattered very thinly through the period of the thirties and forties. The McCarthy era produced a burgeoning of activity in the mid-fifties, but since then the time series have faltered and almost died. The analyst obviously cannot examine these problems as thoroughly as he might like, but still considerable work can be accomplished.[6]

A final type of series is the one where the duration is relatively short and the measurements are few, and the exactness of the replication is also a cause for concern. National data on voluntary association membership are an example. As the case in Chapter V suggests, even these meager resources may lend themselves to the study of change.

The secondary analyst of change must simply tailor his study to the fabrics of data the agencies have woven over the years. There is a wide assortment to choose from, but of uneven quality. If he wishes to work with richer cloth, more yardage, he may have to change his initial problem. If he clings to his choice, he may have to work with thinner cloth, and his fine workmanship will have to compensate for the deficiencies in the material.

In studying change, whatever the substantive area, the secondary analyst's goals may be to describe the process for the aggregate sample or for one or more subgroups, in a sense disaggregating the data. He may focus on the *differential* change across groups, having in mind some model, such as the increasing polarization of groups with time or their convergence. He may examine the *direction* of the convergence, seeing whether one group progressively moves toward the position to which another group has remained anchored.[7] For phenomena that are multifaceted, for example, prejudice, he may examine a family of curves to see whether one aspect changes at a

---

[6] See, for example, H. Hyman and P. B. Sheatsley, "Trends in Public Opinion on Civil Liberties," *J. Soc. Issues*, **9**, (No. 3), pp. 6–16. Douglas K. Stewart, *Support for Dissent; A Study of Trends in the United States* (Unpublished Ph.D. dissertation, Pittsburgh, 1967).

[7] Reed's secondary analysis, cited in Chapter IV, provides a clear illustration. He finds persistent subcultural differences between the South and the North. Insofar as he observes some convergence in values, some decline in the differences over time, it may consist in the South becoming more like the North was, or the North becoming more Southern in style. The latter process seems more frequent. Ironically, one might say that the *distinctiveness* of the region may have declined, but only because its values have *persisted* and pervaded or invaded the North.

different rate than others. And by various means he may try to establish the factors that *explain* any of these processes.

In undertaking such studies the secondary analyst is very much the pioneer. He is traveling toward strange frontiers without benefit of detailed text or guide book, and primary analysts have blazed very few of the trails for him. By contrast, in the study of social groups and phenomena, the quantitative analytical procedures plus the basic logic have been long established, and asserted in books.

Glock states it well in an essay on survey design and analysis. On trend studies, he remarks: "Sociologists, while they have used *other people's data* to pursue the kind of analysis which this design allows, have not had the financial resources to plan and execute such studies *de novo*."[8] Consequently, his one brief example comes from a particular *secondary* analysis, and his technical discussion is sketchy compared to his elaborate review of principles of analysis of single surveys and panel studies.[9]

Given these conditions, secondary analysts of change will have to blaze some technical trails for themselves, taking whatever guidance they can find

---

[8] Glock, *op. cit.*, pp. 51, 53 (italics supplied). The point is underscored if we consider Rosenberg's recent book on *The Logic of Survey Analysis*, *op. cit.*, which contains no treatment whatsoever of trend analysis.

[9] If the secondary analyst is to seek guidance from the example of primary analysts, oddly enough, he should return to the distant past when agencies and analysts occasionally were given the resources to conduct continuing periodic surveys on changes in public opinion. Works before 1950, for example, the previously cited studies by Cantril or Bruner, provide instances. The secondary analyst of sample surveys can also turn for guidance to the field of economics, where the study of time series has been a central topic, and a great deal of sophisticated statistical method has been developed to describe and clarify the temporal patterns, and then to partition the gross change into various component processes. The growth of such methodology in economics underscores our argument. The economists have been *secondary* analysts for many years, living off the long time series on prices, employment, population, etc. produced by the government. If they, too, had been confined to primary surveys, they, no doubt, would also lack for lengthy time series and have been much slower in developing a methodology. We may adapt profitably some of their modes of description, for example, clarifying trend by fitting curves to the pattern or ironing out irregularities by moving averages, or making tests for random sequences, and possibly finding analogies to their adjustments and transformations of raw data, as in the use of index numbers. Their models for partitioning the pattern into a regular or secular trend, plus cyclical and seasonal variation, plus a random or erratic component, may teach us something and perhaps we can adapt some of their statistical procedures. It is difficult, however, to see analogies to seasonal and other cyclical patterns in many of our phenomena. And it is fair to say that the interest of economists in explaining the "erratic" component is low, whereas this may be central in our studies. For a brief statement see Hoel's chapter on "Time Series and Index Numbers" but note his remark on "the difficulty of interpreting the components that have been isolated." P. G. Hoel, *Elementary Statistics* (New York: Wiley, 1960).

only from each other. To simplify their task, we have reviewed some of the studies in the literature, attempting to codify the principles and the procedural steps. Ours is only an approximation to a systematic statement. The steps are presented in a sequence, but the actual research may involve some oscillation back and forth.

Considering Comparability

Accurate description of changes or trends over time and valid explanation, presuppose comparability of the procedures. It would be misleading to evaluate some temporal pattern of results as real change when it simply reflects changing procedures. And it would be foolish to try then to isolate some real explanation of the change when the explanation of it all was simply an artifact, a change produced by some acts of the original researchers rather than by nature and society.

Replication of surveys in all essential respects produces the convenient and ideal set of materials, and this ideal should be pondered as a first step. The term should be regarded in a broad and comprehensive light. As suggested earlier, the *question* or indicator of the variable under study is only one element of comparability, although critical. Its *location* within the questionnaire and the prior context of questions may also affect the responses.[10] If the nature of the *universe,* the design of the *sample,* and the way it actually operated over time—the magnitude and character of the *losses*—had changed,

---

[10] In a succinct and excellent treatment of problems of comparability in the secondary analysis of trends, Glenn mentions a fairly common instance of this element of the problem which might be missed by the secondary analyst. A given question may be identical over time, but have been prefaced on occasion by a "filter" question, the results in the one instance applying to a different portion of the sample than in the other survey. Norval D. Glenn, "Problems of Comparability in Trend Studies with Opinion Poll Data," *Publ. Opin. Quart.,* **34,** 1970, pp. 82–91. Another example is provided by a subtle change in procedure in some of the more recent Survey Research Center surveys. Having arrived at the view that some respondents truly without opinions have been forced into expressing opinions they do not hold by virtue of the "demand character" of an interview, they have more recently added to a question that postscript clause "or don't you have an opinion about that." They also have prefaced a battery of questions with the phrase "Of course people don't have feelings about all of these things. If you don't have an opinion on something, just tell us that." This possibly potent change in the stimulus might not be known to a secondary analyst who did not see the interviewer instructions, know the conventions of the interview, or scrutinize the questionnaire thoroughly. P. E. Converse, personal communication.

the trends in the aggregate or in a subgroup might simply reflect these facts rather than signifying any real changes in a specified collectivity. For phenomena whose occurrence varies seasonally or calendrically—church attendance or attendance at meetings, or leisure-time behavior, for example—the timing of the series of surveys should have been comparable or the *temporal referent* introduced into the question wording should have controlled the problem. The composition of the *field staff* (its social-stimulus character for some or all respondents) and the way it was instructed to and did operate the question, may be important, especially in connection with open-ended questions and for classes of issues and respondents susceptible to interviewer effects.[11] Where refined trends in different subgroups are examined, or where changes over time in the social correlates or causes of a phenomenon are examined, the comparability of wording of such collateral indicators and the associated conventions of interviewing and coding are final elements to consider.[12]

It would be negligent to ignore any of these matters, but it would be defeatist for a secondary analyst to reject wholesale an entire time series which departs in any degree from the ideal. And it is not necessary. He may be able to make some reasonable appraisal of the effect on one or more of the points in the series of a temporary change in the measurement procedures. Indeed, if he is fortunate, the manipulations may have fallen naturally into such an arrangement that he has a pure test in *adjacent* surveys of the influence of operations and instruments unconfounded by changes due to time. If he can afford the luxury of eliminating one or more incomparable points from a lavish time series, he can remove the tainted data without any great loss of information.

---

[11] A poignant example is provided in Stember's study. One of his most lavish time series on antisemitism is based on an open-ended question which was asked in fourteen surveys spanning the nineteen year period, 1940–1959. There is a dramatic discontinuity in the curve, antisemitism dropping radically by this indicator after 1950, the seven surveys thereafter stabilizing at a low level, and the seven surveys before that date all showing a level double or triple in magnitude. But alas at this critical point, he notes that "The surveying task was transferred from one polling agency to another in 1950—precisely the Year in which reports of anti-semitic talk took a sharp drop." Stember, *op. cit.*, p. 61.

[12] One of Blake's special analyses of trends in "family-size ideals" hinges on the quality and comparability of the measures of economic status, since it is critical for her argument to establish the stability of the correlation over time. In some instances, family income was enumerated; in other surveys breadwinner's income; in other surveys, the indicator of the variable is a rating of economic level, the definition itself varying as between surveys. For careful treatment of such sources of incomparability and a reasonable appraisal of their effect on her subgroup findings, as well as care in assessing the validity of the reports of income, see Judith Blake, "Income and Reproductive Motivation," *Population Studies*, **21**, No. 3, 1967, especially pp. 187–188.

If the coding has changed, he may be able to recode or collapse data in such a way as to restore the comparability. If the composition of the field staff or interviewing practices had been changed but only for some locatable portion of the respondents (e.g., Negroes), that stratum could be eliminated by truncating the sample, or the data could be disaggregated and presented separately for the relevant subgroups. Fortuitously, the change in interviewing might have been introduced in such a way as to permit some tests and estimate of its effects on the results.[13] If the phasing of the surveys has varied, creating the danger that seasonal or calendric effects obscure the trend, this too may admit of measurement through fortuitous circumstances and it may turn out that the problem is not of worrisome magnitude.

If the universe has been expanded or contracted in some particular stratum, for example, an age or regional group, the analyst may truncate the surveys, eliminating that stratum and restoring comparability to what is left, although at some loss of generalizability. Alternatively, he may disaggregate the data and present trends for the various strata, thus containing the incomparability which then applies only to one portion of his findings.

Sometimes, a bias occurs in over- or undersampling a stratum in one or a subset of surveys that enter into the time series. The crude changes in the aggregate may then simply represent the *improper* changing weight that stratum added to the total results over time. Even this insidious problem can be ameliorated.

The very long time series of the Gallup Polls constitute a major resource for the secondary analyst, but are marred by this problem. In the early years and up to around 1949–1950 the method of quota sampling was such as to introduce a serious and persistent underrepresentation of the less educated and lower-status segment of the population. One could, to be sure, confine

---

[13] An investigator might apply evidence on the magnitude of interviewer effects obtained from large scale methodological studies to the data he has at hand. For example, studies of variance in the results obtained by different interviewers but from the same agency, NORC, in general showed that the effects were small. See H. Hyman *et al.*, *Interviewing in Social Research* (Chicago: University of Chicago Press, 1954). A few estimates of the effects produced by changing the field staff from that of one agency to another (presumably a combination of the variables of type of interviewer recruited, mode of training, and supervision) have been obtained from occasional large surveys which have been split into interpenetrating half-samples and assigned to two different agencies. For one such study, itself a methodological secondary analysis based on the Stouffer Study of Conformity, half of which had been done by the Gallup Poll and the other half by NORC, see C. H. Stember, *The Effect of Field Procedures on Public Opinion Data* (Unpublished doctoral dissertation, Columbia University, 1955). One other large scale experiment was built into Steiner's national survey on television, half being conducted by Roper and half by NORC. The similarity of the findings was exceedingly high. See Gary Steiner, *The People Look at Television* (New York, Knopf, 1963, pp. 260–318).

his trend analyses to the subset of surveys of more recent years, sacrificing scope but maintaining comparability. Or one could conduct separate trend analyses for the subsets of surveys before and after the major changes in sampling, a procedure followed, in effect, in one of our examples to be presented.

In confronting such problems, Glenn adopts a philosophy that seems a sensible blend of caution and courage, and he develops two effective procedures for working with such imperfect trend data. "Almost as regrettable as the tendency to neglect problems of comparability is the belief . . . that the quota samples used into the 1950's . . . are so poor that trend studies using data from the earlier polls should not be attempted. Such a belief inhibits exploitation of a valuable body of data and leads to undue skepticism . . ."[14] His main procedure is simply to correct for the bias by introducing a new and proper weight (based on population data for that time) for the uneducated stratum obtaining an aggregate time series in which all the points are now adjusted estimates, thus insuring comparability but also generalizability to the national population. He suggests as a prior procedure the cross tabulation of the dependent variable by education to see whether the bias in sampling actually has enough effect on the specific phenomenon to necessitate the introduction of the new weight and a correction of the estimates.

Glenn is aware of the fact that his procedure only corrects for one particular kind of bias. In principle, however, the solution could be extended and weights for other known biases introduced. Although he does not reject all possibility of such additional hazards in using these time series, he remarks that "neither the literature nor my comparisons provide any reason to believe

[14] Glenn, *op. cit.*, p. 83. A secondary analysis we shall not review in this chapter provides a fine example of coping with imperfect and not exactly comparable surveys to produce information on long-term trends in intergenerational mobility between 1945 and 1957. Jackson and Crockett for these purposes juxtapose data from a 1945 quota sample of the white population, a 1947 quota sample of the general adult population, and two later probability samples of the general adult population. The difficulties are compounded by the fact that the 1945 study, although it was nominally comparable to others in sampling the target universe of *noninstitutionalized adults*, eliminated many more young people who were still in the army at that time. In addition, the questions used to measure occupation were not exactly comparable, the original codings were not exactly comparable, and the field staff and agencies involved varied. Yet by dint of careful judgment, reasonable estimates of the effects of such factors, some recoding and collapsing of categories, truncation, disaggregation and corresponding containment of errors, and the like, they manage heroically to mobilize all these data on behalf of a convincing trend analysis. See Elton F. Jackson and H. Crockett, "Occupational Mobility in the United States," A Point Estimate and Trend Comparison," *Amer. Sociol. Rev.*, **29**, 1964, pp. 5–15.

that the samples used by the major polling organizations contained more than one important kind of systematic error."[15]

In the early years of the Gallup Poll and up through 1948, the enterprise was geared to the prediction of elections. Therefore the target universe often was *voters* rather than adults. Correspondingly, it was a desirable feature of the design that the South generally, and additionally, Negroes in the South, were underrepresented, since these strata had a low likelihood of voting. Undersampling *uneducated* members of the population also was a desirable feature to hit the *target universe* better since they had a lower tendency to vote. There is also some suggestion that other methods of screening respondents and allocating quotas over the country may have been introduced so as to underrepresent individuals who had low likelihood of voting in that era, but the evidence is murky and the full truth probably lost in history. Insofar as the later samples were aimed at the target universe of *adults*, and the former weights therefore changed, some additional incomparability is introduced into the trends.

Stember's trend analyses of prejudice, to be reviewed below, are derived partly from the long Gallup time series. He resolves these insidious difficulties by a test similar to one that Glenn proposes. Since the net effect of all these changes is to alter the weight of *"voters"* in the string of samples, he determines if that has any effect on the trend in the phenomena by cross tabulating voting behavior against a series of measures of prejudice. Since seven such tests consistently reveal a negligible association, he can safely regard the changes in sampling as inconsequential for estimating the aggregate trends.[16]

The review of comparability was long but necessitated by its critical importance and the need to suggest cautious but courageous use of data that may initially appear too imperfect for trend analyses. Granted that the threshold of comparability can be crossed, the investigator takes his next steps.

Describing the Trends and Changes

The arrangement and presentation of a series of survey measurements over time might appear to be a simple mechanical step. Yet thoughtless decisions may mislead the investigator and his readers as to the very nature of the

---

[15] Glenn, *op. cit.*, p. 84.

[16] C. H. Stember, *Jews in the Mind of America, op. cit.*, pp. 41–42, 220–221. He does speculate, however, that the problems posed may be more vexatious in the accurate description of trends for certain subgroups.

changes that have occurred, whereas sensitive modes of *description* may lead the analyst more quickly toward the *explanation* of the changes and away from false hypotheses.

CHOICE OF THE CRITERION ATTRIBUTE

The changing magnitude of one or more variables over time is the core of the analysis, but the way to indicate this process presents a dilemma even in the instance of a rudimentary set of data based on a single *opinion* question. Generally, the distribution of the variable has not been measured in the original surveys by merely *two* categories of answers or two alternative attributes. The finding that 39% of a national sample of Americans in 1945 endorsed the position that "Communist Party Members should *not* be allowed to speak on the radio" does *not* imply that 61% were measured and found to be *tolerant*. At that time, 12% expressed no opinion. They were, by one reasonable interpretation of the meaning of this answer, neither tolerant nor intolerant. Only the remainder, some 49%, have definitely asserted their tolerance. The trend describing the course of *one* attribute over time rarely implies the complementary trend, and may well mislead the analyst or the reader and obscure the subtle nature of the process that has unfolded.[17]

Sometimes one polar pattern has gained from attrition at the other pole; in other instances the gain has accrued from the previously undecided who have crystallized their former inchoate views, while the opposing group has remained constant in size. In the most annoying instance, *both* poles may increase their numbers, each drawing into its orbit some of the previously uncommitted, or both may decline as more people withhold judgment. An unwary reader or analyst is unlikely to entertain this last model of change, unless he is alerted to such subtleties.[18]

---

[17] One of the long-term trends that Blake analyzed had profound implications for government population policy. Over the twenty-five year period from 1937 to 1964, several very similar questions have been asked in national surveys on support for dissemination of birth-control information. The time series for the attribute "approval" shows that between two-thirds and nine-tenths of white adults in the child-bearing ages supported such a policy. Lest the reader think that disapproval, although only characteristic of a minority was substantial, Blake is concerned to stress that: "in judging the level of disapproval, one should bear in mind that the remainder of the respondents in all these years includes from 7 to 15 per cent who claim that they have 'no opinion' on the subject, not that they 'disapprove'." Judith Blake, "Population policy. . . ," *op. cit.*, p. 523.

[18] Just such a pattern characterized a portion of the long time series on presidential popularity that Mueller used, and his review of the problem is a model of thoughtful treatment and presentation. *Both* satisfaction and dissatisfaction were low in the first weeks after the Eisenhower and Kennedy elections, because many people withholding judgment said "don't know," and correspondingly *both* the "approvers" and the "disapprovers" increased shortly thereafter as the undecided crystallized a response.

Occasionally, the residual group who show no definite attribute consistently remains neglible in magnitude. Then, effectively, the choice of either one of two definite attributes to describe a trend creates no ambiguity. For example, the long trend of increasing support for school integration between 1942 and 1963 could have been shown accurately, either by the decline in the number of segregationists or the increase of integrationists, since the undecided group in the population has always remained tiny, about 4%. Nevertheless, supplementary reporting of the trend of indecision increased understanding, suggesting, for example, that time and events did not crystallize sentiment, and demonstrating that the great growth of integrationist attitudes came about by the conversion of considerable numbers of the opposition.[19]

One can seemingly eliminate the dilemma by transforming the numbers, repercentaging the three-category distribution after omitting the residual or undecided group. The remaining two proportions then complement each other. Or one can decide on a cutting point and throw the undecided into a common group with one of the original polar groups, regarding them as on one side of the dividing line. Where the question allowed for three or more alternatives over and above the undecided category, one can employ the same technical solution, making some cutting point and dichotomizing the distribution into two amalgamated classes which then complement each other. Such solutions certainly resolve the analyst's dilemmas. The trend that is then plotted is unambiguous in its implication.[20] The choice of the cutting point may have been a rational one, and the elimination of the residual cate-

---

[19] Hyman and Sheatsley, "Desegregation . . . ," *op. cit.* The separate reporting of the "don't knows" also aids in the interpretation of certain kinds of errors. For example, Stember ponders the question of errors arising in the measurement of long-range trends in antisemitism because of "inhibition of prejudiced expressions." In assessing these possibilities he examines the "don't know" trend: "A recent growth, if any, in the inhibition of prejudice could scarcely have been large; if it had been, the inconclusive kinds of response ('don't know,' 'uncertain,' no answer) in which the less than candid presumably take refuge would have shown a steeper rise than they actually do in most of our data." *Jews in the Mind . . . , op. cit.*, p. 44.

[20] But not always to the reader. Stewart's elaborate secondary analysis of trends in tolerance provides an illustration. Trends are differentiated for different aspects of the domain. They are examined carefully in relation to various causes, and for different subgroups. They are manipulated by a high-powered statistical apparatus. Yet throughout, the "proportion tolerant," the attribute that is the vehicle for the analysis, remains opaque in its meaning because the reader is not informed that it is in fact the proportion among those with a definite attitude, the "undecided" having been eliminated and the percentages recalculated. The indicator is unambiguous, and the decision taken was reasonable, but for the reader the meaning of the reported findings suffer from obscurity. The trends, strictly speaking, do not apply to the total collectivity, and ignore some aspects of the gamut of phenomena. Stewart, *op. cit.*

gory or the amalgation of several categories may have been necessary and wise. But these tactics may be evasive and undesirable also. Our argument is essentially toward care in making the decision and explicitness in presentation, but also to stress that a good deal may be learned from subtle inspection of the total distribution prior to any act of collapsing it or curtailing it.

The argument applies equally to the description of a trend based on a single question which yields a variable that can be scored (for example, number of voluntary association memberships) or one based on a battery of questions which also yields a score. The criterion used in describing the trend could be some statistic such as the mean score, or the proportion who have a score higher or lower than some cutting point on the dimension. Assume that the residual group of those who cannot be scored at all because of lack of information is small. Nevertheless, aspects of the distribution which may be highly informative may be lost to sight. For example, there is a major division in the American distribution of voluntary association membership of zero versus any number of memberships. The variable lends itself to obvious dichotomizing at that point. Yet there may be a subtle trend far along on the dimension toward multiple memberships. The "joiner syndrome" and its development over time might well be missed by the exclusive reliance on one criterion. By contrast, in Blake's secondary analysis of long-term trends in "ideal family size," the *low end* of the distribution provides information that would be missed by exclusive reliance on one summary statistic as the criterion. The mean number of children regarded as ideal by Americans is at the center of her analysis and through the years hovers between 2 and 4, but by presenting the total distributions one notes, for example, a dramatic drop in the number who regard "zero" children as ideal, that number being substantial in the thirties and infinitesimal in recent years.

In light of these considerations, a conservative and sensible first approach to the choice of a criterion and the description of a trend is tabular presentation and inspection of the total distribution of attributes or scores on the variable. Then nothing relevant is lost to sight, and *subsequent* modes of description of some selected attribute or statistic do serve to condense, simplify, and clarify the findings without creating any impenetrable obscurity.

DISAGGREGATION OF THE TREND

The changes in a given variable, or criterion attribute, may be described for the aggregate sample, or disaggregated so that the differential trends among subgroups are described. In general, if we ignore any overriding practical or theoretical interest in a particular subgroup or in the total population surveyed, or methodological considerations of comparability which dictate eliminating or inspecting a subgroup, one may recommend, again on conservative grounds, that both the overall trend and the subgroup trends be presented.

The patterns over time for various subgroups are the *components of the net trend* in the aggregate, and therefore provide a more informative description of what has happened, and may give insights into the explanation. No change or little change in the aggregate may conceal a radical change in one sub-group which is but a fraction in the total collectivity and therefore sub-merged in the aggregate findings. Little net change in the aggregate may have come about through many larger changes in several subgroups who have been moving in opposite directions and therefore balance each other out. Consider-able change in the aggregate may even have come about despite little or *no* change in the phenomenon in any subgroup, but simply because some group with a stable but distinctive pattern has substantially increased *its numbers* over time. For example, some of the long-term increase in voluntary associa-tion membership in America may essentially represent a *demographic* process. Since membership is persistently, highly, and positively correlated with socio-economic status, the gradual increase in the proportion of higher-status and better-educated groups in the population could produce a trend toward more membership in the nation, not because various types of individuals have changed their orientation toward participation, but simply because the social composition of the collectivity has changed. The description of the behavior of the subgroups and also the examination of their changing *size* over time provide the necessary evidence.[21]

There are, of course, dozens of dimensions by which to subdivide the pop-ulation, and an elaborate face sheet provides an embarrassment of riches for the analyst about to disaggregate a trend. Shall he divide the sample along racial or ethnic lines, regional lines, social-status lines, lines of sex, or in terms of combinations of characteristics defining multidimensional social groups? Obviously, some judgment has to be exercised, and some restraint applied. Tabular description of the full distribution of change on the dependent vari-able for every conceivable social grouping would defy comprehension and create a grotesque and unwieldy analysis.

The lines of disaggregation will vary depending on the phenomenon and problem under study. Sometimes, the hypothesis dictates a test of the differ-

---

[21] The same kind of model can be employed in the *prediction* of future trends. If one makes the assumption that subgroup patterns will persist, knowledge of the likely changes in future composition of the population can lead to a prediction of a social-psychological nature. Thus Stouffer's 1954 finding that tolerance is greater among the better educated, combined with the rising educational level of the population, leads him to prognosticate greater tolerance in America in the future. Stouffer, *op. cit.*

ential trend in particular subgroups.[22] In other instances, practical, theoretical, and, occasionally methodological considerations point to some particular line of disaggregation.[23] *Age* groupings, for reasons which will become clear, constitute a most valuable adjunct to the analysis of long-term trends. Grouping by *education* is generally a valuable approach for analyzing trends that appear to reflect events and stimuli carried by the media, given the greater attentiveness of the educated and their distinctively high level of communication activity. Analyses directed toward practical or political matters may try to distinguish the trends that characterize more *powerful* groups in the society, the changes in the less powerful having smaller payoff in the real coin of reform. Whatever the groups chosen, when there are multiple indicators of membership (for example, education, occupation, and income as criteria of class), the subgroup trend should be based on the combined use of the several items, thus increasing or estimating the reliability of that finding.

---

[22] For example, a recent study concerned with the "knowledge gap" advanced the rather dismal hypothesis that as the infusion of mass media information increases, the more educated groups will acquire the information at a faster rate so that "the gap in knowledge between these segments tends to increase rather than decrease over time." A variety of tests, including field experiments, were made. One source of evidence is a secondary analysis of trends in knowledge based on three information questions about scientific and health matters which had been asked by the Gallup Poll periodically over spans of time ranging from a six-year interval to a sixteen-year interval during which time relevant information on the topics in the media had increased very substantially. In the aggregate, there was considerable trend toward greater public knowledge, but the central finding was that the slope of these growth curves showed much more rapid rise among the educated, the distance between the subgroups therefore being much greater at the end point of the trends that were plotted. P. J. Tichenor, G. A. Donohue, and C. N. Olien, "Mass Media Flow and Differential Growth in Knowledge," *Publ. Opin. Quart.*, **34**, 1970, pp. 159–170.

[23] This is not to imply that the poor analyst faces terrible problems guided only by these global and vague principles. Sometimes it is almost self-evident what the major lines of group division should be; e.g., trends in prejudice obviously ought to be examined along regional lines, trends in "presidential popularity" along party lines, trends in the area of fertility by religion, and by surveying those in the child-bearing ages. Sometimes the lines are less immediately apparent, but reflection will suggest promising directions. For example, prejudice toward one minority group ought to be examined separately for those who are in the majority and those other minorities who might sense that they share a common fate, e.g., Negro or Catholic trends in prejudice toward Jews ought to be separated from white Protestant trends. There may be a good deal of literature on the major social correlates of many phenomena. Some caution should be suggested about disaggregating by subgroups who show extreme scores on a phenomenon, opening the danger of misinterpreting regression effects as differential trends. It should also be noted that the disaggregated trends may be examined for subgroups refined or controlled on a third variable. Regional trends could be computed for groups matched in religion or race or education, for example.

Where there is a residual category of any substantial size whose group membership cannot be determined, the trend should be reported separately for them so as to reduce ambiguities in the comparison of trends for the several groups. For example, Blake's trends on attitudes in the family planning area are reported not merely for Catholics and non-Catholics but also for those who are enumerated as having "no religion."

In one sense of the term, the disaggregation of the trends shows what is "causing" the aggregate process. The cause is something that has happened, for example, in one group, in one place in the society, or in the numbers that have moved in and out of that social location. In a deeper sense of the term, the disaggregation shows the analyst where to search for the cause. Trends that occur uniformly everywhere, suggest that the explanation may lie in some national or macroscopic factor or fundamental psychological process.[24]

DIFFERENTIATING SPECIFIC ASPECTS OF THE TREND

Where the analyst has several questions or indicators of a single variable, or of a domain of related variables, describing the separate trends for the several aspects is valuable. The specificity or generality of the changes that have occurred in a domain is an important finding in its own right, and leads the analyst further toward a promising explanatory hypothesis. Where the questions are regarded as alternative indicators of the same unitary phenomenon, the differentiated trends for each question provide evidence on the reliability of measurement of the change.

Stewart, for example, described the separate trends in political intolerance in the forties and early fifties on the basis of three related questions that NORC had asked. Tolerance toward Communists showed a much more rapid decline or slope than the decline in tolerance toward Socialists, and support for freedom of criticism by the press showed no decline at all, suggesting that the threat of the Cold War and the spectre that McCarthy had presented to America had not worked wholesale to obliterate all differentiation of objects of attitude in this realm.[25] The erosion of tolerance in that era had not been utterly general.

---

[24] An example shows the insight that comes from such disaggregation. Rosenthal in analyzing a two-year trend in De Gaulle's popularity compares the changes over time for the consolidated four regions that are most "anti" and the four that are most "pro" De Gaulle. Each short-term vicissitude in popularity moves in the same direction for both subgroups, suggesting that short-term fluctuations result from basic responses to the nature of the event or action. But the long-term trend for these two sets of regions shows that the polarization progressively increased.

[25] Stewart, *op. cit.*

Such differentiated aspects of a trend can, of course, be examined not only at the aggregate level but also for subgroups. For example, trends in support of racial integration over a twenty-year period were measured by a battery of questions dealing with schools, transportation, and residential housing. On all three aspects of the issue, and in both the North and the South, the trends were uniformly in the direction of rising support of integration over the years. This uniform and pervasive pattern, revealed by both disaggregation and differentiation in handling the data, suggested some fundamental, sweeping forces, impinging on all and not peculiar to any specific institution. However, there were also particularities observed in the profile or patterning of the three discrete trends in the South versus the North which demanded some supplementary and specialized explanation appropriate to each region.[26]

One certainly should gain the benefit of additional reliability in the measurement of a trend by combining a series of *homogeneous* items that indicate some single aspect or dimension of a phenomenon. But when one combines related items that measure different aspects of a complex domain, such as tolerance or prejudice, and *exclusively* relies on the scale or index score in his analysis of trend, the gain in generality of description is achieved at the price of loss of information on the patterning of the changes within the domain. The two approaches in sequence seem the wise strategy.

DESCRIBING THE TEMPORAL FEATURES OF THE PHENOMENA

It is self-evident that the description of a change or trend, no matter what phenomena and groups are measured or what the mode of analysis, involves the examination of the temporal course of a series of measurements. The dependent variable in every study is change (or stability) over time, and the independent variable always is *time* in some sense of that concept. There is no better guide for the overconfident analyst approaching these tasks than St. Augustine. His perplexity suggests the subtleties involved:

What then is time? I know what it is if no one asks me what it is; but if I want to explain it to someone who has asked me, I find that I do not know . . .

---

[26] Hyman and Sheatsley, *op. cit.*, pp. 4–5. Stewart differentiates trends in discrete aspects of political tolerance and also disaggregates them. The differentiation of the domain—the relatively small decline in tolerance for Socialists and the rapid decline in tolerance for Communists—is sharpest among the educated. "The college graduates were sufficiently less recruitable to cause them to remain essentially constant on Socialists, but they did show a radical decline with respect to Communists." Stewart, *op. cit.*, pp. 18–19. By contrast, Stember examines trends on three different dimensions or aspects of antisemitism (each measured by many questions) and the parallelism of the processes suggests to him that the basic configuration or attitude and belief system toward Jews had undergone a fundamental change. *"Jews in the Mind . . ."* Stember, *op. cit.*, especially pp. 208–209.

it is time passing that we are measuring. For it is impossible to measure the past, which is no longer in existence, . . . unless perhaps one is going to be rash enough to maintain that it is possible to measure something which does not exist. . . . But how do we measure the present, since it has no extent. It is measured while it is passing; when it has passed by it is not measured, for then there will be nothing there to measure. But where does time come from, by what way does it pass, and where is it going to when we are measuring it? . . . . how can the future, which does not yet exist, be diminished or consumed? How can the past, which no longer exists, grow? Only because, in the mind, which performs all this, there are three things done. The mind looks forward to things, it looks at things, and it looks back on things. What it looks forward to passes on through what it looks at into what it looks back on.[27]

St. Augustine ends on a note of perplexity. The secondary analyst must carry on his empirical study as best he can, not forgetting, however, that he deals with a most elusive problem.

The primary survey analyst who studies some particular temporal process has the dilemma, but also the advantage, of choosing to phase his series of surveys at points best suited to illuminate his problem. All that the *secondary* analyst can do is arrange the original surveys in whatever order and spacing they happened to be conducted. Therefore, his description of the *temporal* process would seem to be purely a mechanical task, the measurements simply being anchored in their appropriate location. But it is not that simple.

No survey can be built in a day. The field work generally extends over a few weeks, although on occasion it may drag out interminably over months until the last holdouts are cornered and interviewed. There is, in fact, no single anchorage point, and this may create difficulties for studies of *short-term* change. The vagueness of the anchoring point may introduce ambiguity in testing a hypothesis about the influence of a discrete event in producing change. The date on a questionnaire usually refers only to the *month* and year when the survey was sent into the field. Some of the interviews may in fact have been conducted in the following months. Consequently, it may be difficult to specify the events that impinged upon the respondents and affected their behavior. If the secondary analyst employs only the news releases of polls for his source of data, their dating generally lags behind the actual field dates, and sometimes the exact field dates are nowhere mentioned in a report.

---

[27] *The Confessions of St. Augustine*, Rex Warner translation (New York: Mentor, 1963), Book XI, Chapters 14–31.

Some agencies do code the exact date of each interview, and the distribution of dates provides the basis for anchoring the findings accurately, and relating them to events. It also permits the exclusion of cases prior to a point or even the reallocation of cases that might be closer in time to those contained within another survey. These problems may also distort trend comparisons between subgroups. It is possible that the interval within which one group was interviewed in a survey overlaps little or not at all with the interval during which another group was interviewed, specific events thus being confounded with group differences. Cross tabulation by date of interview provides a routine and desirable check on the problem.

In studies of *long-term* trends over a span of years, by contrast, it is generally of trivial importance that a *point* in a time series is correctly designated as a brief *interval*. Such studies, however, sometimes introduce initially or bring in later an explanatory notion that may create another problem of temporal description and location. The problem is not one of anchoring each survey around a point but rather one of anchoring a string of surveys inside or outside a broader segment of time that corresponds to the concept of an *era* or *period*, for example, "the McCarthy era," "the cold-war period." An interval of time conceptually may be likened to a vehicle carrying or a container holding many variables which really are the causative agents of change. Depending on the length of the interval, a great many external stimuli or events and a variety of psychobiological processes are contained within it. Indeed, following St. Augustine, we realize that the causes of the change wrought in individuals in a given interval include many additional things that preceded the interval but whose residues linger on. His words are old fashioned but he is wise in stressing that the distant past, "the images of those events, . . . in passing through the senses, have left as it were their footprints stamped upon the mind."[28]

The concept of an era or period is, intuitively, appealing. It spares us from selecting arbitrarily one event as causative agent out of the multitudinous ones that are crammed into an interval. We need not worry about pinpointing and connecting that discrete event to the survey data. Instead, we acknowledge an *omnibus* cause—the spirit of the times and its web of institutions—that seems powerful enough to produce even a tidal wave of change in contrast with a single, small event. Other advantages accrue. The analyst, and here we anticipate a later step, can treat the variations among survey results contained *within* the interval as expressive of instability or unreliability of measurement, against which he can evaluate the variation *between* periods.

---

[28] *Ibid.*, p. 271. In this same passage, he reminds us also that our "premeditations," our *expectations* about a future which has not yet presented itself, may be operative causes of a change in a given interval.

Or he can combine surveys within each interval, obtaining for each a more reliable estimate. He can operationalize some incisive criterion of the kind of change that demonstrates the effects of a new era, for example, a sudden, marked elevation or sharp decrease in the phenomena, a discontinuity or radical change in the slope of the curve the process is taking.

The analyst may not have to pinpoint discrete causes and specific surveys, but he still faces problems in segmenting time. He must decide when the era begins that contains the surveys which presumably reflect its influence and which therefore test his hypothesis. Possibly he has to decide when the era has reached its maturity and when it ends, although he may conceive of its effects as lingering on. Perhaps some eras start and end abruptly, and correspondingly the strings of surveys can easily be keyed into these intervals. There may be a signal event—a law, a war, an armistice, or a new presence on the scene, like Senator Joseph McCarthy. Periods are often symbolized in these very terms. Yet, often ambiguity reigns.

Consider the "McCarthy era." Did it begin after his West Virginia speech in February, 1950 when he announced that the State Department was still infiltrated with Communists, or not until he was conducting his Senatorial investigations in 1953? When was his presence and the atmosphere he personified so pervasive that we may regard his era as having reached its height and working its full force to produce a dramatic change in survey findings collected after that date? Perhaps the era really began much earlier and was responsible for bringing him into prominence. Perhaps the year of its birth was 1947, when the problems of internal security became a major concern and led to new Federal regulations and widespread investigation. But perhaps that was the "Cold War period" and not the "McCarthy era." An analyst who invokes such an elastic concept might better think of eras not as separated by sharp boundary lines but rather by border zones of time, when there is a gradual transition and emergence of new forces. This is certainly the safe and conservative approach for the secondary analyst who seeks only to describe a long-run process and tentatively advance an explanation. The analyst who is so bent on proving his hypothesis about an era that he indulges in circularity is thereby restrained. Otherwise he might examine the survey results, adjust the boundary lines of the eras in light of the findings, regroup the surveys that are in the twilight zone, and ergo, prove his theory.[29]

---

[29] The definition of the boundaries of the era when it is introduced as an *explanatory variable* ought to be determined independently by some objective or commonly agreed upon standard or perhaps set in some conservative way so as to handicap the hypothesis. Thus, for example, Stewart simply takes the decade of the fifties as the "McCarthy period" and the forties are conceived of, as the "hot" and "cold war" period. Some McCarthyism, or at least its ancestral equivalent, existed in the late forties, and intolerance was demon-

CONDENSING, SIMPLIFYING, AND CLARIFYING THE DESCRIPTION

The examination of changes and trends in all their complexity, the full distribution on each major aspect for each relevant subgroup for each point in time is informative but may defy clear comprehension and presentation. Attempts at simplification and clarification are certainly desirable and our argument was directed only against the application of such procedures prematurely. A variety of conventional procedures can serve these needs and a brief discussion should suffice.

Graphical plotting or charting of a criterion attribute or score indicating the trend on the various aspects and for various subgroups conveys clearly the general and differential patterns over time. The approximate slopes can be inspected and convergence or polarization more readily seen. By implication, inspecting the graph of such a family of trends suggests by the distance between the curves whether the social correlates of the phenomena have been changing and whether the differentiations in the aspects of the domain have become sharper or more blurred over time. One can also graph the actual changing value over time of some statistic, of the *intercorrelation* or other coefficient of association between aspects, or of the correlation with some group characteristic. Any trend in the internal organization of some constellation or in its social patterning is directly conveyed. Such graphs or charts also juxtapose clearly the short-run fluctuations in the phenomena against the long-term trend permitting better evaluation. They can also carry (as in most of the old, classic trend reports in the survey literature) running entries of events suggesting, although not proving, the influences that may cause the changes or that, unexpectedly, do *not* divert the trend at all from its majestic course over time.

More precise methods can also be employed to clarify the temporal processes. A line can be fitted to the data, providing the best single description of

---

strated in the surveys of that period. It is quite compelling evidence that some aspects of intolerance nevertheless jumped sharply in the fifties, suggesting the potency of McCarthy and his particular era, since other forces with the same vector were already being applied before then. The Rosenthal study of trends in De Gaulle's popularity, by contrast, does *not* invoke the concept of a period and try to test its influence. Therefore, there is nothing wrong with an empirical and inductive determination of a common period from the trend data. By the examination of the distributions and intercorrelating the results of pairs of surveys over time, he establishes that a string of ten surveys all have a commonality, despite the fact that such critical events as a cease-fire, a referendum on Algerian independence, and its final independence all occurred in the interval of the ten surveys. But the same kind of procedure established that surveys after the referendum of De Gaulle in 1962 were not of the same piece. A new period had begun.

the trend for each aspect and group. The slopes then give the clearest picture of the course that the various trends are taking.[30]

Evaluating the Trends

By now the analyst has described the trends. He has yet to explain them, if he wishes to carry his study to that point. But all analysts, even when they stop at the point of description, must pause to evaluate their findings, to read some proper meaning into the patterns of change they have documented. Empirical procedures aid in the task, and the obscurities have already been resolved in part by the previous steps. But an analyst must still ponder his words and judgments carefully, and, no matter what his ponderings and procedures, certain kinds of interpretations will be a risky venture, and predicated on assumptions that may not be testable. There are various realms of meaning that analysts may therefore choose to avoid, but if they enter into them, they are forewarned to be cautious.

EVALUATING BIASES OF SAMPLING AND MEASUREMENT

Consider the paradox that that first step in such studies presents. To insure that the changes were measured accurately, the analyst's first concern was that the series of surveys were replications. Noncomparability created problems for him. Thus the improvement in sampling the population introduced around 1950 increased accuracy of description but reduced comparability over the time series. Less error in generalizing after 1950 introduced the risk of more error in measuring trend and had to be taken into account.

Suppose the trend analyst was fortunate enough to have a long series of comparable national surveys, all of which had a samping bias that was con-

---

[30] Schwartz, for example, fitted linear trend lines, regressing on time the percent of whites favorable to the Negro, for various questions and subgroups, from a series of surveys. The direction of the trends is uniformly toward greater favorability; there are almost "no significant departures from linearity," and particular major events deflect the estimate at that point very little from its position along the line. See Mildred Schwartz, *Trends in White Attitudes toward Negroes*, National Opinion Research Center, Report No. 119, 1967. Tichenor, Donohue, and Olien, whose study of the increased "knowledge gap" between educational groups was cited earlier, tested their trend lines for curvilinearity, and found that the processes were best described as linear, with the slope for the better educated showing a much more rapid growth of knowledge, thereby increasing the gap. Tichenor, Donohue, and Olien, *op. cit.*

stant both in direction and magnitude. He could quickly and accurately evaluate the amount of change over the years, but the minute he ventured to generalize his trend to the nation, he might be in trouble since all of the samples were deficient to some extent. The *replication of error* is a mixed blessing for secondary analysts who aim toward description of trend and generalization about it. Glenn's and Stember's procedures, outlined earlier, were an attempt to achieve that blissful state where one could have it both ways. They appraised and adjusted the noncomparability arising from changes in sampling so as to describe the trends, and they corrected the estimates, if necessary, so as to generalize to the nation.

Consider the paradox presented by comparable *measurement* procedures all containing a constant error. A secondary analyst of trends is pleased when an imperfect instrument or question is exactly replicated, since he then feels confident that he has an accurate measurement of the amount that some phenomenon has *changed.* Thus, Stember makes the reasonable assumptions that questions designed to elicit prejudice are not perfect measuring instruments, but also that there is a response bias whose *direction* can be safely assumed. "While respondents may well disavow prejudices they do possess, they hardly are likely to voice hostilities they do not feel. Insincerity, in other words, consistently causes the prevalence of hostile attitudes to be understated, never to be exaggerated. Thus, comparisons of such attitudes at different times should not be vitiated by this factor."[31] An error, constant in direction and *magnitude,* created by the use of comparable, but imperfect, instruments thus creates no problem in estimating change. The merit of the argument rests on how tenable the assumptions are. We may formulate a principle to guide the analyst at this stage of evaluation. Response biases and sampling biases that are constant in magnitude, create no problem in assessing change, but must be evaluated if one also makes statements about the prevalence of a phenomenon and its generalizability.

The principle is straightforward, but there is, occasionally, a subtle snare in applying it. It is reasonable to assume that the same design and instrument generally has the same effect over time. But, on occasion, a constant procedure may, as time passes, no longer produce accurate data or data marred by the same constant bias. Some critical judgment has to be exercised. For example, Blake based her trend analyses of family size ideals partly on a series of nine Gallup surveys over the thirty-year period, 1936–1966, which asked exactly the same question: "What do you consider is the ideal size of a family—a husband, a wife, and how many children?" Before presenting the findings, she remarks: "There is no particular reason to suspect that the

---

[31] Stember, *op. cit.,* p. 44.

meaning of 'ideal' to respondents had some peculiar set of biases in one year as against the next."[32]

By contrast, Stember deals with trends in anti-semitism over almost the same interval, and appraises the assumptions as less appropriate to his kind of data. In such instances, the admirable caution he exercised is the proper example to follow, as was his attempt to test whether particular questions produced a bias of the same magnitude over time, e.g., by examining the trend in the "don't know" response. How nice if we could tell the analyst when to be confident and when to be suspicious! But there is no simple clue. Stember from long experience has learned to sense danger. As he describes his concerns, we can share his feelings, even though we may not be acute enough to anticipate such problems for ourselves. "It may be of course that inhibition of prejudiced expression has *fluctuated in extent* if not in direction. That avowals of anti-semitism should have become more acceptable than a generation ago seems most unlikely to us; . . . A change of the opposite kind seems more plausible; outright bigotry may well have been driven somewhat underground in recent years. If so, then recent figures may understate the *actual level of prejudice* in the society making *decreases* since earlier days *look larger* than they are . . ."[33]

One way to cope with these uncertainties in evaluation and interpretation is simply to qualify the judgments. Another way is to try to determine by empirical tests the extent of the biases and whether their magnitude is fixed over time. A third way, open to the trend analyst of *social-psychological* phenomena, is to reconceptualize the very meaning of an emergent response bias, so that it is no longer construed as "error" but rather as additional evidence on the process under study. Stember uses all three techniques. He gives little weight to small, apparent trends in antisemitism, since recently introduced biases might account for such magnitudes of change. He uses the "don't know" trend as evidence of such evasion. Thirdly he remarks: "growing reluctance to betray anti-semitism to poll-takers would *in itself* be a noteworthy signal of changed behavior—an acknowledgement that free expression of ethnic prejudices was increasingly frowned upon by the public. If this is what

---

[32] Blake, "Income and Reproductive Motivation . . ." *op. cit.*, p. 187. With respect to the samplings, Blake is very careful to assess the magnitude of the biases and whether they remained constant over the years by comparisons with census data. Thus, for example, she notes that the "later samples are younger than most of the earlier ones, and since younger respondents want smaller families than older ones regardless of time period, this age difference in the samples somewhat obscures the rise" in the trend on ideal family size. "Ideal Family Size," *op. cit.*, p. 166. This problem is controlled by presentation of trends separately for refined age groups.

[33] Stember, *op. cit.*, p. 44 (italics supplied).

happened, it should be viewed as a *real gain*, not merely as an artifact which distorts the data."[34]

EVALUATING RANDOM ERRORS OF SAMPLING AND MEASUREMENT

A difference in the results between two surveys may not represent a change due to the passage of time, but simply the variability that might have occurred if one had drawn two samples of a given population and conducted two *simultaneous* surveys. In principle, the secondary analyst whose surveys were based on probability sample designs can estimate such sampling errors and make the proper inference, although in practice the difficulties for the secondary analyst should not be underrated. The sampling errors may not have been computed in the course of the original inquiry for the characteristics now under study. The details of the sampling design may no longer be known, and if the computations can be made at all at the later date, they may be laborious and costly.

The analyst who has a lavish time series, one with many points from many surveys both bunched and spread, can, however, inspect the data to see whether the long-term trend is of such large magnitude and so systematic in

---

[34] *Ibid.* (italics supplied). This solution is not open to a trend analyst of an *"objective"* reality that cannot change because of people's feelings. A good example of a possible changing bias in reporting, despite constant procedures, and one which ineluctably produces error is provided by a historian of labor force trends. He first reports the evidence of very substantial errors in the reporting of occupation in the census. Then he remarks: "how many times is the factory job upgraded in the interview process, whereas in earlier years the social stigma was less and the impulse to upgrade weaker?" Such incorrect reports, which may have occurred as much as one-third of the time in some occupational groups in the 1960 census, cannot be argued away, if the trend analyst is concerned with changes in actual occupation rather than changes in the prestige of occupations. Stanley Lebergott, "Labor Force and Employment Trends," in Sheldon and Moore, *op. cit.*, p. 133. Jackson and Crockett face the even more subtle problem of appraising such a response bias as it is inhibited or enhanced by slight changes in the questions employed in the several surveys they use for their secondary analysis of occupational mobility. "The questions used in the 1952 and 1957 studies focus on father's occupation while the respondent was 'growing up' but the 1945 and 1947 questions do not specify the period for which father's occupation should be given. Respondents in the earlier studies might have tended to take advantage of the less restrictive question by reporting as father's occupation the most prestigeful job he ever held; this might produce lower rates of upward mobility . . . in the two earlier studies." They might have added up two imponderables—assuming that the greater inclination toward bias in recent years was offset by the tighter question—but instead they acknowledge the imponderability: "The size of this bias, if any, unfortunately cannot be estimated." Jackson and Crockett, *op. cit.*, p. 11.

direction that it seems unreasonable to attribute it to sampling variance. He can use a subset of very closely spaced surveys for an *empirical* estimate of the variability that characterizes such surveys simply because of random errors of sampling plus measurement. These very same procedures come to the aid of the secondary analyst whose time series is based on sampling designs to which the ordinary formulas for estimating sampling errors are not applicable. Glenn has provided just such empirically based estimates for early Gallup samples which used quota-control methods and for their more recent and improved samples.[35] A secondary analyst who has too few surveys for an empirical determination of his own can avail himself of the Glenn estimates, realizing that they are only approximations of the errors that may apply to his particular set of surveys and the particular characteristic he is studying.

The analyst who is concerned with *long-term* change or *trend*, however, is generally in an enviable position. All the empirical evidence suggests that the random errors of sampling plus measurement are nowhere as large as one might fear. Stability of the results even in the primitive days was good.[36]

Whatever fluctuation is observed in his data, or estimated on the basis of previous experience, represents the net effect of random errors of *sampling plus measurement* in the instance of variables that are *conceived* to be relatively unchangeable in the short run. Obviously, everyone conceives of the educational attainment or occupational mobility of the population as changing little or not at all from one month to the next. Therefore any fluctuations observed over a short interval are construed as error and the long-run changes lend themselves to unambiguous evaluation. By contrast, a man may change his mind in a minute, learn something in a flash, switch back and forth on a puzzling issue in the course of a day. Thus some of the short-run fluctuations in the measurement of attitudes or beliefs or knowledge must be regarded as real phenomena, representing natural human instability produced by various causes rather than errors produced by sampling and measurement. It is the very stuff of which the larger trend is made! The ambiguity in interpreting the meaning of such data, however, rarely bothers the analyst in evaluating a *long-term* process. He wishes to see whether some systematic, substantial change has unfolded over a long period which is greater than the perturbations for all causes, natural and artifactual.

Not so the analyst of *short-term* changes in social-psychological phenomena. His entire study may focus on the fluctuations in mood in the public, may be a test of a hypothesis about the influence of discrete events and

---

[35] "Problems of Comparability . . . ," *op. cit.*, pp. 87–89.
[36] H. Cantril, "Do Different Polls Get the Same Results," *Publ. Opin. Quart.*, **9**, 1945, pp. 61–69.

alarms in suddenly changing people's expectations of war, or fear of subversives, or attention to critical issues of domestic or foreign policy. He wishes to estimate the magnitude of instability that is real, but if he is conservative he will recognize that some of the instability observed represents error in sampling plus measurement. The problem of separating the two components of the change—the real from the artifactual—can be difficult, almost intractable, if the analyst is limited to very few surveys and only one indicator of the phenomenon.[37] The puzzlement of the analyst, of course, all depends on the way he conceptualizes processes. The analyst who conceives of a phenomenon as unchangeable in the short run regards all fluctuations as error. The analyst who conceives of a phenomenon as nothing but flux, redefines all observed change as real, in effect claiming that random error of measurement is a fiction, a misguided notion that creates a pseudoproblem. Again we see, as in the instance of the problem of bias, that the assumptions and theories of the analyst have a great deal to do with the evaluation of the data.

The analyst who acknowledges the existence of random error and has at his disposal multiple surveys in a short period may either apply some of the re-

---

[37] Hirschi and Selvin begin with a reasonable statement of our problem, which soon verges on an almost extreme psychologistic position. They remark on "the difficulty of interpreting crude differences between two measurements of the same concept on the same people as indicating the unreliability of the instrument rather than real changes in behavior; without making some assumptions about which sources of error are negligible, it is impossible to interpret such simple before-and-after measurements. . . . Conceptual clarification of the different meanings and sources of unreliability . . . is a good place to start." But where do they end? "The concept of 'unreliability' of the instrument is a *deplorable borrowing* from the physical sciences. Physical instruments may change their properties independently of the observer or the material measured. It is difficult to see how these ideas make sense when applied to lists of questions." Hirschi and Selvin, *op. cit.*, pp. 212–213, p. 215, footnote (italics ours). A secondary analyst who accepts the latter doctrine is of course exceedingly comforted. The error problem has been argued out of existence. The secondary analyst who, despite his awareness that the question is always the same, acknowledges that the interviewers who ask it, and the coders who classify the answers, may make all sorts of clerical and random errors, and that respondents can also answer it almost "at random" depending on their capricious state during the interview, finds the doctrine cold comfort. He must either acknowledge the uncertainty attached to his findings, or if his data are lavish enough he may be able to apply some methodological approaches to separating error from instability. For proposed solutions where there are *three points* of measurement, see James S. Coleman, "The Mathematical Study of Change," in H. and A. Blalock, eds., *Methodology in Social Research* (New York: McGraw-Hill, 1968), escially pp. 453–456; D. R. Heise, "Separating Reliability and Stability in Test–Retest Correlation," *Amer. Sociol. Rev.*, **34**, 1969, pp. 93–101. Any reader of these or similar treatises will soon see how many untested assumptions are made in order to forge a solution or instrument for assessing error. Thus, the secondary analyst who rests his case on his own not unreasonable assumptions is, in a fundamental sense, no worse a sinner or fumbler in the dark.

cent methodological tools to estimating error, or may compare the changes between *pooled* surveys, each "point" thus being based on a more reliable datum, subject to less sampling error. An analyst who has only two surveys, but multiple *indicators* of the very same variable in each survey, can use the intercorrelations between items as an expression of reliability, or can develop an index which attenuates the random errors in the single items or questions. An analyst whose successive, and closely spaced, surveys have each provided only one indicator, but with *slight* variations in question wording, may be fortunate in finding high stability, suggestive of the fact that the measuring instrument itself is unlikely to produce random error.[38]

The analyst who has none of these resources at hand to estimate random errors of measurement is still, in our judgment, not completely lost. His *own* time series may provide none of the methodological tests, but the results of tests with similar or the same questions from other experiments, or from surveys that cannot be incorporated in his time series, can be applied to his conclusions.[39] Even if he is stripped of all these methodological resources, reasoning, theorizing, plus some shreds of relevant evidence, can come to his

---

[38] For example, in a study on trends in popular support for the Korean and the Vietnam Wars, Mueller has available, from about 25 surveys, some variant forms of the basic question on whether the U. S. did the right or wrong thing, made a mistake or not, in entering the Korean War. There were instances where two trivially different wordings (and two different agencies) could be compared on virtually the same dates of inquiry. One may regard these as equivalent indicators of a "generalized support," and as he remarks: "Rather than obfuscating the patterns of support, these question variants, used with care, can help to broaden the trend analysis. . . . The . . . 'right thing'–'mistake' comparison seems to make little difference, as can be seen in a comparison of responses to polls conducted at approximately the same time." Other questions which introduced decisive changes in the way the issue was put did affect the results. Mueller is very careful to treat these as measures of different aspects of the general domain of attitudes engaged by the war. For example, when the question incorporated a reference "to stop the Communist invasion of South Korea," support was increased about 15–20% and there was a drop in the "no opinion" category. When the question was put in terms of "defense of South Korea" but left out the allusion to a Communist invasion, there was no impact on the level of support. By his sensitivity to the value of these natural experiments in question wording, he thus can draw certain inferences about the *causes* of support. In terms of our subsequent discussion of error from overgeneralizing a specific attitude trend, his figuratively stated principle is worth remembering: "Support should be considered a chord, rather than a note." J. E. Mueller, "Trends in Popular Support for the Wars in Korea and Vietnam," *Amer. Polit. Sci. Rev.*, June, 1971.

[39] Blake's study of trends in ideal family size is based mainly on a series of Gallup Polls all of which asked the very same question. In evaluating the errors of measurement created by this instrument, and trying to fix its meaning more precisely, she invokes evidence from a series of tests of variations in wording such questions conducted in Germany, Detroit, and in the surveys of specialized populations known as the Growth of American Families Studies. She remarks on the issue of measurement error, "There are

rescue. If the short-run changes seem to be reflections of some independent variable, such as an event coincident with the change, and some evidence can be adduced that it affected the responses, an assertion that error is responsible seems unreasonable.[40] For example, at *one* point in Mueller's long time series on support for the Korean War, the figures dropped suddenly by over twenty-five percentage points. It so happens that no other short-term shifts ever reach this same magnitude, suggesting that normal stability and reliability of measurement is high. But even if these additional data had not been available, it would have been unreasonable to construe a change of such magnitude as error, especially when it coincided with the entry of China into the war.

More generally, one might expect that unreliability of measurement would attenuate some correlation, but it could hardly account for some demonstrated relationship between changes in the phenomena and some hypothesized cause. Here evaluation of errors in description verges upon a later step in the analysis, the *explanation* of the trends, and other examples will be presented under that heading. But our allusion to multiple indicators versus a single question within each survey also bears upon an additional problem in evaluation of trends.

EVALUATING THE GENERALIZABILITY OF TREND ON A SPECIFIC INDICATOR

In a classic secondary analysis many years ago, Almond examined the trend in the public's attention to foreign affairs as revealed by a question that had

---

no satisfying and elegant answers to such queries for the studies under consideration, since typically only one very general question was asked. Fortunately, however, some experimentation with the phrasing of the question on ideal family size has been done, and this gives a sense of how much hidden variability may exist." Blake, *op. cit.*, p. 160.

[40] Sometimes the concrete findings appropriate to this paradigm lead to the opposite conclusion: that there is *no* real shift. An unexpected finding of this type is available in Stember's trend study of American antisemitism, whch spanned World War II. One might have assumed that the awareness of the extermination of European Jews by the Nazis had an effect on American attitudes. In two surveys in 1945 the sample was directly asked whether this had had any effect. Almost 80% of the sample reported that their feelings toward American Jews had been unaffected. Stember, *op. cit.*, p. 143. Another one of his analyses shows the way shreds of collateral evidence can narrow a field of potential explanations. In examining the trends in the immediate post-war period, 1945–48, it seems reasonable to impute some significance to events in Palestine and the founding of the state of Israel. A series of questions, in fact, indicated a rising awareness and knowledge of the events and developments in Palestine, thus admitting of the possibility that it could have affected the trends (p. 174). By contrast, if these events had not entered the cognitive structures of the individuals, it would have been unreasonable to assert that the trends reflected such influences.

been asked some twenty times by the Gallup Poll in surveys conducted from 1935 to 1949, excluding those surveys conducted during the war years. The particular type of question: "What do you regard as the most important problem before the American people today?" being open-ended, not suggesting any particular theme in its wording, and normally asked as the very first question prior to any specific stimuli, is regarded as an instrument to measure the *saliency* of some entity to an individual. What is spontaneously liberated by a stimulus question so vague and nondirective must be "on the top of the mind."

The dramatic instability over time of the criterion attribute he examined, any reference to a "foreign issue," led him to a now famous formulation about the "instability of mood," about the rapid fluctuations in prime attention to foreign policy in America. Clearly, he did not treat such instability as random error of sampling or measurement or as something trivial compared to the unfolding of a regular secular trend. Indeed, we may put it somewhat paradoxically and say that what was regular or stable about his data was the persistent *instability* over short units of time. Swings of the amplitude that foreign affairs was salient to 81% of Americans at one point in time and to only 11% or 7% at two other points hardly seem consonant with the magniture that errors of measurement assume. To be sure, in terms of the analogy with physical instruments of measurement, this "yardstick" seems to behave like a very elastic rubber band, but it may well be the field of attention that is elastic, sometimes expanding to incorporate foreign affairs, other times contracting.

One feels confident in such an evaluation as one notes the events that were correlative with the shifts. The high point, 81%, was reached in November, 1941, on the eve of Pearl Harbor. The early low point was in 1935 after the conclusion of the Ethiopian War but before the Spanish Civil War. The figures then oscillated back and forth but gradually rose as we moved toward war. Then attention again contracted; the all-time low in his time series was reached in October 1945, when "American interest in foreign affairs collapsed." Subsequently, there was an increasing secular trend of attention but "the responses continue to be highly unstable, suddenly rising in relation to immediate threat and suddenly collapsing in relation to superficial and temporary stabilizations in . . . tensions." In effect we may conclude as he did that it is not the instrument that is unreliable, but the *people*, foreign policy breaking periodically into the focus of attention, but this being only a superficial and transient psychic state.[41]

---

[41] G. Almond, *The American People and Foreign Policy* (New York: Harcourt, 1950), pp. 70–80.

Almond's formulation has been elaborated partly to sharpen the argument that a trend analyst who jumps to interpret fluctuations as error may thereby neglect an important finding on human instability. It is sometimes a difficult distinction to make, but grant that Almond had enough evidence to support his position: that the marked variations over time did not reflect random errors of measurement or sampling, and that the characterization could be generalized, on the basis of the sample designs, to the *population* at large.

This study was presented mainly to illustrate still another dilemma. The analyst whose trend is based on only *one* indicator must finally make a difficult judgment as to the meaning of the finding. It may be a wholly accurate representation of a temporal process, but exactly what process? The findings may be generalizable to a given population, but how generalizable are the findings to other related phenomena? The indicator may be a highly specific one, and the trend may be peculiar to that particular aspect of behavior. Without indicators of parallel processes, one cannot be sure. Therefore, Almond is careful to interpret his findings narrowly, to define the question as a measure of the *saliency* of foreign affairs. It provides "crude indication of the *prominence* of different types of issues," it "tells us about the comparative *salience* of foreign and domestic issues," it speaks to the "changes in the *focus* of attention."[42] Although he does not have extensive evidence based on other indicators, what little he can draw upon is used to determine the specificity or generality of the process that has been charted. "Other questions asked . . . immediately following the war show that a considerable part of the public was ready to give some priority (if not first priority) to American participation in foreign affairs. . . . It can be said, therefore, that questions of foreign affairs were recognized to be of some importance."[43] But on balance he asserts the lack of a pattern of stable attention and concern.

The conservative analyst who stays very close to the strict interpretation of the single indicator is on safe ground, but, of course, there is always some pressure toward enlarging the meaning of one's trend findings. The dangers that Almond might have courted by overgeneralization are well conveyed by Caspary's secondary analysis of trends in attention to foreign affairs and sup-

---

[42] *Ibid.*, pp. 71, 76 (italics supplied). A strict interpretation might also take special note of the phrase, "important *problem*" in the question. Literally what is measured is whether the problematic aspect of foreign affairs is salient to the person. Spontaneous attention to foreign affairs as such might be relatively stable whereas the sharp awareness of a crisis in that realm obviously would fluctuate with the severity of the situation.

[43] *Ibid.*, p. 78. See also the ingenious use he makes of a Gallup split ballot which experimented with alternative phrasings of foreign policy issues to estimate levels of interest (p. 79), and the use of a "knowledge battery" as an index of "effective interest in world problems" (p. 80–81).

port of American involvement based on time series for other variables within this domain. At the time of Almond's analysis (pre 1950), NORC had already begun a series of national surveys which produced several relevant time series and which continued for some years after the publication of his work. These studies, however, had never been given general publication, and Almond, working in the era before data banks, had no access to the materials. With the passage of years, these data entered the public domain, became accessible via the data banks, and Caspary conducted a thorough secondary analysis. His study, published twenty years after Almond's, at last located the empirical limits to the generalizability of the earlier findings. By observation of the differentiated trends for several indicators, and an intercorrelational analysis of the structure of thought and attitude, he determined that Almond's indicator is a measure of "primacy of attention, not of strength of attention." Without contesting the fluctuations in *primacy*, the trends on other indicators show that there is a *"strong and stable* 'permissive mood' toward international involvements. . . . Almond by no means ignored this line of thought. . . . There is no indication, however, that he anticipated the strength or stability of commitment to American foreign policy that our data suggests."[44]

When secondary analysts take a reckless step and move from *description* of some temporal process of the past to *prediction* of the future course of the process, caution seems the best evaluative principle. O. D. Duncan phrases that principle well: "There is nothing about a trend—supposing it to have been reliably ascertained for some specific period—that guarantees its own continuation."[45]

---

[44] W. R. Caspary, "The 'Mood Theory': A Study of Public Opinion and Foreign Policy," *Amer. Polit. Sci. Rev.*, **64**, 1970, p. 546. Caspary argues that Almond's indicator, the saliency question, is of "dubious validity." The invalidity mainly inheres in misinterpreting what it measures, not in the instrument itself. Caspary may intend more, however, by his conclusion, perhaps arguing that it produces a biased and inaccurate measure of what it is intended to measure. Another secondary analysis by Caspary of the previously unavailable NORC time series on American trust of the Soviet Union is a most informative case study. During the period 1945–1949, over twenty such surveys were conducted, and although the long-term trend shows a marked decrement of trust, the short-run fluctuations also reveal considerable instability. The analysis illustrates many of our earlier principles and procedures. The problem of *dating* the surveys is critical to Caspary's attempt to relate the trend to events, and is handled in ways that deserve attention. W. R. Caspary, "United States Public Opinion During the Onset of the Cold War," *Peace Research Society (International) Papers*, **9**, 1968, pp. 25–46.

[45] O. D. Duncan, "Social Stratification and Mobility, Problems in the Measurement of Trend," in Sheldon and Moore, *op. cit.*, p. 679. The published version of Stember's secondary analysis of trends in antisemitism provides a wonderful vehicle for training would-be predictors. His monograph was reviewed by eight commentators whose essays

What perpetuates a trend is the persistence of its former causes or the entry of new causal forces with the same vector. If they can be ascertained, the analyst has better grounds for advancing a prediction. If disaggregation reveals that the cause of the trend, whatever its ultimate nature, is distributed in particular ways in the population or social structure, e.g., by urbanization or education, one may project the future course of the phenomenon on the basis of the likely changes in the population, assuming, of course, some continuity in the processes operative within the groups. It is the inevitable fact of life that the young will replace the old and will determine the future course of any trend. Thus if the young differ from the old, and were to continue to do so despite their own aging, some prediction can be ventured. Thus our later analysis of generations and aging is especially relevant. If other types of causes can be isolated, and some conjectures made about their future occurrence, the risks in prediction are similarly reduced. But this brings us directly to the next stage of trend analysis, and there is little else to be said here except to stress the risks.

Explaining Trends

Throughout our discussion of this phase of trend analysis, we shall be looking at relationships, demonstrated or simply posited, between the changes or trends that have been described and a variety of other variables, conceived as the *causes* of the process. However, we should pause to consider that such relationships may be examined as tests of the opposite causal sequence. Our concern is partly to prevent a fallacious inference, but this poses a less severe methodological problem than is posed in the conventional analysis of causality in a *single* survey. Our concern is rather to insure that secondary analysts of trend do not neglect to explore an important facet of the relation between institutional change and mass behavior.

---

are incorporated in the published work. They focus periodically on his *tentative* prediction, and bring to this critical exercise the apparatus and perspectives of such varied disciplines as history, demography, social theory, and social psychology. The persistent decline of antisemitism over almost a twenty-five year period in America seems to Stember to provide considerable foundation for a prediction, albeit qualified. To one of the historians, whose perspective is the centuries and the world, Stember has brought into scope but a tiny point in time and space, and the prediction in light of the vast historical chronicle appears dubious. The published symposium may be read with great profit not only on styles of approach to prediction, but also for the hypotheses that men from different disciplines invoke to explain trends. Stember, *op. cit.*

Blake was sensitive to these opportunities in her secondary analyses of trends on issues relating to family planning. Apart from the time series on family size preferences, the attitude toward the dissemination of birth control information had also been asked in thirteen national surveys beginning in 1937. Support had risen over the years, but, as she stresses, the time series "contradict the notion that Americans have only recently ceased to regard birth control as a tabooed topic. As far back as 30 years ago, almost three-quarters . . . approved having the government make birth control information available to the married."[46] Her interest is not to explain the trend or the persistently high level of popular support. She turns the problem around, to see whether the "popular will" is the cause of government policy or not. She remarks: "The notion that the American public has only recently become willing to tolerate open discussion of birth control has been assiduously cultivated by congressmen." She quotes a 1966 statement by Senator Tydings: " . . . Ten years ago, even five years ago, this was a politically delicate subject. Today the nation has awakened to the need for government action." Fortunately, the time series long preceded such assertions and provides the evidence that "if birth-control information has in fact been unavailable . . . the cause has not been a generalized and pervasive attitude of prudery on the part of the American public . . . most Americans of an age to be having children did not regard birth control as a subject that should be under a blanket of secrecy and, as far back as the 1930's, evinced a marked willingness to have their government make such information widely available."[47]

The hypothesis that the officials have advanced to explain their own behavior makes the popular will and the changes or lack of changes in it the prime cause. Blake has tested it by her time series, and found it unsatisfactory as an explanation. This is not necessarily to suggest that there has been a conscious deception: Although the surveys were long available, Blake's thorough and trenchant secondary analysis was not published until 1969. She asks: "Is the government being misled?" and she remarks that "public officials may have misjudged American opinion" partly under the influence of those who "have been acting as self-designated spokesmen for 'public

---

[46] J. Blake, "Population Policy . . . ," *op. cit.*, p. 2. The time series from 1938 to 1947 is based on a question which specified married women. Between 1959 and 1963, the question was changed, but this lack of comparability does not impair her conclusion. The newer question mentioned that the provision of such information has been illegal in some places, and asks whether the respondent favors making such information available to *anyone*, not just married people. Support of such an unrestricted policy in opposition to a statute on the books obviously is a more permissive attitude, and yet the trend had risen, rather than declined.

[47] *Ibid.*

opinion'."[48] The complete explanation of the political behavior thus leads one into subtle matters of the false definition of the situation and how it became perpetrated, and into questions of whether officials respond to the view of *strategic* publics rather than the aggregate public. But understanding begins with examining opinions, revealed by the time series, as a causal agent, rather than as a phenomenon itself to be explained, and can be pursued further by disaggregating the data and presenting separate time series for such strategic groups as Catholics and non-Catholics, poor and rich, etc.

Blake's analysis establishes that the behavior of officials in this area cannot be explained by the popular will. One can now turn the problem around again. One can eliminate the hypothesis that the trend in the public's attitudes can be explained by government policy, unless one accepts a theory of such human perversity that what the government persists in prohibiting is what the public wants all the more. The gradual growth hardly seems a response to prolonged government inactivity. But this is not to suggest that the introduction of a new law or policy might not cause some additional acceleration of the trend. The existence of a time series prior to legislative acts provides the baseline for studying just such effects, either through secondary analysis or *semi*secondary analysis, in which a new point is deliberately added in order to estimate the effect of some institutional or legal force. Such a force is only one of the types of factors that can account for the trends and changes described, and we turn to a more detailed review and illustration of the problems at the stage of explanation.

TYPES OF CHANGE PROCESSES AND APPROPRIATE MODELS OF EXPLANATION

Testing some hypothesized explanation of the changes or trends that have been described is difficult, but first of all the analyst must have his hypothesis. Often, there are *too many* from which to choose, and the problem is somehow to narrow the choice down to those that are promising. Hanson, a philosopher–historian of science, reminds us "that the ingenuity, tenacity, imagination and conceptual boldness which has marked physics since Galileo shows itself more clearly in *hypothesis-catching* than in the deductive elaboration of caught hypotheses.[49] The secondary analyst of trends also needs the gift to catch the right hypothesis. Character and intellect count, as Hanson says, but close watch for clues presented in the careful description of the trend itself helps the analyst to search for his specific hypothesis in the right places.

---

[48] *Ibid.*

[49] N. R. Hanson, *Patterns of Discovery* (Cambridge: University Press, 1958), p. 72 (italics supplied).

As the analyst scans his data, some image of the type of change appears before his eyes, and, correspondingly, some general model of the process is suggested to him. Some factors just do not seem logically compatible with, or capable of, explaining the kinds of changes he observes. Other factors, in principle, could fashion the pattern. By theorizing about the kind of model that has a goodness of fit with the observed pattern of change, the analyst narrows his search for an explanation, is more likely to begin his testing in a fruitful area, and finally catches up with a hypothesis that pays off.

Recall an earlier example. Instability over short units of time, irregular oscillating changes, such as Almond observed, seem to reflect a *fickle* model of man and to fit with *intermittent events and transient* circumstances as forces that play upon him. They intrude and deflect his pattern; they depart and the process veers back; another distinctive event occurs and the process veers off in another direction. By contrast, a longer-run trend that unfolds in a systematic direction for a considerable time could suggest a *run* of discrete events as the cause, but all of the *same thematic* character. There is a vector which cumulatively pushes the trend along on a regular course.

An orderly trend plotted for a long enough time may reveal phases or describe a curvilinear course. It may move progressively in one direction over some time, then inflect and move in regular fashion in another direction for a considerable time. Stember observed such a pattern by tracing antisemitism from 1937 to 1962. "Though anti-semitism was much less prevalent at the end of the quarter-century studied than at its outset, the trend during the intervening years was by no means uniformly downward. According to our evidence, hostility against Jews actually *increased* from the beginning of the period until the final phase of the war, turned down sharply toward the later 1940s and has consistently ebbed since."[50] The model of eras or periods comes to mind, although, as earlier noted, it is not easy to be an honest operator in testing such a model, and the global nature of the concept may not satisfy those who like refined dissection of causes.

An alternative model, compatible with trends that move steadily in one direction is a single event of prolonged duration, or one that is short but so powerful that its effects are lasting. A law on the books illustrates one; a sudden crisis the other. The latter model is reminiscent of *trauma* on a collective scale. Nobody will ever be the same again after some one shocking experience. A long-term trend that unfolds regularly in one direction, but with occasional bumps in it, suggests a mixed model. Some cumulative force or set of parallel forces is at work. Discrete events intrude, however, and interfere occasionally to produce a temporary perturbation.

---

[50] Stember, *op. cit.*, p. 210 (italics supplied).

These are only images derived from a *single, aggregate* trend and some of the corresponding explanatory models that come to mind. A family of curves produced by differentiating trends for various aspects of a phenomenon may evoke other images and models. When Stember looks at trends in *twelve* different measures, a clearer image comes into view and he is emphatic: "Anti-semitism *in all its forms* massively declined in the United States between the pre-war or war years and the early 1960s. . . . Each of these measures registers a substantial diminution of anti-semitism . . . no matter whether it is the affective, cognitive or conative aspect that is gauged."[51] The explanatory model must either be a force that is broad and general enough to impinge directly on all the different aspects, or a narrow and specific force that impinges on a critical aspect, changes in which ramify to other aspects. What is in turn implied is the assumption of an interdependent structure of attitude or system of belief which topples when one foundation stone is shaken. Stember's theorizing partakes of such concepts. "Ideas about a given group of people reinforce one another." "Our data do not identify the particular component in which a change first occurred, but the parallelism . . . is such as to suggest that a major change in any one is bound ultimately to affect the other. . . ."

When trends are disaggregated, and a family of curves examined for different subgroups, new images and models are suggested. A trend that is pervasive suggests some macroscopic force diffused enough to touch everyone. When the trends are observed in some places and groups, but not elsewhere, several models suggest themselves. An event of a more circumscribed nature, impinging only on some, could account for the differential pattern.

One can also invoke some model of differential susceptibility to or insulation from a pervasive event. It is almost a fundamental principle that individuals and groups bring their special predispositions to encounters with events. The same event has more or less relevance to different population and status groups, and different implications and consequences for their welfare and interests. Such arguments are so *axiomatic* that an analyst who finds a pervasive trend, despite individual and group differences in predisposition, can regard it as evidence of some *compelling*, if unknown, force to which they all respond. It sweeps all groups along, overriding those who were disinclined to budge as well as those who welcomed change.[52]

---

[51] *Ibid.*, p. 208 (italics supplied).

[52] A striking example is provided by the trend studies of attitudes toward desegregation, where the changes among white Southerners and Northerners moved in the same direction toward integration, and, by some indices, might be regarded as having moved at a more accelerated pace in the South. Certainly, this suggests that the cause was fundamental and powerful, rather than an insignificant, circumscribed factor. Hyman and Sheatsley, "Attitudes toward Desegregation," *op. cit.*

Differential patterns among age groups, especially for the young versus the older members of the population, have a special importance for the analyst who is concerned with explaining and projecting trends. But often more than one model is appropriate. Competing explanations are tenable, and testing their respective merits is so complex and difficult a problem that we shall reserve it for separate discussion later. Some issues and policies, e.g., draft or pension laws, impinge on the special, current interests and welfare of given age groups, and may account for their respective stands and the trends in their responses.[53] These issues aside, the models of the trend analyst tend to be shaped by his underlying theories. He may argue simply for the greater plasticity of the young, their openness to stimulation, or he may invoke some doctrine of generations, theorizing that a particular age cohort became permanently marked by the prior experiences and events in its formative years, and thereafter responds differentially to subsequent events in light of its stable predispositions.

Some analysts, observing different trends among social groups and age groups, tend to think of particular historical events as the formative influences that have created their respective predispositions. Others, more sensitized to notions of social structure and demography, look at other types of factors which have gradually shaped the predispositions of particular groups— the urbanization or industrialization of a region, or the exposure of an age cohort to greater schooling or to military experience.[54] These factors do not intrude suddenly or all at once, and their plausibility as explanations thus can be undermined or strengthened by reference to the pace at which the trends have moved.

---

[53] Even here, plausible hypotheses derived from a theory of "interest groups" are sometimes not borne out by empirical data. For example, repeated comparisons of older and younger age groups in the U.S. showed only small differences in support of old age pensions and extensions of the social security laws, and consistently documented somewhat *less* support among the old, even when education and income were controlled. See Schiltz, *op. cit.*, pp. 38 and 78.

[54] For example, Jackson and Crockett observed somewhat greater mobility in their 1957 survey than in their 1945 survey and entertain the following hypotheses: ". . . the effect of military service on many men was to broaden their occupational aspirations and, in the form of post-war assistance in technical and academic training, provide for implementation of some of these aspirations. In many cases, too, by interrupting careers, military service might also have produced downward mobility. In other words, the war might have loosened the ties between father's occupation and son's occupation for the cohorts beginning their careers at that time . . . the 1957 sample might . . . have had a higher mobility rate, since it includes those veterans after the effects of military service have had time to emerge." Jackson and Crockett, *op. cit.*, p. 13.

Analysts who observe differential patterns among population groups and who are inclined toward demographic models may also, as earlier noted, have a basis for explaining an *aggregate* trend. It may be regarded as the *net* result of the subgroup differences, and therefore the changing size and weight of a population group can contribute to the outcome.

Those who are inclined to explain trends in terms of demographic and structural factors are not limited to models of such processes going on *internally* within those who are themselves changing their ideas and behavior. The *object of the attitude* may itself have been undergoing some demographic or structural change. By way of illustration, Stember entertained as causal factors such events as the rise of Nazism and World War II, which may have affected the attitudes of Christians toward Jews. But competing explanations entertained by a demographer include such a long-running event as the rise and decline in Jewish immigration (which not only changed the size of the Jewish group in the U.S. but also their nativity composition) and changes in the geographical and occupational distribution of Jews. Both of these changes may have affected Gentile–Jewish contacts, the beliefs about Jews, and the kinds of relations between the groups.[55] Similarly, an analyst of trends in white attitudes toward Negroes could entertain such an event as the 1954 Supreme Court decision, or alternatively such a slow demographic event as the changes in the occupational and geographical distribution of Negroes.

Demographic and structural changes in the group that is the *object* of attitudes are slow-moving events and also occur in certain locii rather than uniformly throughout the nation. The disaggregated trends also should show some parallels to the locus of the changes in the minority. Gutman, the commentator on Stember's study who entertained these demographic models, remarks: "Certainly between 1939 and 1962—the period for which poll data broken by region are available—shifts in the geographical distribution of Jews were not great enough to account for the vast reported reduction in anti-semitism. . . . Perhaps the most striking aspect of the findings is how much anti-semitism has declined in *all* regions, independently of the changing residence of Jews."

When competing models such as the role of historical events and demographic events seem equally tenable, one probably falls back on some underlying theory in weighing their respective merits. Those who see the motivational sources of intergroup attitudes in terms of projective or ego-defensive functions for the individual would find the demographic model less plausible

---

[55] R. Gutman, "Demographic Trends and the Decline of Anti-Semitism" in Stember *et al.*, *op. cit.*, pp. 354–375.

than those who stress the object appraisal or knowledge function of attitude. Those who see the sources and maintenance of attitudes in terms of value-expressive functions and their functions for relating the individual to his membership and reference groups would be likely to generate still other models explaining the trends in terms of some sweeping value change and the promulgation of the corresponding norms among many groups.[56]

Some secondary analysts are so set from the start on a specific hypothesis about a change or trend they set out to describe and explain that they skip the experiences of model building, and, in turn, hypothesis catching. By sparing themselves the pains of such intellectual labors, they may eliminate alternative, equally plausible, explanations, and form premature judgments or conclusions. Indeed, as we shall suggest, sometimes it is not possible to make a convincing *direct* proof of a hypothesis about change. In such instances, one has at least strengthened his case if he has shown that other explanations are dubious.

For those who do need to catch their hypothesis along the way, there is no better approach than to examine their descriptive data carefully, entertain alternative models or classes of explanation, reject those that do not withstand logical examination and critical scrutiny, and finally set out to test one or more specific hypotheses that conform to the appropriate model. Mueller describes the experience of "hypothesis-catching" very well: "If one stares at Presidential popularity trend lines long enough, one soon comes to imagine one is seeing things. If the things imagined seem also to be mentioned in the literature about the way Presidential popularity should or does behave, one begins to take the visions seriously and move to test them."[57] We now turn to that phase of the analysis.

ATTEMPTS TO TEST HYPOTHESES

One of the favorite models for analysts trying to explain short-term change implicates some discrete event contiguous with the change. It is easy enough to *disconfirm* particular events which have been advanced predictively as likely to cause some change in attitude or belief, since one often finds by subsequent inspection of the data that they have not made the slightest difference in the pattern. Many trends seem to move imperturbably, unaffected by events which analysts, who did not have the benefit of hindsight, would have regarded as potent forces. For example, in three different NORC surveys conducted in 1956 which repeated the battery of questions on desegregation, the variation in support of integration was less than 1% despite three inter-

---

[56] For such a model, see the commentary by Robin Williams in Stember, *op. cit.*
[57] Mueller, *op. cit.*, p. 19.

vening crises over the issue in Southern cities which were widely publicized. Three other measurements of the trend in 1963 again showed a variation of less than 1% despite the fact that the assassination of President Kennedy intervened one week before one of the surveys and might well have been an event traumatic enough to convert the opinions of many.[58]

Stember's study provides other illustrations. The steady downward course of antisemitism from the late forties to the sixties remained unperturbed by a number of major events which seemed "likely to worsen the public's attitudes toward Jews. One was the birth of Israel, which according to some observers was sure to cast doubt on the loyalty of American Jewry. Another was America's growing concern about Communist espionage and subversion, culminating in the trial and conviction of several Soviet spies, some of whom bore Jewish names . . . . Israel's subsequent invasion of Egyptian territory, an act which directly challenged policies of the United States Government" was a third event which did not alter the trend.[59]

Disconfirming the immediate impact of an event is easy and a frequent experience for trend analysts. What about confirmation? That too appears simple—deceptively so. Earlier we alluded to the common practice of analysts inclined toward such models to look at their time series, observe a shift, and then fasten on a discrete historical event coincident with the change. The juxtaposition is then taken as evidence of cause and effect. To be sure, the analyst can have confidence that *some* variable is causing the shift. He can rely on the general evidence of the high reliability of the measurements, of the normal imperturbability of trends. His own long time series may provide additional evidence. Thus, it is eminently reasonable to adjudge the shift as real and the product of some powerful force. But when he identifies a particular contiguous event, and regards the mere coincidence as evidence, it often is a reckless, not a reasonable, inference. Unless he has some supplementary qualitative evidence to guide and support him, he has no basis for choosing which one of several contiguous events is causal. And it is even possible that none of the contiguous historical events were important. Long experience with the *disconfirmation* of many causal hypotheses involving particular events should make one wary. Why regard one event as a potent force at a particular point when *similar* events have proven so impotent at other times?

The *two* meanings of coincidence come to mind. The event and the change coincide in time, but their joint occurrence may be accidental, a coincidence in the second sense of that word. When the particular event is treated as a

---

[58] "Attitudes toward Desegregation," *op. cit.*
[59] Stember, *op. cit.*, p. 210.

unique, concrete instance, the analyst has no way of resolving the dilemma.[60] If one had only totaled up the other instances where a similar event produced no shift in the trend, then one might really see that the effect of such a causal variable *generally* was nil, or at best a rather capricious force sometimes working its effects, sometimes not. To be sure, similar events are not identical in all respects, and a particular entity, in its distinctive nature and magnitude impinging at one particular historical juncture, truly might have worked a change which similar events had never produced before. But then again it might be sheer coincidence. The cautious analyst so regards it, realizing that he might be ignoring a real finding, but playing it safe unless he has some auxiliary evidence to strengthen his argument. If, however, he is fortunate enough to demonstrate that the general variable, a class of similar events, recurrently produced the same kind of changes, then he really feels confident that the joint occurrence at one point is not coincidence and that he has isolated a dependable cause.

Such a strategy is exemplified in Mueller's study of trends in presidential popularity. As earlier noted, the Gallup Poll had asked national samples: "Do you approve or disapprove of the way _____ is handling his job as President?" several hundred times from the beginning of Truman's presidency in 1945 to the end of Johnson's in January, 1969. This provided the lavish supply of episodes of change or stability in popularity for making the repeated tests of the causal significance of various classes of variables which had recurred during the 24-year period. And the long time series and the corresponding historical chronicle provided the raw materials, the food for thought, that

---

[60] After-the-fact arguments about the *direction* of the shift, or the *sign* of the association between the event and the change, are not very reassuring. An analyst might muse that the trend went just in the direction he would have predicted and thus must reflect the influence of the event, since chance might have led to shift in the opposite direction. But, often one can rationalize a plausible hypothesis about either direction. Carry out the honest "thought experiment" relevant to the Stember trends during World War II. It seems highly likely that one would have *predicted* that the Nazi holocaust and the ideological nature of that war would have worked to reduce antisemitism. Yet knowing that Stember found that antisemitism actually *increased*, one could have produced a theory to explain that also, leaning on any number of specific hypotheses: e.g., Americans might have distinguished the plight of European Jews as distinctive, unrelated to their attitudes toward American Jews. They might have been hostile to American Jews on grounds that the latter group were "war mongers;" "draft-dodgers," etc. They might have responded to the antisemitic appeals of the native agitators in the U.S. whose arguments so paralleled their European Fascist counterparts. These are only some of the possibilities one could have invented to rationalize what might otherwise have seemed bizarre findings moving in a strange, unexpected direction. What strengthens Stember's interpretations is empirical evidence from many other survey questions of the links in the hypothesized dynamic processes. Stember, *op. cit.*

led Mueller to the general concepts under which he classified discrete events, although he tells us how long and hard he stared before he caught some of his hypotheses.

History, to be sure, just happened to repeat itself during those 24 years with respect to very major kinds of events: There were, alas, two wars, not just one; there were, sadly, several economic slumps, not just one; there were four instances of a new president assuming office.[61] The number of repeated tests of a variable, however, depends not only on the acts of history, but also on an act of *mind*, on the way the investigator conceptualizes events. Thus, instead of making a *single* test of each of 34 discrete and unique events, or a few tests of each of 6 smallish and separate classes of similar events (for example, 4 tests of sudden American military intervention versus 6 tests of meetings between the President and the head of the Soviet Union), Mueller conceptualizes all 34 as instances of similar international events which start a general variable, a "rally 'round the flag" into motion. Thus, he can make a great many tests of the hypothesis that such events always boost popularity, though briefly, as the public moves to support a president facing a crisis.[62]

These tests, no matter how plentiful, can still be deceptive, unless one avoids circularity and classifies events in an objective fashion. If one redefines an event when it does not produce the hypothesized effect as no longer belonging in the original class, the negative evidence disappears. And as Mueller emphasizes: "There is a terrible temptation to find a bump on a popularity plot, then to scurry to historical records to find an international 'rally point' to associate with it. This process all but guarantees that the variable will prove significant." And so he "adopted a definition of what a rally point should look like on . . . *a priori* grounds. . . . Most of the points are associated with bumps . . . but quite a few are *not*."[63]

Mueller saw many *upward* "short term bumps and wiggles" reflecting rallies 'round the flag, but he also saw, partly in his mind's eye, an "inexorable descent" in popularity. He conceptualized this long-run process in terms of a "coalition of minorities" variable. Inevitably, the argument goes, a president creates by his actions "intense, unforgiving opponents [out] of former sup-

---

[61] Mueller, *op. cit.* Since Mueller's analysis, the time series has been extended by frequent measurements of President Nixon's popularity, providing opportunities for additional tests of the same variables he employed, and some tests of new factors and of the general process under still a fifth president.

[62] This is not to suggest that secondary analysts should ignore finer distinctions simply to build up a superfluity of tests. In fact, Mueller separates the 34 rally points into 2 subclasses, the "good" class hypothesized to create larger boosts and a "bad" class. Interestingly, the public seemed "to react to 'good' and 'bad' events in much the same way." *Ibid.*, p. 22.

[63] *Ibid.*, p. 21 (italics supplied).

porters. . . . From time to time there arise exquisite dilemmas in which the President must act and in which he will tend to alienate both sides no matter what he does."[64] Mueller takes as problematic the rate of descent, the shape of its course—whether it is curvilinear gathering speed or tapering off with time in office or linear, and whether there are differences depending on the particular president and his starting level, but assumes that the coalition must grow ever larger. Again, what should be stressed is that this iron-clad law governing the fortunes of any president, however operationalized in particular hypotheses, is subjected to *repeated* tests. The pessimistic prediction is indeed confirmed, although the rate of descent is found to be more precipitous for some presidents than others. A highly general cause of the trends is thus established, with one notable exception: No matter what subtleties of index construction and analysis are introduced, "President Eisenhower's rating uncooperatively refuses to decline at all."[65]

Mueller's explanatory model is not limited simply to an inexorable descent periodically retarded or bumped upwards by rally points. Two other variables are introduced which are hypothesized to be major factors that accelerate the *downward* course. The factor of war is entered into the analysis in an undifferentiated way, its sheer presence at any point creating a further decrement in popularity.[66] The "economic slump" variable is measured by a refined index: At each point in the time series on popularity, the rise in the percent unemployed since the President's term began is computed. What Mueller is arguing, most interestingly, is that the sense of *relative deprivation* or worsening of the economy and not the absolute level of conditions is the potent variable. Furthermore, the index ironically is scored in such a way, and the analysis seems to document that rising employment does not help popularity. "There is punishment but never reward."[67]

At every point in the time series, each of these two variables and the previous two can be given a value to denote the presence or the magnitude of its

---

[64] *Ibid.*, p. 20.

[65] *Ibid.*, p. 27.

[66] This is not to suggest that the war variable is handled crudely. Relevant to our earlier discussion of "timing" the initiation of a protracted event, the Vietnam war is not regarded as begun and present as an operative variable until June, 1965. The Korean War is given a "zero" value, treated as absent, during Eisenhower's administration, although it, in fact, continued, presumably because the public blamed its presence on the previous administration from whom he had inherited it. That Mueller is not unmindful that a war can worsen or better when it is "present" is suggested by his study of trends in support of the Korean and Vietnam wars, where the vicissitudes of the wars are given very precise values. Mueller, *op. cit.* And that some wars are worse than others and may have different effects on the public is not ignored in his analysis.

[67] *Ibid.*, p. 23.

force, and thus many repeated tests can be made. The joint and separate contribution of the several variables was then determined by multiple regression methods. This procedure provides protection against the reckless practice mentioned earlier of selecting arbitrarily as *the* cause only one element out of a complex of factors that impinge at some point in a trend.

The complexities of Mueller's theorizing are not conveyed adequately by this brief account. The four major variables were translated operationally in a variety of interesting ways. Other subsidiary variables incorporated are of considerable interest—for example, a variable for the presence of major strikes, a variable denoting the atmosphere of "moral crises," measured most ingeniously by a content analysis of trends in periodical literature. Nor have we described the full refinements of the analysis. But our summary should serve well enough to suggest the way a complex explanatory model can be formulated, the hypothesized causes of change measured objectively, and their effects put to repeated and dependable tests.[68]

Other literature that we might review shows the varied ways in which the general principles already presented can be applied, and thus would serve to improve the secondary analyst's abilities to describe and explain trends.[69] Rather than elaborate on the same body of principles, however, we turn from conventional trend analysis to a set of new designs, some most intricate in structure, which greatly enlarge our power to analyze social and psychological processes of change.

---

[68] We have not reviewed the question of comparability of the trend measures, which is presupposed in any attempt to explain the changes as due to real factors. Mueller does stress that the question was exactly replicated through all these hundreds of surveys, and the use of data from only the one agency, the Gallup Poll, would suggest that the field work was also a constant. He does not raise the issue of the location of the question, but it might be noted that this presents no problem. For many years, the question has always been the opening one in the interview, thus being constant in position and the response not influenced artificially by any prior issues posed. Occasional anomalies in popularity or deviation of a point from the regression line are considered by Mueller in terms of sampling error or accidental variations in procedure. As earlier noted, the Gallup Poll introduced a systematic change in its sampling procedures around 1950, and Mueller does not review this problem explicitly. But it is certainly a reasonable assumption that all the trend examined in the more recent years is based on comparability in sampling, and that the trend within the Truman years is also based on a set of comparable samples. Mueller's mode of analysis, in effect, handles the problem by the introduction of a dummy variable for administration and corresponding calendar years.

[69] For example, Mueller's study of trends in support of the Korean and Vietnam wars illustrates ways to treat difficult problems of comparability of question wording and sampling, and the choice of a criterion attribute. Despite surface differences, the long-term pattern can be explained in both instances by a general process. Initial support reflects the "rally 'round the flag"; long-term decline is rarely a response to specific events and mainly a function of the *logarithm* of the total number of casualties. Mueller, *op. cit.*

VII

Age Comparisons
and Cohort Analysis
in the Study of
Long-Term Change

THE FIRST DESIGN TO BE PRESENTED HAS A SPECIAL APPEAL. IT MAKES NO STRIN-
gent demands for lengthy, comparable time series. It is simple to implement
and it provides an inferential avenue to the study of long-term change. Thus,
it increases the power of the deprived but gifted analyst. For those who had
never entertained it, new vistas will open. But for those who feel impelled to
apply it recklessly and interpret it carelessly, a review of its limitations is
essential.

Comparisons of Age Groups Drawn from the Same Surveys

Let us begin by picking up some threads left dangling in our discussion of
trends and in our earlier chapters. These threads usually weave themselves
together into an elaborate, tight pattern that describes and explains a complex of social and psychological phenomena and processes. The difficulty
arises when one wishes to untangle them.

In Chapter IV we reviewed the many possibilities for the focused study or
broad characterization of social groups and categories within a society, all
brought within the reach of the secondary analyst through the routine information on the face sheet. We hardly paused there to note that the *age* of the
individual is almost invariably recorded. We cited not a single example of a
secondary analysis of a discrete age grouping, the "old" or the "middle-aged"
or the "young adult," nor any comparison of such groups, although there are

endless possibilities for such studies.[1] Age groups surely are as important to study as groups varying in sex, or religion, or class. Age implicates a massive form of stratification in that the old may have power and wealth, perhaps privilege and deference accorded to them, which the young may fiercely want to share. All sorts of theoretical questions on the concomitants of position in the age structure of a society could be addressed by broad or focused secondary analyses, and that currently popular topic, the "generation gap," could be illuminated by data establishing the extent and nature of the differences

---

[1] The problem generic to all studies of social groups, error arising in the sampling of a group or in the measurement of the defining characteristic, cannot be ignored in the study of age groups. But the mythology should not be taken as the fact. In most surveys the individual is taken at his word, reports his own age, and is rarely checked upon by any battery of questions. Yet the reliability of such reports of age is high. In a classic study of response error based on a sample of about a thousand cases in Denver, reports of exact age on two different questions within the interview were consistent within one year in 95% of the cases. In one panel study where the respondent reported his age on a second interview conducted some six months later, age in gross categories was consistently reported in 98% of the cases. In another panel study of a more specialized local population reinterviewed after a lapse of three years, age in fine categories was consistently reported in 88% of the cases. In the Denver study, validity of report as checked against two criteria, exact age reported in drivers' license records and election registration records was accurate within one year in 92% and 83% of the cases, respectively, and the residual errors were completely *random* in direction. See H. J. Parry and H. M. Crossley, "Validity of Responses to Survey Questions," *Publ. Opin. Quart.,* **14,** 1950, p. 78; H. Hyman *et al., Interviewing in Social Research, op. cit.,* p. 247; P. Haberman and J. Sheinberg, "Education Reported in Interviews," *Publ. Opin. Quart.,* **30,** 1966, pp. 299–300. In connection with errors arising from sampling, there is some evidence that older individuals are more likely to refuse, and that young men are less likely to be found at home to be interviewed, but the critical issue is whether those who are lost differ from those who are interviewed with respect to the phenomena under study. Such subtle evidence of sampling bias is hard to obtain, but the occasional findings are reassuring on this score. See Norval Glenn, "Aging, Disengagement, and Opinionation," *Publ. Opin. Quart.,* **33,** 1969, p. 31; B. S. Dohrenwendt and B. P. Dohrenwendt, "Sources of Refusals in Surveys," *Publ. Opin. Quart.,* **32,** 1968, p. 81; R. Williams, "Probability Sampling in the Field," *Publ. Opin. Quart.,* **14,** 1950, p. 320. There is, as earlier noted, a possible problem in the fact that most sampling designs are restricted to the population living in private dwellings, and therefore the very young and the very old contained within institutions are missed. One should be careful not to generalize beyond the boundaries of the target population, but even if one exceeded his proper bounds, it does not follow generally that the institutionalized members would differ from the non-institutionalized with respect to the phenomenon under study and that the conclusion would be in error. In any case, the magnitude of the losses of very old and very young is at worst small when compared with census data on the total population, this discrepancy representing the net effect of differences in the universe, noncompletion, and response error in the enumerations. For illustrative findings, see G. Almond and S. Verba, *The Civic Culture* (Princeton: Princeton University Press, 1963), pp. 518–521.

in outlook between age groups. So, too, eternal questions of social policy about which there has been endless speculation could be clarified. Are the old wiser by virtue of long experience and the status they have slowly arrived at? Or, as Gergen and Back, in one of the few secondary analyses of age, couch the hypothesis: perhaps "the aged are often petulant, unreasonable, and insensitive to changes in the contemporary world."[2]

Ironically, we really study age a good deal of the time in our conventional social comparisons in primary survey research or in secondary analysis, often without realizing what we are doing. Men and women, the native born and immigrants and Black and white in America, those with much and little education, differ substantially in age. Yet we rarely bother to control age in such analyses, although we are alert to control other variables that might confound our conclusions. The problem, as we shall see, is double-edged. Some of the differences between age groups might be "spurious" and reflect the other social characteristics that accompany a certain age status, rather than the *intrinsic* effect of age as such. That difficulty can be handled, when demanded by one's need to refine the constellation labeled "age," by straightforward technical means, and should deter no secondary analyst from applying the many research designs of Chapter IV to the *description* of an age group, or of the entire age structure and stratification of a society. Indeed, if that is all one wishes to establish by his studies, those designs are ideal. The portrait of the aged or the young can be made as comprehensive as one wishes. The reliability of the evidence can be strengthened by pooling or replicating the observations. The pools of cases can be built up so that one can examine a constellation of characteristics. One can establish what it is to be a young man, or young women, or young, black man rather than just a youth.[3]

A series of such controlled comparisons opens the door to a fascinating problem. Is there more continuity or change in some subcultures and strata than in others? Are young Southerners, for example, more like their elders than young Northerners, young whites more so than young Negroes? Something is then suggested about the potency of the socialization process in some places and about the disjunctive forces of social change in other places which attenuate the transmission of the old culture.[4] Why then were studies so feasible and informative not reviewed in Chapter IV?

---

[2] K. J. Gergen and K. W. Back, "Aging, Time Perspective and Preferred Solutions to International Conflicts," *J. Conflict Resol.*, **9**, 1965, p. 177.

[3] We need not stress the egregious error one could perpetrate if he employed a "pseudo-comparative" design examining only one discrete age group, and simply imputed a difference to some contrasted group he had not studied empirically.

[4] John Reed's demonstration of the persistence of a Southern subculture by the secondary

Such studies do open a door—but to a Pandora's box of puzzling problems.[5] Analysts who employ the design often wish to go far beyond the sheer description and comparison of age groups to draw confident conclusions about the meaning and explanation of the findings. The threads they then spin out weave many problems mentioned in Chapters V and VI inextricably into their studies. By deferring discussion until now, we shall better understand the complexity of the findings, the risks in interpretation, and the care that must be applied in operating the design.

VARIETIES OF INTERPRETATION OF COMPARISONS AMONG AGE GROUPS

Some analysts, although they have not, in fact, traced any changes in individuals by repeated measurements spaced out over time, nevertheless treat the set of descriptions of groups contrasted in age as if it were a continuous picture of the process of *aging*. In their hands, a cross-sectional design is bent into the form of a *quasilongitudinal* design. They assume that the mystery of what a thirty-year old, for example, will be like when he has aged twenty years, can be solved without waiting around all that time, simply by looking at the profile of a fifty-year old in their current surveys. By the same token, they can turn back time and infer what the fifty-year old was like twenty years ago without benefit of an empirical measurement from back then, simply by inspecting the thirty-year olds in their current surveys.

The central assumption is that the groups being compared represent *equivalent* individuals differing only in the point in the life cycle or in the aging process they have reached. To be sure, the analyst must apply one basic precaution. Since men (and, in America, Negroes and some other minority groups) die earlier, the old and young in any gross comparisons are not equivalent in social composition. Moreover, because educational opportunity has expanded, and waves of immigration occurred at certain historical points in the past, the old and young differ in ethnicity and level of education also. The age groups must be made equivalent in such respects by introducing conventional controls or by multiple standardization, when the phenomena under study are influenced by such social variables and the analyst wishes to establish the intrinsic effect of aging. But that, as already mentioned, is read-

---

analysis of trends in the difference between South and North leads him to just such a discussion of the respective socialization agencies. Reed, *op. cit.*

[5] The encyclopedic review of age groups by Riley *et al.*, shows the utility of the designs in Chapter IV. But the limitations of all such designs and the appropriateness of each for the study of different aspects of the complex subsumed under the rubric "Age" are analyzed in a general introduction. Riley, *op. cit.*

ily accomplished. The findings then would seem well protected, and would appear to speak with precision on such questions as what happens for example, when women grow old, or the poor and lowly educated grow old. A whole series of developmental curves or aging processes could presumably be mapped. Admittedly, the number of points that could be plotted along the course of life is dependent on the refinement with which age was enumerated and coded in the original surveys, but we have an abundant supply to choose from. If some surveys were too crude for our purposes, others can be found which did measure age with sufficient refinement.

Comparisons of age groups, applied carefully and treated in this inferential manner, squarely belong in Chapters V and VI. Nothing could be more universal than aging. By this simple and feasible design, we can expand our agenda of studies of fundamental phenomena. Without it, our powers as secondary analysts are weakened. Panel designs are rare resources in survey research, and generally of such short duration that they only trace a brief segment in the lives of individuals, a few months or at best a few years. Often they are limited to a single community, and their generality is severely limited in another way. Panels are truly longitudinal designs, and indeed demonstrate how a given sample has aged over a specified interval of time, but the process may reflect the peculiar conditions present during that particular period when the sample has aged. Time is being sampled also, and the findings, therefore, may not be representative of the general process of aging.[6] Perhaps the design that employs comparisons of age groups can be freed from this limitation. The sampling of time surely is critical for its power and success, but may also turn out to be its hidden vulnerability.

Contemplating the process of aging and bringing it under inferential observation by the comparison of age groups also enlarges our ability to study change comprehensively. Chapter VI dealt essentially with *social* change, a change in a huge collectivity, such as a nation, or in a very large group within it, such as a stratum. When we described social change, whether in the short or long run, discrete events or strings of events or certain kinds of aggregative processes were treated as the major determinants of the change, although, occasionally, in a most allusive way, reference was made to the disaggregation of the trend by age groups.

Treated purely as *independent* processes, driven by different types of forces, the study of long-term social change in a collectivity and the study of aging,

---

[6] This is not to argue against making maximum use in secondary analysis of those conventional panels that are available. Moreover, as suggested in Chapter II, the design of experimental empanelling in which samples from old surveys are followed up years later by new surveys would contribute a great deal to the study of aging, although by *semi*-secondary analysis.

the long-term changes within the *individual,* lead together to more comprehensive research. Both deserve study. But certainly, the two processes must be
interdependent; different patterns among age groups must contribute somehow to the aggregate changes observed. The explanatory model that links
these two levels of change could even be based on the simple, but rarely considered, fact that the proportion of older individuals in a society may change
over time. In the United States their weight has gradually but substantially
increased over a long interval. Whatever distinctive effect aging might *always*
have had on the individual would thus weigh more heavily upon the collectivity in recent years and could, in theory, account for some aggregate trend.
Some might elaborate this same model in a more subtle way, entertaining a
"contextual" effect. Perhaps the effect of aging on any single individual is intensified when there are more aged individuals surrounding him. Thus the
increase in their weight in the collectivity might contribute to the aggregate
trend almost geometrically, not additively.

In this light, the comparison of age groups seems to be a design of excep-
tional merit, enlarging our understanding not only of individual change but
also of social change. Why withhold its discussion for so long? Consider some
radically different conceptions invoked by other analysts to understand and
link the two levels of change. Surely, they say, the pattern of aging must be
shaped in some ways by the times into which people are born, the events they
then live through as they are aging, and not merely by the fact that they are
all moving in uniform manner, inexorably along the course of life.

Whatever influence a particular cohort of aged individuals might have on
the aggregate changes observed, by virtue of their special characteristic or
their number, must inevitably wane as they die and are replaced by another
cohort who have aged under different circumstances and have been shaped by
the events of newer times. If aging is a fundamental and universal phenomenon, so too is the endless succession of cohorts who are presumed to age in
different ways. In this formulation, the dynamics are reversed.[7] Social change,
and the forces that push it, in turn shape the aging process; in the earlier one,
the generic process of aging and the numbers involved shape the pattern of
aggregate change.

This formulation, if authoritative, raises serious questions for those who
employ a simple comparison of age groups to study pure *aging.* Groups who

---

[7] Ryder summarizes it well: "Each new cohort makes fresh contact with the contemporary
social heritage and carries the impress of the encounter through life. . . . The members
of any cohort are entitled to participate in only one slice of life—their unique location
in the stream of history. . . . The new cohorts provide the opportunity for social change
to occur. They do not cause change; they permit it." N. Ryder, "The Cohort as a Concept in the Study of Social Change," *Amer. Sociol. Rev.,* **30,** 1965, pp. 844.

differ in age at the time of a particular survey may have been equated in social composition, but that does not make them equivalent in the experiences they will all have lived through when they reach a certain point in life. The fifty-year olds do not necessarily give us a preview of what the thirty-year olds will become. They are older but were born into a world and have already lived through a set of events which probably is different from the world the thirty-year olds entered and will experience in their years to come. Analytically, we might play with the question of what would happen to people as they aged, if we could stop the world from moving, but empirically the two processes seem intertwined in this design and jointly responsible for the net effects. Unless buttressed in some way, conclusions about aging per se seem shaky and the design seems fraught with uncertainty.

In pondering the several processes, social change in the wider world and the aging of successive cohorts who have entered the scene at different historical points, some analysts invoke a special theory of *generations*. Each cohort is presumed to be shaped distinctively and primarily by the conditions during the *formative* years. Thereafter, to be sure, the members may change in some respects as a result of the fundamental process of aging and the events of later years, but a generation is presumed to be relatively rigid or fixated in its pattern and somehow insulated from later experience. Social change, history, is again the potent factor, but only during a limited interval.[8] The generation, so to speak, has been imprinted by the events and features during one critical, narrow phase of its development.

Ironically, the generational theorist also employs the comparisons of matched groups, contrasted in age, and drawn from the *same* survey to test his theory, just as others draw their conclusions about aging using the very same design.[9] Of course, the old in any survey were reared in an earlier period

---

[8] Just as age groups may vary in their numbers, so, too, a particular generation may have many members and great longevity. Thus it could have a great weight for a long time on the aggregate pattern and account for the subsequent social changes. Again Ryder puts it well: "A cohort's size relative to the size of its neighbors is a persistent and compelling feature of its lifetime environment. . . . Any extraordinary size deviation is likely to leave an imprint on the cohort as well as on the society." Ryder, *op. cit.*, p. 845. On the complexities of the doctrine of generations, see, for example, G. and K. Karlsson, "Age, Cohorts, and the Generation of Generations," *Amer. Sociol. Rev.*, **35**, 1970, pp. 710–718; H. Hyman, *Political Socialization* (New York: Free Press, Paperback edition, 1969), Chapter 6.

[9] The controls are not necessarily applied in the same way, and in no case should be applied or interpreted thoughtlessly. No one can change sex, or color or place of birth as he ages, nor can he change the amount of schooling he received during his childhood. Thus all these controls make good sense in a test of aging. Becoming richer or poorer, however, is a normal accompaniment of aging, and would not be controlled, unless one wishes for analytic reasons to examine aging, purified of such an accompaniment. To test

than the young, but they also have aged more. The cross-sectional design seems to implicate both processes. The generational theorist, like the student of aging, needs a *longitudinal* design, but of a different type. If he had a series of comparable *trend* surveys spaced out over a long span of time, he then could compare the young across the *different* surveys. They are equated in age and caught at an early point in life before the process of aging has set in, but they were reared at different times and are samples from different generations historically. This same design lends itself to the intricacies of cohort analysis, to which we shall come. It will then yield evidence also on the generic process of aging and on the specificities of the process for cohorts aging in different eras and under the influence of different events. Lacking such long-term trend designs, the generation theorist bends the cross-sectional design into his own form of quasilongitudinal design. He assumes so to speak, that he had stopped the aging process somehow, and that the old and young reflect essentially the respective conditions prevailing in their formative years.

The secondary analyst sometimes uses the cross-sectional design not merely to test a specific generational hypothesis, but also as a *quasitrend* to make inferences about the aggregate, or general pattern of social change, despite the lack of long-term trend data. If young and old adults bear the imprint of their formative years, they can be regarded as the living embodiment, the epitome, of those earlier times. The fifty-year olds in a survey in 1950 implicitly must be telling us about life and society in 1910; the seventy-year olds in the same survey carry us back to the last century. They are the carriers of that old culture. Though we may lack the surveys that should have been conducted long ago, they inform us as to what the earlier survey would have shown.

How can the one design which, in reality, intertwines so many processes serve two or more different masters equally well? It seems two-faced, or at least ambiguous. The design seems to capture the poor secondary analyst in a tangled web of threads woven into an intricate, almost seamless fabric of change. He may decide to leave it at that, simply describing the final fabric, unless he inherits some rare, longitudinal design ideally suited to a refined analysis of change. But perhaps there are special ways to operate the design critically and creatively so as to dissect some of the processes.

THE CASE OF GLENN VERSUS GERGEN AND BACK

Observe the way two of the highly successful and experienced analysts, mentioned in Chapter III, handle the assignment.

---

the general influence of being brought up in a certain era, similarly, requires controls on sex and color and ethnicity. But the distinctive feature of the experience of a particular generation may well be the educational opportunities it had, and thus one would not introduce a control on education, unless, again, one wished to eliminate that aspect from the complex of factors to be examined.

Back, and his associate Gergen, as noted earlier, have been engaged in extensive secondary analyses on such fundamental features of the person as self-conception, time and spatial perspectives, perception of causality, body image, etc., and on aging generally and as it affects such orientations. In order to document enduring, central features of personality, one must use many different questions and find persistent regularities; otherwise a discrete finding might reflect simply the particular content of a given question. By the same token, a great many different questions are grist for one's mill, since the deeper personality should intrude into almost every sphere of attitude and response providing one finds a way to abstract the variable. In one of their papers, therefore, they examine for some 46 different questions, contained within 4 different surveys, the "no opinion" response, treating the lack of opinionation as a formal index of "disengagement" from social life.[10] Variations in the magnitude of this index are then examined over all 46 questions for three age groups, young, middle-aged, and old adults. Summarized briefly, the analysis reveals a consistent decline in opinionation as one moves from the young through the middle aged to the old that is pervasive over most of the questions and all four surveys. Gergen and Back interpret the findings as indicative of the general process of *aging*.

What warrant do they have for rejecting alternative explanations? Perhaps the respective groups are simply showing the distinctive marks of their generation. The sixty-year olds, for example, mgiht have been a less opinionated generation and answered that very same way when they were in their twenties, as, correspondingly, might the middle-aged group. Or why regard the process as generic? It might be peculiar to the influences surrounding these several cohorts as they aged. Gergen and Back are careful to note the possibility that the "results simply reflect generational differences," and they entertain still other alternatives, which they review and test, but their tentative conclusion is in terms of *aging*. What in their handling of the design buttresses their confidence?

The first thing to be stressed is the *content or nature* of the dependent variable. In our judgment, the thoughtful analyst should ponder the choice and sampling of items in his implementation of the design and the weighing of the conclusions. If the items employed had dealt with some particular area, for example, preferences in clothing or music, or child rearing, it would be plausible that the variations might reflect the currents of fashion when

---

[10] "Communication in the Interview and the Disengaged Respondent," Back and Gergen, *op. cit.* We omit for present discussion the use they make of other formal indices in this and other papers, e.g., the tendency to give extreme or undifferentiated responses. Nor do we raise the question, posed by Glenn as to the validity of the index as a measure of disengagement, who argues that *involvement* in matters of opinion might imply a *greater* disengagement from intimate social life.

the several cohorts were growing up, and during the respective periods when they were aging. A persistent and *pervasive* lack of opinion seems to be something timeless that is hard to explain by the flow of events or the fads and the doctrines of a period. To be sure, such judgments are not fool-proof evidence. Upon further reflection, a variable that seemed unsusceptible to temporary fashions or external events may often be seen in another light. For example, the doctrine that the "young should be seen and not heard" has become less fashionable. It is plausible that the more recent generations have been encouraged to express their views on anything and everything. Indeed, the virtuosity of survey analysts in finding a plausible *post hoc* explanation of an unexpected finding suggests that the criterion of plausibility is no guarantee that one has interpreted the findings from age comparisons correctly. Nevertheless, the *wide and thoughtful sampling* of items does reduce the ambiguities in the interpretation of age comparisons.[11]

In a similar vein, it seems, to us, that covering a wide range in age, the use of many refined age groups and the choice of appropriate cutting points are aids to the interpretation of findings from such a design. When Gergen and Back find a decrease in opinionation progressively through three stages of aging, it suggests a continuous process that is difficult to reconcile with circumscribed events that might impinge on only one generation or cohort. Certainly the aging process may show sudden spurts or inflections, and conversely a long string of events may impinge with cumulative force on a series of successive adjacent cohorts. The device is not insurance, but its intelligent use, and especially a wise selection of cutting points on the age continuum in light of the historical chronicle, may reduce ambiguities in interpretation.[12]

---

[11] Our argument is underscored in the course of the critique and replication of the study by Glenn, to be reviewed shortly. He suggests that an appropriate test would be based on *current* items, that would not be manifestations of long-standing issues. "Even if their attention to current issues were to decline considerably, aging persons probably would not give up opinions which crystallized when they were younger." N. Glenn, "Aging, Disengagement, and Opinionation," *Publ. Opin. Quart.*, **33**, 1969, p. 25.

[12] A cautionary note on the use of the two devices, the selection of items and the handling of the age variable, is provided by a secondary analysis of frequency of religious attendance by age. A very large pooled sample from the Detroit area surveys for a period of years permitted the comparison of age groups for very fine groupings. It would have been most plausible to expect either a regular increase as a function of aging, or an abrupt increase after some critical point when old age had made other-worldly concerns urgent, and before extreme enfeeblement prevented attendance. Yet when it turns out that there is no consistent change with age in the aggregate or for more refined subgroupings, it is easy to invoke the notion that various stimuli impinging on particular groups and cohorts account for their religious behavior and overlay any effects from sheer aging. See H. L. Orbach, "Aging and Religion," *Geriatrics*, October, 1961, pp. 530–540.

In their several studies of the problem, Gergen and Back stress another factor that supports their conclusions about aging. Against the argument that the findings represent generational differences, or are peculiar to the mature experiences of specific cohorts, they invoke "the fact that the results . . . were taken from surveys conducted over a fifteen-year time span."[13] And items on which the age groups are compared are taken *about equally* from each of the four surveys separated over this time interval. Although the various age groups are homogeneous in age, some of the old were already old when the first survey was taken, and others did not reach that same age until the last survey was taken, fifteen years later. The individuals in any particular age group are drawn from several cohorts and generations. The force of the defense could be blunted, if one regarded a fifteen-year span as too narrow to transcend the single era of one generation or cohort. But a valuable general principle has been suggested. If one can sample surveys widely spaced in time, one may be able to disentangle the several processes.

How the principle can be put into operation at all in the course of such a design, and made to work properly, must be reviewed. Gergen and Back did not have a series of trend surveys, in which the very same questions had been repeated, and could not trace a given cohort as it responded over time to the item. But by abstracting from the different questions and different surveys, a common property—*opinionation*—a formal index could be computed, and they could consolidate evidence from all the surveys. Then, in order to argue faithfully that the evidence really is based on a sampling of surveys widely spaced in time, the items themselves had to be about equally spread across the surveys. Further, in combining the evidence, they could not give undue weight to the differences obtained from any particular questions within a single survey. They protect themselves by presenting the comparisons separately for each of the four surveys, and by using a sign test, the findings from any single question—no matter how big the difference between age groups— being given no greater weight than the findings from each of the other 45 questions.

These cautionary measures, plus others against error afflicting the conclusions, were taken. But what about the most basic precaution of all, that the age groups be made equivalent in social composition. Gergen and Back take measures, which seem not to have gone far enough. On *one* of the four surveys, education is controlled by subdividing each age group into two parts, those with only grammar school backgrounds and those with more education. We shall not review the detailed findings, and note only that the basic finding by age did persist among the better educated.

---

[13] Gergen and Back, *op. cit.*, p. 395.

In a subsequent study, Glenn reexamined the age differences in the very same survey, but modified the earlier analysis in one respect. The controls instituted by Gergen and Back seemed to him too few and too crude to insure that the age groups were equivalent in social composition. Among those who had had some high school, the old nevertheless had had less years of education than the young. So Glenn introduced a more refined control, subdividing each age group into many small subgroups more homogeneous in education, and he added controls on sex and race, before examining differences in opinionation by age. Within the various equivalent groups, Glenn found *no* consistent evidence of any changes in opinionation with age. Considering the findings in their most severe light, they simply give stern warning that the most stringent precautions must be taken to insure equivalence. However, that should not disturb any future secondary analyst. It is thoroughly practical, as Glenn's analysis itself proves.

Something else is disturbing and should make us pause. Somehow, completely *negative* findings seem inconceivable. The aged certainly should have become less opinionated as they grew weary. If not that, they should have grown more opinionated with wisdom and experience. Or the recent generation must have been socialized to talk more—or to talk less. That there is *no* regular pattern at all seems truly startling.

Another look at these anomalous findings may lead to better understanding of the general properties of the design. They are based on only *one* survey. Perhaps some artifact of procedure in the original inquiry distorts the true picture or some subtle variation in the modes of secondary analysis accounts for the confusing and contradictory findings obtained by the several investigators. With one possible, but improbable, exception these ideas must be rejected. Glenn entertains such possibilities and his careful scrutiny satisfies us that the finding is real, not artifactual.[14]

The finding seems real enough, but still it may be true for only *one* survey. Perhaps it applies only to the strange haphazard sample of *issues* contained

---

[14] For example, Glenn hypothesizes that "many disengaged oldsters may exclude themselves from the samples by refusing to be interviewed." But he is able to marshall evidence against such a sampling bias distorting the true findings. Similarly, by ingenious selection of questions, he can reject the possibility that there is a response bias, in which the old do not want to reveal their true decline to the interviewer. Since Glenn followed the principle of "not peeking" at the cross-tabulations by aging when he selected the arrays of questions for his later aanlyses, this potential source of bias is controlled. The one procedural problem that remains is that Glenn synthesizes the findings from the series of questions by a different method of index construction than Gergen and Back used. Glenn computes the *average* value of "non-opinionation" over his sixteen questions. Thus an occasional extreme value could distort the mean level, whereas the earlier investigators simply used a sign test, thus giving each item equal weight.

within the sixteen questions. The careful review of the discrete findings from questions of different content argues against this hypothesis.[15] The finding, however, might still apply only to the *one* survey, because of the tiny sampling of historical *time*. Gergen and Back had forty-six questions, but, more important, *four* surveys. One wishes they had introduced refined controls into the analysis of all their surveys, or that Glenn had reexamined all four with his degree of refinement. Then one would know whether the odd, negative finding remains to plague us.

As we recall the basic ambiguity in the design, especially when applied to a narrow sampling of surveys and historical time, an unpleasant possibility must be entertained. Two processes, the imprinting of a particular generation and the changes with aging, are implicated and could work at cross purposes. It might appear that nothing at all is happening when, in reality, everything is happening behind the facade of the data.

For example, there could in fact be a general tendency for opinionation even to *increase* with aging. But suppose in the instance of this one survey conducted in 1957, the youngest cohorts sliced out of an endless stream, just by the accident of cutting the age continuum a certain way (at age 39), happened to be those reared in the Depression—an especially opinionated generation. Then the old, when compared with *this* young group, would appear not to have changed at all, when in fact they had changed greatly from the way they *themselves* were when they were young. Alternatively, Gergen and Back might indeed be correct that opinionation declines generally with aging, but Survey #580 might have cut out a young generation that was especially *passive*. Then, when the two age groups are compared, no change is observable. The several processes could translate themselves in all sorts of ways so as to show a net change of zero. So many possibilities boggle the mind. The perplexity of St. Augustine contemplating the meaning of time comes to mind.

Glenn, fortunately, comes to our aid. He follows up his analysis of the survey by age comparisons, with refined controls, of responses to 29 items from 14 surveys spanning the 16 year period, 1948–1964. Unless the critic pushes the argument hard, Glenn has transcended the times and events of particular

---

[15] This portion of Glenn's analysis is rewarding reading for future secondary analysts and underscores the earlier recommendation that the design be applied to a wide sampling of issues. In this particular survey, a considerable number of questions dealt with religious matters and "one might suspect that aging persons become more interested in religion . . . even if their general level of opinionation declines. In fact, increased involvement in an other-worldly religion would be consonant with the disengagement hypothesis" (p. 21). Therefore Glenn analyzed separately the subset of questions on politics, and the original finding persisted. But as we shall see, when he samples a much broader range of items in his subsequent analysis, a new finding emerges.

generations and cohorts, and the pattern that shines through should provide a relatively clear picture of the effects of aging.

His finding is consistent, and perhaps surprising. Aging, studied (as he did) up to those who are sixty or older, brings with it a small *increase* in attention, knowledge, and opinionation in public affairs. The decline that Gergen and Back reported seems, therefore, to be the product of the lack of controls for other characteristics, rather than a product of aging. However, their other three surveys were not incorporated in the new batch of fourteen that Glenn examined, and the indicators he employed, although incisive, are not identical. Thus some controversy could persist until someone carried out the specific and refined empirical tests on all the original data. However it is not the contradiction, but rather the inherent uncertainties of the general design that lead Glenn on to search for a longitudinal test of the theory. He finds it by means of cohort analysis. We shall turn to this new design shortly, and especially his application of it to the present problem. Given the inferential nature of the cross-sectional design and the ever present danger of a false conclusion, any longitudinal study that validates or invalidates the findings is valuable information on the safest way to operate and interpret the cross-sectional design. However, one more case of the cross-sectional design is worth special attention, before turning to a new topic.

Glenn clearly is aware of all the ambiguity in the comparisons of age groups. Yet at many points in his career as a secondary analyst, he has also relied on it to work for him. An important question compelled an answer; no better design was then available to provide it; and the risks presumably could be reduced by special care in applying the procedures and in drawing conclusions. It is instructive to examine one example of his strategy.

The grand theme implicit in so many of his studies has been the comprehensive description of the pattern of differentiation between groups in American society, which he has traced along the lines of region, race, religion, class, etc. As he has documented these differences, the further question presses for an answer: Has there been a *trend* away from differentiation, in his words, toward *massification*? Have such forces as the mass media, travel, mobility, urbanization, industrialization, and education erased the old differences and moved us closer to a homogeneous "mass society"? Ideally, one would want comparable long-term data for the nation, then disaggregated for various groups so that one could examine whether the patterns are converging, but "no one has conducted repeated national surveys for the purpose of tracing . . . trends in a wide variety of values and beliefs, and not enough comparable questions have been asked at different times . . . to make possible an adequate trend analysis using existing data. No one is likely to conduct the type of study that is needed, and even if such research were started today, reliable results would not be available for several years." But as remarked in the example to be examined: "Fortunately, however, there is a more economical and less time-consuming alternative that can cast light upon trends in regional differentiation: an analysis by age of responses to questions asked on recent national surveys. If regional differences have diminished, it is to be expected that they are greater among older people than among the younger people."[16]

Glenn and his co-worker, Simmons, are building the case upon the generational model, and thereby using the comparison of age groups as a quasi-longitudinal design to infer trend. The old people can tell us about the old South. Therefore Glenn and Simmons examine 44 diverse questions drawn from 10 surveys conducted during the period 1950–1961, and in each instance compare the difference between regions, once for the residents who are old and once for the residents who are young. The age categories used are such that many of the "old" were reared very early in the century and some even experienced their childhood before the turn of the century. Almost all the young, by contrast, were reared before World War II but most of them were born and shaped by events after World War I. There is a consistent "trend" of a rather surprising nature. The differences are greater among the *young*. There appears to have been a *divergence* in the culture of regions, not a convergence, in the recent period.

We shall not review all the subtleties of the analysis. There is again the standard problem of how comprehensively the domain of culture has been covered by the 44 questions, and the need to select them by proper criteria and without "peeking." Also, there are problems of index construction and appropriate statistical treatment to synthesize voluminous and diverse data, not giving undue weight to one variable rather than another. Errors of sampling must be evaluated in appraising the findings. The care exercised assures the reader that the paradoxical findings cannot be explained away on such grounds.

The reader should ponder the way controls on other social characteristics were introduced or omitted from the comparisons of the regional age groupings. The samples were truncated, and the entire analysis, for many good methodological reasons, confined only to whites. No controls were instituted for sex, and the reader may pause to ponder this specific question. That no controls were instituted for education, which as we know is more characteristic of the younger cohorts in America, deserves special attention. The general enlargement of educational opportunity as well the *relative* slowness of its expansion in particular regions, is central to the social and historical changes that have occurred. Glenn wants its imprint to be present when he examines the generations in the several regions. In this light, finding a "diver-

---

[16] Glenn and Simmons, *op. cit.*, pp. 177–178.

gence" appears even more compelling. Despite the so-called "educational factory" working now to turn out mass-produced products, the regions have
maintained their distinctiveness, and seemingly increased it.

There is a special and puzzling problem that arises in this particular application of the design. An assumption critical for the entire study might seem
to be that the various age groups were *reared* in the specified regions. But, in
fact, Glenn and Simmons classify the individuals on the basis of their *current*
residence. The old and young "Southerners" or "Northerners" may be reflecting the culture of the region of their childhood, but it is indubitably true that
many of them, as migrants, were reared in another region from where we find
them at the time of the survey. They may be telling us about life in the old
days, but where? Such a problem, by definition, could never arise when the
same design is applied to the study of trends in the differentiation between
sex or racial groups, and would be of trivial magnitude if the focus of study
were religious groups.

One way of operating the design therefore would be to introduce region of
origin in the comparisons, but that item of information is rarely available.
One could try to adjust the survey findings in light of external knowledge on
the magnitude of migration in and out of regions over time. In the absence
of such procedures, some might quickly judge the entire study to be shaky.
Glenn and Simmons do none of these things and yet are thoroughly sensitive
to the possibility that migration is a factor at issue. Indeed, they present a
table to show that the Western region has a much higher proportion of
migrants than all other regions, especially within the *older* cohort, and then
invoke this fact to explain why there is such a marked "trend" toward distinctiveness and divergence of that region. However, they comment: "This
partial explanation . . . does *not* mean that the differences *do not reflect
change*; rather, it means that a growing indigenous Western population is
probably an important factor underlying the apparent rapid "liberalization"
of the West. However, this explanation can be used only for the West, since
in each of the other regions the older people were at least as homogeneous in
regional background in 1960 as the young ones."[17] They could have purified
their data, but preferred the design to operate in such a way that the trends
reflect the net result of the two forces, the variations over time in the indigenous cultures that are transmitted, and the contamination of the culture of
a region by virtue of historic waves of migration. After all, the theory to be
tested claims that geographical mobility is one force toward increasing homogeneity. Therefore, it should be reckoned into the balance sheet rather than
subtracted.

---

[17] *Ibid.*, pp. 191–192 (italics supplied).

Everything seems settled and clear, until we recall the most fundamental property of the design. A third factor may contribute to the net result, and might even be regarded as accounting for all of it. The old tell us something about the old culture, but they also tell us something about *aging*. The apparent divergence of regional cultures observed among the young may simply mean that there has been a process of *convergence* among the *old*. Perhaps the old representatives of the region were equally divergent when they themselves were young. If there is a "culture of the aged," peculiarly potent in producing uniformity, aging has simply obliterated the distinctive regional culture that the old formerly exhibited.

Glenn and Simmons, despite all their care and ingenuity, cannot escape this dilemma. They finally must rest their case on a chain of logical argument. As of then, they had exhausted all empirical solutions to the problem, and they end with the admission that "it is very probable, though not certain, that the regions recently have diverged . . ."[18]

Glenn would not leave the case moot indefinitely, realizing that "convergence with aging could mask the effect of a massification trend, or divergence with aging could create false evidence for such a trend."[19] He wished to strengthen the tentative conclusions from his *quasitrend* design by a true trend study. He therefore continued to search and finally found 13 diverse questions that had been repeated on national surveys. The interval between the measurements averaged 16 years, the first measure almost always prior to 1946, and the second measure generally around 1960 or later. The trend in the differences between regions was then examined over the range of questions and summarized by an overall index. This direct test establishes a small but *greater* difference in the recent period and is thus a validation of the inferential measurement of social change by the comparison of age groups. Subsequently, Reed in his secondary analysis of Southern culture found trend data on several additional questions, and was able to extend the time series on several of the questions Glenn had employed. He also finds by this direct test no general evidence for recent convergence of the regions, and indeed on some questions a growing divergence.[20]

---

[18] *Ibid.*, p. 190.

[19] "Massification versus Differentiation . . . , " Glenn, *op. cit.*, p. 173.

[20] Reed, *op. cit.* In one notable sphere, however, Reed and others have documented a convergence, Southern white attitudes toward desegregation moving towards the more liberal Northern position. By the use of multiple standardization, Reed is able to document the fact that the distinctiveness of Southern culture is not the product of the region's lesser urbanization, industrialization, and education, and must inhere in some resdual, unknown features of social life. On an ingenious use of ths procedure to *predict* future cultural trends as structural changes continue to unfold in the South, see especially his Appendix.

Twice, the direct measurement of trends has validated a particular way of applying the age-comparison design to the study of social change. Our confidence should certainly be bolstered, but, of course, more evidence would be desirable. And when applied in another way, the validity of the design for the study of aging has still not been established by agreement with empirical evidence from direct longitudinal studies. We turn to the long postponed topic of designs involving cohort analysis.

Cohort Analysis

The secondary analyst lacks the long-term panel suited to the longitudinal study of changes in individuals as they are aging. But he has something almost as good for the purpose, imbedded within a set of *trend* surveys, if only he is sharp enough to see it and skillful enough to extricate it. It is like the hidden design or figure contained within an old-fashioned puzzle that becomes visible only when the child joins in pencil the correct series of discrete points on a page. The secondary analyst also must join the right set of discrete units across the surveys in order to create the beautiful design which represents the course of aging in individuals. It is not child's play, however; tracing this process is far more complicated. But as with many puzzles, the solution starts by adopting a new and unconventional way of looking at things.

Consider, for example, an imaginary investigator interested in aging, so fortunate as to operate a long-term, large-scale *panel* on a national sample of American adults over a twenty-year period, 1940–1960. What in effect he has done at Time 1 is to draw a sample of individuals who are twenty-one years of age in 1940, put another way, a sample of the cohort of individuals who were born in 1919; correspondingly a sample of the individuals who are some specified older age in 1940 and who thus represent an earlier cohort born prior to 1919 and so on. The one sample is really composed of many subsamples of birth cohorts, each measured at the particular age it has reached in 1940. To trace the effect of aging, he must know what has happened to them at Time 2, for example, in 1950 after ten years, or at Time 3 in 1960 after twenty years.

When he remeasures the *same* individuals, for example, the 21-year olds who later became 31 and subsequently 41, he has brought the *same* particular sample representative of that cohort under repeated study as it ages. If instead he had drawn a *new* sample in 1950 representative of all individuals who were 31 at that point, and still a third new sample in 1960 of individuals who were 41 at that point, all three samples if drawn properly would be equivalent to each other and representative of the total population of that birth cohort—those born in 1919. In this example, we have defined a cohort in very narrow terms of a single birth year, but, of course it can be defined in terms of birth during an interval of several years or in grosser terms, a decade, etc., and the logic applies equally well.

Looking at matters in this new light, all that the secondary analyst of aging has to do is locate within a series of trend surveys the respective groups who have reached the age at each of the survey times that defines their common membership in a given birth cohort. Then, although he does not have a panel of the very same individuals within the cohort, he has, to use Evan's suggestive term, a *quasipanel*.[21] By joining together the discrete samples of the right age groups, changes in the same cohort can be traced over whatever phase of its life has been covered by the timing and span of the surveys and in relation to its experiences. In trend surveys that sample a wide range of ages, many such cohorts can be isolated and traced by joining the right units, each treated as a quasipanel to examine various phases of the life course and the influence of historical forces impinging at those stages of its development.

Ryder's image may help us to envision the new design. "The cohort record, as *macro-biography*, is the aggregate analogue of the individual life history."[22] The full beauty of the design still remains to be revealed, but since no design is without blemish, first let us examine some of its troublesome methodological features. We shall describe them briefly since recent studies by secondary analysts provide an excellent review of the principles and procedures and illustrations of fruiful applications of the design.[23]

---

[21] William M. Evan, "Cohort Analysis of Survey Data: A Procedure for Studying Long-Term Opinion Change," *Publ. Opin. Quart.*, **23**, 1959, p. 66. Recalling the property of a true panel, the reader can realize that if one portion of the cohort were to change in one direction, and the other portion in an opposing direction, the net change observed could be zero. The cohort analyst cannot examine *turnover* at the individual level, although he can examine differential change within subgroups of the cohort, e.g., men versus women.

[22] Ryder, *op. cit.*, p. 859 (italics supplied).

[23] N. Glenn and M. Grimes, "Aging, Voting, and Political Interest," *Amer. Sociol. Rev.*, **33**, 1968, pp. 563–575; N. Glenn and R. E. Zody, "Cohort Analysis with National Survey Data," *Gerentologist*, **10**, 1970, pp. 233–240; R. E. Zody, "Cohort Analysis: Some Applicatory Problems in the Study of Social and Political Behavior," *Soc. Sci. Quart.*, **50**, 1969, pp. 374–380; J. Crittenden, "Aging and Political Participation," *West. Polit. Quart.*, **16**, 1963, pp. 323–331; J. Crittenden, "Aging and Party Affiliation," *Publ. Opin. Quart.*, **26**, 1962, pp. 648–657; N. E. Cutler, *The Alternative Effects of Generations and Aging Upon Political Behavior: A Cohort Analysis of American Attitudes toward Foreign Policy, 1946–1966* (Oak Ridge: Oak Ridge National Laboratory, 1968, mimeo). For a brief summary, see his "Generational Succession as a Source of Foreign Policy Attitudes," *J. Peace Research*, 1970, No. 1, pp. 33–47. An exchange be-

MORTALITY AND MIGRATION

The sampling, though well designed and consistently applied, is more properly described as representative of those members of the cohort who are alive, at large, and accessible at each life stage within the geographical boundaries covered. Those who have entered institutions, died, or departed the domain obviously cannot be sampled. Attrition and defection, certainly, are legitimate aspects of the *macro*biography of a cohort. So, too, is infusion from members of the birth cohort, born elsewhere, who have migrated into the domain under study. However, for the analyst who wishes to draw conclusions purely about aging, who treats the design as a quasipanel of *individuals*, changes in the composition of the cohort can, in principle, confound his interpretations.

This is an old set of problems, familiar to us from our previous discussion, which simply has insinuated itself again into cohort analysis. We already know that it can be dealt with. Migration in and out of the United States in the last forty years has been so little that it is a trivial concern for analysts working with *American national* samples, and at worst affects few cohorts. It could, however, seriously affect conclusions drawn from national surveys of other countries that have had substantial migration recently, or from local and regional surveys in the United States, since geographical mobility has been of great magnitude. Birthplace would be an essential face-sheet item for those analysts in dealing with the problem.

Differential mortality of social groups is again familiar and controllable. The samples can be truncated and the analysis confined to one homogeneous group in terms of sex and race; multiple standardization can be applied to the data, or the cohorts can be subdivided by sex and race, thereby gaining information on differential patterns of aging.[24]

Selective losses from those entering institutions are of small magnitude and only likely to distort conclusions about aging, if at all, when the analyst tries to trace the aging process far out to old age or far back to early stages of adult life. Selective losses at various life stages, because of inability to be interviewed, refusal, or not-at-homeness are probably only a minor source of error. Controls by sex and race automatically help, and original records from the surveys can provide empirical evidence about the nature and magnitude of the sampling losses by age.

---

tween two of these secondary analysts provides a most instructive case. See N. Cutler, "Generation, Maturation, and Party Affiliation," and J. Crittenden, "Reply to Cutler," *Public Opin. Quart.*, **33**, 1969, pp. 583–591.

[24] Differential mortality, despite such measures, can occasionally present vexatious problems of inference. See, for example, Glenn and Zody's thoughtful treatment of a cohort analysis of changes in drinking habits with aging. *Gerontologist, op. cit.*

NONCOMPARABILITY IN THE DESIGN OF THE SAMPLES IN THE TREND SURVEYS

The cohort analyst can separate influences due to aging from influences due to changes in the population of the cohort, and in the sample thereof that can be studied at various stages of life. Such change in the *obtained sample* with age can be regarded, like vital changes in the population, as part of the natural course of life. Just as there is death and migration, so, too the old end up in institutions or become too infirm to be interviewed, and the young go off to college or the army, or are "never-at-home." Inevitably, some members eliminate themselves from a cohort that anyone can actually trace, no matter when or how carefully the survey was conducted. All these troubles afflicting every cohort analyst were gathered together under Problem 1, and generally turn out to be neither severe nor intractable of solution. Another problem may confront those cohort analysts who have had to select a set of surveys especially appropriate in content and length of time series, but which suffer from changes in the *design* of the sample. Here again we are on familiar ground, an old problem insinuating itself again to trouble the cohort analyst.

Over the years, as noted, the Gallup Poll and other long-established survey agencies have improved their sampling designs so as to reduce the former bias of undersampling the low socioeconomic strata of the population. The switch from the universe of voters to that of adults has had the same effect of increasing the weight of the lower strata in the recent surveys. Since changes attributable to aging are inferred by joining together the appropriate age groupings from different surveys done over the years, the findings might reflect the fact that different strata within the cohort are being compared across the life stages. This danger would be greatly reduced if the analysis were confined to surveys since 1950, the approximate time at which the major changes in sampling design were instituted.

For the cohort analyst, like the trend analyst, comparability of the procedures in all important respects prevents confusing artifactual change and real change. One can treat this as an absolute principle, only selecting surveys in the most fastidious way, and thus, denying to oneself many opportunities. Fortunately, as will be recalled, one can often work effectively with imperfect data appraising or correcting noncomparability. When the cohort analyses are made separately for groups homogeneous in education, the changing bias in the sampling of various social strata is brought under control, and the analyst can also examine whether aging has different effects in the different strata. Glenn and Grimes, and Glenn and Zody, present various ways of introducing controls so as to correct the results for the changing sampling bias.[25] Comparability with respect to procedures other than sampling will be reviewed later.

PROBLEMS IN CHOOSING, LOCATING, AND TRACING COHORTS

Skip quickly over the problem: Which particular cohorts born in what years or periods and thus exposed to particular slices of experience at certain critical stages of life would be fruitful to distinguish for study and comparison? It is of course central to those who wish to test a generational theory, but it presents the same deep, perhaps imponderable, questions to every cohort analyst, whether he be a primary researcher or secondary analyst. Those who use the design to examine the generic process of aging need only to trace a series of successive cohorts or several widely separated in the times of their births and the events of their lives, and again the choice presents a common dilemma to all who employ the design.[26]

The secondary analyst, assuming he had made some choices of desirable cohorts to study, faces special difficulties, on occasion, in locating and separating the specified cohorts within the surveys available to him, and then in tracing each of them through time. He must accommodate himself to the intervals between the trend surveys available to him. He must accept the categories under which age was originally coded, and they may be too gross to isolate particular cohorts mixed in with others in a broad age band. They may be incompatible with the intervals between the surveys and prevent joining up the members of the cohort across all the surveys (unless age was *enumerated* in a refined way, and the original questionnaires could be recoded to make the codes compatible).

Figure 1 presents a hypothetical example of the difficulties an analyst might face who had three trend surveys of special appeal to him, conducted in 1960,

---

[25] The controls should not be applied mechanically or interpreted thoughtlessly. For example, although formal education is concentrated in the early years of life, some individuals within any cohort pursue their education into late life. Controls for education may therefore subtract not only the changing sampling bias but also a genuine, if very small, component of the aging process. Since individuals obviously change their economic position with age, and education indirectly controls that variable, one may implicitly be subtracting some natural economic changes that accompany aging. And if successive cohorts are compared, the controls could be applied in such a fashion as to eliminate from the reckoning the different educational handicaps respective generations had.

[26] Cutler poses the questions vividly. Is the World War I cohort "the cohort *born during the war*, the cohort of persons *about ten years old* during the War or those *about twenty-one years* old during the War?" In one study, Cutler and Bobrow single out two additional cataclysmic forces implicit in the labels: the "Nuclear Era" and the "Great Depression" cohorts, defining the victims as types who were "approximately twenty years old at the beginning of the events." *op. cit.*, 1968, p. 29 and 146.

1964, and 1968, where age was uniformly coded in the designated categories, each defining a cohort born during a specified 8-year period. Suppose that he wishes to distinguish two relatively homogeneous cohorts, those aged 21–24 in 1960 and those aged 25–28 in 1960. He would have to sacrifice that refinement because both were coded under the same broad category and adjust the cohorts to suit the categories. Having made that sacrifice in the 1960 survey, he wishes to trace the revised cohorts on into the 1964 survey and plot the patterns they exhibited after four years of aging. Unfortunately, because age is coded in both surveys in a *broader* interval than the lapse of 4 years, he faces, as Zody puts it, "cohort overlap." Each cohort has aged 4 years, but his code categories require him to jump 8 years at a clip or not at all. Cohort A has been split down the middle. Some of the members properly belong now under code 2, but if so located they are mixed in with half of cohort B, and others who properly should be left behind in category 1 then are mixed in with the wrong age mates. He cannot advance or "age" the cohort by the proper amount. Fortunately, by 1968, things are back in phase. He can locate the cohorts precisely since the codes are now compatible with the interval.

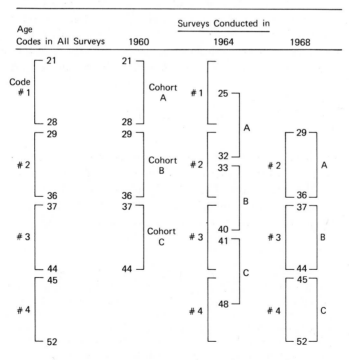

FIGURE 1   *Cohort overlap because of gross age codes.*

Under such conditions, the secondary analyst must move back and forth and compromise, dropping some trend points, revising cohorts, trying to get the best fit possible.

Zody, fortunately, presents a sensible strategy for such situations and some ingenious tactics to help.[27] And the problem has become less common as survey agencies have adopted refined age codes; some to coding exact years of age. Cutler, for example, found 45 surveys containing variables of interest to him over a twenty-year period which had coded exact age. Under these new, very pliable circumstances, the cohort analyst can rush himself into new dangers. If he were to try to trace many tiny cohorts, defined in terms of *single* birth years, he would be overwhelmed and dealing with very flimsy amounts of data in plotting the course of aging. Breaking the age continuum in a survey to yield fifty or so cohorts then traced over three surveys would produce a matrix of over 150 cells to be examined. Introducing controls for social composition would then double or quadruple the number of cells. Some would contain only a handful of cases and thus be subject to much sampling error. Indeed, even with sensibly defined cohorts—not too narrow, not too broad—the *primary* analyst might still have too few cases in his cells to draw reliable conclusions about the course of aging in any given cohort or the difference in the process between contrasted cohorts. The secondary analyst sometimes is better off in these respects. He may be able to *pool* several adjacent and comparable surveys thereby improving the estimates for that time point, and having a total number big enough to be subdivided into refined cohorts.[28]

COMPARABILITY OF INSTRUMENTS: THE SUPPLY OF TREND SURVEYS

We seem to have neglected the most pressing, practical problem of all. Cohort analysis makes the same severe demands as conventional trend analysis for surveys that are comparable not only in sampling, but also in terms of instruments and measurement procedures. On top of those stringent demands, the time series must be extended if we are to trace aging over a long

---

[27] Zody, *op. cit.*

[28] This still begs the question of where to make the subdivisions. One could indeed split a distinctive cohort apart and lose a fascinating finding by the accident of badly chosen cutting points on the age continuum, even though one had introduced great refinement and examined many cohorts. Thus in one study, Cutler outdoes the poet. Instead of dividing the continuum in terms of the seven ages of man, he marks it off in five-year increments thus producing *twelve* refined birth cohorts, but as he stresses: "there is no theoretical reason for assuming that any generational experiences . . . which might be uncovered . . . will fall neatly into five-year intervals." Cutler, *op. cit.*, p. 147.

course, following a cohort for example for ten or twenty or, ideally, thirty or more years. And finally, the surveys must also provide age codes that are compatible with the interval under study and sensitive to our problem. What a stringent set of demands? How often can they be met?

The moral, again, is to make the most of what we have. As earlier noted in the brief inventory of the kinds of time series available, we are not so poverty stricken as we might think, the secondary analysts have hardly begun to apply the design and exploit the resources available. As earlier noted, canons of comparability can be applied rigorously but yet reasonably, and we shall soon see some new ingenious, somewhat tricky, ways that clever cohort analysts have overcome apparent noncomparability of instruments.

Potential cohort analysts have a number of extended time series right under their noses, in the items routinely incorporated on the face sheets of surveys spanning many years. Using these simple staples, Alston has shed new light on that perennial problem, *The Protestant Ethic*.[29] Four national surveys dating from the early fifties were pooled to provide a big enough sample, and four others by the same agency from the decade of the sixties were pooled. The samples were truncated, and the analysis confined to white males. A Protestant and Catholic cohort of the same age were traced over the ten-year interval to observe whether there were differential improvements in occupation with aging, and a more recent and younger cohort was compared to document any generational changes in the phenomenon. The findings suggest that Catholics, as they age—at least for the basic cohort studied, aged 25–44 in the early fifties—rise more quickly than Protestants and close most of the gap exhibited at the start of their occupational careers. The pattern persists in the younger cohort, beginning its occupational career in the sixties, suggesting that there has been no generational change among the religious groups, at least for the two successive cohorts. Other secondary analysts could easily follow Alston's lead and pursue the process on into later stages of aging, and back into earlier cohorts or generations of Catholics and Protestants.

The cohort analyst need not restrict himself to routine face-sheet items. Other variables of enduring interest are measured many times over the years. Many appear in election surveys, and a number of secondary analysts have exploited these materials. Glenn and Grimes examined changes with age in *turnout or voting* for a series of cohorts followed from 1944–1964, and over the six presidential elections in which they had opportunity to participate.[30]

---

[29] J. P. Alston, "Occupational Placement and Mobility of Protestants and Catholics, 1953–1964," *Rev. Relig. Res.*, **10**, 1969, pp. 135–140.

[30] Glenn and Grimes, *op. cit.*

Obviously, the most recent cohorts of adults incorporated in the later elections had not yet reached their majorities at the beginning of the period. For other cohorts it was possible to trace changes as they aged from their majorities into middle age, and for several it was possible to trace the life cycle out to the farthest reaches of old age.

We shall reconsider these facts later, and only review here the *combined* findings on the several older cohorts or earlier generations on whom the full brunt of aging has already fallen. Since controls are introduced for sex, the voting estimates standardized by education, and the samples truncated to exclude Negroes, the results cannot be obscured by differential mortality, changes in sampling designs, nor by any institutional changes in the enfranchisement of Negroes or their political mobilization.

The findings are dramatic. "The cohort aged 70 through 79 in 1964 shows an almost *constant* turnout through the six elections." This cohort entered the analysis at about age 50. But the same stable pattern is observed for another cohort traced as it aged from its thirties onward, and for the adjacent cohort traced from its forties into its sixties. For the earliest cohort (already "old" in 1944), traced into its *eighties*, there is still no decline in voting. Unfortunately, that pattern can only be traced through the first four elections and a twelve-year period, since presumably most had expired thereafter or been beyond the reach of any interviewer.

In drawing conclusions, Glenn and Grimes acknowledge a built-in bias, an inherent limitation. The aged who are too feeble to be interviewed would, no doubt, be too weak to engage in the *physical act* of getting to the polls. With this particular indicator, there is no *direct* way out of the trap.[31] Perforce, they must qualify their interpretation but construe the many findings as evidence that there is no decline in political involvement with aging, at least among those who have retained a modicum of health.

Crittenden employs another indicator, not subject to this limitation, in a cohort analysis of four off-year election surveys within the same period.[32] The

---

[31] The indicator has another limitation which must be taken into account. The young in truth, might have greater involvement, but have no way of showing it if they are legally disfranchised by virtue of greater residential mobility. The handicap is not controlled in any comparisons based on this indicator. Glenn and Grimes very neatly resolved the question by using estimates of mobility for age groups from the Census, to correct for any differential handicap. The indicator also is biased in that respondents tend to inflate their reports of voting, but Glenn and Grimes make the reasonable assumption that the bias is of constant *magnitude* in all the surveys and does not impair the comparisons. It is only a *changing* bias that is critical, as earlier noted, for trend analysis and, in turn, cohort analysis.

[32] Crittenden, *op. cit.*, 1963, Table IV. The code on age uses an eight-year step interval. Correspondingly, Crittenden must advance his cohorts eight years at a clip. Since the

percent who are identified with *any* party is examined for a series of cohorts as they age. The index permits a cohort to be fickle, to change its party loyalty, but to reveal the level of involvement by an attachment to either party, rather than a "disengagement" from both. Only modest controls on changes in social composition or in the sample design are introduced but function *de facto* to reduce most such artifacts. As far as he can trace the process, into those who have aged well into their sixties, the overall pattern is toward higher involvement.

The findings based on two different indicators confirm each other. Let us digress to note an important fact. The findings also agree with the earlier conclusions Glenn drew from comparisons of *opinionation* among age groups drawn from the *same* survey. It is comforting that this inferential design, when carefully controlled and applied to many surveys, can yield valid conclusions about aging. Still more comfort is ahead. Glenn and Grimes apply the inferential design to a string of election surveys containing the question on voting, and those findings, in principle ambiguous, agree with their more rigorous cohort analysis of the same datum. Crittenden independently examined the effects of aging on the act of voting and on party identification by the inferential design, applying the safeguards in a somewhat different way. Again, the results agree with the several cohort analyses in suggesting no decline, but rather an increase.[33]

One last validation will bring added comfort and bring us back to the general practical problem of the resources available for cohort analysis and the methodological issue of comparability of instruments. Since he had based most of his conclusions about *opinionation* on the cross-sectional design, Glenn sought to bolster his evidence by a cohort analysis of that very same variable.[34] He searched for opinion questions carried on trend surveys separated by a long interval of time. Obviously, saying "don't know" on any *single* issue can hardly be taken as a global index of a pervasive trait of disengagement. And saying "don't know" to some questions cannot blithely be assumed to be equivalent to "don't know" on other questions. Some issues are just more difficult to judge than others. The equivalence of the indicators that get joined across surveys, pooled into composite indexes, or compared across studies must be carefully appraised. Perhaps their level of difficulty must even be calibrated in some empirical manner; their conceptual content assayed. But certainly the cohort analyst should entertain the prospect that

---

four elections only span a twelve-year period, the best he can do is trace a cohort over eight years of aging. Crittenden plays his hand cleverly. Realizing that he holds *two pairs* of elections, alternate ones spanning an eight-year interval, he replicates the analysis.

[33] Crittenden, *op. cit.* Table 1.

[34] "Aging, Disengagement. . . . , " Glenn, *op. cit.*, pp. 23–24.

he may strike rich resources if only he can treat a variety of questions as equivalent indicators of some abstract, underlying variable. At any rate, Glenn finds four questions, each of which had been repeated on a pair of surveys separated by about ten years time. Changes in opinionation are examined as a cohort ages from its fifties to its seventies, and the results are averaged over the four items to obtain a generalized measure of the process. There is a slight increase in opinionation with old age, again confirming the other conclusion.

Once one begins playing with the pleasant thought that nominally different questions may be equivalent indicators, one also entertains the terrible thought that nominally *identical* questions may become conceptually different with time. As Glenn and Grimes note, it is easier to vote in some elections than others; at least, the nation's turnout in some of the elections they joined together in their cohort analysis of voting suggest that. The question wording was comparable in the several surveys, but the acts to which it referred were different in some respect. What may appear in their data as the increased participation among the old may simply reflect the fact, for example, that a measure obtained late in life coincided with the Kennedy election which impelled a great many people to vote. We shall not review the way they handle the problem. Clearly they have six elections to play with and many cohorts moving through these various political arenas in which it is easy or hard to act. Glenn and Grimes are not stuck with an indicator or estimate based on any *one* peculiar instance. They can capture a general picture from all the cohorts and elections, and can also take special particulars into account.

An approach to the problem of noncomparability is suggested by Crittenden in one of his cohort analyses. He examines changes in the affiliation with the Republican party to test the common theory that conservatism increases with age, excluding the Southern stratum, introducing a control for education, and following the principle of "no peeking" in selecting the surveys.[35] But the actual measure analyzed is not the *raw* percentage change, but rather an index *corrected for the secular trend*. During the period, one might say it became "harder" to remain or become a Republican (and perhaps to admit that one was) since the nation was being swept toward the Democrats. History had changed the meaning of the item even though the question was constant. The logic of the index might be phrased in several ways. As Crittenden remarks, the uncorrected index will show "Republican

---

[35] Crittenden, *op. cit.*, 1962. The same analysis is repeated, using as the indicator the party voted for in the particular election. Each index has its virtues and deficiencies, and the two employed together are more powerful evidence than either one alone.

'aging' effects over periods of increasing Republicanism, but Democratic 'aging' effects when the trend is Democratic."[36] Put another way, a cohort that had moved *slightly* toward the *Democrats* as it aged might, nevertheless, be regarded as showing a strong drive toward conservatism, since it had resisted much of the larger tide sweeping all others into the Democratic party. A cohort that moved only a *fraction* toward the *Republicans* must have had an even stronger drive toward conservatism, since it overcame and conquered the general trend.

Crittenden's example inspires a most attractive, versatile, perhaps too seductive, invention which the cohort analyst can employ either to clarify or purify his findings on "aging," or to remove forms of noncomparability that seem at first to make some time series unusable. He might derive from the overall trend data, or from external sources of information, a correction factor representing the contribution of some change in survey *procedure* or some change out in the *real* world. Subtracting it from the raw scores then leaves in the final reckoning only the influence of pure "aging." Along these lines, Glenn and Grimes, for example, could have tried to subtract from the gross change in voting with age the amount due to some secular trend in participation or to some abrupt change in registration procedures or to some insidious variation in the ways the successive surveys were operated. Their supposition that the *elections* differ might have been expressed in the form of transformed scores: the meaning of a certain absolute level of voting as an indicator of "high" or "low" involvement being expressed relative to the general level in that election.

There is almost no limit to how far one can carry these kinds of thoughts and construct all sorts of correction factors and transformations of the data. We cannot pursue the intricacies involved. We simply suggest that a cohort analyst can be so inventive that he befuddles himself and his readers, and empties "aging" of so much of its normal contents that he is examining a pure abstraction. He should apply corrections for *real* factors with restraint, interpret the results with care, and be very, very clear about his purposes and his concept, "aging." All of us age in the course of something—a Democratic party in the ascendant, a change in occupational structure, a change in electoral laws, whatever it may be. No one ages apart from the real world. If the analyst is after a naturalistic description of aging, he may decide properly to leave these things in the balance and interpret his results accordingly. If he is after some generic aspect of aging, he could purify it analytically by various corrections, but know it is not the way people age in real life. And he could

---

[36] "Reply to Cutler," *op. cit.*, p. 589. See also Cutler's critique for a different formulation of the process that must be exhibited if the hypothesis is to be confirmed or rejected.

also arrive at the generic process by abstracting the common pattern he has observed over the uncorrected analyses from a series of cohorts.

Corrections for changes in the survey *procedures* by contrast seem highly desirable, providing they can be derived. Cutler suggests one approach to transforming raw scores into equivalent indices of an underlying variable, despite changes in the questions asked in successive surveys. With this novel tool, admittedly controversial, the cohort analyst might study change despite the fact that the trend surveys were not identical instruments, and there is almost no limit to his wealth.

Briefly summarized, judges, guided by a set of rules and a taxonomic scheme of concepts, classify a very large batch of questions as falling along a set of attitudinal dimensions. In this way, Cutler arrived at initial clusters of questions representing twelve dimensions of the belief system or ideology about foreign affairs. Granted that questions fall on a common dimension, they still may be located at different points along it. The question, for example, "Do you think the United States should declare war on . . . . . . now?" seems easier to answer "yes" to (although very hard for many) than "Do you think the United States should start an all-out war with. . . . ?" Both, by inspection, fall within the dimension "advocacy of war," but the change in the percentage "yes" if the respective questions were used on successive surveys would hardly be a safe measure of the change in bellicosity as a cohort aged.

Cutler transforms the raw percent for the cohort at each point into a Z score or standard score, expressing its attitudinal position relative to the average position on the question over all cohorts in the sample, computed in standard deviation units. As in classical psychometrics, scores from the different test items are now regarded as comparable, since they are expressed in equivalent units from a fixed, central reference point. Put in other words, if a question makes it artificially easy for people to seem to advocate war, one has to be unusually extreme in his answer properly to be called an "advocate." All the subsequent analysis is worked with Z scores, thus revealing the way cohorts move with age toward more or less relative extremism on each of the twelve dimensions.[37]

Some may be skeptical about Cutler's specific technique for resolving initial noncomparability and determining scale scores, and prefer to stick to strictly identical items for their cohort analyses. Even they do not lack resources, and their task of searching is made progressively easier by each cohort analyst who has preceded them. He has already located for them a pool of trend surveys, where the age codes are flexible and suited to the design, and

---

[37] See Chapters V and VI of his monograph for a detailed treatment. The procedure automatically corrects also for secular trend.

which treat some domain of variables that can be further explored. Indeed, the special pool may have been conveniently deposited in some data bank for the next analyst to draw upon.[38] For those who are sympathetic to a methodology of transformations applied in one specific way or another to overcome noncomparability, the horizons for cohort analysis are greatly widened, and in very desirable directions. Then a cohort might be traced not only with respect to one discrete attribute or characteristic, but along multiple dimensions of change. One could examine the profile of aging, or the degree to which a set of attitudes become more or less consistent with age—more coherently organized into a system or more fragmented; one can trace whether a particular typological construct or pattern grows or wanes with aging. We conclude with a last set of problems, set off against one potentiality not yet emphasized, so as to end with a balanced view of the general prospects.

INHERENT LIMITATIONS OF CURRENT SUPPLY—PROBLEMS AND PROSPECTS

Consider Figure 2, which represents the situation of current analysts (to be more precise, the generation of secondary analysts working around 1970), born a bit too soon and whose worldly wealth is about fifteen years worth of good surveys of American adults. The cohort matrix shows the total resources: the life course of each cohort being shown as a diagonal stream bounded by solid or dotted lines along which it moves and ages from survey to survey.

Assume the best of worlds. The surveys are of excellent quality, exactly comparable, have exact codes on age, and contain measures of many variables. The figure is simplified. Their resources might permit the analysts to mark off the course of aging through adult life at many more intervening points than the four shown, but this, for sure, will not affect the argument. If the reader wishes he can extend the matrix forward in time, closing the broken lines, to represent the situation of the later analyst who has inherited a brand new, comparable survey for 1971. That will reduce, but not eliminate, the problem. The reader might also extend the matrix backward in time, closing those broken lines. The history of surveys does go back to around 1936, but that might convey the situation of only the most fortunate and skillful cohort analysts. 1950 marks the general turning point around which sampling de-

---

[38] Thus the specialized archive of over 100 national surveys on foreign affairs which Bobrow and Cutler developed, and the 40 or so surveys finally used for the cohort analysis, was located at Oak Ridge, but a duplicate archive now also exists at the University of Pennsylvania. The surveys have been reformatted for convenient machine processing; they are now "machine-readable" for easy searching.

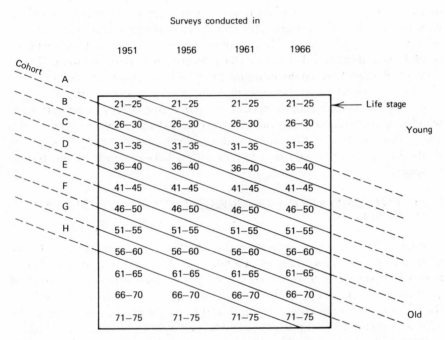

Surveys conducted in

	1951	1956	1961	1966

Cohort

A

B	21–25	21–25	21–25	21–25	← Life stage
C	26–30	26–30	26–30	26–30	Young
D	31–35	31–35	31–35	31–35	
E	36–40	36–40	36–40	36–40	
F	41–45	41–45	41–45	41–45	
G	46–50	46–50	46–50	46–50	
H	51–55	51–55	51–55	51–55	
	56–60	56–60	56–60	56–60	
	61–65	61–65	61–65	61–65	
	66–70	66–70	66–70	66–70	
	71–75	71–75	71–75	71–75	Old

FIGURE 2   *The approximate extent of the cohort matrix for a secondary analyst working before 1970.*

signs had improved and stabilized, and the assumption about high quality of research becomes warranted. But stretch the matrix, if you wish, back to 1946. Fill in the dotted lines and entries in the figure to trace the life course for all the cohorts via surveys over a twenty-five-year period from 1946 to 1971. The problem of the most fortunate of current analysts still remains unchanged fundamentally.

The macrobiographies of all the cohorts have missing chapters. For the younger cohorts, the last chapters have still to be written and wait upon the surveys of the distant future. For the oldest cohorts, the last chapters are in, but the first chapters can never be written; they predate the beginnings of survey research. The biographies of the youngest and oldest cohorts are but fragments of the story. The current cohort analyst can write a complete, but *synthetic,* biography, piecing together chapters about different cohorts into a picture of the total life history, composing, as can be seen, many chapters for the middle years to examine the varieties of experience during that phase of aging. No one should underrate the important works that can already be written, but let us recognize this inherent limitation of the present day. The secondary analyst of the future will be less limited, and should be able to write longer, strictly authentic, biographies of cohorts as the agencies extend their trend surveys. He can insure these better prospects by a strategy of *semi*secondary analysis, making the continuity of particular time series and the study of aging a primary goal.

No one should think that the current analyst has to be utterly arbitrary, simply concocting an inauthentic life history, by joining segments of aging from cohorts whose histories must take different courses because, in fact, they are separate generations being moldded in different ways. The matrix at his disposal already contains a great deal of information by which he can test empirically the implicit assumption and obtain a general understanding of both generational and aging processes.

Note, for example, that we can compare the pattern as cohort C ages from 36 to 46 with the pattern exhibited by cohort D, an earlier generation; or the segment 46 to 56 for successive cohorts E and F, to see whether the aging process shows uniformities that transcend generations. Summarizing the information *somehow* within each *diagonal* stream and then combining or abstracting it would provide a generalized picture of the aging process. Inspecting each *row* would show whether there is a uniformity produced by that life stage no matter which cohort or generation the individuals are recruited from. Summarizing the information within each row and combining it provides a generalized picture of the series of life stages. The heterogeneity within each row, since age is constant, expresses generational influences. The heterogeneity within each diagonal stream expresses aging influences, since generation is constant.

There is a great deal of information contained in the current matrix if we can figure out ways to extract it and express it. Again we are reminded of a basic theme in secondary analysis: the need for formal indices that synthesize or summarize elaborate data. And the need becomes more pressing as we realize that any one matrix will expand with future surveys, that there is one for each dependent variable under study, that each matrix can be partitioned into several to examine the patterns of aging and generation in different groups, men versus women, white versus Negro, etc., and that ultimately we shall want to compare parallel matrices for Americans and Europeans. The large prospects imply a large methodological problem. Fortunately, the technical procedures of index construction have been developed, and the reader can find guidance in the literature.

The secondary analyst now has three major designs for the study of change: replication of surveys and trend analysis, age comparison within a survey, and cohort analysis, to add to the earlier list of designs for the study of social groups and phenomena. We move now from comparisons across time to comparisons across societies, to explore cross-national designs in secondary analysis. One of the examples to be presented will show, incidentally, a new way to reduce the ambiguity in age comparisons and to use that design for the study of generational differences and social change.

VIII

Cross-National Studies

KNOWLEDGE BASED ON COMPARATIVE NATIONAL STUDIES HAS LONG BEEN A GOAL of social scientists. Although the methodology is well established, many barriers—financial, diplomatic, and organizational—obstruct those who undertake *primary* cross-national surveys. Only those who are very gifted and also endowed with abundant funds can realistically entertain that pathway to the goal. Through secondary analysis, the goal is brought within the reach of many who can exploit the prior accomplishments of the fortunate few. With the available data, they can help establish the transnational contours within which generalizations hold, and the way phenomena vary over a wider range of conditions than can be represented in a survey of a single society.

Yet cross-national research is the last place for the inexperienced secondary analyst to begin his career. He is freed from practical problems, but the same methodological difficulties that primary investigators face along the way are faced by the secondary analyst after-the-fact in the selection of surveys and evaluation of data. He cannot take the original investigator's word for the deed and assume that comparability was in fact achieved. Since there are few large-scale cross-national surveys available, the secondary analyst cannot rely exclusively on these resources. He must often exploit surveys conducted independently in different countries, joining separate but parallel studies together as if they were pieces of a large common survey. Following this strategy presents the issue of comparability of procedure in an even more acute form. And the issue of the comparability of the events and circumstances at the time of the respective inquiries, not to be ignored even in a *simultaneous* cross-national survey, becomes an obvious concern for those who join surveys from different times, and a difficult problem whichever strategy is followed.

Thoughtful interpretation of different findings for several countries demands depths of substantive knowledge which the secondary analyst may lack. Primary analysts face the same demands but at least can draw upon their first-hand experience in the several countries and upon the collective knowledge of the participants in the original studies. Intimate knowledge of procedures is essential in weighing the possibility that some of the observed differences are merely artifacts of the survey rather than products of real societal forces. In contrast with secondary analysts who stay close to home and primary analysts who wander abroad, the adventurous secondary analyst is handicapped in learning about the workings of distant agencies operating under field conditions remote from his own normal experience.

Cross-national research should be the last chapter in the career of a secondary analyst. This being the last chapter in the book, now is the time to enter upon that phase. The secondary analyst, having lived vicariously through the experiences presented in previous chapters, has become acquainted with the wide range of data and its potentialities, and with the various research designs he can employ, albeit in a single country. These are precious resources. They do not lose one penny in value when the secondary analyst starts his mental travels. Occasionally, the contemplation of a cross-national survey may suggest an utterly novel substantive problem, a set of variables that one had never thought of before or ever studied back home. More often, it is simply the study of an old problem placed in a new range of settings, an extension of a single-country design to several national contexts. The secondary analyst now starts this phase of his career with a fund of essential ideas and designs, not having to generate problems from scratch or master the full intricacies of these designs-within-designs all at once. He can concentrate all his attention on the new features to be learned.

The studies presented here will document that cross-national secondary analyses often grow by a process of proliferation. But Chapters IV–VII, although devoted to single-country studies, already imply the same process. Ponder a whimsical thought: Most of the earlier examples were based on American surveys and thus *American* readers probably regarded them as no contribution whatsoever to comparative studies. Understandably, we are unlikely, as Americans, to adopt the comparative perspective of another society when we look at survey data on our *own* country. By contrast, the analysis by Broom and Hill of class differences in Australian society was probably seen as an exotic case, comparative in character. No doubt the scholar from Australia would see it all in reverse perspective. He would regard Broom and Hill's study as not comparative at all, but would probably juxtapose every American study reported against his knowledge of Australia and therefore regard them as comparative. Thus any single-country study can be incorporated within the comparative sphere providing one adopts the right vantage point.

"To see ourselves as others see us" is not only poetry, but a source of inspiration for cross-national analysts. To be sure, an analyst so inspired must not indulge in *pseudo* cross-national research, filling in the missing cells for other countries simply by an act of imagination. In the form of musing and tentative hypothesis, such behavior should be encouraged, as long as the analyst does not take himself too seriously. Ultimately the cells must be filled with empirical data from actual surveys. And if this cannot be accomplished by pure secondary analysis, then as Chapter II suggested, a desirable strategy is *semi*secondary analysis, in which some cells of the design are represented by available surveys and others based on data collected in a primary inquiry.

We shall now turn to specific problems. In contrast with the discussion of studies of change in Chapters VI, there is no need to present a detailed statement of the general methodology since there is an ample literature on such primary surveys.[1] We stress only the distinctive aspects of the secondary analysis of cross-national data.

Comparative Studies of Social Groups

The standardization of the face sheet, as suggested in Chapter IV, creates endless sources of data for studies of social groups, and insures that knowledge can be enlarged through designs involving pooling and replication. All of the examples presented, however, were limited to single-country studies, even though some achieved almost unlimited scope in combining twenty or more surveys with common face-sheet information. The tendency toward worldwide uniformities in the face sheet truly creates unlimited opportunities for replicating studies of specified social groups cross-nationally.

SOCIAL CLASSES IN CROSS-NATIONAL CONTEXT

The study of social classes serves here to illustrate the possibilities, and immediately presents the classic and perplexing problem of *comparability* in cross-national research. If, instead, we had chosen the comparative study of *sex* differences, the variable, sex, is incorporated in surveys everywhere, measured in the identical way and with negligible error in classification, and refers to the very same underlying concept. This is not to suggest that the correlative sex roles implicated in different societies are regarded as identical. That is left problematic and indeed is what the analyst is trying to determine. By

---

[1] See, for example, the references cited in footnote 17 in Chapter I.

contrast, although some conception of class is implicit in practically all face sheets, it may be measured in different ways from country to country, by those variables and categories that seem best suited to convey the realities of the particular social structure. Education, occupation, subjective class identification, income, interviewer ratings of standard of living, material possessions, size of house, rent, diet eaten, etc., are some of the indicators employed. The cutting points along these dimensions generally are chosen so as to render the harsh facts of life in the particular society. Yet these variations should not distress an investigator who penetrates beneath the concrete surface of things and can think abstractly about the underlying meaning in particular cultural contexts. He will realize that *nominal identity* may obscure a conceptual difference, and that *conceptual equivalence* may be carried by nominally different indicators. There is no need to pursue these matters since they are a perennial topic in the literature, except to stress that apparent dissimilarities in face-sheet data may not be as hampering as might at first appear, whereas surface similarities may not always be such a boon.

A few examples, however, will illustrate the point. There probably is no American survey that provides a separate category for the "illiterate." They do exist but in such negligible magnitude as not be noted on the face sheet. By contrast that large group is distinguished on many surveys in India. An investigator however might regard it as equivalent to the category "no school" or "some" elementary school in the U.S. Given its prevalence in India, the correspondingly disadvantaged American might even be anyone who had not gone on to high school. The classifications "those who sleep on the ground, on straw matting, in hammocks, cots, vs. beds" or "who walk barefoot, in sandals, or in shoes" were found to be meaningful in surveys in Mexico, but hardly apply to the circumstances of people in more affluent societies. Although there may be no absolute counterparts, there may be equivalent underclasses.

Such radical variations on the common theme of class have not obstructed secondary analysts who have been thoughtful in handling the data from sharply contrasted societies. And those analysts who have followed an alternative strategy of selecting for their studies countries that are *similar* face little or no problem of comparability at the level of the measures employed or the concepts implicated.

The comparability of a single face-sheet datum on some specified social characteristic is not sufficient to implement such cross-national secondary analyses. The social groups have to be characterized on one or more dependent variables, and some may question whether comparable cross-national measures of these variables can be found. Many such items do recur in surveys everywhere, although not all of the time, and various solutions to the shortages that might occur will be presented. No one should neglect the array of items that appear within the face-sheet itself. Is it not ironic that all ten studies of *The Protestant Ethic* cited in Chapter IV examined the problem in the United States. To our knowledge, only one such secondary analysis for other countries is in the literature, despite the fact that religion like class, is on the face sheet in many countries. A comparative study in Holland or Switzerland or Germany for example, would be a welcome addition to our knowledge, easily accomplished, and perhaps a better test of Weber's theory.[2]

Dyadic Successive Design with Multiple Surveys Introduced Symmetrically— Baker's Study of Class Differences in Values in Japan and the United States. An analysis by Wendell Baker, prior to the founding of archives, will show the way a cross-national study can grow by a process of a proliferation, and some desirable strategies for inquiry. Using a number of different surveys conducted in Japan between 1949 and 1953, he replicated as closely as possible an earlier secondary analysis of American class differences in beliefs and values by Hyman based on surveys conducted around 1947, some, however dating back to the thirties.[3] In effect, two separate chains of surveys, each composed of several links, were joined across the two contrasted cultures to form the new cross-national study.

Within his string of national surveys, Hyman had multiple indicators of class position, and multiple questions on beliefs and values relating to mobility and occupational choice. Baker had to find comparable data for other countries, but he notes sadly that *primary* cross-national surveys of that early period, lacked the appropriate dependent variables. But he found what he sought in Japan: a series of surveys containing multiple indicators for the major variables, some being almost identical through fortunate accident, with the items employed in the American surveys.

The final design may properly be described as *dyadic* (limited to two countries), *successive* in that the timing of the inquiries was not simultaneous in the two countries, and *internally replicated* in *symmetrical* fashion in that multiple surveys and measures were employed in *both* countries. A dyadic

---

[2] Two secondary analyses to be cited below examine the influence of religion and class, separately and jointly, on voting behavior in some twenty-five surveys in four countries. This certainly documents the ample data available, but, ironically, neither one focuses on the "The Protestant Ethic." Bendix and Lipset report findings from one national sample survey in Germany, *op. cit.*, p. 53. I omit from my count two studies of specialized samples in England and Holland, that they cite, which admit of no generalization and which seem not to have been secondary analyses at all.

[3] W. D. Baker, "A Study of Selected Aspects of Japanese Social Stratification: Class Differences in Values and Levels of Aspiration," unpublished doctoral dissertation, Columbia University, 1956; H. Hyman, "The Value Systems of Different Classes: A Social Psychological Contribution to the Analysis of Stratification," in R. Bendix and S. M. Lipset, *Class, Status, and Power* (New York: Free Press, 1953), pp. 426–442.

study, of course, does not have the scope of a triad or the grand sweep of a multination study, but it should not be depreciated simply on that account. And it should be noted that a successive design can grow ever larger by later replications which extend the chain to other countries since one does not impose the stringent requirement that all the surveys be simultaneous. A not inconsiderable advantage is that the dyad does not strain the substantive knowledge of the investigator to the breaking point; all that he must master is two cultures in interpreting the findings.

What led Baker, an American, to choose Japan? And how then did he learn the necessary background knowledge, and also of the existence of the surveys—no easy task in a period when surveys were not conveniently indexed and accessible in archives. The answer is that he already knew everything he needed to know about Japan, and that was a prime reason for the choice. He had lived there, had special training in the history and language, and had had association with survey agencies. Any investigator who neglects such over-riding advantages in choosing a country would be foolhardy. So, too, the United States was a country he knew well and had studied, and more important, the analysis was already in hand, saving him half the work involved. To be sure there should be some good theoretical reason for the choice of countries, but fortunately, such reasons pointed him in the same direction. When compared with higher classes, Hyman had concluded that the American "lower class individual doesn't want as much success, knows he couldn't get it even if he wanted to, and doesn't want what might help him get success" (p. 427). In contrast with the United States, Japan had a feudal history and aristocracy, no long tradition of an open-class structure, a system of beliefs presumably encouraging resignation and acceptance of one's station in life, and an institution of local public records identifying for all who wished to see one's lowly social origins. Until its abolition, one could not conceal one's past even if he had been upward mobile. Such factors led Baker to expect that the class differences Hyman had reported for America would apply to Japan, but be even greater in magnitude and his secondary analysis did provide empirical confirmation of the hypothesis. Thus, Baker was able to extend the generalizability of the basic American finding, but also to demonstrate certain particularities and relate them to culture and social institutions.

How can Baker be sure that the national differences reflect enduring cultural and social factors? Might they not simply be transient differences reflecting the situations present in the respective societies only at the times the respective surveys were conducted? An impulsive critic might underscore the point by stressing that the design was successive; the timing was not a constant in the comparison. But a second thought will suggest that a simultaneous design would in no way have resolved the difficulty. All that would have been held constant would have been the worldwide events that impinged on both societies. The *domestic* events occurring within each society at the same chronological point might still have been different in character and made the classes depart from their normal pattern of values and beliefs.

There are only two ways to protect the inference. One is the internal replication symmetrically built into the design. The finding in each nation is based on several surveys and thus transcends a narrow point in time. One may still argue that it is peculiar to the total interval or historical period spanned. The second line of protection can be used against this danger and lies in the knowledge of the period the analyst can bring to bear upon the interpretation. Such knowledge would be mandatory and the *only* protection in a simultaneous or a successive, but nonreplicated, design, since all the findings are then anchored to a singularly narrow time point.

Baker's choice of Japan insures that he is on familiar ground and can invoke the requisite knowledge. He stresses that the findings "represent the thinking of Japanese in a period of reconstruction following the chaos of World War II. And there are a variety of factors relative to aspiration in the post-war Japanese situation which are not typical of Japanese society." Given the "collapse of traditional leadership . . . the extensive educational reform . . . [and] the extensive legal reforms [that] gave new civil rights to many segments of the population which had been previously disadvantaged,"[4] these circumstances should have produced an unusually heightened awareness of opportunity and motivation toward mobility. The findings of sharp class differences under such conditions are even more compelling; they are a conservative estimate of the normal differences.

One ambiguity remains to be resolved. Perhaps the respective differences between the classes in Japan and the United States are not an accurate picture of the societies, but simply reflect the respective survey procedures employed. Even when they are nominally identical, measures of the dependent variables may not be truly comparable. Perhaps the classes are not defined in comparable terms. Perhaps the instruments in some way have located within the Japanese structure classes that are further removed from each other in station and therefore further apart in belief. Again, the basic protection against the danger is the internal replication and variation built into the design. The finding in each country is based on multiple surveys and multiple indicators of the independent and dependent variables, and thus is not peculiar to any single instrument. Unless one were to adopt the extreme argument that the entire set of American instruments and surveys is biased in some persistent and strange fashion, and the Japanese set in some persistent and different fashion, it is hard to defend this interpretation of the findings. Never-

---

[4] Baker, *op. cit.*, pp. 13–14.

theless, Baker entertains these possibilities and can appraise them in light of his knowledge of the languages and the survey procedures. But he does not rely exclusively on his own judgment, no matter how well informed.

He arrives at the meaning of the measures by various methodological tests. For example, the various measures of class are intercorrelated to establish what constellation of status characteristics accompanies position along any dimension and compared with the corresponding pattern previously obtained from the American matrix. Thus he determines whether an indicator functions in the same way cross-culturally. And one might add that this methodological excursion yields *substantive* findings on status crystallization in the two societies. He also appoints a group of Japanese "judges" and assigns them various tasks of coding and ranking a long series of occupations in order to check upon the meaning of his measures and their comparability to the American indicators. What is worth stressing again is that he can operate such experiments easily because of his special language facility.[5] However, the general approach of providing methodological underpinnings for what might be idiosyncratic or shaky assumptions could be followed by others. Certainly internal, quantitative analyses of measures could be implemented by analysts who lack language facility and judges, if they were bilingual, could be used by ordinary analysts and the tasks adapted to the special problem.

Triadic, Successive Design with Symmetrical Internal Replication: Hamilton's Comparative Studies of Marginal Middle Classes.   Richard Hamilton's career was cited in Chapter III as an example of long and productive secondary analysis, and several of his studies of *American* classes were cited in Chapter IV. His comparative explorations in a theory of *marginality* deserve brief treatment here, and add to our knowledge of the way cross-national secondary analysis can grow by proliferation and desirable strategies and principles of inquiry.[6] In contrast with Baker, Hamilton forged all the links in a chain of replications by himself, moving successively by a career of wandering from French to American to German surveys. Like Baker, his earlier experience plus his later travels provided valuable knowledge of the languages and cultures, and facilitated the location of surveys and their appraisal. That one can create a triadic design containing symmetrical internal replication by oneself,

---

[5] One must express sadness at the premature death of Wendell Baker, not only for reasons of personal loss, but because of the loss to the profession of secondary analysts. He had fine intellectual gifts and the rare skills needed for effective cross-national research on a great body of Japanese survey data. The dissertation monograph actually incorporates a number of other secondary analyses, for example a comparative study of mobility rates in Japan and the United States, and "A Portrait of the Japanese Underdog," a replication of the Knupfer study of the American underdog.

[6] Hamilton, *op. cit.*

and obtain wide-ranging evidence that a theory of marginality of given occupational groups has little generality should encourage others to a nomadic
and productive career in cross-national secondary analysis.

In these studies, unlike Baker, Hamilton did not employ the entire samples
nor examine patterns across the entire class structure. He focused on certain
occupational groups who were presumably in marginal positions between the
larger working class and middle class (for example, white-collar workers, or
such highly skilled manual workers as foremen). Such groups are readily
located by face-sheet data, although the usual thorny problems arise as to the
heterogeneity of the occupational codes, the meaning and rank position of
specific occupational terms, and the comparability of the statuses implicated
from country to country. Like Baker, Hamilton could bring his background
knowledge to bear upon such questions.

Hamilton generally did *not* restrict himself, however, to the examination of
a *single*, "marginal" group whose values and ideology he examined and then
compared *directly* from country to country, and this brings up a useful principle for cross-national inquiry. If he had followed that design, he would have
had to make arbitrary judgments as to how prevalent a given belief had to
be to warrant the assertion that a particular group felt marginal or not marginal. More than that, even when the question or indicator of a dependent
variable was nominally identical in several countries, any assertion that a
group was relatively more marginal in one country than another might have
been criticized on the ground that the indicators were not conceptually equivalent. Or the argument could have been advanced that equivalent indicators
were nevertheless operated by the agencies in such ways in given countries
that the estimate was artifactually inflated or deflated. And the criticism
could be applied with special force, since Hamilton often had to settle for
different indicators of such abstract dependent variables as ideology, from
country to country, which might well by their wording and character have
yielded peculiar magnitudes.

His general procedure was to compare the particular occupational group of
interest with one or two other adjacent groups in the same country—to survey, for example, highly skilled workers versus white-collar workers or semiskilled workers to see how far the highly skilled deviated from one pole or the
other or where they fell along the distance between the two. He followed the
practice Rokkan and Campbell have recommended even under the more
controlled conditions of primary cross-national research of making *"indirect
'second-order' comparisons of regularities."*[7] In effect the absolute percentage

---

[7] S. Rokkan and A. Campbell, "Norway and the United States of America," *Internat. Soc.
Science Journal*, Vol. 12, No. 1, 1960, p. 15 (italics supplied).

is converted into a relativized score or deviation from a statistical norm. Thus transformed, it is freed from whatever constant forces affect that instrument and sample survey and occurrence of the variable in that country. It is these scores that are then compared across nations.[8]

However a finding might have turned out—for example, showing very little "marginal middle class" pattern among one or more national groups of workers—it might have been assailed as representing the peculiar circumstances that temporarily changed the consciousness of the group, or as applying only to the discrete dimension of thought or particular sample examined in that one particular survey. Again, the internal replication adds stature to the findings. Hamilton uses about four American surveys spanning a ten-year period. Two German surveys span an eleven-year period. In this fashion he transcends time and is also able to provide more comprehensive coverage of the domain of middle-class ideology and characteristics.

The studies taken together as a long chain, to which, of course, still further links could be added, move in the direction of generality. In this connection, one last feature of his design is relevant. Hamilton usually truncated the initial sample, eliminating at various times such groups as *young* workers or Negro workers. Otherwise his comparisons within and between countries mgiht have been confounded by characteristics other than class, and various ambiguities would have reduced the sharpness of the test of the theory. For example, a youthful worker might have had too short an experience to become fixed in the ways of thought of his class. Truncation is a tool that is useful not only in single country studies but also in cross-national studies. But as was noted, for the reduction in ambiguity, one pays a price of some loss in generality.

Multinational Design Through Secondary Semianalysis: Inkeles' Broad Characterization of Industrial Man.   This last study of class differences represents a very different style of work, forced perhaps upon the investigator who aspired to study grand problems with meager data resources in the era before archives.[9] It is a kind of adventure story about dangerous living in hard times.

---

[8] Although the formal modes for transforming scores that Cutler employed, reviewed in Chapter VII, or that Glenn and Alston or Broom and Glenn employed, reviewed in Chapter IV, were different, a similar logic and purpose governed those manipulations. It may also be noted, in effect, that Baker's procedure is a parallel. A particular class is not compared directly in Japan and the United States, but the *differences* between classes in Japan and in America are compared. For a general methodological discussion see Murray A. Strauss, "Phenomenal Identity and Conceptual Equivalence of Measurement in Cross-National Comparative Research," *J. Marriage and the Family*, May 1969, especially pp. 235–237.

[9] A. Inkeles, "Industrial Man: The Relation of Status to Experience, Perception and Value," *Amer. J. Sociol.*, LXVI, 1960, pp. 2–31.

To some the moral may be cautionary. But to those heroic enough, it will suggest how much can be accomplished purely by the method described in Chapter II as *semianalysis*, the use of published reports.

It is not easy to write a simple, accurate label for the contents and design. In the terms of Chapter IV, it is a synthesis of many surveys so as to portray the distinctive psychic profiles of social classes. The study then proliferates wildly across many countries to test whether the contrast in the class profiles is universal. Some features of the profiles are examined only in a pair of countries. Other features of the profiles are examined across six, or even twelve countries. If we ignore which features are examined where, Inkeles finally has tested his general hypothesis over a grand total of *sixteen* countries. Some of the *specific* tests are replicated internally in one or more countries; others are not. But since every test bears upon the same general hypothesis, the design may be described as replication on a massive scale. However, if one remains specific, he might describe the replications as scattered almost in random fashion.

Inkeles chained together bits of data already cross tabulated by class, mainly from brief releases or compilations of tables, from surveys conducted independently in many different countries. Quality sometimes and comparability often were dubious. The reported breakdowns by class often contained obscurities; such rudiments as sample sizes and specific dates of inquiry sometimes remained unknowns, although all of the data seem to fall in the interval 1948–1958; many of the survey procedures remained a mystery; the questionnaire itself was usually missing and only the specific question known. Confusing findings were subject to little clarification since the background documents and cards were unavailable. But since the published reports were in front of him, in the nature of the case, "peeking" was unavoidable. Fortunately, Inkeles was able to enrich this mixture of materials with data from a 1948 study involving comparable surveys in nine countries and from other periodic comparable surveys in a large series of countries, these surveys being simultaneous in design. But in these instances, again he was limited to semianalysis, the extraction of findings only from the published reports.

Whether one regards it as an encouraging or cautionary tale, it will suggest the risks in such an undertaking and how to hedge them. It will surely show that success was dependent partly on good luck, on the fortunate shape the findings took. But, in part, success was dependent on sagacity, on the very special way Inkeles formulated his problem.

Inkeles theorized that no matter what culture it penetrated, industrial society, and more particularly a man's consequent position within it (his class), would shape his psyche in standardized ways. "Industrial man" is superimposed on the Englishman, or Frenchman, or any man. Clearly, the problem is formulated so that *any* country, so long as there has been the slightest intrusion of industrialization, is a relevant case if surveys are available to make the tests. Indeed, *many* countries are necessary—the more the better—since positive evidence from one or two would hardly be proof of a theory stated in such sweeping terms. Admittedly, some countries would provide more crucial tests, depending on how long and wide the influence of industrialization had been and how contrary and strong its traditional culture in the face of such forces. Inkeles suggests that the entire *distribution* of psychic types could be displaced by cultural forces, but in every country he posits a regular pattern of variation related to class position in the hierarchy of industrial society.

Since the changes are supposed to pervade the psyche, molding it in many respects, any survey—whether it measures attitudes, feelings, values, or character traits—is relevant. The more variables covering the domain, the better the test. Some surveys certainly would be better than others in measuring variables that play a central role in psychic life, because of the high quality of the data and scope of the sample. Some, however relevant, would be harmful for him to use if they provided severely distorted evidence against or for the theory. And if he had included too many of one such bad ilk, he really would have been in deep trouble. Inkeles needed a very sharp eye and nose for such things, since very little background knowledge of the survey procedures was available. But, in some degree, he acted like a gambler who keeps on playing in the belief that he cannot have an endless streak of bad luck and draw only bad cards. Indeed, given the uncertainties and obscurities, Inkeles was forced to make the assumption that he was not being dealt his hand all the time from bad decks of IBM cards. Errors there would be, but they would be diluted in the total bulk and they would not all run in the same direction. Replication was his prime resource.

Every survey, of course, had to incorporate a measure of class position, and the corresponding publication had to report the cross tabulation.[10] In this respect he could safely count on some indicator of class being a universal on the face sheet, although the indicators often varied and he had to treat the different ones available to him as if they were interchangeable. Inkeles also had to accept the class groupings that were reported, not being able to purify

---

[10] It seems plausible that the releases of survey agencies, being journalistic in purpose, tend to report dramatic findings. It would seem hardly "news" that something is *not* correlated with class. So, too, one may suspect a tendency for scholarly investigators to omit negative findings. A semi-analysis thus might overstate the merits of the theory, since the reader would have no way of determining the number of tests that went contra the hypothesis. However, given the great many positive findings, it seems hard to believe in this instance that there could have been all that many negative ones in the missing materials. The same problem, of course, could not occur in a true secondary analysis.

the categories in any way. And this adds one more obscurity. Taking Hamilton's lead, one might argue that young workers had not borne the impress of industrialization long enough to show the psychic effects, or that the housewives should not show the full effects simply by virtue of their husband's position. Any such line of speculation is cut short by the fact that Inkeles can introduce no such refinements. But under these crude conditions, he can argue persuasively that any *positive* evidence for his theory is most compelling, since the refined classes would have shown even bigger differences. If the gross differences had been *negligible*, however, the conclusions would really have been indeterminate, since the picture might have reversed itself by further refinements. Inkeles again has to count on his luck, and hope that positive findings would fall his way.[11] What very great luck this was for him still remains to be shown!

Inkeles, in dealing with the endless string of tests bearing upon his general hypothesis, had to cope with sixteen countries, ranging from Latin America, through Western Europe, to Russia and then to Japan and Australia. No single scholar could possibly master the substantive knowledge of history plus circumstances at the times of the surveys needed to interpret the national differences he might encounter over such an incredible range of societies. It would have been superhuman to have mastered the knowledge of the procedures used in all the surveys and places in order to reject that explanation of any variation in the findings: Moreover that information was unavailable. But Inkeles would only have to face these perils if he found national *differences,* and with rare exception, he found only uniformities. What a gamble, and what a streak of luck! Yet, it is not all luck.

Inkeles, and any clever scholar, controls these perils to some degree by the way he formulates his task and orients himself to the data. In any comparison one can point to the similarity or the difference. Inkeles remarks: "A more serious criticism is that we unduly stress the regularity in the pattern across national lines while slighting the impressive difference in the absolute proportion. . . . Choice of emphasis is largely a consequence of one's purpose; the concern here is to discover regularity. . . . This is not to say that for some purposes the location of and analysis of differences is not more important."[12]

---

[11] Of course, luck will not come to his rescue in connection with other characteristics confounded with socioeconomic status which could either mask or produce spurious evidence of class differences. For example, education, one of his indicators of class, has tended to be reserved for males in many of the less-developed societies. Some of the apparent characterological effects of class position on such variables as sense of mastery or values in child rearing might be nothing but sex differences.

[12] Inkeles, *op. cit.,* p. 7.

In some instances Inkeles had to base his comparisons on questions of dubious comparability from independent surveys which also varied in unknown respects. This increased his risk of finding national differences that would be false evidence against his hypothesis. He controlled the risk, in part, by the procedure already familiar to us. He did not compare discrete classes across nations in terms of absolute percentages. The occupational hierarchy within each country was the first unit of analysis, and only the *changes* as one moved through the hierarchy were then compared across the nations. The scores of the given classes were relativized and protected from the artifacts that might influence their absolute magnitudes in the particular country.

He controls in one more way any puzzling national differences he still might encounter. When they appear, he will discount them since he has made the reasonable assumption that they probably reflect the unknown variations in procedure. By the same token, when uniformities occur he will give them weight since "any consistent pattern really there would be muted and muffled."[13] Since his hypothesis is handicapped, the evidence he obtained in favor of it is regarded as compelling. To some this may appear an invulnerable way to prove a point. But clearly it is not. Inkeles still had to find empirical evidence to support the theory, although it could be weak in character. And if he had found massive negative evidence, he could not have ignored that, although he could have discounted some of it as artifact. Like a gambler, he took his chances in a dangerous game of cross-national, semianalysis, and he was both clever and lucky.

Multinational Design Through Semisecondary Analysis, a Six-Country Comparison Produced by Addition of One Link.   Goel, an Indian political scientist was familiar with the surveys of the Indian Institute of Public Opinion. Thus he was sensitive to the errors that might arise from particular procedures and from difficulties in the field, and could also interpret the findings in light of the cultural patterning of politics. Within the large pool of over 125 surveys, at least 7 were appropriate to his problem, and he produced a string of carefully worked studies, each of which is juxtaposed against comparative findings from Almond and Verba's primary cross-national surveys in 5 other countries.[14] Thus a 6-country chain was produced.

What a testimonial to the value of *semisecondary* analysis, of merging primary and secondary studies. Goel was even able to test some of the earlier

---

[13] *Ibid.*, p. 29.

[14] M. L. Goel, "The Relevance of Education for Political Participation in a Developing Society," *Compar. Polit. Studies*, **3**, 1970, pp. 333–346; "Distribution of Civic Competence Feelings in India," *Soc. Sci. Quart.*, **51**, 1970, pp. 755–768; "Urban-Rural Correlates of Political Participation in India," *Polit. Scientist*, 1969, pp. 49–56; *India: Political Participation in a Developing Nation* (Delhi; Asia Publishing House, in press).

findings on the political patterns of socioeconomic groups by internal replications over the 7 surveys spread over a period of years, and with multiple indicators some of which are identical to those used by Almond and Verba. He extends the generalizability of some of their findings which, although based on 5 countries, had been limited, apart from Mexico, to western, modernized societies. But he also documents departures from the previously established patterns, some where the relationships are reversed in direction and others taking a curvilinear shape, which he then interprets in light of his knowledge of the Indian social structure.

Since surveys around the world incorporate measures of class and often focus on politics and ideology, other comparative secondary analyses that have exploited such materials effectively could be presented. One of these shows an unusual economy of effort. Lenski examined the generalizability of the theory that status inconsistency increases leftist voting by tests based on twenty-five surveys from Australia, Britain, Canada and the United States. Thus the design introduces a great deal of internal replication in all the countries.

The point to be stressed is that this was a *semianalysis*, based on already published tables, but these were extracted from a previous *secondary* analysis and not from one or more reports of *primary* research. Alford had previously done an ambitious work focused on other problems which we shall describe later, and incidentally had provided the essential tables Lenski exploited to test the theory.[15] With minor exceptions, the evidence was consistently positive, and Lenski therefore did not have to ponder puzzling problems of national differences. However, if fate had dealt him a less kind blow, it should be noted that he was in no instance dealing with exotic countries completely outside of his experience and in every instance with data produced by long-established agencies operating in rather uniform fashion, whose procedures were easily known and in which one could place some confidence. Moreover, some of the endless sourcs of national variation had been controlled initially by restriction of the earlier design to *similar* countries, Anglo-American democracies, thus reducing the complexity of interpretation. Some primary or secondary analysts select countries so as to maximize the number of variables that differ and the range of variation on each, thereby netting certain advantages. Other analysts select contiguous countries, or ones similar in many respects. This strategy for designing cross-national research nets many advantages, one of which is clear from the case, but is bought at a price of other disadvantages. The respective strategies are reviewed at length in the literature.

---

[15] G. Lenski "Status Inconsistency and the Vote: A Four Nation Test," *Amer. Sociol. Rev.*, Vol. 32, April 1967, pp. 298–301.

Several studies go so deep that they examine *changes over time* in the comparative patterns of behavior of social groups, and therefore belong in our later discussion. Other instructive cases simply must be omitted.[16]

Studies of Fundamental Phenomena

Chapter V described a long series of fundamental phenomena that had been studied by secondary analysis in particular countries. In principle, all of these phenomena could be examined cross-nationally because the coverage of such important variables is common in the surveys of many countries, but, in practice, many topics have been neglected. We shall review only two of the areas where fruitful work on important problems can be accomplished, and where the studies add to our general principles for cross-national secondary analysis.

CROSS-NATIONAL STUDIES OF INTERNATIONAL RELATIONS

Much attention was devoted in Chapter V to studies of the patterning of attitude and belief, of knowledge and thought, over a very broad domain of issues, and to smaller sets of disposition having a circumscribed relevance to a class of issues, for example to civil liberties or minority groups. All of these studies take us inside the minds of men. But many of them by virtue of their focus help us understand only the *domestic* life of a society as it is regulated by interior forces—not that anyone should construe that as trivial. When such studies are carried out cross-nationally, they contribute greatly to basic theory, to establishing a comparative social psychology, but they add little to *applied* research over what would be obtained from a discrete *single*-country study. For example, we do not need to know what the average Indian thinks about his domestic social problems to ameliorate our problems in the United States. Nor do Indian applied researchers need to know the way ordinary Americans pattern their ideas, although comparative findings may shake accustomed modes of thought and problem solving.

Other studies described in Chapter V dealt with dispositions in the *international* sphere—toward war or the United Nations, for example. A single-

---

[16] By pooling almost 13,000 cases from seven German surveys, almost 6000 from four British surveys, and about 11,000 cases from eight American surveys, Janowitz and Segal had enough cases to examine relative political polarization along a refined scale of social class, and to compare the way other forms of social cleavage reinforce or reduce the class cleavage. M. Janowitz and D. Segal, "Social Cleavage and Party Affiliation: Germany, Great Britain, and the United States, *Amer. J. Sociol.*, **72**, 1967, pp. 601–618.

country study contributes both to theory and application. But cross-national research in these spheres, apart from adding to basic theory, raises the *applied* value to a much higher power. Such problems are at an intersection where many countries meet, and a single country study is a picture of only *one* party to the transactions. Ultimately we shall need to know what is in the minds of many peoples if we are to resolve our common problems.

This is a high priority for secondary analysis, but ironically it seems to have had low priority thus far. It cannot be from sheer lack of data. Surveys in many countries deal with aspects of international relations, or on global matters such as war and the United Nations, or matters of foreign trade and aid, emigration and immigration, cultural exchanges, beliefs about other national groups, down to such microcosmic equivalents of international relations as personal foreign travel.

Self-imposed stringent requirements impede the secondary analyst. It is taken as so axiomatic that dispositions in these matters are influenced by events sweeping over the world, that scholars exploring these realms often restrict themselves to data from comparable cross-national surveys conducted *simultaneously*. They fear, understandably, that any attempt to draw conclusions about real national differences could be confounded not only by variations in the procedures but in the foreign events at the time of the respective surveys. Their cautions are deepened by the sense that opinions in connection with these distant problems may be lightly held and especially susceptible therefore to variations in the instruments, in contrast with bedrock issues in the immediate environment of the ordinary man. One strategy would be to make more use of the few simultaneous multination surveys available. However, it seems wise to be less dogmatic about the need for simultaneity, and to build up empirical tests that would gradually establish when (one would hope at least part of the time) the joint stringent requirements of exact comparability of procedures and circumstances could be relaxed. Perhaps only one, perhaps both, could be waived at times, or at least made allowance for in various ways. A few studies provide evidence.

Brouwer's Cross-National Experiments on Comparability via a Split Ballot Contained within a Simultaneous Study.   Brouwer prefaces his secondary analysis: "The problem of European unification in the military, economic and political fields has always had, as one of its most important aspects, the question of how the *peoples* of Western Europe thought about each other, and about the plans for unification."[17] Among other sources of data, he is fortunate to locate comparable surveys on the topic conducted in March, 1951

---

[17] Marten Brouwer, "Some Data from a Six-Country Split Ballot Survey on European Military Cooperation Anno 1951," *Gazette*, **5**, 1959, pp. 249 (italics supplied).

in six western European countries. But his analysis in 1959 focuses not on the historic substantive findings and their social determinants, important as they may be, but rather on the unusual parallel experiments built into the studies in all six countries. By splitting the ballot into two forms, the original investigators had insinuated into the minds of *half* the respondents rather strong stimuli which made the role of the United States salient in the consideration of European conflicts. These manipulations of the inquiry might influence the attitudinal responses on certain questions, and Brouwer tests tne experimental effects.

One should note that this secondary analysis is informative not only on the technical problem of comparability of question wording and sequence in cross-national research, but also on the need for simultaneity. One may regard the experimental manipulation as the symbolic equivalent in words of the real events that might have penetrated into the minds of respondents differentially if the timing of surveys had differed. Chapter V has already suggested that the many surveys containing split ballots provide an avenue to the general study of language and thought processes, but here their greatest utility is methodological. Alas, in this instance, the experimental effects are substantial in most of the countries, giving us empirical grounds for caution about waiving comparability. But the findings, considering the strong manipulations, may not apply to weaker symbols and events and perhaps are an extreme expression of the usual effects.[18] Our next case broadens the range of the evidence.

Almond's Cross-National Analysis of the Effect of Events Via a Replicated Series of Simultaneous Surveys in Four Countries. Almond's secondary analysis of 1959 is prefaced: "Opinion reactions to recent developments in space technology . . . may affect the policies and politics of the *major participants* in the international political system. Popular opinion may be viewed as 'latent policy.' "[19] The very nature of his formulation requires that he seek cross-national and simultaneous surveys, and, ideally, multiple time series spaced at the same points in all the countries. Not only did he find one set of appropriate surveys for *four* European countries. Depending on the specific question on foreign policy, he found no less than two sets, and more usually three sets of trend surveys spaced as far apart as a three-year interval 1955–1958. The

---

[18] At least seven sets of such parallel experiments varying in the strengths of the manipulations, were conducted in four European countries in the course of the USIA program of periodic surveys. The basic data on the effects are presented in tabular form in Merritt and Puchala, *op. cit.*

[19] G. A. Almond, "Public Opinion and the Development of Space Technology," *Publ. Opin. Quart.*, **24**, 1960, p. 553 (italics supplied).

309 Studies of Fundamental Phenomena

substantive finding was: "In general we may say that space competition has an importance for public opinion that is perhaps out of proportion to its over-all technological and military significance."[20] But he also observes on the basis of the trends on specific questions that "estimates of over-all military capability, while fluctuating in the same way as estimates of scientific capability, have not fluctuated as extremely."[21]

The fact that Almond found data satisfying the complete requirements, sets of comparable and simultaneous cross-national surveys spaced out over the same series of time points, is comforting. But the methodological implications once again dampen hope that one can relax the requirement of simultaneity. Some opinions in the international sphere do seem most susceptible to the influence of some events. Yet the findings should not be overgeneralized: "The only other event in recent history which can match Sputnik was the explosion of the atom bomb in 1945."[22]

Davis and Verba's Semianalysis of French and British Opinions on Foreign Policy and Their Relations to Party Affiliation. The studies so far seem to inflict nothing but pessimism on the secondary analyst hoping to make easy contributions to international problems. The last case may raise his hopes. From many releases of Gallup Polls cross tabulated by party affiliation, Davis and Verba synthesized a comprehensive profile of French and British public opinion on international matters over the period 1947–1956. There are all the inherent limitations on knowledge characteristic of *semi*analysis, but it should be stressed that they can play that dangerous game with a relatively strong hand. They are dealing, in contrast with Inkeles, with only two countries whose political cultures are familiar. The surveys were conducted by long-established, *affiliated* agencies working in somewhat parallel fashion, whose general procedures are not unknown and in which some confidence can be placed.

Focus only on the two difficulties that are critical in secondary analyses of *internationalism*. The questions employed in Britain and France as indicators of attitude were not identical. The exact times at which they were asked are not specified and simultaneity cannot be assumed. They do fall within the same decade, but what a lively period and what a flux of events! Pairs of parallel questions in the two countries cannot be regarded as located on the same pinpoint of time, and the respective respondents as replying at the same gunpoint. Although Davis and Verba[23] are themselves cautious and warn the

---

[20] *Ibid.*, p. 571.

[21] *Ibid.*, p. 558.

[22] *Ibid.*, p. 555.

[23] M. Davis and S. Verba, "Party Affiliation and International Opinions in Britain and France, 1947–1956, *Publ. Opin. Quart.*, **24**, 1960, pp. 590–604.

reader to absorb the findings with a grain of salt, their study also provides a string of safeguards against these difficulties, which we shall try to explicate.

The analysis is based on 100 specific questions for Britain and 75 for France. Although these may differ *nominally* in the two countries, sets of them, perhaps even all of them, may be conceptually equivalent in that they tap the same latent disposition. The implicit model is somewhat like a long scale of items, all of which are presumed to measure the same underlying variable, and in which the misleading evidence from a few bad items is diluted in the mass of other measures. With so many items in the two countries, it is hard to believe that they drew such an unlucky hand that the French items are persistently peculiar in some respect and the British items in another respect producing distorted comparisons. And it seems unreasonable to assume that all the French items over this long period were timed in apposition with particular events that would repeatedly push opinion in one direction, and that the timing of the British questions would repeatedly push these opinions in another direction.

They institute special precautions, nevertheless, against the non-comparability of the items, engaging in a simple method of scale construction. The items in both countries are classified by reference to their content into seven categories indicative of more specific aspects of foreign policy. The comparisons are thus based on more homogeneous sets of items, and the "subscales" are themselves comprised of multiple indicators, sometimes including twenty or more questions in each country. An index expressive of the position of the French or English on that latent dimension of foreign policy summarizes the data. Since the scores on all dimensions, whatever the aspect involved, can in turn be seen to express a highly general orientation for or against one basic ideology on foreign affairs, a composite index to represent this most generalized position is then constructed in such a way that no undue weight is given to one aspect or another, or to any subset of items that might be especially error prone. The index scores, and the composite score serve not only to tap the latent dispositions, but, as in all secondary analyses of many surveys reduce a huge bulk of data to manageable proportions, and do the work of synthesis. Otherwise Davis and Verba would have faced not merely 175 sets of marginals, but, as will be seen, an even greater multiplicity of arrays of data representing the foreign policy positions of the adherents of six French political parties and three British parties on the 175 items.

One last point about the methods of index construction deserves special note. Those answering "don't know" are eliminated initially, and the indices are computed only on the basis of those who express definite opinions. There is considerable evidence of national variations in the tendency to express an opinion. Of course, an analyst might regard this phenomenon worthy of study or inclusion in any comparisons of national ideologies.[24] But apart from the difficulty of scoring such individuals on a dimension, there are other good reasons for their exclusion. Agencies and their interviewers vary in the tendency to push uncertain people into apparent opinions or leave them undecided. The French and British positions examined are based only on those who equally felt pushed or were pushed into a view, and the undecided vote cannot drag down either score. There also is much cross-national evidence that the lack of opinions as well as knowledge is much more characteristic of the uneducated strata in most populations. Insofar as it is incorporated into the scores, any national differences are heavily weighted by the differing proportions of educated people in a society. Some analysts may wish to have such variations in social composition entered into comparisons between nations, but by eliminating "don't knows," others simplify their interpretation of findings, and can focus on other sources of the differences.[25]

There is a final protection against the twin risks of noncomparability of events and procedures which inheres in the very formulation of the problem. Davis or Verba do not compare the *aggregate*, marginal distributions of opinions in the two countries on discrete issues, which despite all their precautions could be distorted. They are concerned rather with "the *general and lasting effects of party affiliation*" on international attitudes, and they note that "there have been relatively few attempts to combine in one such study data from many surveys."[26] Primary researchers obviously lack the resources for enough surveys to cover the broad domain, and span of time.

They wish to see whether there is a polarization of opinion created and maintained by the parties, and whether such processes are general to both countries or differ between them. If they had explored this problem on only one or a few issues, then indeed they would have required simultaneity and

---

[24] For example, from a simultaneous cross-national study on knowledge of and opinion about international issues conducted in France, Norway and Poland, Sicinski presents evidence on "cultural variation in the readiness to admit lack of knowledge or opinion . . . a problem of varying 'response styles' creating difficulties in cross-national comparisons" (p. 126). A Sicinski, " 'Don't Know' Answers in Cross-National Surveys," *Publ. Opin. Quart.*, **34**, 1970, pp. 126–129.

[25] For example, in another cross-national secondary analysis of differences in international opinions, Brouwer finds a substantial correlation between formal education and the expression of opinion in each of four countries. To be sure, eliminating the "don't knows" does not eliminate the influence of education on the *direction* of opinion, and the compositional effects could be eliminated completely by conventional controls or by standardization of the data. However, the exclusion of don't knows has the desirable properties described. See M. Brouwer, "International Contacts and Integration-Mindedness: A Secondary Analysis of a Study in Western Europe," *Polls*, **1**, No. 2, Summer, 1965, pp. 1–11.

[26] Davis and Verba, p. 591 (italics supplied).

comparability in the foreign events which might have been of such a nature as to temporarily aggravate the polarity. The findings might then have been unambiguous, but hardly adequate to support any generalization. By comparing party scores *within* each country over all the classes of issues presented over a decade, they obtain the appropriate data. A specific foreign event might have coincided with a survey in only one of the countries, but over the many surveys of the decade its influence on the scores would have been attenuated or negligible. Indeed if our image of these processes is that of *cumulative* forces modifying the views of adherents and the positions of parties, a later survey in one country would have reflected the influences caught by an earlier survey in the other country.

This mode of analysis automatically applies a now-familiar protection against noncomparability of procedures. Since the differences between the index scores of the parties in each country are compared, the scores have been relativized and protected against any constant error of procedure that would have moved the distribution and average level. In all these ways their comparative secondary analysis yields conclusions which, although stated tentatively, provide substantial evidence on international problems and the contribution of party structures to their aggravation or amelioration.[27] Our three cases together suggest that exact comparability may truly be a stringent requirement in the study of some problems of internationalism, but that it can be met, and in other instances that the requirement can be circumvented by thoughtful formulation, design, and procedure.

CROSS-NATIONAL STUDIES OF AUTHORITARIANISM

We turn to one last fundamental phenomenon where fruitful work may be accomplished by secondary analysis, and one on which there has been much speculation in discussions of the differences between nations. Some conceive of authoritarian relations between people simply as one ideology or specialized system of ideas and beliefs and attitudes among many; others give it the status almost of a master disposition, a fundamental character structure, which shapes other more political ideologies: some see it working through the socialization process, penetrating into the early family life of the individual and then controlling much of his later political life. Whichever formu-

---

[27] We omit from our review the fact that the findings on polarization are obviously affected by the six parties analyzed in France and only the three parties examined in England. The difference between the scores, of course, is dependent on the ideological distance between the parties that are compared, but Davis and Verba can readily take such matters into account, and do examine "the yawning chasm that separates the Communists from *all* other French parties (p. 597) as a special problem.

lation, many assume for reasons obscure or because of history and culture that its presence is far more felt in some societies than others, and in some strata more than others within any society.

This is a grand and appropriate theme for cross-national secondary analysis. We shall examine some of the ways it was explored by Elder, whose career was described in Chapter III as an example of productivity.[28] As noted, in his search for surveys containing reports of actual relations within the family, he was led accidentally by an informant to Almond and Verba's surveys conducted comparably and concurrently in five nations. In contrast with studies of internationalism, few would regard *simultaneity* as an essential. Domestic events, fads or fashions in child rearing within a country might be situational determinants of the phenomenon, but it would be bizarre to regard some worldwide event as penetrating into the bosom of the family and ordering those relations. Indeed, if one realizes that the samples in each survey include people who by virtue of their ages were socialized over a period of 50 years, the timing of the *survey* is only incidental to defining the temporal circumstances surrounding the family relations that are reported. The other variables that enter into his several studies, depending on their nature, however, may be more or less sensitive to influences keyed to the survey dates, and this should be kept in mind.

The key variables Elder used in all of his studies were whether the respondent as a child was subjected to authoritarian or democratic treatment by the parents, and whether the conjugal family structure was equalitarian or dominated by the husband. In one study the influence of such patterns on subsequent educational attainment is examined, the face-sheet item on education serving to measure the dependent variable and the five countries serving to test whether there is cross-national uniformity in the findings.[29] We shall skip over the problem of response errors in the reports about family relations and educational attainment, although it cannot be ignored in evaluating any differences between nations, or strata, or age groups, or in appraising the merits of the overall finding. Also, we shall omit any reference to the special sampling design employed in Mexico versus the other four nations, which, by its omission of major strata, could account for a differential pattern there, except to note that Elder is most sensitive to these technical problems. We note

---

[28] Since Chapter III was written, Elder has written several more chapters in his own career as a secondary analyst. One study, not yet published, was accomplished by "piggy-backing" a brief set of questions on a 1970 Gallup survey, thus updating trends dating back through 1958, 1954, and 1946 on attitudes toward the discipline of children within the school and family. This semisecondary analysis will be reported in a late 1971 issue of *Youth and Society*.

[29] Elder, "Family Structure and Educational Attainment," *op. cit.*

only in passing that Elder *truncated* the American sample, omitting the Negro stratum from his comparative analysis, since the presence of that group uniquely in the one survey might otherwise have accounted for differential findings.

Educational attainment, of course, could have been influenced by the structural context of a society, by the sheer opportunity to get an education in some nations and strata within any society. That is exactly what Elder wants represented in his comparative design, not excluded. If the influence of authoritarian upbringing had varied, he would have had to entertain such factors in his interpretations, but he is hoping that the key variable will be powerful enough to show its force under all the different national conditions, and that is exactly what he observed. In addition, these analyses are made separately in every nation for men and women born in rural and urban areas. Thus any variations in population structure or its sampling cannot account for the national differences examined, and it is possible to document that the influence of the family structure shines through in all the strata, although in differential degree. In Germany and the United States, where the composition of the population is of sufficient heterogeneity, Elder repeats the analyses separately for Catholics and Protestants. This permits the specification of the basic relationship by such a social characteristic, incidentally enlarging by secondary analysis our knowledge about *The Protestant Ethic*,[30] and insures that any difference in the basic pattern in the two nations cannot be due to the variations in the religious composition of the populations.

The ambiguities attending the comparison of age groups contained within the same survey were heavily documented in Chapter VII, but Elder employs them in these analyses, and with good effect. Since the measures have an *explicit temporal location in past time* (the schooling one had as a child and the family pattern when one was growing up), there is no problem, ignoring issues of memory, of interpreting the responses of very old adults as referring to an early historical period and of very young adults as revealing a recent point in history. By these simple means Elder can examine whether there have been secular changes everywhere and in what degree in authoritarian practices, and whether these practices have had less potent influence on educational attainment as the larger society changed its provision of education over time and in other respects as well.[31]

---

[30] The analysis is also specified by birthplace, thus controlling any variation in rurality in the comparison of religious groups.

[31] Elder also does the analysis of religion separately for younger and older age groups, thus examining whether there have been historic changes in the patterns of family life of such groups. In connection with our earlier discussion of conceptual equivalence, it perhaps should be noted that Elder defined his criterion variable, *high* educational attainment, in the same way everywhere as "having reached secondary school." This was an

We will not review the intricacies of the other secondary analyses Elder accomplished with the same set of surveys, but we can quickly convey how many aspects of the complex problem lent themselves to exploration. In one paper, Elder used many fine age groups to trace the detailed secular trend over about forty years toward democratic treatment of the child in the five countries.[32] The historic onset is dated earlier in some of the countries, and the subsequent speed of change varies. The processes are traced separately for social strata, regional, and religious groups by reference to the face-sheet items. Although all the trends move toward the democratic norm, there is no single, unitary curve, but rather a whole family of differentiated curves. The points at which there are the sharpest shifts, for example in Italy and Germany shortly after World War II, suggest interpretations in terms of historical factors that precipitate change.

In another paper, a web of interrelations is woven by combining the key variables with data available from other questions. This analysis is relevant to much of the theorizing about the fundamental importance of authoritarianism. For example, in each nation, and sometimes within more finely specified groupings, the relation between authoritarian treatment from parents and the respondent's own endorsement of authoritarianism in family life is examined. The sins of the grandfathers indeed seem visited upon the grandchildren, although the pattern is modified by the particular national context and by the respondent's formal education. The relation between the respondent's own authoritarian ideology in the sphere of family life and his authoritarianism in the *political* domain is then examined cross-nationally and in various social strata. An ideological consistency or "spread" is demonstrated, but the consistency across spheres is dependent on both structural and national factors.[33]

Studies of Social Change: Cross-National Trend and Cohort Analysis

A few of the examples have already suggested the possibility of studying a problem not only comparatively but also as it changes over time. It may be

---

advised decision on his part, and given the detail with which education was enumerated, he could, if he had wished, chosen different cutting points for different countries and age groups.

[32] Elder, "Democratic Parent–Youth Relations in Cross-National Perspective," *op. cit.*

[33] Elder, "Role Relations, Sociocultural Environments and Autocratic Family Ideology," *op. cit.*

hard to imagine that one could satisfy the stringent requirements for several sets of comparable cross-national surveys spaced out over time. The studies now to be presented will document how lavish the resources of secondary analysis are in some spheres, and provide knowledge of special procedures. There is no need to review the general methodology presented in Chapters VI and VII.

TREND ANALYSIS OF THE CHANGING INFLUENCE OF CLASS IN DIFFERENT SOCIETIES: ALFORD'S STUDIES

Alford examined the degree to which voting patterns show cleavages along class lines (and also other lines of social structure) in Australia, Canada, Great Britain, and the United States. His "basic concern is with relatively enduring constellations of political cleavages, not with the vicissitudes of particular elections."[34] Obviously, evidence adequate for this formulation required many surveys. All told, he employed fifty-three surveys over the four countries. Appropriate cross tabulations from fourteen of these were already available in published accounts, this portion of the study being accomplished by semianalysis. Another thirty-nine constitute the heart of the study and were selected with "no peeking" and the appropriate cross tabulations and complete secondary analyses accomplished. For Australia, eight surveys spanned the period 1943–1961; for Canada, eleven spanned 1940–1961; for Great Britain, nine spanned 1943–1962; and for the United States, eleven covered 1936–1960. In each of these, the dependent variable was voting preference in the respective *national* elections, and the central independent variable was class as indicated by occupation of the respondent or breadwinner.

One may conceive of the inquiry simply as a multinational design with internal symmetrical replication. The lavish scale of the replications suggests how uniform the face sheet is across the world, and, for better or worse, how much survey agencies everywhere have concentrated on the study of elections. How really abundant the replications can be still remains to be suggested. Five years after the completion of his monograph, Alford found that eleven more surveys had become available, making a grand total of sixty-four surveys. Thus he extended his comparative analyses further in time and repeated them for three more elections per country, with the exception of Great Britain where he could only add two to his string.[35] One may label this simply as some external replications piled on top of the earlier replications.

Many of the surveys, though not all, contained in addition to the measure of occupation up to four more indicators of social class, e.g., education, in-

---

[34] R. R. Alford, *Party and Society* (Chicago: Rand McNally, 1963), p. x.
[35] R. R. Alford, "Class Voting in the Anglo-American Political Systems," in S. M. Lipset and S. Rokkan, eds., *Party Systems and Voter Alignments* (New York: The Free Press, 1967), pp. 81–89.

come, subjective class identification. Thus Alford could base an analysis on each of these discrete indicators and on a composite index of class. One may label this intrasurvey replication using multiple indicators. Since the surveys contained face-sheet data on other group memberships of the respondent (e.g., religion, region, etc.), Alford could examine the class patterns, controlling or specifying them by these other variables. Alternatively, he could focus on these other sources of political cleavage, controlling class.

Alford is interested not only in the basic uniformity that *persistently* characterizes the political behavior of classes everywhere, and the *stable* differences in the patterns in different societal settings, but also in the changes over the long-time span. Thus he examines the trend in the political cleavage of classes in each of the countries.

It may appear that the giant dimensions of the design in space and time impose corresponding colossal demands for knowledge of culture and history and of the survey procedures on the secondary analyst. But a principle of design comes to his rescue. The selection of countries reduce his problems from the start. They do differ in some respects, but they are all "Anglo-American democracies," with cultural heritage and political institutions in common. Alford must master only *one* language—his own—to evaluate the survey questions and procedures, and he is dealing with long-established research agencies whose work is not a mystery and whose level of performance is not a terrible source of anxiety. One is again reminded of the advantages of choosing countries in terms of a principle of *similarity*, rather than in terms of endless variations whose influences might never be untangled. And the secondary analyst is also reminded to apply the principle of *familiarity* so that one does not deal with endless variations in societies and survey procedures whose character is not even *known*.

Alford is protected in two other ways. A basic uniformity that transcends nations and times requires no specialized explanations, and fortunately he finds class cleavages everywhere. But beneath this surface uniformity, there are variations in the sharpness of the cleavages by place and time, and these present problems of interpretation. Alford employs a strategy so simple and sensible, but perhaps neglected, that it should be stressed. The secondary analyst needs no team of collaborators, and can manage a far-flung study all by himself. He reaps these economies but he then suffers by working alone. However, he can always call in advisers later. "Since I cannot claim detailed familiarity with the political and social systems of the Anglo-American countries, I have prevailed upon persons in each country to comment upon various chapters."[36] There follows a list of ten advisers.

---

[36] Alford, *op. cit.*, p. xiii.

We will skip quickly over the many conventional problems that must be treated in such an analysis. There are the usual issues of the comparability of the procedures both over time and place, and of errors in the various findings arising from sampling biases and response error. For example, indefinite responses and refusals to report vote varied over time and country from about 2% to 30% of the sample, and had to be omitted from the calculations. If these persons came disproportionately from one social class and could have been allocated, some of the findings might change appreciably. The lavish replication, at each time point and overall, provided protection against errors, and presumably attenuated the weight on the findings of any badly and peculiarly biased survey. Whether truncation should have been employed to eliminate Negroes, poorly sampled in the past, from the American analysis to reduce noncomparability with other countries and error in the American trend is worth consideration.

The method of index construction deserves brief note. To compress the gigantic volume of data and to permit orderly analyses of trends and differences between countries in the aggregate, and for regions and religions within countries, a simple, but sensitive, index was needed that expressed essential class cleavage. After careful pondering of the formal properties and the conceptual equivalence of indicators of "leftism" and class across nations, Alford based his index on the difference in percent voting for parties of the left between manual and nonmanual groups, generally excluding farmers from the computations. Certainly, the use of multiple measures of class which reproduced the basic findings allays concern.

Nations do not standardize the calendar dates on which they hold their elections, and correspondingly the specific dates for each survey vary across the four countries, although the four *series* of surveys span approximately the same twenty-five-year period. No one should apply the doctrine of simultaneity narrowly and mechanically in evaluating or designing such an inquiry. What is under study is the long-term process which is affected in great degree by the domestic events unfolding in each place, and in lesser degree by the worldwide events that unfold. The *points* in the time series are not identically dated, but the trend lines that have been drawn through them describe the course of the long process under the influence of the same historical worldwide forces. The domestic events that need to be entered into the interpretation could not have been forced to become the same just by making surveys on particular dates. Alford is most thoughtful, however, in selecting surveys that occurred at comparable developmental stages, approximately three months before the respective elections. Otherwise class factors might have been intensified or dampened from survey to survey and country to country by the fact that the campaigns had not reached the same points of intensity.

Alford's study is one of the rare instances of multinational comparisons carried out with long-term trend data, but this is not to suggest that he has exhausted the potentialities for such secondary analyses. Cutler has recently developed a specialized archive, labeled the *Western European Macro-Survey* containing comparable data on international opinions from annual surveys conducted between 1957 and 1967 in France, Italy, West Germany, and Great Britain.[37] This pool of data, originally obtained at the request of the USIA, will permit comparisons between nations and over time. If one wishes to think big, one may even regard the entire pool as a *single*, macrosurvey describing the quintessential features of Western European thought over a decade of problems of internationalism. The materials even lend themselves to cohort analysis, as revealed by our final case.

COHORT ANALYSIS ON A CROSS-NATIONAL SCALE

At many points in his analyses, Alford examines class differences among refined age groups, demonstrating in general that the cleavages occur at all age levels, that any *national* differences in the influence of class could not be dependent simply on any variations in the age composition of the national populations, and that age cannot account for the overall class cleavages. After all, people's fortunes can grow as they age although, unfortunately, sometimes they decline, and the two variables can be confounded in any gross analysis of class. But the meaning of the age differences as such still remains obscure, since the groupings vary both in how long they have lived and what generational forces have molded them. The variables that enter into these analyses, and the long series of trend surveys available imply, however, that cohort analysis could have been applied to enlarge our knowledge. That such a methodology can, indeed, be used rigorously in a cross-national secondary analysis is readily documented by two other studies.

Abramson's Study of the Changing Role of Class in Four Western European Countries.   Comparable surveys in 1955 by the USIA in France, Germany, Italy, and Great Britain contained measures of party preference, social class, and age.[38] Since two such waves had been conducted within that year, Abramson could pool the data to obtain larger cells. The degree of class cleavage was expressed by an index almost identical to Alford's, and examined

---

[37] N. E. Cutler and E. S. Cutler, "The USIA Western European Macro-Survey: A Tool for Cross Time/Cross-National Comparative Research." Paper read at the Annual Meeting of the International Studies Association, March, 1971.

[38] Paul R. Abramson, "Social Class and Political Change in Western European Politics: A Cross-National Longitudinal Analysis," *Compar. Polit. Studies*, **4**, No. 2, July, 1971, pp. 131–155.

separately for three age cohorts. Given only this one set of data, any age differences were ambiguous and could reflect either the life stage a group had reached at the point of that survey, or the distinctive persistent politics of a generation. Another set of such surveys conducted ten years later, in 1965, contained measures of the same variables, and fortunately *exact age* had been coded. Thus Alford could trace whether or not the previous patterns of cleavage changed with further aging or remained distinctive among generations born and socialized during certain historical periods.

Although Great Britain is common to both the Alford and the Abramson studies, it is posed against different countries of comparison in the two studies, and Alford's findings speak to a somewhat earlier period than Abramson's. Nevertheless, it might be noted that the general finding of a persistent class cleavage is documented in the two studies, despite the fact that they are based on the surveys of different agencies. In evaluating these particular data, it should be stressed that Abramson has the advantage of special knowledge, his previous work (cited in an earlier chapter) having involved field experience in England and association with the British Gallup poll, the contractor for the USIA surveys in England.

In Italy, Germany, and France, by contrast, the cohort analysis documents a decline, though far from a disappearance, in class polarization among the young. It is here where Abramson must reach for some appropriate explanation in the circumstances surrounding the experiences of the recent generations on the continent. However, he does not have to proceed simply by dragging in untested, if plausible, interpretations. Some of his hypotheses can be subjected to empirical tests by data contained in other questions within the surveys.

Only one other point should be noted. Following the procedures described in Chapter VII, Abramson executes these cohort analyses twice, once with the absolute scores on the index of cleavage, and secondly with the index transformed into a Z score, thus correcting the scores for any secular trend in cleavage over the decade, and expressing the distinctiveness of a cohort relative to the average level of cleavage at that point.

Choosing Countries and Interpreting the Meaning of National Contexts

We have described the many types of patterns and processes that can be examined across a range of national settings. The designs and principles presented earlier should provide ample guidance to the secondary analyst in the systematic study of his problems once he has pursued them across national boundaries. But the critical questions of where to travel mentally and how many countries to visit have been given only passing treatment. This brief concluding statement abstracting some of the earlier points contained within the cases and adding to them may aid the secondary analyst.

The review of these basic questions in the general literature on *primary* cross-national research helps greatly, but the circumstances of the secondary analyst may alter their application. He is, of course, well off in being able to incorporate many countries, each one costing him so little, but still he must choose from among those that have been made available. And he is constrained in both decisions by the fact that his knowledge is frequently second-hand and often inadequate to the evaluation and interpretation of data from various and many countries. The principle of *familiarity* is especially valuable for him.

If the secondary analyst has his eye on the big payoff, the universal generalization, and he has a gambler's gift for making a good bet, then *maximizing the number and diversity of countries* is a good principle, but a dangerous one. If he has bet on the wrong hypothesis and finds differences, he may not be able to interpret them in the midst of all the bewildering variety he has incorporated into the design. His intellectual assets plus all the assets he has accumulated in the course of the research may be inadequate to resolve the confusion, and he then ends up, like the unlucky gambler, a bankrupt.

The principle of *similarity* is wise, although it is the slow and conservative way to wealth. Choosing countries that are similar in many respects, although contrasted enough in some other one or few respects to represent in a design some variation in a national variable, is a way to hedge one's bet. If differences are found, they are easier to interpret. The possible explanations have been reduced in number, and the design may have been tight enough and big enough to provide a reasonably good test of one of them. If uniformities have been demonstrated they might not hold, admittedly, over other more diverse nations, but it is no trivial accomplishment to have arrived at any degree of generalization across societies, and one can enlarge that generalization gradually by further studies taken in easy steps.

We still need much guidance in selecting specific countries and their number. The principle of similarity does not operate itself. Its apparent simplicity is deceptive, and it is truly simple only for those who know very little about the nations they are considering. An encounter with one learned man and heavy-weight authority may consternate any naive secondary or primary analyst who has operated by this principle. The tragicomic dialogue is easy to write: "Norway and Sweden, Australia and England. Each pair may look like fraternal twins to you—the same in almost all respects. But how dare you neglect the totemism in the Australian past, or the presence of the coalminers of Spitzbergen in the Norwegian body politic in explaining your findings?" On and on it can go. Nations are contexts of great complexity. Even when one thinks abstractly about it, they seem to vary along many dimensions. And if one is highly concrete about it, each is composed of endless particularities. Nevertheless, the principle of similarity is surely most useful, if only we learn to operate it carefully and with sophistication. We shall learn something from advances in contextual analysis involving units smaller than nations. But first consider two other principles for selecting countries implicit in the earlier cases, and a strategy there suggested that evades difficulties and promotes fruitful cross-national research.

The secondary analyst may make his contributions to *applied* research rather than to theory. Then the design does not have to be an unambiguous test of an hypothesis, but only an avenue to useful knowledge about international relations. Here the principles of *contiguity* and *importance* guide the selection of countries. Some nations control the fate of the world more than others, and from any practical point of view, they are more important to study. To be sure, there are partners and adversaries in all such transactions, and they too enter the design in accordance with their importance. Contiguity, which commends itself as a principle in theoretically oriented studies for reasons reviewed in the general literature, is also useful in the design of applied cross-national studies. It insures similarity in not unimportant respects. Additionally, neighboring nations often interact in international transactions and surveys among them illuminate the problems.

Contextual analysts of such small units as counties or communes or cities or precincts have shown by the mere catalogue of information on these units how many modes of variation are implicated in such studies. Some of these activities were described in Chapter II. Recall that the American cities in Turk's archive are catalogued on some 300 different variables, and the communes in a Finnish archive are classified on 80 variables. If *micro*contexts have such levels of complexity, is it not likely that *macro*contexts, nations, will have equal if not greater complexities of variation?

It is in the fortunate nature of their circumstances that analysts working, whether with primary or secondary materials, on small contextual units, have from any *single* survey a great many such units to allocate over a design. They may have sixty counties, twenty-five states, a dozen very large cities, almost an endless number of smaller units such as neighborhoods in a large sample. With these numbers they can find units to represent many different contextual variables or combinations of variables, and each such contextual pattern can in turn be represented by more than one actual unit. By contrast, the cross-national analyst has too few national units, perhaps two to five, or if from this special point of view he is unusually lucky, perhaps a dozen nations.

He cannot possibly represent all the constellations of variables at many levels in a kind of factorial design, let alone have duplicate units representing the constellations. Certainly, the cross-national analyst should recognize the inherent limitations, and perhaps not spread his national resources too thin and too wide. If he moves toward greater similarity he may represent less of the gamut but do it better and with more duplication of units in particular cells.

Durkheim, who pioneered contextual and secondary analysis so long ago, faced all these problems. Selvin summarizes his predicament very well and guides us toward one solution.[39] In treating anomic suicide, Durkheim reports:

"There is very little suicide in Ireland where the peasantry leads so wretched a life. Poverty-stricken Calabria has almost no suicide; Spain has a tenth as many as France." Here is an association between groups [countries] and individual behavior, in which the relationship is attributed to one property of the groups—their poverty. But Calabria, Ireland, and Spain are not only poorer than France; they are also more Catholic than France and, as Durkheim was at pains to show in his analysis of egoistic suicide, less educated. There is no necessary reason why poverty should be singled out as the cause of the lower suicide rate in these countries. Religious or educational differences would have accounted equally well for the variations in suicide.

The source of this difficulty is clear. It is the oversimple description of a group [nation] according to a single variable. What can be done to avoid such problems? One answer is to hold the other group characteristics constant by cross-tabulation, just as one does with individual characteristics. To study the influence of poverty on suicide, Durkheim would have had to find areas that were alike on other variables, such as religion, urbanization, and education, and different only in relative wealth. As a practical matter, this is impossible.

If groups [nations] differing in only a single characteristic are practically impossible to find in survey research and if large numbers of groups are impossibly expensive, is there any alternative? The most attractive alternative— perhaps the only one—is to abandon the attempt to deal with one group characteristic at a time and to describe the groups with as many variables as necessary. . . . Calabria, Ireland, and Spain would have been described as poor, Catholic, and having a low level of education. Theoretical simplicity is thus sacrificed for theoretical and empirical accuracy. These countries would differ from France on three or more independent variables instead of one, but they would be described in all their relevant aspects.

---

[39] H. Selvin, "Durkheim's Suicide: Further Thoughts on a Methodological Classic," in R. Nisbet, ed., *Emile Durkheim* (Englewood Cliffs, Prentice-Hall, 1965, p. 135.

Some analysts, whether working with small or national units, have guided us to another solution. Perhaps the endless complexity can be simplified and the many dimensions of variation reduced to a simpler structure of fewer but more fundamental factors. For example, one factor analysis of data on about forty dimensions along which Finnish areas or communes varied yielded seven more fundamental factors, and in another solution the many factors were reduced to five dimensions. Long ago, a matrix of data on seventy nations measured on seventy-two different variables was reduced by R. B. Cattell to five major factors that accounted for most of the variance. More recently, Sawyer et al., examining 236 variables over 82 nations, found that three factors accounted for most of the variance.[40] Nations need only be represented along very few abstract dimensions, perhaps by their basic profile of "factor scores," to capture their many concrete modes of variation. With such catalogues already available to him and these basic coordinates already drawn for him, the secondary analyst makes a more informed and comprehensive judgment as to what may account for any differences he has found, and he can make sounder choices of similar or contrasted nations for his designs.

In these several ways, guided by a set of principles and the growing body of knowledge about the multiple patterns among nations, the secondary analyst will produce more and better cross-national research on a wide range of problems.

---

[40] Erik Allardt and Olavi Riihinen, "Files for Aggregate Data by Territorial Units in Finland," in Rokkan, *op. cit.*, pp. 128–135. R. B. Cattell, "The Dimensions of Culture Patterns by Factorization of National Characters," *J. Abnorm. Soc. Psychol.*, **44**, 1949, pp. 443–469. See also R. B. Cattell, H. Breul, and H. P. Hartman, "An Attempt at More Refined Definition of the Cultural Dimensions of Syntality in Modern Nations," *Amer. Sociol. Rev.*, **17**, 1952, pp. 408–421; Jack Sawyer, "Dimensions of Nations: Size, Wealth, and Politics," *Amer. J. Sociol.* **73**, 1967, pp. 145–172. See also H. C. Selvin and W. O. Hagstrom, "The Empirical Classification of Formal Groups," *Amer. Sociol. Rev.* **28**, 1963, pp. 399–411.

IX

Conclusion

WE HAVE COVERED THE MAJOR CLASSES OF PROBLEMS THAT CAN BE TREATED BY secondary analysis of sample surveys, and reviewed many specific studies of social groups and fundamental phenomena, and of their stable patterns and changing character over a range of historical and societal conditions. We have not tried, however, to present an exhaustive list of all the specific ways secondary analysis can be applied to each of the classes of problems, although we have aimed to be comprehensive about the general types of problems and the basic methodology.

Any attempt to be exhaustive as to particulars would defeat itself. The present archives are already huge and become larger everyday as agencies busily continue their production of surveys. Given the almost infinite variety of the data, the potentialities in secondary analysis, for men of imagination and skill, are myriad in number. The scientific community has not yet exploited the present resources. Who can envision all the specific directions that future explorations in secondary analysis will take as men penetrate more deeply into regions of knowledge that are already accessible, or what new frontiers for exploration will open in the natural course of future surveys? We have emphasized adherence to particular standards of research, but our stress has been on creativity in the choice of problems, not conformity to particular prescribed paths of study. Any idea that the previous examples exhaust the potentialities of secondary analysis would be contrary to the spirit of this book.

The examples dealt mainly with the interests of sociologists, psychologists, and political scientists. Secondary analysis, of course, can be applied to the concerns of other fields—economics, medicine, and public health, education, social work. Workers in those fields, with any spark of creativity, can formulate their own problems which can then be illuminated by applying the principles generic to all secondary analysis.[1]

There is one additional class of problems, not yet treated, which is amenable to secondary analysis. In all the previous examples, secondary analysis has served to study problems of a substantive or theoretical nature. It can also serve to study the *methodology* of surveys. We do not mean the methodology of *secondary* analysis. We refer, rather, to the possibilities for abstracting general methodological principles from the multiplicity of existing surveys and from the accompanying descriptions of their operating procedures that have been kept systematically by the better agencies.

Bits of knowledge about method naturally accumulated in the course of the daily round of surveys, and prudent researchers, like frugal housekeepers collecting crumbs, have not allowed them to go to waste. Such methodological by-products, incidental in the production of all kinds of surveys, usually were fed back into the work of the given agency rather than being subjected to systematic analysis and abstracted into statements of general principles. But by making and keeping the records of the functioning of their procedures on all their surveys, the established agencies, in effect, hoarded the crumbs of knowledge for future methodologists who might examine systematically how procedures perform under varied circumstances.[2]

A compendium of comparative findings on losses in sampling, or on nonresponse and other kinds of difficulties with various kinds of questions administered by different types of interviewers to different populations, or on validity of responses as checked against an external criterion, or a comparative analysis of interviewer ratings of status, race, and other characteristics—these and similar codifications go far beyond the special purposes of each original

---

[1] The contributions by Morgan, Trow, Massarik, and Suchman on survey research in economics, education, social work, and public health and medicine, respectively, in Glock's *Survey Research in the Social Sciences* will suggest a great many potential studies. *op. cit.*

[2] Primary investigators may also abstract the methodological findings implicit in the records of their own surveys, and, again, could best be described as semisecondary analysts. For example, prefatory to analysis of the findings derived from the interviewer report forms used by NORC over several years, Sheatsley remarks that such forms "were used mainly as a means by which interviewers could air their complaints. But . . . new and important uses for interviewer-reports have been *discovered.*" P. B. Sheatsley, "Some Uses of Interviewer-Report Forms," *Publ. Opin. Quart.*, 11, 1947, p. 601 (italics supplied). In another example, where the records of one survey provided an unusual opportunity for an analysis of sampling problems, the original investigators remark that "such methodological problems were secondary to the substantive content of the survey," D. Manheimer and H. Hyman, "Interviewer Performance in Area Sampling," *Publ. Opin. Quart.*, 13, 1949, p. 83.

record keeper and could yield methodological contributions.[3] Indeed, one codification of a relatively small number of the surveys conducted only by a single agency, the review by Kendall and Lazarsfeld of studies analyzed in *The American Soldier*, led to a widely used formalization of the general modes of multivariate analysis.[4]

Occasionally, entire surveys have been designed to incorporate true field experiments in which a procedure is systematically varied and other factors are held constant. The use of different forms of a questionnaire by the same crew of interviewers on equivalent subsamples, described in Chapter V, is one example of such experimental designs. The allocation of two crews of interviewers from different agencies to equivalent half-samples in a survey, cited in Chapters IV and VI, is another example of an experimental design that has been used on a number of occasions. Although methodological purposes obviously inspired such experiments initially, much of the data still await secondary analysis. In some instances the results from the different experimental procedures contained within a survey have simply been averaged, rather than compared, the aim being to make the final conclusion less vulnerable to the errors that would operate if only one procedure had been used. And even when the original analysts have examined the comparisons, they often used only a small portion of the data for its immediate relevance to their substantive findings, the general methodological implications of other

---

[3] Such studies could serve two purposes in addition to enlarging general methodology. The many secondary analysts engaged in *substantive* studies would have a convenient reference work on the usual quality of the procedures of the agencies on whose data they rely, and could better select and appraise the original surveys. And there is also an implicit substantive meaning to be drawn from the way various populations react to the request to be surveyed. The interview simulates experimentally the natural processes of social interaction, of communication of information and opinion, and stable patterns of response to such a situation therefore tell us something about the cultural and subcultural definitions of social and political behavior in particular groups.

[4] P. L. Kendall and P. F. Lazarsfeld, "Problems of Survey Analysis," in R. K. Merton and P. F. Lazarsfeld, eds., *Continuities in Social Research: Studies in the Scope and Method of "The American Soldier"* (New York: Free Press, 1950), pp. 133–196. With the publication of this volume containing several notable secondary analyses, and the earlier publication of *The American Soldier*, itself a collection of *semi*secondary analyses, it is fair to say that knowledge of the wartime surveys and their potentialities for secondary analysis is probably universal among social scientists. Ironically, the continuation of the program of such surveys after World War II seems to be hardly known and the potentialities for parallel secondary analyses, especially for the comparison of attitudes of the military in peace and war, have been neglected. In the period, 1946–1953, almost 150 reports based on a large number of surveys were issued by the research division that was the successor to the wartime unit.

possible tests remaining unexplored until some secondary analyst grasps the opportunity.[5]

There is a third empirical source of methodological findings which in type falls between the two contrasted sources already suggested. Instead of codifying the cumulative historical record of the functioning of procedures over many surveys, or analyzing the rare surveys containing true experimental tests of procedures, the sensitive analyst may stumble periodically upon surveys which contain an unusual set of variables or an unusual distribution of scores, or an accidental *quasi*-experiment approaching the true experiment one would ideally design, these circumstances then serving to illuminate some methodological question. It is not easy to describe these opportunities by any general formula, but we can illustrate them.

Ehrlich and Riesman, for example, sensed the opportunity inherent in a study of adolescent girls conducted by the Survey Research Center of the University of Michigan. The interviewers were all women, homogeneous in class but varying widely in age, and this permitted a test of age disparities between respondent and interviewer on the responses to questions about the authority of the parents. The fact that various personality measures on the interviewers were also available added to the attractiveness of the data. So they "followed on the heels of the original interviewing" with a secondary analysis.[6]

The fact that a particular survey provides an unusual opportunity for a secondary analysis of a methodological problem may also strike an investigator after the fact as he stumbles upon a serendipitous finding in the course of his own *primary* analysis of the substantive data. For example, Shapiro realized, while inspecting a matrix of data for a factor analysis of a large number of variables in which the entries just happened to be arranged spatially by interviewer, that one factor was best interpreted in terms of the interviewer's

---

[5] One of the surveys in which crews of interviewers were allocated to equivalent subsamples was the subject of an extensive secondary analysis, but others still await analysis, and the synthesis of the findings from the entire series is still to be done. See Stember, *op. cit.*

[6] June Ehrlich and David Riesman, "Age and Authority in the Interview," *Publ. Opin. Quart.,* **25,** 1961, p. 39. That the term "quasi-experiment" is apt is suggested by their remark. "Our conclusions and reconstructions are based on the usual small cells and uncomfortably fragmentary tendencies that researchers must often depend upon in trying to push subtle ideas through a crude mesh of cross-tabulations" (p. 41). Also note the way routine records of the functioning of procedures may contribute a methodological datum. From the interviewer report forms, they quote the interviewer who described her approach to the task: "I explained that I was a mother of a sixteen-year-old girl somewhere in each interview" (p. 41).

probing behavior since the component items had no congruence of content. As he remarks: "The discovery of interviewer bias reported here was not anticipated," but he was able to pursue the problem because of the particular elaborate structure of measures he had and the quasi-experimental arrangement he could impose upon them.[7]

Sometimes, awareness of the opportunity for a secondary analysis of a methodological problem may come to a primary investigator at an earlier stage of his research. He may realize that a design being employed primarily for some substantive purpose provides naturally a quasi-experiment which approximates the planful experimental design one would use, or which has been used, to examine some procedures. Obviously, knowledge of the experimental models and sensitivity are the prerequisites for such accidental discoveries and the subsequent secondary analysis.

Such would seem a fair reconstruction of the process that led Haberman and Sheinberg to their secondary analysis.[8] In a longitudinal study in which a panel was reinterviewed after an interval of three years, formal education was enumerated twice, the respondent in some cases making the report for himself both times and in other cases another family member providing the information in one of the two interviews. This led to their study of the reliability of reports of factual data and an evaluation of the use of household informants in obtaining such information. They note high agreement between their "adventitious" findings and the literature that had been derived from deliberate use of this same design. But what should be especially stressed is that they *replicated* their first analysis on another panel study which had followed the same design. The general strategy suggested is that secondary analysts can be searching the archives with particular models of methodological experiments in mind, and thereby increase the yield of such studies, and more particularly, that past panel surveys on file may be one fruitful place in which to apply the strategy to studies of response error.

This brief discussion will suggest the potentialities of secondary analysis for methodological studies and the kinds of survey data appropriate to these purposes.

---

[7] M. J. Shapiro, "Discovering Interviewer Bias in Open-Ended Survey Responses" *Publ. Opin. Quart.*, **34**, 1970, p. 412. The survey approximated an experimental design in one other respect. Respondents had been assigned randomly to the interviewers. Consequently variations in the results could not be attributed to initial differences in their respective samples.

[8] P. W. Haberman and J. Sheinberg, "Education Reported in Interviews: An Aspect of Survey Content Error," *Publ. Opin. Quart.*, **30**, 1966, pp. 295–301.

A List of Archives

We have now treated the many kinds of studies that can be undertaken by secondary analysis of existing sample surveys, and the methods for accomplishing such studies.[9] Although we have tried to convey familiarity with the range of content of past surveys, and occasionally have mentioned particular archives in the course of our discussion, we have not specified the many places where the scholar may find rich deposits of data on which he can draw.

A selected list of archives may be a helpful addition to his knowledge, and, although an unconventional conclusion, seems to us the most useful ending to this work. We emphasize once again that a so-called "archive" is not essential to secondary analysis. Every primary survey researcher should think of himself as fortunately endowed with a small data bank, and should not forget that he is potentially a rich man who need borrow from no one else. And every academic scholar working outside of the survey agencies should think of those individual agencies as a host of friendly institutions lending data. They may be less conspicuous in that role than the well-known archive, and their separate assets may be small relative to the giant, consolidated holdings of the major archives. Yet a small agency may have a unique set of precious data, especially desirable to some scholar. The wise secondary analyst does not ignore these prospects, but neither does he neglect the major archives. He entertains all the possibilities, sometimes having to search far and wide for an elusive and rare set of data, but, at other times, knowing exactly where to start in light of his past experience with the holdings of particular archives and the special emphases and practices of particular survey agencies.

---

[9] Our entire text, as its title suggests, focuses on the analysis of data derived from sample surveys. The archives have also accumulated a great deal of data on various features of *collectivities* of different sizes and types, obtained originally from sources other than surveys of samples of individuals. For example, *aggregate* characteristics of the populations of cities, counties, regions, and nations derived from censuses or from historical statistics such as voting records have been filed. *Global* characteristics of the collectivity, the presence of various kinds of organizations, or institutions, the occurrence of events such as conflicts, wars, riots, outbreaks of violence, etc., have also been filed. Some of these materials were mentioned in earlier chapters. When they have entered as *contextual* data into secondary analyses which focus on individuals and are merged with sample survey materials, they have been given review. However, there is an entire realm of research giving *exclusive* attention to studies of collectivities, accomplished by the analysis of available data, which we have omitted from our text. To be sure, some of the methodological matters we raise apply equally well to these other kinds of secondary analysis: the appraisal of errors in the original data, problems of slippage in index construction, and the rearrangement of data sets into research designs. But the substantive problems are very different in content and formulation from the range of topics we have treated. Several of the symposia cited in Chapter I review this realm of problems, and the reader is referred to those sources.

The archives listed were functioning around 1970 and have policies that are not unduly restrictive with respect to access. They all have substantial collections of data, some specializing in surveys of particular populations and problems, but, nevertheless, appearing to serve the interests of more than a narrow group of scholars. Some that are so specialized that we have excluded them may in fact be of considerable interest to a larger constituency than we have judged. We have excluded official agencies of governments which often function as archives accessible to secondary analysts as well as producers of the original data.

In the future, some that are now listed may have ceased to exist. More likely, a future listing will be even longer. New archives will, no doubt, come into being to meet local needs as funds become available and secondary analysis as an activity establishes its merits in more places. At present, the geographical distribution is very uneven, most of the ones listed being located within the United States. But this does not mean that the surveys in their files relate only to American populations. Many American archives are truly international in their holdings. Similarly, the archives located in other countries are international, often including, for example, surveys of American populations.

The brief descriptions merely suggest the contents and emphasis of the respective archives. The scholar can obtain detailed information on the holdings and the procedures for obtaining data by direct correspondence, and acquaint himself with the entire array and the overall resources by consulting the several articles and brief directory cited in the early chapters.

Bureau of Applied Social Research, Columbia University, New York City

A general collection of the agency's own surveys, mainly dealing with samples of special areas, groups, or organizations within the United States of America.

Carleton University Social Science Data Archives, Ottawa, Canada

A large general collection limited to data on Canada, but including, in addition to sample surveys, data on the social and political characteristics of the country and on the political elite.

Columbia University School of Public Health and Administrative Medicine Research Archives, New York City

The collection is limited to surveys and other data related to matters of public health, with special emphasis on the New York area, although data for other parts of the United States and Puerto Rico are included.

Data Repository Section, Survey Research Laboratory, University of Illinois, Urbana

The collection focuses on Illinois and includes, in addition to sample surveys, historical data on economic, social, and political characteristics of the area.

International Data Library and Reference Service, Survey Research Center, University of California, Berkeley

A large international collection with special emphasis on surveys of Asian and Latin American countries.

Inter-University Consortium for Political Research, University of Michigan, Ann Arbor, Michigan

A large general collection with special emphasis on political surveys of the United States. Holdings also include cross-national surveys and historical data on the social and political characteristics of areal units, e.g., counties, and data on political elites.

International Development Data Bank, Michigan State University, East Lansing, Michigan

The collection focuses on studies of modernization conducted primarily in the developing countries.

Laboratory for Political Research, Social Science Data Archive, University of Iowa, Iowa City

The collection focuses on Iowa and includes, in addition to sample surveys, data on the social and political characteristics of the state and of its elites. Some comparative data for other states, for the Federal level, and for other countries are included.

Louis Harris Political Data Center, University of North Carolina, Chapel Hill, North Carolina

The collection houses sample surveys of the American population conducted by the Louis Harris agency.

National Opinion Research Center, University of Chicago, Chicago, Illinois

A general collection of the agency's own surveys of the U.S. national population and of special areas within the country.

Public Opinion Survey Unit, University of Missouri, Columbia, Missouri

The collection focuses on Missouri and includes, in addition to sample surveys, data on the social and political characteristics of the state and its elites.

Roper Public Opinion Research Center, Williams College, Williamstown, Mass.

The largest general collection containing thousands of sample surveys from many countries.

Social Science Data and Program Library Service, University of Wisconsin, Madison, Wisconsin

The collection focuses on economic data and includes, in addition to national sample surveys, historical data on economic variables for the United States, and especially for the state of Wisconsin. Comparative economic data for Holland, and a data file on the characteristics of American cities are included.

Social Science Research Council Data Bank, University of Essex, England

A large general collection of surveys, and other types of machine readable data, for England and localities within the country.

Steinmetz Institute, University of Amsterdam, Amsterdam, Netherlands

A large general collection focusing on studies of the Netherlands.

UCLA Political Behavior Archives, University of California, Los Angeles

The collection focuses on the politics of California, but includes comparative data for other countries. In addition to sample surveys, historical data on the social and political characteristics of small areal units within California and on the political elites are included.

Zentralarchiv für Empirische Sozialforschung, University of Cologne, Cologne, Germany

A large general collection focusing on surveys of West Germany and of German speaking populations in Austria and Switzerland.

By the use of these archives and other sources of survey data, and practicing the principles and procedures presented, it is our hope that many students and scholars will begin to realize the full potentialities of secondary analysis.

Appendix

The Survey of Users of the Archives

A BRIEF DESCRIPTION OF THE SURVEY DESIGN AND PROCEDURES SHOULD SUFFICE. Our aim was not to make statistical generalizations about the population of all users of all archives of sample survey data. This would have involved drawing samples from over a considerable time period from more than twenty archives located not only all over the United States but in other parts of the world, some of which have very small and specialized holdings and very limited numbers of clients. We did not plan to place exclusive reliance on the survey findings for source materials for the codification of general principles of secondary analysis. That was to be based largely on the extensive review of the published literature and on our own research experience and experience in teaching the topic over many years. Consequently, the stringent requirements of a conventional survey could be relaxed and the size of our sample reduced to manageable numbers.

The survey certainly did serve to locate literature reported by the respondents that we might otherwise have neglected and works in progress not yet ready for publication. But mainly, it was intended to serve one unique function. Published studies generally are orderly and polished accounts of the successful completion of a research plan and rarely describe the difficulties experienced along the way or the accidental circumstances that may have inspired a discovery. Those who started research but who experienced such intractable difficulties that they could not finish obviously never publish. The survey was intended to locate this otherwise buried world of aborted research and to reveal the experiences of those analysts, although it also yielded cases of highly successful analysts. The inquiry among the two groups was conceived as a set of case studies on the process of research and on the variety of factors that impede or facilitate discovery and productivity in secondary analysis.

The sample was drawn from the users of two archives. The Roper Public Opinion Research Center as the largest and longest-established general-purpose archive was the obvious, first choice. The Inter-university Consortium for Political Research was also chosen. It was established as long ago as 1962 and has large holdings. Active use of its materials would be facilitated by the network of over 100 member institutions who are entitled to various free services and to send students and staff to regularly held training seminars. The samples were drawn systematically from the files of correspondence, and, wherever possible, from within various strata of users, the particular procedure being dependent on the way the files were kept at the respective centers. From the correspondence itself, the purpose of the request usually could be inferred. Users of data for purposes unrelated to individual research, e.g., stockpiling of surveys for training students, were eliminated. Certain strata of users whose requests seemed less fruitful for our purposes were sampled less heavily than other strata. For example, institutional representatives who were intermediaries between the archive and other unknown scholars at the member institution were sampled lightly. Such cases, however, generally did refer us to an ultimate user who was then contacted. In general, we also undersampled individual users from "member institutions"; our assumption being that some were simply taking advantage of the free services and perhaps stockpiling data for some possible, uncrystallized future purpose, and if involved in research would be less likely to experience difficulties along the way because of the many supportive conditions in their milieu.

About 170 names were drawn from the two archives, restricting the selection to those who had requested data in the period around 1966, so that the experiences would be still fresh enough to be recalled (the survey was done in 1968), but not so recent as to have precluded finishing the studies. By the choice of the two well-established centers, the recent time period, and the particular strata, it was assumed that the individual respondents would be active, motivated researchers working under conditions that would represent a relatively advanced and efficient stage of archival operations; our interest being to highlight problems of methodology rather than obstacles of technology.

Instead of a questionnaire, a personal letter on a university letterhead was sent to each respondent, stating that this was an independent scholarly study of secondary analysis, and giving assurances that they would not be quoted without their consent. (A copy of the letter generally used is attached, and minor variations in wording were introduced where the respondent was a personal friend or acquaintance. Occasionally, an individual fell into both samples, having drawn on data from the two archives. In such instances, the one letter that was sent was modified to refer to both sources of his data.) Those who did not reply were sent reminders in the form of additional personal letters, less to increase the rate of return than to encourage those who perhaps were reticent to report their failures and problems, whose omission from the survey would have detracted greatly from our knowledge of critical problems. Those who did reply and described works in progress, but at a preliminary stage, were also generally sent follow-ups after some months had passed to determine their subsequent experiences and the eventual product.

The results of the survey were gratifying. The overall response rate was 83%, the rates of the separate samples from the two archives being almost identical—81% and 83%. Inspection of the nonrespondents does not suggest that they were any distinctive homogeneous type in terms of geographical or institutional location or discipline in contrast with the repliers, although they appear to be less well established and notable figures in the disciplines. Perhaps the difficulties they experienced, which were lost to our survey, were more severe in light of their lesser proven accomplishments, but this remains moot. Indeed, among the best-established scholars who replied, some reported serious technical difficulties and aborted investigations, and among the respondents who were still in the status of student, some reported no difficulties and completed their studies. The obstacles, as Chapter III will suggest, are not dependent on the *absolute* level of technical expertise alone, but often on the happy choice of a problem that is compatible with the data available and on the match between the methodological skill the problem and data demand and the competence of the investigator. Ironically, an experienced investigator may choose his problem and set his aspirations in such a way as to strain his resources more than a beginner.

The responses were generally long and highly informative accounts of experiences in secondary analysis, some successful, others unsuccessful, and these varying from the tragic to the comic in the difficulties encountered. Respondents answered from nearby places and from remote distances around the world; some were students, some were distinguished scholars. There appeared to be great interest in telling their experiences and much honesty in reporting their varied difficulties. Some did put the onus on the archive or the original producer of the surveys, but many located the difficulty within themselves.

The group of "highly productive" secondary analysts described in Chapter III came in part from the sample of users. The scholars who had long careers and many accomplishments in secondary analysis were readily located by the survey. They generally reported their full bibliography of studies.

One of the archives had a separate classification within its files for "heavy users" and this group was oversampled so as to net a larger number of "successful" analysts. However, some analysts were added to this category on the basis of our judgment of their published work, even when they did not fall into our sample. Letters were then sent to these individuals requesting a report of their experiences. The cases reported in Chapter III are but a selection from the total number available, chosen on the basis of judgment as to productivity and because they were unusually articulate.

The courtesy of the archives in making their files accessible, and the cooperation of their staffs is gratefully acknowledged. John S. Reed, Jr., was responsible for the drawing of the final samples in the course of field trips to the two Centers, and he and Miss Margaret Gannon were responsible for the follow-ups on the respondents. Their assistance is greatly appreciated.

COPY OF LETTER

Dear

I write to you in connection with our mutual interests in sample survey methods and findings. One of my long standing concerns has been the problems and potentialities of Secondary Analysis of survey data, and I am now engaged in writing a monograph on the subject. An approach that comes naturally to my mind is to conduct a small survey among those individuals who have used data from previous surveys on file in the Archives of the Michigan Inter-University Consortium (Roper Public Opinion Research Center) for scholarly research.

The National Science Foundation was generous enough to provide a small grant to me for the purposes of such an inquiry, and your name was drawn in a sample of past clients, kindly made available to me by the staff of the Consortium (Center). The research use you made of the data obtained, the analytic procedures you found appropriate; and the methodological difficulties you may have encountered, in combination with the experiences of other users, would be most valuable information of benefit to social science.

If your use culminated in some publication, I would greatly appreciate knowing the exact citation, and if it is available in article or report form, 1-2 reprints would be helpful to me. By examining such writings myself, I can attempt to abstract some general conclusions. But if you were to take the additional time to write me a brief chronicle or letter describing your experience in that secondary analysis, it would be even more helpful.

It may be that your work with the data did not result in any publication. Then, the only way in which such experiences can become useful to the larger profession is by your own account, and I hope very much, if you are among this category of users, that you will write me a brief statement.

I can assure you that any information you wish to have treated as confidential will be so regarded and that your anonymity will be protected in anything I write if you so instruct me. Needless to say, appropriate citations and acknowledgement will be made in my monograph.

If you acted simply as a representative to transmit your colleagues' requests for data, I would appreciate your passing my letter on to one major user for whom you acted. If you analyzed the data yourself, but also know of another colleague who made a major attempt at secondary analysis, I would welcome his name as a way of expanding my sample. With the hope that I may hear from you soon.

Yours sincerely,

Herbert H. Hyman

HHH/mag

We are grateful to the following authors and publishers for permission to use certain material.

Prentice-Hall, Inc.

Selvin, H.,"*Durkheim's Suicide: Further Thoughts on a Methodological Classic,*" in Robert A. Nisbet, Ed., *Emile Durkheim*, 1965.

American Psychological Association

Samelson, B., "*Mrs. Jones's Ethnic Attitudes: A Ballot Analysis,*" **J. Abnorm. and Soc. Psychol.**, 40, 1945, pp. 205, 214.

American Sociological Association

Glenn, Norval and Ruth Hyland, "*Religious Preference and Worldly Success; Some Evidence from National Surveys,*" **American Sociological Review**, Vol. 32, 1967.

Jackson, Elton F. and Harry J. Crockett, Jr., "*Occupational Mobility in the United States: A Point Estimate and Trend Comparison,*" **American Sociological Review**, 29, 1964, pp. 11, 13.

University of Chicago Press

Schatzman, L. and A. Straus, "*Social Class and Modes of Communication,*" **American Journal of Sociology**, 1955, p. 330.

The Belknap Press of *Harvard University Press*

Key, V. O., Jr., *The Responsible Electorate*, 1966, pp. 18, 52, 53.

The Macmillan Company

Bogue, Donald J., **The Population of the United States**, 1959, p. 688 and 703.

Hirschi, Travis and Hanan Selvin, **Delinquency Research**, 1967, Chapters 6 and 8.

Planck, R. E., "*Public Opinion in France After the Liberation, 1944-45*" in M. Komarovsky, editor, **Common Frontiers in the Social Sciences**, 1957, p. 214.

Princeton University Press

Hamilton, Richard F., **Affluence and the French Workers in the Fourth Republic,** 1967, pp. 8–9, 14.

Russell Sage Foundation

Glock, Charles, editor, **Survey Research in the Social Sciences,** 1967, pp. 52–53.

Yale University Press

Converse, Philip E., *"The Availability and Quality of Sample Survey Data in Archives within the United States,"* in R. Merritt and S. Rokkan, **Comparing Nations: The Use of Quantitative Data in Cross-National Research,** 1966, p. 431.

Basic Books, Inc.

Stember, C. H., *et al.,* **Jews in the Mind of America,** 1966, p. 44.

PUBLIC OPINION QUARTERLY
Columbia Univ. Press

Bobrow, Davis C., *"Organization of American National Security Opinions,"* **Public Opinion Quarterly,** 1969, p. 223.

New American Library

Warner, Rex, Trans., **The Confessions of St. Augustine,** 1963, Book XI, Chapters 14–31.